THE NEW CAMBRIDGE SHAKESPEARE

GENERAL EDITOR
Brian Gibbons

ASSOCIATE GENERAL EDITOR
A. R. Braunmuller, *University of California, Los Angeles*

From the publication of the first volumes in 1984 the General Editor of the New Cambridge Shakespeare was Philip Brockbank and the Associate General Editors were Brian Gibbons and Robin Hood. From 1990 to 1994 the General Editor was Brian Gibbons and the Associate General Editors were A. R. Braunmuller and Robin Hood.

AS YOU LIKE IT

Shakespeare's *As You Like It* can appear bright or sombre in performance: a feast of language and a delight for comic actors; or a risk-taking exploration of gender roles. An updated introduction provides an account of what makes this popular play both innocent and dangerous. There is a new section on recent critical, stage and film interpretations of the play, an updated reading list and a new appendix on a possible early court performance of *As You Like It* in 1599. Mapping the complexities of the play's setting – a no-man's-land related to both France and England – the edition also includes detailed commentary on its language and an analytical account of performance.

THE NEW CAMBRIDGE SHAKESPEARE

All's Well That Ends Well, edited by Russell Fraser
Antony and Cleopatra, edited by David Bevington
As You Like It, edited by Michael Hattaway
The Comedy of Errors, edited by T. S. Dorsch
Coriolanus, edited by Lee Bliss
Cymbeline, edited by Martin Butler
Hamlet, edited by Philip Edwards
Julius Caesar, edited by Marvin Spevack
King Edward III, edited by Giorgio Melchiori
The First Part of King Henry IV, edited by Herbert Weil and Judith Weil
The Second Part of King Henry IV, edited by Giorgio Melchiori
King Henry V, edited by Andrew Gurr
The First Part of King Henry VI, edited by Michael Hattaway
The Second Part of King Henry VI, edited by Michael Hattaway
The Third Part of King Henry VI, edited by Michael Hattaway
King Henry VIII, edited by John Margeson
King John, edited by L. A. Beaurline
The Tragedy of King Lear, edited by Jay L. Halio
King Richard II, edited by Andrew Gurr
King Richard III, edited by Janis Lull
Love's Labour's Lost, edited by William C. Carroll
Macbeth, edited by A. R. Braunmuller
Measure for Measure, edited by Brian Gibbons
The Merchant of Venice, edited by M. M. Mahood
The Merry Wives of Windsor, edited by David Crane
A Midsummer Night's Dream, edited by R. A. Foakes
Much Ado About Nothing, edited by F. H. Mares
Othello, edited by Norman Sanders
Pericles, edited by Doreen DelVecchio and Antony Hammond
The Poems, edited by John Roe
Romeo and Juliet, edited by G. Blakemore Evans
The Sonnets, edited by G. Blakemore Evans
The Taming of the Shrew, edited by Ann Thompson
The Tempest, edited by David Lindley
Timon of Athens, edited by Karl Klein
Titus Andronicus, edited by Alan Hughes
Troilus and Cressida, edited by Anthony B. Dawson
Twelfth Night, edited by Elizabeth Story Donno
The Two Gentlemen of Verona, edited by Kurt Schlueter
The Two Noble Kinsmen, edited by Robert Kean Turner and Patricia Tatspaugh
The Winter's Tale, edited by Susan Snyder and Deborah T. Curren-Aquino

THE EARLY QUARTOS

The First Quarto of Hamlet, edited by Kathleen O. Irace
The First Quarto of King Henry V, edited by Andrew Gurr
The First Quarto of King Lear, edited by Jay L. Halio
The First Quarto of King Richard III, edited by Peter Davison
The First Quarto of Othello, edited by Scott McMillin
The First Quarto of Romeo and Juliet, edited by Lukas Erne
The Taming of a Shrew: The 1594 Quarto, edited by Stephen Roy Miller

ILLUSTRATIONS

AS YOU LIKE IT

Updated edition

Edited by

MICHAEL HATTAWAY

Professor of English, New York University in London

CAMBRIDGE
UNIVERSITY PRESS

CAMBRIDGE
UNIVERSITY PRESS

University Printing House, Cambridge CB2 8BS, United Kingdom

One Liberty Plaza, 20th Floor, New York, NY 10006, USA

477 Williamstown Road, Port Melbourne, VIC 3207, Australia

314-321, 3rd Floor, Plot 3, Splendor Forum, Jasola District Centre, New Delhi - 110025, India

79 Anson Road, #06-04/06, Singapore 079906

Cambridge University Press is part of the University of Cambridge.

It furthers the University's mission by disseminating knowledge in the pursuit of education, learning and research at the highest international levels of excellence.

www.cambridge.org
Information on this title: www.cambridge.org/9780521732505

© Cambridge University Press 2000, 2009

First published 2000
Updated edition 2009
Reprinted 2011
10th printing 2017

A catalogue record for this publication is available from the British Library

Library of Congress Cataloging in Publication data
Shakespeare, William, 1564–1616.
As you like it / edited by Michael Hattway. – Updated ed.
    p.   cm. – (The new Cambridge Shakespeare)
Include bibliographical references.
ISBN 978-0-521-51974-8
1. Fathers and daughters – Drama.   2. Exiles – Drama.   3. Shakespeare, William, 1564–1616.
As you like it.   I. Hattaway, Michael.   II. Title.
PR2803.A2H35   2009
822.3'3 – dc22   2009025024

ISBN   978-0-521-51974-8   Hardback
ISBN   978-0-521-73250-5   Paperback

CONTENTS

PREFACE TO THE UPDATED EDITION

The popularity of *As You Like It* over the last 260 years has generated a myriad of productions. There are not as many editors, but their accumulated industry means that each successor can make only a modest contribution to what has been revealed and explained. It is therefore appropriate to begin with a tribute to my predecessors, especially H. H. Furness, whose acute common sense shines through the verbosities that convention dictated he transcribe in the notes to the first New Variorum edition (1890), to his successor, Richard Knowles, whose revised work in the same series (1977) is magnificently full, sagacious, and accurate, to Alan Brissenden, who generously offered encouragement just after his own Oxford edition had appeared (1993), and to Juliet Dusinberre whose Arden 3 edition (2006) prompted a deal of revision in this second edition (see, especially, Appendix 1). This volume is supported by recent encyclopaedic works of reference: Stanley Wells and Gary Taylor, *William Shakespeare: A Textual Companion*, 1987, Kenneth S. Rothwell and Annabelle Henkin Melzer (eds.), *Shakespeare on Screen: An International Filmography and Videography*, 1990, and Bryan N. S. Gooch, David Thatcher, Odean Long (eds.), *A Shakespeare Music Catalogue*, 5 vols., 1991. James L. Harner's online *World Shakespeare Bibliography*, together with the *Oxford English Dictionary*, *Literature Online*, *Early English Books Online*, and the visual riches of *Designing Shakespeare*, produced under the aegis of the Arts and Humanities Data Service (UK), not only enable an editor to move more swiftly and with more assurance, and support scholars and students taking up the references that derive from them, but also will serve to expose the lacunae that any editor knows dot the surface of her or his endeavours. Conversely, for much of what had to be imported into earlier editions – analogous word usages, dutiful accounts of run-of-the-mill productions, transcriptions of song settings not associated with the earliest performances – the curious reader can be directed to these great repositories. These add to the earlier works, George C. D. Odell's *Shakespeare from Betterton to Irving*, 2 vols., 1920, for example, upon which we all relied so much.

This edition appeared after the explosion of theory-led re-examination of the texts and culture of the early modern period. Whether in my Introduction I paid too little or too much attention to the studies of gender, insurrection, and social praxis generally, I have to leave my readers to decide. I started my work convinced I wanted to protect the innocence of the play, to remind the users of the edition that comedy should be fun. I end with the sense that *As You Like It* is both a more dangerous and a more cautious play than I would have thought. It is dangerous in its exposure of gender instability, cautious in its invocation of a sanctified polis as the basis for civic order. I still think it is fun, full of exuberance and wit, and that any serious points are made with a light touch that is enjoyable yet sharp.

Librarians at the University of Sheffield, the Warburg and Shakespeare Institutes, the Shakespeare Centre (particularly Sylvia Morris), the British and London Libraries, and, especially, the Folger Shakespeare Library have been always helpful, and to my former colleagues at Sheffield I was grateful for generous sabbatical leaves that hastened the completion of this work. An award from the Auber Bequest, Royal Society of Edinburgh, supported my stay in Washington DC while I worked on this edition, updating its introduction and supplying a survey of recent criticism and productions, as well as a new appendix (Appendix 1). The late Professor Don McKenzie kindled my interest in textual studies when I was a student. Later I learned much from my students at the Universities of Kent and Sheffield who worked with me on productions of the play. Dr Malcolm Jones shared with me his research into early modern sexuality, the late Rex Gibson offered memories of productions we had both seen, and Professor Carol Chillington Rutter rendered trenchant but positive criticism of early drafts of the Introduction. Juliet Dusinberre's Arden 3 edition (2006) provocatively challenged my earlier account of the play's genesis – and for that I am truly grateful. Professors Al Braunmuller, Madalina Nicolaescu, and Andrew Gurr generously sent me helpful information. Conversations with Professors Patrick Collinson, John L. Murphy, Richard Wilson, and Dr Pamela Mason reminded me of how much I didn't know. Professors Richard Knowles and Steven F. May sharpened my discussion of the play's date and occasion in this second edition, and Dr Peter Roberts shared his incisive knowledge of patrons and playing companies. M. Michel Bitot kindly invited me to try out some of my work in Tours; Paul Chipchase, Margaret Berrill, and Chris Jackson copy-edited the text with the attention and diligence I have come to expect and welcome, and Brian Gibbons, my general editor, and Sarah Stanton were wonderfully supportive of my work. My wife Judi has given me inestimable encouragement during the preparation of this book.

Arborfield, Berkshire M. H.

ABBREVIATIONS AND CONVENTIONS

Shakespeare's plays, when cited in this edition, are abbreviated in a style modified slightly from that used in the *Harvard Concordance to Shakespeare*. Other editions of Shakespeare are abbreviated under the editor's surname (Latham, Dyce) unless they are the work of more than one editor. In such cases, an abbreviated series name is used (Cam., Johnson Var.). When more than one edition by the same editor is cited, later editions are discriminated with a raised figure (Collier²). All quotations from Shakespeare use the lineation of *The Riverside Shakespeare*, under the textual editorship of G. Blakemore Evans.

1. Shakespeare's works

Ado	*Much Ado About Nothing*
Ant.	*Antony and Cleopatra*
AWW	*All's Well That Ends Well*
AYLI	*As You Like It*
Cor.	*Coriolanus*
Cym.	*Cymbeline*
Err.	*The Comedy of Errors*
Ham.	*Hamlet*
1H4	*The First Part of King Henry the Fourth*
2H4	*The Second Part of King Henry the Fourth*
H5	*King Henry the Fifth*
1H6	*The First Part of King Henry the Sixth*
2H6	*The Second Part of King Henry the Sixth*
3H6	*The Third Part of King Henry the Sixth*
H8	*King Henry the Eighth*
JC	*Julius Caesar*
John	*King John*
LLL	*Love's Labour's Lost*
Lear	*King Lear*
Luc.	*The Rape of Lucrece*
Mac.	*Macbeth*
MM	*Measure for Measure*
MND	*A Midsummer Night's Dream*
MV	*The Merchant of Venice*
Oth.	*Othello*
Per.	*Pericles*
PP	*The Passionate Pilgrim*
R2	*King Richard the Second*
R3	*King Richard the Third*
Rom.	*Romeo and Juliet*
Shr.	*The Taming of the Shrew*
Son.	*The Sonnets*
STM	*Sir Thomas More*

Temp.	*The Tempest*
TGV	*The Two Gentlemen of Verona*
Tim.	*Timon of Athens*
Tit.	*Titus Andronicus*
TN	*Twelfth Night*
TNK	*The Two Noble Kinsmen*
Tro.	*Troilus and Cressida*
Wiv.	*The Merry Wives of Windsor*
WT	*The Winter's Tale*

2. Other works cited and general references

Abbott	E. A. Abbott, *A Shakespearian Grammar*, 1878 edn (references are to numbered paragraphs)
AEB	*Analytical and Enumerative Bibliography*
Aeneid	Virgil, *Aeneid*, ed. H. R. Fairclough, *Virgil*, Loeb Classical Library, 2 vols., 1986 edn
Andrews	*As You Like It*, ed. John F. Andrews, The Everyman Shakespeare, 1997
Arber	E. Arber, *A Transcript of the Registers of the Company of Stationers of London 1554–1640*, 5 vols., 1875–94
Armstrong	Edward A. Armstrong, *Shakespeare's Imagination*, 1963 edn
Baldwin	T. W. Baldwin, *Shakspere's 'Small Latine and Lesse Greeke'*, 2 vols., 1944
Bell	*Shakespeare's Plays*, ed. J. Bell, 9 vols., 1774
Bentley	G. E. Bentley, *The Jacobean and Caroline Stage*, 7 vols., 1941–68
Brand	*Brand's Popular Antiquities of Great Britain*, ed. Henry Ellis and William Carew Hazlitt, 2 vols., 1905
Brewer	E. C. Brewer, *The Dictionary of Phrase and Fable*, n.d.
Brissenden	*As You Like It*, ed. Alan Brissenden, The Oxford Shakespeare, 1993
Bullough	Geoffrey Bullough, *Narrative and Dramatic Sources of Shakespeare*, 8 vols., 1957–75 (unless otherwise specified, page references are to vol. II)
Cam.	*Works*, ed. William Aldis Wright, 9 vols., 1891–3 (Cambridge Shakespeare)
Capell	*Mr William Shakespeare his Comedies, Histories, and Tragedies*, ed. Edward Capell, 10 vols., 1767–8
Cercignani	F. Cercignani, *Shakespeare's Works and Elizabethan Pronunciation*, 1981
Chambers	E. K. Chambers, *The Elizabethan Stage*, 4 vols., 1923
Chambers, *Shakespeare*	E. K. Chambers, *William Shakespeare: A Study of Facts and Problems*, 2 vols., 1930

Collier	*Works*, ed. John P. Collier, 8 vols., 1842–4
Collier²	*Plays*, ed. John P. Collier, 1853
conj.	conjecture
Cowden Clarke	*Plays*, ed. Charles and Mary Cowden Clarke, 3 vols., 1864–8
Curtius	Ernst Robert Curtius, *European Literature and the Latin Middle Ages*, trans. Willard R. Trask, 1953
Dent	R. W. Dent, *Shakespeare's Proverbial Language: An Index*, 1981 (references are to numbered proverbs)
DNB	*Dictionary of National Biography*
Drayton	Michael Drayton, *Works*, ed. J. W. Hebel *et al.*, 5 vols., 1961
Dusinberre	*As You Like It*, ed. Juliet Dusinberre, *The Arden Shakespeare*, 2006
Dyce	*The Works of William Shakespeare*, ed. Alexander Dyce, 6 vols., 1857
Dyce²	*The Works of William Shakespeare*, ed. Alexander Dyce, 9 vols., 1864–7
Dyce³	*The Works of William Shakespeare*, ed. Alexander Dyce, 9 vols., 1875–6
Eds.	Various editors
ELH	*English Literary History*
ELN	*English Language Notes*
ELR	*English Literary Renaissance*
ES	*English Studies*
F	*Mr William Shakespeares Comedies, Histories, and Tragedies*, 1623 (Corrected sheets of First Folio)
Fᵘ	*Mr William Shakespeares Comedies, Histories, and Tragedies*, 1623 (Uncorrected sheets of First Folio)
F2	*Mr William Shakespear's Comedies, Histories, and Tragedies*, 1632 (Second Folio)
F3	*Mr William Shakespear's Comedies, Histories, and Tragedies*, 1664 (Third Folio)
F4	*Mr William Shakespeares Comedies, Histories, and Tragedies*, 1685 (Fourth Folio)
Farmer	Richard Farmer, in Johnson Var. (see below)
FQ	Edmund Spenser, *The Faerie Queene*, ed. A. C. Hamilton, 1977
Furness	*As You Like It*, ed. H. H. Furness, New Variorum, vol. VIII, 1890
Gilman	*As You Like It*, ed. Albert Gilman, Signet Shakespeare, 1963
Globe	*The Globe Edition, The Works of William Shakespeare*, ed. W. G. Clark and W. A. Wright, 1864
Greene	Robert Greene, *Works*, ed. A. B. Grosart, 15 vols., 1881–3
Halliwell	*The Complete Works of Shakespeare*, ed. James O. Halliwell, 16 vols., 1853–65

Hanmer	*The Works of Shakspear*, ed. Thomas Hanmer, 6 vols., 1743–4
Harbage	*The Complete Works of William Shakespeare*, ed. Alfred Harbage, 1969
Hattaway	Michael Hattaway, *Elizabethan Popular Theatre*, 1982
Heath	B[enjamin] H[eath], *The Revisal of Shakespear's Text* [1765]
Henslowe	R. A. Foakes and R. T. Rickert (eds.), *Henslowe's Diary*, 1961
Hilton	John Hilton, *Catch that Catch Can*, 1652
HLQ	*The Huntington Library Quarterly*
Hogan	C. B. Hogan, *Shakespeare in the Theatre, 1701–1800*, 2 vols., 1952–7
Hudson	*The Complete Works of William Shakespeare*, ed. Henry N. Hudson, 11 vols., 1851–6
Hudson²	*The Complete Works of William Shakespeare*, ed. Henry N. Hudson, 20 vols., 1880–1
Hulme	Hilda M. Hulme, *Explorations in Shakespeare's Language*, 1962
JEGP	*Journal of English and Germanic Philology*
Johnson	*The Plays of William Shakespeare*, ed. Samuel Johnson, 8 vols., 1765
Johnson²	*The Plays of William Shakespeare*, ed. Samuel Johnson, 10 vols., 1766
Johnson Var.	*The Plays of William Shakespeare*, ed. Samuel Johnson and George Steevens, 10 vols., 1773
Jones	Malcolm Jones, 'Sex and sexuality in late medieval and early modern art', in *Privatisierung der Triebe? Sexualität in der Frühen Neuzeit*, ed. Daniela Erlach, Markus Reisenleitner, and Karl Vocelka, 1994, 1, 187–267
Jonson	*The Works of Ben Jonson*, ed. C. H. Herford and P. and E. M. Simpson, 11 vols., 1925–52
Keightley	*The Plays of Shakespeare*, ed. Thomas Keightley, 6 vols., 1864
Knowles	*As You Like It*, ed. Richard Knowles, New Variorum Shakespeare, 1977
Kökeritz	Helge Kökeritz, *Shakespeare's Pronunciation*, 1953
Laroque	François Laroque, *Shakespeare's Festive World*, trans. Janet Lloyd, 1991
Latham	*As You Like It*, ed. Agnes Latham, Arden Shakespeare, 1975
Lettsom	See Walker
Long	John H. Long, *Shakespeare's Use of Music*, 1955
Mahood	M. M. Mahood, *Shakespeare's Wordplay*, 1957
Malone	*The Plays and Poems of William Shakespeare*, ed. Edmond Malone, 10 vols., 1790
Malone²	*The Plays and Poems of William Shakespeare*, ed. Edmond Malone, 16 vols., 1794

Marshall	*As You Like It*, ed. Cynthia Marshall, Shakespeare in Production, 2004
Mason	John Monck Mason, *Comments on . . . Shakespeare's Plays*, 1785
Metamorphoses	Ovid, *Metamorphoses*, trans. Arthur Golding (1567), ed. J. F. Nims, 1965
MLN	*Modern Language Notes*
MLQ	*Modern Language Quarterly*
Morley	*The First Book of Airs . . . to Sing and Play to the Lute*, 1600
Nashe	Thomas Nashe, *Works*, ed. R. B. McKerrow, 5 vols., 1904–10, revised by F. P. Wilson, 1958
Noble	Richmond Noble, *Shakespeare's Biblical Knowledge*, 1935
NQ	*Notes and Queries*
obs.	obsolete
Odell	George C. D. Odell, *Shakespeare from Betterton to Irving*, 2 vols., 1920
OED	*The Oxford English Dictionary*, 1987 edn
Oxford	*William Shakespeare: The Complete Works*, ed. Stanley Wells and Gary Taylor, 1986
Panofsky	Erwin Panofsky, *Studies in Iconology*, 1939
Partridge	Eric Partridge, *Shakespeare's Bawdy*, 1968 edn
PBSA	*Papers of the Bibliographical Society of America*
PMLA	*Publications of the Modern Language Association of America*
Pope	*The Works of Shakespear*, ed. Alexander Pope, 6 vols., 1723–5
PQ	*Philological Quarterly*
Rann	*Dramatic Works*, ed. Joseph Rann, 6 vols., 1786–94
Reed	*The Plays of William Shakspeare*, [ed. Isaac Reed], 21 vols., 1803
Ren. Drama	*Renaissance Drama*
RES	*Review of English Studies*
Ridley	*Works. The New Temple Shakespeare*, ed. M. R. Ridley, 40 vols., 1934
Ritson	[J. Ritson], *Cursory Criticisms on the edition of Shakespeare published by Edmond Malone*, 1792
Riverside	*The Riverside Shakespeare*, ed. G. Blakemore Evans, 1974
RORD	*Research Opportunities in Renaissance Drama*
Rosalind	Thomas Lodge, *Rosalind*, ed. Donald Beecher, 1997
Rowe	*The Works of Mr William Shakespear*, ed. Nicholas Rowe, 6 vols., 1709
Rowe²	*The Works of Mr William Shakespear*, ed. Nicholas Rowe, 2nd edn, 6 vols., 1709
Rowe³	*The Works of Mr William Shakespear*, ed. Nicholas Rowe, 3rd edn, 8 vols., 1714

RQ	*Renaissance Quarterly*
RSC	Royal Shakespeare Company
Rubinstein	Frankie Rubinstein, *A Dictionary of Shakespeare's Sexual Puns and Their Significance*, 1984
Sargent	*As You Like It*, ed. Ralph M. Sargent, Pelican Shakespeare, 1959
SB	*Studies in Bibliography*
Schmidt	Alexander Schmidt, *Shakespeare-Lexicon*, 1886 ed
SD	stage direction
SEL	*Studies in English Literature*
Seng	Peter J. Seng, *The Vocal Songs in the Plays of Shakespeare: A Critical History*, 1967
SH	speech heading
Shaheen	Naseeb Shaheen, *Biblical References in Shakespeare's Comedies*, 1993
Shakespeare's England	*Shakespeare's England: An Account of the Life and Manners of His Age*, ed. Sidney Lee and C. T. Onions, 2 vols., 1916
Shattuck	Charles H. Shattuck, *The Shakespeare Promptboo* 1965
sig.	signature(s) (printer's indications of the ordering pages in early modern books, used here where pa numbers do not exist, or occasionally for bibliographical reasons)
Singer	*The Dramatic Works of William Shakespeare*, ed. Samuel Weller Singer, 10 vols., 1826
Singer²	*The Dramatic Works of William Shakespeare*, ed. Samuel Weller Singer, 10 vols., 1856
Sisson	*Works*, ed. Charles Sisson, 1954
Sisson, *New Readings*	C. J. Sisson, *New Readings in Shakespeare*, 2 vols 1956
Smallwood	R. L. Smallwood, *As You Like It*, Shakespeare a Stratford, 2003
SQ	*Shakespeare Quarterly*
S.St.	*Shakespeare Studies*
S.Sur.	*Shakespeare Survey*
Steevens	*The Plays of William Shakespeare*, ed. Samuel Johnson and George Steevens, 10 vols., 1773
Steevens²	*The Plays of William Shakespeare*, ed. George Steevens, 10 vols., 1778
Steevens³	*The Plays of William Shakespeare*, ed. George Steevens and Isaac Reed, 10 vols., 1785
subst.	substantively
Sugden	E. H. Sugden, *A Topographical Dictionary to the Works of Shakespeare and his Fellow Dramatists*, 1925
SV	*sub verbum* (Latin for 'under the word', used in dictionary citations)
Theobald	*The Works of Shakespeare*, ed. Lewis Theobald, 7 vols., 1733

Theobald²	*The Works of Shakespeare*, ed. Lewis Theobald, 8 vols., 1740
Theobald³	*The Works of Shakespeare*, ed. Lewis Theobald, 8 vols., 1752
Thomas	K. V. Thomas, *Religion and the Decline of Magic*, 1971
Tilley	M. P. Tilley, *A Dictionary of the Proverbs in England in the Sixteenth and Seventeenth Centuries*, 1950 (references are to numbered proverbs)
TLN	through line numbering
Walker	William S. Walker, *Critical Examination of the Text of Shakespear*, ed. W. N. Lettsom, 3 vols., 1860
Warburton	*The Works of Shakespear*, ed. William Warburton, 8 vols., 1747
Wells and Taylor, *Textual Companion*	Stanley Wells and Gary Taylor, *William Shakespeare: A Textual Companion*, 1987
White	*Works*, ed. Richard Grant White, 12 vols., 1857–66
White²	*Mr William Shakespeare's Comedies, Tragedies and Poems*, ed. Richard Grant White, 3 vols., 1883
Whiter	Walter Whiter, *A Specimen of a Commentary on Shakespeare*, 1794
Wiles	David Wiles, *Shakespeare's Clown: Actor and Text in the Elizabethan Playhouse*, 1987
Wilson	*As You Like It*, ed. Arthur Quiller-Couch and John Dover Wilson, New Shakespeare, 1926
Williams	Gordon Williams, *A Glossary of Shakespeare's Sexual Language*, 1997
Yale	*The Yale Shakespeare*, ed. Helge Kökeritz and Charles T. Prouty, 1974

Unless otherwise specified, biblical quotations are given in the Geneva version, 1560 (see 1.1.29 n.).

INTRODUCTION

Journeys

As You Like It, like most of Shakespeare's comedies, presents a world apart: a 'forest' to which the principal characters are exiled from court or country estate. The action begins in an orchard and moves to the forest or, as it is sometimes designated in the text, a 'desert'. It ends with the main characters – with the exception of Jaques, who claims to be heading for a monastic life – returning to court. Almost all of the action takes place within that shadow-land elsewhere, which, given that it is peopled with characters out of pastoral, may not satisfy romantic expectations of wilderness, and in which customary patterns of characterisation and plausibility do not obtain. In this world at the fringe of civilisation there is courtliness, hospitality, and cure, whereas in what we might have expected to be the serenity of Oliver's country estate we witness violence and seeming injustice. For the characters who have escaped from the court, the forest is a place imaginatively familiar and also a metonym for values, particularly those allied with Nature; for those that live there, it has material associations with property and with work.[1] But, somehow, in that slightly anarchic – and very literary – realm of fancy, love blooms: not only, and as we should expect, between heroine and hero as atonement for persecution, but also between familiars (Orlando and Adam), between strangers (Oliver and Celia), between the scornful Phoebe and the poetical Silvius (eventually), and between the cynical Touchstone and the trusting Audrey (probably).[2] In some ways *As You Like It* demands to be apprehended as something 'light, and bright, and sparkling',[3] a play to breed both delight and laughter. Its romantic assertions are displaced by a fool, enhanced by song, dance, and spectacle, and laced by the subversive irony and eloquence of Rosalind, who alternately revels in and then repudiates the games of love. For Orlando the forest is a place in which he serves an apprenticeship in honour and explores the impulses and idiocies of love-prate.

This good play of courtship, therefore, may need no prologue. However, as Ben Jonson remarked, comedy can be no laughing matter (see below, p. 44): the play interrogates matters of gender, rank, and the social order, and we might even – given the ways in which it brings some characters near death, eschews punishment in its resolution, is written in a mixture of styles, and is resolved in part by a

---

[1] For the history of 'soft' and 'hard' versions of primitivism see Erwin Panofsky, '*Et in Arcadia Ego*: Poussin and the elegiac tradition', in *Meaning in the Visual Arts*, 1970, pp. 340–67; for the contrasts between city and country in Renaissance romance see Walter R. Davis, 'Masking in Arden: the histrionics of Lodge's *Rosalynde*', *SEL* 5 (1965), 151–63; for an analysis of recent design choices for courts and Arden at Stratford-upon-Avon, see Smallwood, pp. 19–71.

[2] See Fiona Shaw in Carol Rutter *et al.*, *Clamorous Voices: Shakespeare's Women Today*, 1988, pp. 97–8.

[3] A phrase Jane Austen applied to *Pride and Prejudice* in a letter to her sister of 4 February 1813.

god – want to consider aspects of it as pertaining not just to comedy but to tragicomedy, a genre newly fashionable in the 1590s.[1] Some modern directors have chosen to mark these departures from the pursuit of happiness by using sombre stage settings or by demonstrating that the play's humour depends upon its men and women having to play many parts that attend upon hierarchies of rank and gender.

'Forest' in Elizabethan times was a legal term as well as being a topographical description or a site licensed for the sports of love: the word designated a domain preserved for the noble sport of hunting.[2] Moreover, such forests were not necessarily expanses of woodland but could include pasture, as well as sparsely inhabited tilled and untilled terrain – England in Shakespeare's time was, in fact, not much more forested than it is now.[3] In literature, however, woods and forests were ubiquitous, figuring not just as settings for romantic sentiment, for endurance, and to house glamorous bandits like Robin Hood, but also as sites where contradictions of the primitive converged. Forests challenged economic and cultural expansion and also kindled nostalgia for civilisation's origins in a lost golden world.[4] The 'forest' in *As You Like It* turns out to contain tracts that are both 'desert' and given over to husbandry: one meaning for the play's riddling title may have to do with the imagining of topography and landscape – or even of 'reality'. For some in the play, the forest enables the exploration of escapist fantasies and alternative gender roles within a world of 'if' (see 5.4.84–8); for others, it is a place for the enduring of social inequalities and the briars of the 'working-day world' (1.3.9).

The mixed economies of this poetic terrain make the text's images of nature immediately complex: the 'natural' has much more to do contesting patterns of culture in Elizabethan England than with geographic difference or with the

---

[1] 'A tragi-comedy is not so called in respect of mirth and killing, but in respect it wants deaths, which is enough to make it no tragedy, yet brings some near it, which is enough to make it no comedy . . . so that a god is as lawful in this as in a tragedy, and mean people as in a comedy' (John Fletcher, Epistle to *The Faithful Shepherdess* (1608?), Fredson Bowers (ed.), *The Dramatic Works in the Beaumont and Fletcher Canon*, 1976, III, 497). Fletcher, like Jonson, was much influenced by Guarini's *Il Pastor Fido* (1590) and *Compendium of Tragicomic Poetry* (1590 and 1593). Part of the latter is reprinted in Michael J. Sidnell (ed.), *Sources of Dramatic Theory*, 1991. Guarini also uses pastoral in his play and writes about it in the *Compendium*. For the effect on Jonson, Fletcher, and the later Shakespeare, see Arthur C. Kirsch, *Jacobean Dramatic Perspectives*, 1972; see also Lee Bliss, 'Pastiche, burlesque, tragi-comedy', in A. R. Braunmuller and Michael Hattaway (eds.), *The Cambridge Companion to English Renaissance Drama*, 2003, pp. 228–53.

[2] 'A forest is certain territory of woody grounds and fruitful pastures, privileged for wild beasts and fouls of forest, chase, and warren, to rest and abide in, in the safe protection of the king, for his princely delight and pleasure' (John Manwood, *A Treatise . . . of the Laws of the Forest* (1598 edn), f. 1); there is a commentary upon this work in Richard Marienstras, *Le Proche et le lointain*, 1981, and in Robert Pogue Harrison, *Forests: The Shadow of Civilisation*, 1992, pp. 70–5. A. Stuart Daley notes that twelve out of the sixteen 'forest' scenes in the play take place on a farm ('Where are the woods in *As You Like It*?', *SQ* 34 (1983), 172–80).

[3] So Michael Drayton writing of Warwickshire: '. . . of our forests' kind the quality to tell, / We equally partake with woodland as with plain / Alike with hill and dale; and every day maintain / The sundry kinds of beasts upon our copious wastes / That men for profit breed, as well as those of chase' (*Polyolbion*, XIII, 34–8, in Drayton, IV, 276); compare Oliver Rackham, *Trees and Woodlands in the British Landscape*, 1996, pp. 76–86.

[4] See John Hale, 'The taming of Nature', *The Civilization of Europe in the Renaissance*, 1994, pp. 509–83; compare *Aeneid*, VIII, 415–29; *Metamorphoses*, I, 103–28; Harrison, *Forests*, *passim*.

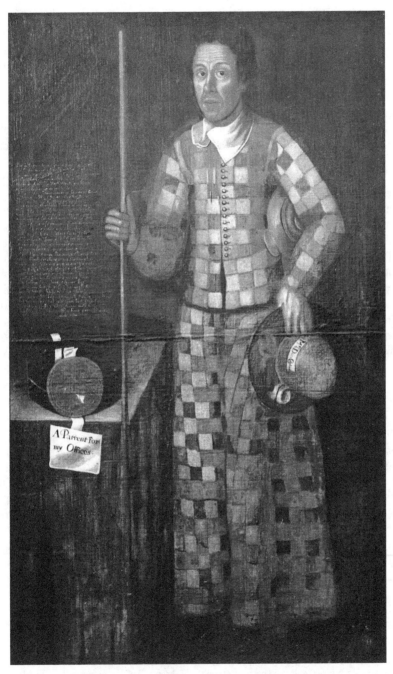

1   The jester Tom Skelton: see Eric Ives, 'Tom Skelton: a seventeenth-century jester', *S.Sur.* 13 (1960), 90–105; for Touchstone's costume, see Wiles, pp. 186–7

actualities of contemporary behaviour. Ideas of nature in the play define those ideological concepts of the natural which contemporaries used in order to fix identity and legitimate the social and political order – the natural, when not associated with 'great creating Nature' (*WT* 4.4.88), generally designates what one social or political group takes to be the normative or, antithetically, the primitive and authentic.[1] As well as generating fun for the audience as the characters overcome difficulties, social and psychological, the play raises questions of authenticity and value that turn upon encounters with the 'other'. Court impinges upon country, feminine encounters masculine, youth joins with age (old Adam). The elite mix with shepherds (Corin, Silvius, and Phoebe), with a rustic 'clown' and his lass (William and Audrey), and with a fool (Touchstone), to all of whom the designation 'natural' might apply.[2] Some, notably Celia and Rosalind, discover their 'other' selves: Aliena means 'other', and 'Ganymede' was the name of Jupiter's male lover, associated since antiquity with homo-eroticism (see below, pp. 39–41). And built into the language of the play is a series of oppositions: winter against spring, Nature against Fortune (see Plate 2), pastoral fantasies against rural realities, Christian orthodoxy against classical humanism (see Plates 3 and 4) and the white magic of Rosalind (3.3.288–9, 5.2.47–9), oppositions that can be dissolved into paradox as when Rosalind exclaims, 'the wiser, the waywarder' (4.1.129–30), or as when Touchstone is reported to lament, 'And so, from hour to hour, we ripe and ripe, And then, from hour to hour, we rot and rot' (2.7.26–7). From the outset, therefore, we realise that there can be no monolithic meaning in the text; we find rather a set of paradoxes and contradictions that can be turned into a multitude of coexistent interpretations. The first task for both directors and readers is to decide upon their forms for this 'forest', because the perspectives established upon these will, in part, create their particular webs of meaning for the play.

Nineteenth-century productions of *As You Like It* offered romanticised settings using the conventions of the realist stage,[3] and certain screen versions have been shot on location (see below, pp. 75–6, 80–1): these demonstrate the difficulties of fixing the constitution of the forest, a place which is obviously neither normal nor 'real' but a field of play for disguise-games, charades, hunting pageants, and revelry. It is not possible to reproduce or even map the 'worlds' conceived for the non-illusionistic stages of the Elizabethan period: court and country estate, arable unenclosed 'champian' on the one hand and forest and enclosed pasture on the other, the material boundaries of farms and the symbolic margins of dukedoms, are all inscribed upon one another. The effect is that the court characters migrate not from one location to another, but from one mode of theatrical representation to another: the 'pastoral' mode of the 'forest' represents a condition – or state of mind – rather than a place. There Orlando can play the role of the Petrarchan lover, and Rosalind, within the guise

---

[1] See 1.1.13, 4.3.119; see in this respect the account of Jonson's 'To Penshurst' in Raymond Williams, *The Country and the City*, 1973, pp. 27–34.

[2] See 1.2.41–2, 3.3.17 and *OED Natural*, *sb* 2; for these characters at Stratford from 1952 to 2000, see Smallwood, pp. 167–88.

[3] See Plate 9, p. 61.

2 'The Wheel of Life which is called Fortune', a block-print of about 1460 (British Library, I.C. 35); compare R. Klibansky, E. Panofsky, and F. Saxl, *Saturn and Melancholy*, 1964, plates 58 and 79. Figures depict the Seven Ages of Man (see 2.7.139–66)

3 Hymen, who is crowned with flowers and who carries a torch and a marriage veil, from Vincenzo Cartari, *Le Imagini dei Dei degli Antichi* (1580), p. 189

4   John de Critz (attributed), Lucy Harrington Countess of Bedford attired for Ben Jonson's masque *Hymenaei* (1606); see W. Friedländer, 'Hymenaea', *De Artibus Opuscula* 40 (1961), 153–6

of a witty adolescent male, can explore roles that might be open to women.[1] *Space* in the playhouse does not have to be configured to represent *places* named in the text: Elizabethan scenic devices were used as much to establish genre as location – the 'two mossy banks' found in the list of properties owned by the theatrical impresario Philip Henslowe presumably signalled to their audiences 'pastoral' rather than 'woodland', as did costumes and properties such as the grey or white cloaks, sheep-hook, scrip (bag), and bottle that the attendant shepherds may have borne.[2]

Because Shakespeare's texts were not written for playhouses that attempted scenic verisimilitude it has proved difficult for his poetic topographies to be translated into modern theatrical landscapes for audiences who are likely to relish spectacle and who often still expect elements of realism to compose that spectacle – as Jonathan Miller remarked, 'It is invariably true that nature looks atrocious on stage.'[3] If a modern director decides to represent the forest in *As You Like It* by the use of trees, these had best be stylised to signal the artificiality of the setting. In those modern productions that do eschew theatrical realism it is common for audiences to collude delightedly with a Rosalind who, appearing on a stage with not a leaf in sight, proclaims, 'Well, this is the Forest of Arden' (2.4.11).[4] Moreover, with its allegiances to utopias and lost golden ages of innocence and justice, pastoral occupies not just a special place but a special time, what Mikhail Bakhtin termed a 'chronotope'.[5] Time in this forest without a clock, where 'some kind of social space replaces a physical landscape', and where no explanations are needed for encounters between characters,[6] is a measure for play rather than for work, delineates time as it is imagined and remembered rather than as it is calibrated in a regulated society.

Yet if the theatrical location was geographically alien, Elizabethan players appropriated the narrative from its mythical past by using the costumes of the present – gentlemen, it is reported, sometimes willed their finest clothes to their servants

[1] For Orlando and Rosalind at Stratford from 1952 to 2000, see Smallwood, pp. 99–134.

[2] Henslowe, p. 320; Henslowe lists 'two white shepherds' coats' (p. 317); for the grey cloaks see the Epistle to Fletcher's *The Faithful Shepherdess*, p. 497; for the staff and bottle, see *Orlando Furioso*, 561, in Greene, XIII, 141; see also Martha Ronk, 'Locating the visual in *As You Like It*', *SQ* 52 (2001), 255–76.

[3] Jonathan Miller, *Subsequent Performances*, 1986, p. 82; for Giambattista Vico's notion of 'poetic geography', see John Gillies, *Shakespeare and the Geography of Difference*, 1994, pp. 4–7. 'Ancient Britain' has always been a problem for modern directors of *King Lear*, a play that uncannily remembers aspects of *As You Like It*: see Helen Gardner, '*As You Like It*', in J. Garrett (ed.), *More Talking of Shakespeare*, 1959, pp. 17–32.

[4] Werner Habicht, 'Tree properties and tree scenes in Elizabethan theater', *Ren. Drama* n.s. 4 (1971), 69–92; in 1985 Bob Crowley at Stratford-upon-Avon successfully made Arden a looking-glass world by the use of mirrors, through one of which Jaques stepped back at the end of the play (see Smallwood, pp. 34–5).

[5] Arden is equivalent to the first kind of chronotope in ancient novels, 'adventure time': see M. M. Bakhtin, *The Dialogic Imagination*, trans. Caryl Emerson and Michael Holquist, 1981, pp. 86–110; see also Bart Westerweel, 'The dialogic imagination: the European discovery of time and Shakespeare's mature comedies', in Jean R. Brink and William F. Gentrup (eds.), *Renaissance Culture*, 1993, pp. 54–74; Maurice Hunt, 'Kairos and the ripeness of time in *As You Like It*', *MLQ* 52 (1991), 113–35; Paul Glennie and Nigel Thrift, *Shaping the Day: A History of Timekeeping in England and Wales, 1300–1800*, 2009.

[6] Katerina Clark and Michael Holquist, *Mikhail Bakhtin*, 1984, p. 282.

who then sold them to the players.[1] This meant that the action was not *historically* remote, and that witty interplay between the imaginative and the real allowed for both topical reference and the re-definition of social and cultural issues.[2]

The codes of theatrical representation are complicated by problems of reading and naming: should we designate the forest 'Arden' or 'Ardennes'? 'Arden' is a name that not only signifies a 'real' local habitation in Shakespeare's Warwickshire but also alludes to the *topos* of the 'greenwood' that was venerated in idylls and in ballads and romanticised settings for Robin Hood and his outlaws,[3] echoes of which sound throughout the text. *La Forêt des Ardennes* is a location with a geographical identity on the border between modern France and Belgium, but was similarly mythologised in prose romance: 'Nowe our Marriners Pilgrimes . . . discoured Calleis [Calais] where, hauing taken land, they determined to finishe the voyage on Horsebacke . . . Thus the Princes . . . approched the Countery of Arden [*sic*] . . . and there . . . they founde the famous fountaynes, whiche, will they, nill they, inuite the passengers to drinke, engendryng in them the one loue, and the other hate.'[4] Oliver says of Orlando, 'it is the stubbornest young fellow of France' (1.1.111–12), and Robin Hood is referred to as 'the old Robin Hood of England' (1.1.93–4): these would suggest a setting in France.[5] However, accommodating as it does lions and olive-trees, Arden possesses the conventional attributes of the *locus amoenus* of

[1] Hattaway, p. 86.

[2] Juliet Dusinberre, 'As *who* liked it?', *S.Sur.* 46 (1994), 9–22, argues subtly that the play's 'fictions of sexuality . . . draw some of their vitality from the complex relationship between [Sir John] Harington and the Queen'; she also cites older authorities who directly linked Jaques with Harington (p. 12 n. 19); for the possibility that Jaques is based on John Marston, see *The Poems of John Marston*, ed. Arnold Davenport, 1961, p. 27.

[3] See, for example, 'Robin Hood and Guy of Gisborne' in Thomas Percy (ed.), *Percy's Reliques of Ancient English Poetry*, 2 vols., Everyman, n.d. I, 115–24; *Polyolbion*, XXVI, 286–359, in Drayton, IV, 528–30.

[4] Henry Wotton, *A Courtly Controversy of Cupid's Cautels* [Tricks] (1578), p. 224.

[5] If we decide that 'Arden' is English, then it is the only comedy – apart from *Wiv.* – 'set' in England. Joseph Hunter insisted upon a French setting (*New Illustrations of Shakespeare*, 2 vols., 1845, I, 332, and a similar case is argued by Stanley Wells, *Re-Editing Shakespeare for the Modern Reader*, 1984, pp. 28–30). Details of the setting are obviously conventional: there is a palm-tree (compare 3.3.146) to be seen in a print of about 1569 by Étienne Delaune, which foregrounds a shepherd with bagpipes and a goatherdess with a distaff (British Library, Reg. 1834, 0804.197). Shakespeare also often uses 'Monsieur' in place of 'Master', especially for Le Beau and Jaques. In Harington's translation of Ariosto's *Orlando Furioso* there are two magical fountains of love and hate in 'Ardenna' (i.78); Spenser refers to 'that same water of Ardenne, / The which *Rinaldo* drunck in happie howre' (*FQ*, 4.3.45), and to 'famous Ardeyn' in 'Astrophel' (line 96), his lament for Sir Philip Sidney published in *Colin Clout's Come Home Again* (1595). A couplet in a poem attributed to Michael Drayton, 'Dowsabell', would indicate that Arden and 'Ardenne' were pronounced identically: 'Farre in the country of Arden / There won'd a knight, hight Cassamen' (Percy's *Reliques*, I, 261); A. Stuart Daley, 'Observations on the natural settings and flora of the Ardens of Lodge and Shakespeare', *ELN* 22.3 (1985), 20–9, notes that in Henry Roberts' *Haigh for Devonshire* (1600) there is a forest of 'Arden' to the north-east of Bordeaux in Périgord. In the text of *AYLI* the word occurs only once in a verse line (1.3.97), but, unfortunately, in a passage of very free rhythm where scansion does not provide evidence for stress. At 2.4.12 Touchstone's pun suggests the word was stressed on the second syllable. A succinct counter-argument for reading 'Arden' is given by Fiona Carlyon: 'In political terms . . . this play was promoting the conception that a foreign court was full of injustice and cruelty, where love or desire could not flourish, whilst England, as represented by the forest of Arden, was where injustices were righted, love and desire were fulfilled' ('The significance of homosexuality in Christopher Marlowe's *Edward II*', unpublished MA dissertation, University of York, 1997, p. 15).

classical Arcadias and the exotic worlds of Renaissance romance. This latter milieu is the kind of romance forest (also nominally in France) that we find in the play's source, Thomas Lodge's prose romance *Rosalind* (1590), as well as being the kind of location evoked in the anonymous play *Thomas of Woodstock* (1604–6).[1] In that text's 'anticke' or masque the goddess Cynthia arrives and proclaims:

> From the cleere orbe of our Etheryall Sphere
> Bright *Cinthia* comes to hunt & revell heere.
> The groves of Callidon and Arden woods
> Of untamd monsters, wild & savadge heards,
> We & our knights have freed . . .[2]

In Spenser's pastoral works, there is often an exotic setting peopled with characters with 'English' names.

It could also be that Shakespeare was thinking etymologically, in that contemporaries associated the word 'Arden' with generic or mythological labels for woodland. The Warwickshire Arden is celebrated in Drayton's *Polyolbion*, XIII, but the author notes that 'the relics of [Arden] in Dene of Monmouthshire and that *Arduenna* or *La Forest d'Ardenne* by [near] Henault and Luxembourg shows likelihood of interpretation of the yet used English name of woodland'.[3] This is partly reinforced by a meaning offered by the *OED* for the component of many English and Scottish place names, 'dean' or 'dene': 'now, usually, the deep, narrow, and wooded vale of a rivulet'.[4] William Camden writes of Warwickshire being divided into the 'Feldon [champian or open ground] and the Woodland', and of the latter says 'it is at this day called Woodland, so also it was in old time known by a more ancient name Arden: but of the selfsame sense and signification . . . For it seemeth that Arden among the ancient Britons and Gauls signified a wood, considering that we see a very great wood in France named Arden [*sic*]'.[5] Since the inset world of *As You Like It* is, like Sir Thomas More's *Utopia*, a 'no place' – the literal meaning of 'utopia' – it seems likely that Shakespeare wittily linked both English and French references to this quasi-allegorical place and, riddlingly, gave us a Jaques as well as a Jacques, an Oliver Martext as well as an Oliver de Boys. Shakespeare's Arden is both an Arcadian sylvan landscape and a location for working arable and pastoral farms, a place for Hymen, the classical god of wedding, and for 'English' rustics like Audrey and William, as well as the hedge-priest Sir Oliver Martext, who is there to remind the audience obliquely of the forms of Christian marriage. Lyly's pastoral drama *Gallathea* (1585) contains a similar mix of characters from Virgilian pastoral and the 'English countryside'. *A Midsummer Night's Dream* and *Much Ado About Nothing* name Greece and Sicily for their settings while nevertheless containing

---

[1] For the date, see Macd. P. Jackson, 'Shakespeare's *Richard II* and the anonymous *Thomas of Woodstock*', *Medieval and Renaissance Drama in England* 14 (2001), 17–65.
[2] 4.2.2096–2100, reprinted in Bullough, III, 483; see also Curtius, pp. 183 ff.
[3] Drayton, *Works*, IV, 286.
[4] *OED* Dean[2] b.
[5] William Camden, *Britain*, trans. Philemon Holland (1610), pp. 562, 565. The equivalent passage is on pp. 316–17 of the first edition (William Camden, *Britannia sive . . . Chorographica Descriptio* (1586)).

English 'mechanicals' and cultural allusions. The setting of *The Tempest* is both in the New World (Bermuda) and on some anonymous Mediterranean island. Shakespeare (or his compositors) printed 'Arden', but whenever we encounter the word we must remember that this is an imaginary location, as 'French' as it is 'English', as fantastic as it is familiar.

Plays within the play

The dukedom in *As You Like It*, like those in *The Comedy of Errors*, *A Midsummer Night's Dream*, and *Measure for Measure*, licenses a space for revelry and pastime where, distinctively, the power of dukes is set apart from an emotional life which, as G. K. Hunter remarks, 'the dukes are unable to engage with because they see it only from the standpoint of public control'.[1] In *As You Like It* not only does this narrative pattern create a political frame that sets ethical systems against status systems but also, given the nature of the play's resolution, it suggests that much that is worked out in the forest is provisional. Likewise, more than in those other comedies, many of the inset episodes are metatheatrical, set-piece performances before on-stage audiences. These include the wrestling at the court of Duke Frederick (1.2), the elegy of Jaques and the sobbing stag enacted before the forest court (2.1),[2] Jaques' speech upon the ages of man (2.7), the 'pageant' of Silvius and Phoebe watched by Rosalind and Celia (3.6), the wooing by Orlando of 'Ganymede' with Celia as spectator (4.1), Oliver's tale of his rescue from the lioness by Orlando (4.3), and the song by the pages before Touchstone and Audrey (5.3).[3] In the last scene alone, in Touchstone's speech about the lie we hear him satirise, before all the forest court, masculine honour codes; we witness the mass ceremony of four betrothals solemnised by Hymen; and, finally, we hear the narrative of Duke Frederick's conversion delivered by Jacques de Boys. The sequence is rounded off by Rosalind's epilogue,[4] which reminds the audience that, just as the actors have done, they have themselves played many parts. In some ways these rituals and revelries constitute 'a kind of borderland between everyday life and the stage';[5] in others they generate what René Girard calls 'mimetic desire' – 'The sight of lovers feedeth those in love' (3.5.48).[6] They remind us yet further of the processes of fiction-making that the play enacts.

Yet we live by these very fictions – of authenticity, of innocence, of desire, of gender, and of ending and resolution. The inset narratives serve as figures of the

---

[1] *English Drama 1586–1642: The Age of Shakespeare*, 1997, p. 317.
[2] The speech was transformed into an icon of sentiment by William Blake, William Hodges, and John Constable: see Stuart Sillars, *Painting Shakespeare: The Artist as Critic, 1720–1820*, 2006, pp. 169–73, 281–4, 303–4.
[3] Hanna Scolnicov, '"Here is the place appointed for the wrestling"', in François Laroque (ed.), *The Show Within*, 2 vols., 1992, II, 141–53; for Celia's crucial role in 4.1, see Rutter *et al.*, *Clamorous Voices*, pp. 115–16.
[4] See below, p. 226.
[5] Leo Salingar, *Shakespeare and the Traditions of Comedy*, 1974, p. 9.
[6] *A Theater of Envy: William Shakespeare*, 1991, chap. 11.

larger narrative, and many are stories of travesty or, sometimes, reversal or change. By virtue of being framed within the action they remind us, by their fictitiousness, that this motif of transformation, so prevalent in earlier comedies like *A Midsummer Night's Dream*, needs to be considered anew in relation to the action of *As You Like It* in its completeness. After this play has ended, Jaques will remain Jaques; William, Audrey, and probably Touchstone will remain untransfigured and untouched by Fortune – 'strange beasts', as Jaques calls them (5.4.36). The lovers, on the other hand, ought to have purged the inconstancies and 'supposes' of 'moonish youth' (3.3.338) and become authors of themselves. For them, transformation has modulated into a new concept of voluntary conversion (see below, p. 45). However, these main characters have bound themselves within an artful and possibly unstable contract that is defined by the multiplicity of 'if's that stud the play's conclusion – 'If truth hold true contents' (5.4.114), as Hymen sums it up.

Theatrical genres

The play's central story of the wooing of Orlando and Rosalind, a tale in which, in the manner of classical New Comedy, love and virtue overcome adversity and oppression, is of the slightest: the heroine and hero experience love at first sight as she watches him prove his manhood in a kind of trial by combat with the champion of a wicked duke.[1] The play's simplicity of plot, made even more spare by the pruning of the intrigue that generally characterises this genre, is one source of the delight that it may provoke, although Rosalind's wit and the games the lovers play with gender roles make it, in the words of a modern actor, a 'dangerous' play.[2] In New Comedy the usual pattern is for an eloquent hero with the help of a witty slave to win his loved one from the guardianship of a 'humorous' or hypocritical order: here, it could be argued, an ironic woman and her best friend usurp this customary masculine role, and here it is the 'hero', Orlando, who has to be purged of a sentimental romantic humour.

The text also announces its kinship to an 'old tale' (1.2.94), drawing not only upon comedy and tragi-comedy but upon folktale and romance:[3] there are three sons (the youngest being the most virtuous),[4] a mixture of the quotidian and the foreign, brushes with death, hints of magic, and miraculous deliverances. (Perhaps the unequal bequest of Sir Roland was a variation upon the folk-motif of a father giving an equal amount of money to each of his sons as a test: Orlando must prove

---

[1] For New Comedy, see Salingar, *Traditions of Comedy, passim*.
[2] Juliet Stevenson, quoted in Rutter *et al.*, *Clamorous Voices*, p. 97; for Sidney on delight, see Sir Philip Sidney, *An Apology for Poetry*, ed. G. Shepherd, 1973, p. 137.
[3] For ancient romances, see Bakhtin, *Dialogic Imagination*, pp. 86–110.
[4] This is mirrored by three sons of the franklin in Lodge (*Rosalind*, p. 170); for Ben Jonson's disdain for romance, 'All the mad Rolands and sweet Olivers', see his *Underwood*, 'Execration upon Vulcan', 79 (*Poems*, ed. Ian Donaldson, 1975, p. 196); for an actor's account of playing Orlando in a production by Terry Hands that dealt with the play as a fairy-tale, see John Bowe, 'Orlando', in Philip Brockbank (ed.), *Players of Shakespeare*, 1985, pp. 67–76.

himself, as he does by wrestling a champion and slaying a lion.)[1] There may be residues of the often misogynist jigs that ended performances of Elizabethan plays.[2] Elements of its plot are variations upon romance chronicles exemplified by a play of about 1570, *Sir Clyomon and Clamydes* (attributed to Thomas Preston), as well as upon what G. K. Hunter calls 'romantic adventure plays'. At the time that *As You Like It* was being written, such plays (which, unlike Shakespeare's text, tended to exclude romantic love) comprised the stock in trade of Henslowe's Admiral's Men, rivals to Shakespeare's company – this could be another explanation for its title (see below, p. 51). These tend to be

> stories of enforced adventure imposed on virtuous noblemen . . . forced into exile by unscrupulous families. They lose their social status and are separated from their families; they are obliged to live with boors, devious foreigners, and cynical (though loyal) clowns; but they bear all this with Christian cheerfulness, and eventually change of circumstances uncovers the plot against them; the hero can then recover (usually by military means) the status he lost. The king or other ruler, who has been misled by villains, now confirms . . . the return of justice to the deserving individual.[3]

Although this synopsis may outline the action of the play, it does not match its plot. Most of the turning-points of the story are narrated rather than enacted – as though Shakespeare was seeking to strip bare and make strange the conventions of the genres he had adopted. Moreover, the setting makes it a pastoral (see below, pp. 18–21) and, like many pastoral poems, Shakespeare's pastoral comedy is lacking in event or action. Apart from the set-pieces of the wrestling, the song (and dance?) after the killing of the deer (4.2), and the masque and dance at the end of the play, it is mainly a play of talk and song, a feast of language that, in some of its registers, looks back to the comedies written in prose for the Elizabethan court by John Lyly from about 1583 for Oxford's Boys and revived at about the time of *As You Like It* by the Children of the Chapel and the Children of Paul's.[4] (Prose in these contexts is certainly no index of the 'real' or the natural.) If, as it might have been, *As You Like It* was written for the opening of the Globe rather than for a court performance,[5] Shakespeare was perhaps deliberately conjuring for his audience not only the stories of romantic adventure popular in public playhouses but also the linguistic styles of court theatre. In Lylyan drama, as in the play's source, Lodge's *Rosalind* (the subtitle of which, *Euphues' Golden Legacy*, pays homage to Lyly's prose romance of that name), talk serves not merely to express turmoils of feeling but also, as in

---

[1] Relevant analogies can be found in Stith Thompson, *Motif-Index of Folk-Literature*, 6 vols., 1955–8, H331.6, H501.3, and H1161.3.

[2] Mary Thomas Crane, 'Linguistic change, theatrical practice, and the ideologies of status in *As You Like It*', *ELR* 27 (1997), 361–92.

[3] Hunter, *English Drama*, pp. 364–71 at 364.

[4] Lyly's pastoral comedy *Love's Metamorphosis*, originally performed by Paul's Boys in 1590, was revived by the Blackfriars Boys in 1600 (see Andrew Gurr, *The Shakespearian Playing Companies*, 1996, pp. 229 and 341); the anonymous pastoral comedy, *The Maid's Metamorphosis* (written in heroic couplets by Lyly or Day?) which, like *Love's Metamorphosis*, contains a breeches part, was performed by Paul's Boys in about 1600 (see below, p. 40 n. 3).

[5] See Date and Occasion, p. 52, and Appendix 1.

Lyly's plays, to analyse and re-define themes of desire and romance. An apposite example of this technique is to be found in *Gallathea* (1588). Gallathea and Phyllida greet each other: they are both daughters of shepherds and both had been disguised as boys by their fathers so that they might not be sacrificed to a monster in order to appease the wrath of Neptune. At their first encounter they had become enamoured of one another:

> PHYLLIDA   ... I say it is pity you are not a woman.
>
> GALLATHEA I would not wish to be a woman, unless it were because thou art a man.
>
> PHYLLIDA Nay, I do not wish thee to be a woman, for then I should not love thee, for I have sworn never to love a woman.
>
> GALLATHEA A strange humour in so pretty a youth, and according to mine, for myself will never love a woman.
>
> PHYLLIDA It were a shame, if a maiden should be a suitor (a thing hated in that sex), that thou shouldst deny to be her servant.
>
> GALLATHEA If it be a shame in me, it can be no commendation in you, for yourself is of that mind.
>
> PHYLLIDA Suppose I were a virgin (I blush in supposing myself one), and that under the habit of a boy were the person of a maid: if I should utter my affection with sighs, manifest my sweet love by my salt tears, and prove my loyalty unspotted and my griefs intolerable, would not then that fair face pity his true heart?
>
> GALLATHEA Admit that I were as you would have me suppose that you are, and that I should with entreaties, prayers, oaths, bribes, and whatever can be invented in love, desire your favour, would you not yield?
>
> PHYLLIDA Tush, you come in with 'admit'.
>
> GALLATHEA And you with 'suppose'.[1]

The situation matches the falling in love of Phoebe with 'Ganymede', as well as the game of supposes between Orlando and Rosalind, and the matter resembles the set-piece anatomies of love that stud the play. On occasion Shakespeare imitates the particulars of Lyly's euphuistic style, its parallel and correspondent clauses and balanced antitheses.[2] The play also looks forward to the modes of Restoration comedy in which epilogues were often spoken by women and where theatrical speech provided a licensed mode for independent women and young men to escape from the tyranny of fathers (see below, p. 36).[3] Shakespeare plays both within and with these generic conventions, now granting them credit, now exposing their excess, so encouraging the audience to attend to the tones of wit and fancy. Between the larger tableau scenes there is a series of fillers: the courtship of Touchstone and Audrey, the putting-down of Sir Oliver by Jaques, the bringing home of the deer-slayer, and the 'two unexplained Pages whose pertness sets off the sweetness of

---

[1] John Lyly, *Gallathea*, 3.2.6–28 in *'Gallathea' and 'Midas'*, ed. Anne Begor Lancashire, 1970.

[2] Examples of Lodge's euphuism in *Rosalind* are given in Appendix 2, pp. 227–38; for Lyly's style, see Peter Saccio, *The Court Comedies of John Lyly*, 1969, pp. 40–51; and for an account of how the play's 'feast of rural antitheses' might be approached by actors, see John Barton, *Playing Shakespeare*, 1984, pp. 72–3.

[3] For epilogues, see Elizabeth Howe, *The First English Actresses: Women and Drama, 1660–1700*, 1992, pp. 93–4. The unadapted text of *AYLI* was performed for the first time after 1642 only in 1740–1 (see Stage History, p. 57 below), which may indicate something about the power of Restoration patriarchy.

their song. In all this there is an undertone of parody, as if Shakespeare were well aware that the filler scene was a hoary theatrical device.'[1] Players are therefore called upon to use not only representational but presentational skills – the skills of ironic delivery, elocution, singing, and dance. Because the story and situations are so familiar, players will kindle for their spectators not just those emotional responses we expect from surprising turns of plot but varieties of knowingness – ranging from the enjoyment of feats of seeming improvisation to reflection upon the way that sports of love in the forest will change in style when their players return to court. Celia and Rosalind return from their forest exile to a court that may have been purged of its iniquities but not of its gendered inequalities. Before this happens we are prepared to accept, as nodal points in the action, those occasions when characters turn without motive or reason against others – Oliver's abomination of Orlando, Duke Frederick's sudden hatred of Rosalind, and subsequently, equally unexpected, his conversion from his old self – and then attend to the rhetorical consequences of these moments.

From other aspects *As You Like It* is a 'humour' play where the plot consists of sets of conversational encounters between stock 'characters', sometimes deployed for the purposes of satire: Ben Jonson's satirical comedy *Every Man in his Humour*, which had been performed by the Chamberlain's Men in 1598, is a play that exposes, among other follies, fashionable melancholy of the kind affected by Jaques.[2] The play was contemporary with a flurry of publication that invoked a notorious act of censorship in June 1599 by the Archbishop of Canterbury, John Whitgift, who prohibited further printing of certain named satires in verse and prose (those that had been printed were to be burnt), and ordered in particular that no history plays be printed unless they had been allowed by the Privy Council and that other plays be permitted only 'by such as have authority'.[3] In the public and private (boys') playhouses Jonson and Marston were competing with parodic and satirical plays that seem designed to appeal to the particular tastes and prejudices of young adult males, particularly the students of the Inns of Court.[4] Shakespeare, perhaps in response to these new modes, added to the characters that people Lodge's romance narrative not only comic types like the hedge-priest Sir Oliver Martext and the bucolic innocents William and Audrey, but also two satirical agents, Touchstone and Jaques, who serve as both embodiments of affectation and castigators of folly

---

[1] M. M. Mahood, *Bit Parts in Shakespeare's Plays*, 1992, p. 28.

[2] In *The Sad Shepherd* (1637?) Jonson returns to the theme in a more sympathetic mode, setting his tale in a world of Robin Hood and the greenwood.

[3] See 1.2.70–1 n. and Richard A. McCabe, 'Elizabethan satire and the bishops' ban of 1599', *Yearbook of English Studies* 11 (1981), 188–94; the ban may have prevented early publication of *AYLI*: see Textual Analysis, p. 215 below.

[4] Hunter, *English Drama*, pp. 282–300; but see Ann Blake, '"The humour of children": John Marston's plays in the private theatres', *RES* n.s. 38 (1987), 471–82. Dialogues between Rosalind and Celia and Rosalind and Orlando contain, as the commentary to this edition reveals, a remarkable amount of salaciousness; compare Lynda E. Boose, 'The 1599 bishops' ban, Elizabethan pornography, and the sexualization of the Jacobean stage', in Richard Burt and John Michael Archer (eds.), *Enclosure Acts: Sexuality, Property, and Culture in Early Modern England*, 1994, pp. 185–200.

and vice in others.[1] Jaques' melancholy – which was signified by his dressing in black and associated with the stock figure of the traveller as well as with the melancholy madness of Homer's Ajax[2] – contrasts with Silvius' love-sick melancholy, and is disconcerting. Although he professes that 'motley's the only wear' (2.7.34), instead of the fool's bauble he seems to be addicted to the scourge of the satirist, applying it not only to city pride (2.7.70–87) but to the innocent follies of love, as well as improvising, in the 'Ducdame' sequence (2.5.41–51)[3] for example, against the exiled noblemen with a degree of sardonicism that borders on the misanthropic. He narcissistically luxuriates in death and its coming – we might not expect Death to stalk in Arcadia (see Plate 5)[4] – and, supposedly a reformed libertine, seems to be stalking the forest on some kind of undisclosed sexual quest – a 'philosopher in search of sensations' as Oscar Wilde called him.[5] In fact melancholy was not just a picturesque literary topic or psychological aberration but was regarded by contemporaries as a dangerous malady. Seneca's account of the topic (translated by Ben Jonson) fits Jaques:

Periculosa melancholia. – It is a dangerous thing when men's minds come to sojourn with their affections, and their diseases eat into their strength; that when too much desire and greediness of vice hath made the body unfit, or unprofitable, it is yet gladded with the sight and spectacle of it in others; and for want of ability to be an actor, is content to be a witness. It enjoys the pleasure of sinning in beholding others sin, as in dicing, drinking, drabbing, etc. Nay, when it cannot do all these, it is offended with his own narrowness, that excludes it from the universal delights of mankind, and oft times dies of a melancholy that it cannot be vicious enough.[6]

---

[1] See *OED* Hedge-priest; Spenser's Fifth (May) Eclogue in *The Shepheardes Calender* (1579) and his complaint *Prosopopœia or Mother Hubberds Tale* (1591) had lampooned unlettered Elizabethan clergy and dumb-dog priests like Sir Oliver. Touchstone is generally described in the text as a fool (although named in the speech prefixes as 'Clown'), and there is no reason but to believe that he would have worn the conventional costume described by a contemporary: 'before I went out of Rome, I was again taken by the English College and put there into the holy house three days, with a fool's coat on my back, half blue, half yellow, and a cockscomb with three bells on my head' (*Edward Webbe . . . his Troublesome Travels* (1590), ed. Edward Arber, 1868, pp. 30–1); the clown's part is taken by Much in Chettle and Munday's Robin Hood plays (1598).

[2] See Z. S. Fink, 'Jaques and the malcontent traveler', *PQ* 14 (1935), 237–52; Jaques resembles the travellers Macilente and Carlo Buffone in Jonson's *Everyman out of his Humour* (1599), Bruto in Marston's *Certain Satires* (in Davenport (ed.), *Poems of John Marston*, pp. 76–7, ll. 127–56), and fits the type of the 'hick scorner', a scoffing and travelled libertine like the hero of the interlude of that name (1513) – see *OED* Hick scorner; see also Roger Ascham, *The Schoolmaster* (1570), *English Works*, ed. W. A. Wright, 1904, pp. 228–37; for the melancholy of Ajax, see R. Klibansky, E. Panofsky, and F. Saxl, *Saturn and Melancholy*, 1964, pp. 16–18; Frances A. Yates, *The Occult Philosophy*, 1979, p. 153; for an actor's account of the part, see Alan Rickman, 'Jaques in *As You Like It*', in Russell Jackson and Robert Smallwood (eds.), *Players of Shakespeare 2*, 1988, 73–80.

[3] See Richard A. J. Knowles, 'Ducdame', *SQ* 18 (1967), 438–41.

[4] See Poussin's '*Et in Arcadia Ego*', Plate 5, p. 17; compare Douglas Trevor, 'John Donne and scholarly melancholy', *SEL* 40 (2000), 81–102.

[5] Gamini Salgādo (ed.), *Eyewitnesses of Shakespeare*, 1975, p. 165; for Jaques at Stratford 1952–2000, see Smallwood, pp. 135–66. In Chettle and Munday's *The Downfall of Robert Earl of Huntington* (1598) Robin Hood and his men have taken a vow of chastity (3.2): it is notable that there are no women in Duke Senior's entourage.

[6] Seneca, *Epist.*, CXIV, 23–5 in Jonson, *Timber or Discoveries*, VIII, 608; compare John Weever's epigram 'What beastliness by others you have shown, / Such by yourselves 'tis thought that you have known' (*Faunus and Melliflora*, 1600); see also the important appendix, 'Seventeenth-century melancholy' to L. C. Knights, *Drama and Society in the Age of Jonson*, 1937. Knights wrote, 'In this world, when a humanistic philosophy was current, death appeared more terrible than in the past' (p. 265).

5   Nicolas Poussin, *Et in Arcadia Ego*, *c.* 1630, Devonshire Collection, Chatsworth. Shepherds are uncovering an overgrown tomb. The motto ('I too am in Arcadia') is to be imagined as an utterance by Death: it is one of Jaques' functions to remind the characters to remember their ends. See Erwin Panofsky, '*Et in Arcadia Ego*: Poussin and the elegiac tradition', *Meaning in the Visual Arts*, 1970, pp. 340–67

Jaques may be saved at the completion of his pilgrimage from libertinism by the espousal of a holy way of life, but Duke Senior's stern rebukes remind us that melancholics were closely related both to malcontents and to dissidents like Shakespeare's Hamlet or Webster's Bosola who insisted upon seeing the calamities that beset the age – plague, dearth, and political disorder – as emblems of corrupt government.[1] Melancholy can have its origins as much in the social and economic conditions of the time as in individual psychology.

Jaques is remembered above all for his speech on the seven ages of man (2.7.139–66). It is for director and actor to decide whether this is the incarnation of a mature if pessimistic wisdom, whether his speech is a Hamlet-like *memento mori*, a reminder to the Duke that he is but dressed in a little brief authority,[2] whether the speech is imbued by a world-view that valued life in terms of commercial worth (an old man is 'sans everything'),[3] or whether the biting sentiments are coloured by his inability to find ease in company and the consequent projection of the disease of a 'fantastical knave' (3.4.82) onto his listeners. He may disdain his own eloquence, an interpretation chosen by many productions in which the malcontent munches an apple as he speaks. Whatever his effect, it may be felt that the entrance of good old Adam immediately afterwards, exhausted but scarcely 'sans everything' (2.7.166), gives the lie to his sardonicism.

Pastoral

In opposition to the scenes of court cruelty, Shakespeare sets the bulk of the play in the country, thus submitting comedy, romance, and satire to the decorum of pastoral.[4] The court is never forgotten, however, and the narrative of Jacques de Boys (5.4.135–50) reminds us that it was only by the miracle of meeting the old religious man that Duke Frederick, in the manner of tragi-comedy, was diverted from his intention of invading the forest with a mighty power in order to put his brother to the sword.[5]

Pastoral is established in a literal manner by the presence of the shepherds, Silvius, Corin, and Phoebe, who are given speeches that praise the worthy toil of

---

[1] Jaques gives the impression of having had, like them, a university education which did not, as it did not for many contemporaries, lead to preferment (see Knights, *Drama and Society* pp. 268–74).

[2] See Karin Coddon, '"Such strange desygns": madness, subjectivity, and treason in *Hamlet* and Elizabethan culture', *Ren. Drama* n.s. 20 (1989), 51–75.

[3] Changes in meaning of 'the theatre of the world' are plotted in Jean-Christophe Agnew, *Worlds Apart: The Market and the Theater in Anglo-American Thought, 1550–1750*, 1986, pp. 14–16, 55–6.

[4] The anonymous anthology of pastoral verse, *England's Helicon*, appeared in the same year as the play; B. Loughrey (ed.), *The Pastoral Mode: A Casebook*, 1984, offers a useful anthology of Renaissance and contemporary critical texts; see also Girard, *Theater of Envy*, chap. 10. Brian Gibbons, 'Amorous fictions and *As You Like It*', in *Shakespeare and Multiplicity*, 1993, pp. 153–81, offers a subtle reading of the play in relation to Sidney's *Arcadia*; see also Juliet Dusinberre, 'Rival poets in the Forest of Arden', *Shakespeare Jahrbuch* 139 (2003), 71–83.

[5] In this aspect the play anticipates the miraculous endings of Shakespeare's later romances; for the theme of *felix culpa*, 'the achievement of joy not only through suffering but partly because of it', in Guarini's *Il Pastor Fido* (1590), see Kirsch, *Jacobean Dramatic Perspectives*, pp. 10–12.

country life and pageants that depict the joys and pangs of rustic love. But pastoral is, of course, by no means a naive form, not simply 'about' the natural innocence of the countryside: it is a species of allegory, the characters in which, shepherds and not peasants, are anti-types of landlords or the privileged.[1] What perhaps distinguishes pastoral from other forms of lyric or narrative is that in pastoral there is always an implied comparison with another culture, court or city, or another kind of vocation or material production. This *différance*[2] may make the choice of theatrical setting particularly difficult for pastoral drama. However, although the play may offer a social critique (see below, pp. 22–6) and although few directors these days would choose to present Arden as a simple vision of a golden age, there is little mud and no artisanal labour in pastoral – certainly no rural work is *enacted* on stage by its refined characters who, in this case, speak with the accents and tone of the courtiers.[3] As William Empson wrote:

> The essential trick of . . . pastoral, which was felt to imply a beautiful relation between rich and poor, was to make simple people express strong feelings (felt as the most universal subject, something fundamentally true about everybody) in learned and fashionable language (so that you wrote about the best subject in the best way). From seeing the two sorts of people combined like this you thought better of both; the best parts of both were used.[4]

The increasing political and economic dominance of the court and the city in early modern England may explain why the realities of the country are seldom if ever represented directly on the stage.[5] The countryside is generally a fictive place of resort, a festive, 'green', or comic world to which characters migrate while in some state of unsettledness and from which they return to the city having achieved a measure of recognition in the course of their rustic revelling. At the end of *The Tempest* Gonzalo sums up the movement:

> Prospero [found] his dukedom
> In a poor isle; and all of us, ourselves,
> When no man was his own.   (5.1.211–13)

In Arden, by analogy, most find their 'selves'. Yet we have to remember that that world of pastoral, so closely associated with 'nature', is self-authenticating: pastoral

---

[1] Examples are provided by Spenser's *The Shepheardes Calender* (1579) and George Wither, *The Shep-herds Hunting* (1615), which was written 'during the time of the author's imprisonment in the Marshalsea' (title page), where the satirist was imprisoned for writing *Abuses Stripped and Whipped* (1613), and which begins with an epistle that exposes the rise and fall of courtiers. In the January Eclogue of *The Shepheardes Calender*, Colin complains that his country lass Rosalind does not love him, although he is loved by another shepherd, Hobbinol. The gloss to the poem by 'E. K.' notes that it proves that 'paederastice [is] much to be preferred before gynerastice, that is the love which enflameth men with lust toward woman-kind' (Edmund Spenser, *The Shorter Poems*, ed. William A. Oram *et al.*, 1989, p. 34).

[2] The term is from Jacques Derrida, *Writing and Difference*, trans. Alan Bass, 1978.

[3] The text of Preston's *Clyomon and Clamydes* indicates that in the play the shepherd Corin was to speak, as was often the case for rustic characters, in a 'Mummerset' West Country accent (Hattaway, p. 72); in Golding's Ovid, Mercury adopts the same accent when in disguise (*Metamorphoses*, II, 869–72).

[4] William Empson, *Some Versions of Pastoral*, 1935, p. 17.

[5] Michael Hattaway, 'Drama and society', in Braunmuller and Hattaway (eds.), *English Renaissance Drama*, pp. 106–8.

worlds, where 'nature' invokes a myth of political equality, serve to define those elements of 'civilised' life that are 'unnatural', cruel, or concerned with social climbing. The earliest pastoral is arguably the Garden of Eden, and the rather stark world of *As You Like It* is itself infused with nostalgia for the lost paradises of the Bible and the classical Golden Age as described in Ovid's *Metamorphoses*.[1] It also looks back to a less distant feudal world where social status depended upon kinship rather than upon wealth, a change that we see Orlando refusing to accept in the play's first scene. Arden is a place of cure and re-creation if not recreation: the forest magic associated with Rosalind[2] eventually extends as far as the court, where the usurping Duke is converted to the religious life so that Duke Senior can find his dukedom again and justice be restored.

Counter-pastoral

It is characteristic of Shakespeare, however, that he is as much concerned with undercutting his literary techniques as with flaunting them. The shepherd Corin describes not the pleasures but the labours of the country, and the play's fools, Jaques and Touchstone, establish a kind of reality principle, both demonstrating a derisive scepticism about the satisfactions of country as opposed to pastoral life.[3] Touchstone's discourse belongs in the humanist tradition of the paradoxical encomium, exemplified by Erasmus' *Praise of Folly* and the *Gargantua and Pantagruel* of François Rabelais, in which fools are used to expound upon the follies of the world.[4] He deploys an intricate and elaborate rhetoric to make the point that the artificiality of court life is more 'natural' than life in the country:

> CORIN And how like you this shepherd's life, Master Touchstone?
> TOUCHSTONE Truly, shepherd, in respect of itself, it is a good life; but in respect that it is a shepherd's life, it is naught. In respect that it is solitary, I like it very well; but in respect that it is private, it is a very vile life. Now in respect it is in the fields, it pleaseth me well; but in respect it is not in the court, it is tedious. As it is a spare life, look you, it fits my humour well; but as there is no more plenty in it, it goes much against my stomach.   (3.3.1–8)

---

[1] For memories in the text of a lost Eden and references to the parable of the prodigal son, see Armstrong, pp. 125–7; Russell Fraser, 'Shakespeare's Book of Genesis', *Comparative Drama* 25 (1991), 121–8; for the Golden Age, see 1.1.95, 2.1.5, 3.3.197–8 and, for the topic, Salingar, *Traditions of Comedy*, pp. 288–93.

[2] See Christopher Hill, *The World Turned Upside Down*, 1975, pp. 46–7, for the associations between forests and witchcraft. The old religious man who converted Duke Frederick may be Rosalind's mentor, an un-named uncle (see 5.4.144 n.): in Lodge usurpation is rectified by an armed uprising; for the figure in general, see 'The hermit in an Elizabethan textbook of chivalry', Frances A. Yates, *Astraea: The Imperial Theme in the Sixteenth Century*, 1975, pp. 106–8.

[3] The term 'counter-pastoral' comes from Williams, *The Country and the City*, chap. 3. It is to be found from earliest times: see Theocritus, *Idylls*, xx, in which Eunica despises the young goatherd for his coarse features and foul breath; compare Nicholas Breton's *The Court and the Country*, 1618, and A. Stuart Daley's important article, 'The dispraise of the country in *As You Like It*', *SQ* 36 (1985), 300–14; Renato Poggioli reads the pastoral impulse as a projective mechanism for the sublimation of civilisation's discontents; see *The Oaten Flute*, 1975.

[4] See Walter Kaiser, *Praisers of Folly*, 1964; Rosalie L. Colie, *Paradoxia Epidemica: The Renaissance Tradition of Paradox*, 1976.

Other lines are studded with proverbial lore: they are not, however, folksy, since many of them derive ultimately from Erasmus' *Adages*. The ritualised scene after the killing of the deer (4.2) hovers exactly on the border between pastoral and counter-pastoral, being a celebration of rustic sports deployed for the purposes of survival and of masculine bonding, as well as offering a memory of death and pain and the decay of marriage into adultery.[1]

Roland Barthes distinguished between the *lisible* and the *scriptible*, 'readerly' and 'writerly' texts.[2] As the above description of its generic indeterminacy reveals, *As You Like It* is a 'writerly' text; in the context of theatre, it requires of both actors and spectators a keen observance of style, detail, and tone in order to identify a gamut of meanings. These are compounded by gender indeterminacies: an original boy-player, an apprentice actor, had to speak as a woman, as a woman dressed as a man, as a male playing a woman dressed as a male pretending to be a youth enacting a woman's part (4.1.55–157), indeed, on occasion, as himself! Even the play's title is profoundly and teasingly ambiguous: does its 'you' designate a distinguished patron, even the Queen herself,[3] or perhaps a public playhouse audience, aspiring to – or reacting against – the tastes of a theatrical coterie? Does it suggest handing the play over to spectators – or the players – as a text to be re-produced at will? Does it imply that Shakespeare disowns the form and content of what he produced? Does it invoke a trans-historical, trans-cultural, trans-generic concept of pleasure, uncontaminated by social form and pressure? Does it refer to the play's content, the kinds of tales it tells, or to its form, the manner of its performance, its play of styles, its exposition of social roles, its simultaneous invocation and subversion of decorum?[4] Is the play sexually provocative? Precisely because this invoked pleasure is not embedded in any one specific context, historical, cultural, or aesthetic, the title problematises not only the experience of pleasure but its use, its relation to individual happiness and to its social functions of containment and subversion.

Perhaps Rosader (Orlando) in Lodge's *Rosalind* can be taken to speak for understanding onlookers as well as himself when he reflects, 'I take these follies for high fortunes, and hope these feigned affections do divine some unfeigned end of ensuing fancies.'[5]

---

[1] It is notable that there is no mention of poaching, no reason to link the scene to the feasts of poached venison celebrated in legends of Robin Hood (see below, pp. 27–9).

[2] Roland Barthes, *S/Z*, trans. Richard Miller, 1970, pp. 3–4.

[3] See below, pp. 51–2, 221–6.

[4] For the popularity of pastoral plays in the years 1597–1600 see A. H. Thorndike, 'The pastoral element in the English drama before 1605', *MLN* 14 (1899), 228–46; Samuel Daniel's *Hymen's Triumph*, described on its title page as 'a pastoral tragi-comedy', was performed at Somerset House in 1615. Heywood's *The Four Prentices of London*, performed by the Admiral's Men in 1594, has a heroine who disguises herself as a page and later plays the part of a woman (Michael Shapiro, *Gender in Play on the Shakespearean Stage: Boy Heroines and Female Pages*, 1994, pp. 120–2; see also p. 52).

[5] *Rosalind*, p. 83.

The condition of the country

Although the play is in cheerful dialogue with dominant theatrical genres of the period, it also addresses contemporary civil and economic issues. England in the 1590s was undergoing some measure of social stress, although the political and social order did remain basically stable. Plagues and bad harvests were compounded by dearth caused by the pursuit of gain, by profit-taking by lords like Oliver cutting down on their households, and by landlords and usurers evicting or buying out tenants like Corin from their holdings.[1] There was much crying out against the death of hospitality and 'housekeeping', exemplified in the text by Oliver's casting-out of his father's old servant Adam. Contemporaries often compared 'The constant service of the antique world' (2.3.57) with the unemployment and vices of their own age.[2]

On the part of certain landowners financial success generated a desire for upward mobility. In 1600 Thomas Wilson castigated the ambition of elder sons,

not contented with their states of their fathers to be counted yeomen and called John or Robert (such a one) but must skip into his [*sic*] velvet breeches and silken doublet and, getting to be admitted into some Inn of Court or Chancery, must ever after think scorn to be called any other than gentleman; which gentlemen indeed, perceiving them unfit to do them service that their fathers did, when their leases do expire, turn them out of their lands.[3]

Since the first-born inherited everything and younger sons had to make their own way, the lot of younger brothers like Orlando could worsen as they became alienated from their older siblings not only by wealth but by rank: in *1 Henry IV* Falstaff leads a company of 'discarded unjust servingmen, younger sons to younger brothers . . . the cankers of a calm world and a long peace' (*1H4*, 4.2.27–30). Not surprisingly, younger sons were often prominent in plays of the period – Edmond in *King Lear* (1605?) and Will Smallshanks in Barry's *Ram Alley* (1608?) are examples – just as they had been in medieval romances.[4]

---

[1] John Walter and Keith Wrightson, 'Dearth and the social order in early modern England', in Paul Slack (ed.), *Rebellion, Popular Protest and the Social Order in Early Modern England*, 1984, pp. 108–28; Margaret Spufford, 'The disappearance of the small landowner', in *Contrasting Communities: English Villagers in the Sixteenth and Seventeenth Centuries*, 1974, pp. 46–57; Sir Henry Lee (1530–1610), who arranged the Accession Day Tilts for Queen Elizabeth, was also a notorious enclosing landlord (see Yates, *Astraea*, pp. 88–111, and 'Sir Henry Lee' in *DNB*); for the figure of a usurer who deprives poor farmers of their land and cattle, see Greene and Lodge's play, *A Looking-Glass for London and England* (1588), 1.3.

[2] See, for example, Anon., *The English Courtier and the Country Gentleman* (1586), repr. in Roxburghe Library, *Inedited Tracts* (1868), pp. 34 ff.; Joseph Hall, *Virgidemiarum* (1597), Book v, in Joseph Hall, *Collected Poems*, ed. A. Davenport, 1949, pp. 75–86; Gervase Markham (?), *A Health to the Gentlemanly Profession of Servingman* (1598); Philip Stubbes, *Anatomy of Abuses* (1583), ed. Frederick J. Furnivall, 1879, p. 54.

[3] *The State of England Anno Dom 1600*, ed. F. Fisher, 1936, p. 19.

[4] See, for example, *The Tale of Gamelyn*, the source of *Rosalind*; in 'Of Brotherly Love or Amity' Plutarch remarks that 'the amity of brethren [is] as rare as their hatred was in times past' (*Moralia*, Everyman Library, trans. Philemon Holland [1603], n.d., p. 209; see also Samuel Taylor Coleridge, *Coleridge's Criticism of Shakespeare*, ed. R. A. Foakes, 1989, pp. 97–8.

Another cause for contemporary social and moral concern was the complaint, laid early in the century by Sir Thomas More, that sheep were eating up men:[1] in Arden the forest is inhabited not by freeholders but by tenants, reduced to a subsistence level by tending other men's sheep. Sheep-raising was increasingly profitable for landowners; it generated not only wool but manure, which was used to increase arable production. Inequalities were becoming greater as the wealth of the Tudor gentry steadily increased during the first half of the sixteenth century at the expense of customary tenants and the wage-dependent. By 1608 John Fletcher, in a Preface to his tragi-comedy *The Faithful Shepherdess*, was inclined to spurn the kind of pastoral that was peopled by 'country-hired shepherds, in grey cloaks, with curtailed dogs in strings, sometimes laughing together and sometimes killing one another; and [including] Whitsun-ales, cream, wassail and morris-dances'. He boasted that his shepherds would be 'such as all the ancient poets, and modern, of understanding, have received them; that is, the owners of flocks, and not hirelings'.[2] Shakespeare, however, does give us 'hirelings' – although they scarcely speak in a rustic dialect. He also exposes the real economic hardships of shepherd's lives when Corin, describing his lot to Rosalind, spells out the dire effects of enclosure, the seizure of common land for the purposes of wool production:

> I am shepherd to another man,
> And do not shear the fleeces that I graze.
> My master is of churlish disposition
> And little recks to find the way to heaven
> By doing deeds of hospitality.
> Besides, his cot, his flocks, and bounds of feed
> Are now on sale, and at our sheepcote now
> By reason of his absence there is nothing
> That you will feed on.   (2.4.71–9)[3]

This registers the loss of an English Eden remembered, for example, in George Puttenham's *Art of English Poesy* (1589): Puttenham quotes Aristotle's *Politics* to the effect that 'pasturage was before tillage, or fishing, or fowling, or any other predatory art or chevisance [resource to get money] . . . for before there was a shepherd-keeper of his own or some other body's flock, there was none owner in the world – quick [living] cattle being the first property of any foreign possession'.[4] It also resembles the radical and vitriolic indictment that we find in '*Leicester's Commonwealth*' (1584): '[the Earl of Leicester] hath taken from the tenants round about their lands, woods, pastures, and commons, to make himself parks, chases, and other commodities therewith, to the subversion of many a good family, which

---

[1] *Utopia*, ed. J. Rawson Lumby, 1885, pp. 32–3; for a succinct account of the appropriation of arable land for pastoral use between 1561 and 1740 see Ann Kussmaul, *A General View of the Rural Economy of England, 1538–1840*, 1990, pp. 1–13; James R. Siemon, 'Landlord not king: agrarian change and interarticulation', in Burt and Archer, *Enclosure Acts*, pp. 17–33.
[2] *The Faithful Shepherdess*, p. 497; for Jonson's disdain for Guarini and Sidney, whose shepherds spoke in the registers of their authors, see Jonson, *Conversations with Drummond*, I, 132, 134.
[3] For statistics on enclosure and patterns of farming around 1600, see D. M. Palliser, *The Age of Elizabeth: England under the Later Tudors, 1547–1603*, 1983, pp. 162–70.
[4] *The Art of English Poesy* (1589), p. 30.

was maintained there, before this devourer set foot in that country.'[1] The trend was deplored by Francis Bacon, who saw a threat to the greatness and safety of the realm when 'dwellers' were reduced to beggars or 'cottagers'.[2] And, in a poem published a couple of years before the play:

> Sheep have eat up our meadows and our downs,
> Our corn, our wood, whole villages and towns,
> Yea, they have eat up many wealthy men,
> Besides widows and orphan children,
> Besides our statutes and our iron laws
> Which they have swallowed down into their maws:
> > Till now I thought the proverb did but jest,
> > Which said a black sheep was a biting beast.[3]

Complaints like these, based upon a moral economy, were commonplace: Christopher Hill analysed the ways in which those reduced to wage labour considered themselves little better than slaves.[4] Enclosure was the most popularly perceived cause of dearth: it had helped generate Kett's rebellion in 1549 and helped catalyse not only food riots but, particularly among rural artificers (many of whom lived in forest areas), the radicalism that irritated the Tudor and Stuart regimes between 1586 and 1631.[5] Poverty on rural estates was further compounded by the absenteeism of landlords (of which Silvius complains), their withdrawal 'from face to face relations with their servants and the people of their village'.[6] Overall, therefore, the play registers contemporary movements from a late feudal agricultural economy to a rentier system run by capitalist landlords, as well as agrarian innovations that turned peasants to labourers and concentrated on production for the market. It is notable that, at the play's end, the exiled courtiers make no attempt to rectify the effects of enclosure. But although it is true to say that the text aligns itself with a concept of the English Renaissance stage as 'a laboratory of and for the new social relations of agricultural and commercial capitalism',[7] it may be that the demands of the marriage sequence at the end of such a tragi-comedy make the accommodation of these matters impossible.

The fact that the miseries consequent upon enclosure were taking place in a 'forest' adds an extra resonance to the issue. For forests marked out the margins

---

[1] [T. Morgan?], *A Copy of a Letter written by a Master of Art in Cambridge* [*Leicester's Commonwealth*], ([Paris], 1584), p. 83; Sir Philip Sidney was a member of the Leicester circle, and the topic of enclosure is conspicuously lacking from his *Arcadia*; for Lodge's account of the shepherd's lot, see Appendix 2, p. 232; see also Knights, *Drama and Society*, pp. 89–100.

[2] *History of the Reign of King Henry VII*, ed. J. R. Lumby, 1881, p. 72.

[3] Thomas Bastard, *Chrestoleros* (1598), IV.20, p. 90; see also Hall, *Poems*, pp. 85–6.

[4] *World Turned Upside Down*, p. 53; see E. P. Thompson, 'The moral economy of the English crowd in the eighteenth century', *Past and Present* 50 (1971), 76–136; see Robert Greene's lament for the loss of Hospitality, Neighbourhood, and Conscience, *A Quippe for an Upstart Courtier* (1592) (Greene, XI, 209–10).

[5] See the account of Kett's rebellion (1549) printed in 1615: Alexander Neville, *Norfolk's Furies, or A View of Kett's Camp*, trans. R[ichard] W[oods] (1615), sigs. B1ᵛ–B2ᵛ, and Buchanan Sharp, *In Contempt of All Authority: Rural Artisans and Riot in the West of England, 1586–1660*, 1980, pp. 38–42.

[6] Anthony Fletcher and John Stevenson (eds.), *Order and Disorder in Early Modern England*, 1985, pp. 21–2.

[7] Agnew, *Worlds Apart*, p. xi.

of civil and civilised life. In early modern England they were, as we have seen, generally demesnes held by royal prerogative and set aside for hunting.[1] They were as a consequence likely to become sites of contest between royal or noble and artisanal or common interests. According to David Underdown, 'In the early seventeenth century . . . the Forest of Arden . . . experienced a marked increase in the number of landless poor, squatting on commons and wastes . . . Between 1590 and 1620 the Henley-in-Arden court leet regularly presented people for engaging in violent affrays, in numbers out of all proportion to the population.'[2] Woodland areas were outside the parochial system, its denizens free from parson as well as squire (Sir Oliver Martext has to be sent for from the 'next village' (3.4.31–2)). Because forests were associated with mythical figures of disorder, with the 'wood-woses' and 'savage men' from literature – the word 'savage' derives from the Latin word for 'wood', *silva* – and with the actual vagabonds, outlaws, and masterless men of Elizabethan times, 'deforesting' and the resultant increase in land for the raising of sheep could be legitimated by the gentry. In 1610 King James was to suggest that action should be taken against cottages on waste grounds and commons, especially forests, which were 'nurseries and receptacles of thieves, rogues, and beggars'.[3] Deforesting, therefore, for men of the early modern period as for those of Mesolithic times, was an index of the triumph of civilisation.[4]

Throughout the play conditions of the present are set against those of the past so that we realise that pastoral is a kind of history, not an escape from politics but a reading of politics. Moreover, the English pastoral tradition that culminates in Spenser's *Shepheardes Calendar* (1579) derives not just from the classical and neo-classical tradition marked out by the *Idylls* of Theocritus (ca 316–260 BC), the *Eclogues* of Virgil and, later, of Mantuan (1448–1516), but from a native tradition of satire and complaint. Sir Philip Sidney, in his defence of pastoral, noted: 'sometimes, under the pretty tales of wolves and sheep [the pastoral poem] can include the whole considerations of wrong-doing and patience [suffering]'.[5] The play may begin on a country estate, but we encounter immediately a power struggle between brothers

---

[1] Manwood, *Laws of the Forest*, ff. 3^r, 7^v–9^r; compare John Cowell, *The Interpreter* (1637), sigs. Gg2^r– Gg3^v.

[2] *Revel, Riot, and Rebellion: Popular Politics and Culture in England 1603–1660*, 1985, p. 34; 31° Eliz.c.7, 'An act against erecting and maintaining of cottages', had been deployed against the equivalent of rural squatters, although the act did not cover cottages for common herdsmen or shepherds (*Statutes*, IV.2,804–5). The word 'desert' is frequently used in the text to designate the forest: see 2.1.23, 2.4.65, 2.6.13, 2.7.110, 3.3.100, 4.3.136; see Hill, *World Turned Upside Down*, p. 44 for radical traditions associated with the Warwickshire Arden.

[3] Hill, *World Turned Upside Down*, p. 51; see E. R. Foster, *Proceedings in Parliament, 1610*, 1966, II, 280–1; A. L. Beier, *Masterless Men: The Vagrancy Problem in England 1560–1640*, 1985, pp. 37–9.

[4] See 'The wild wood', in Keith Thomas, *Man and the Natural World*, 1983, pp. 192–7; also Sharp, *In Contempt of All Authority, passim*. William Harrison, however, regretted the loss of England's forests: see *The Description of England* [1577], ed. G. Edelen, 1968, pp. 275–84.

[5] Sir Philip Sidney, *An Apology for Poetry*, ed. G. Shepherd, 1973, p. 116; J. Peter, *Complaint and Satire in Early English Literature*, 1956, pp. 40–59; for the use made by the Queen of pastoral forms, see Louis Adrian Montrose, '"Eliza, Queen of shepheardes", and the pastoral of power', *ELR* 10 (1980), 153–82; for Spenser and Sidney, see David Norbrook, *Poetry and Politics in the English Renaissance*, 1984, pp. 59–108; for a general study of the politics of pastoral, see Annabel Patterson, *Pastoral and Ideology: Virgil to Valéry*, 1987.

as fierce as that in *King Lear* between Edgar and Edmond.[1] Like that tragedy, *As You Like It* includes a narrative of usurpation: the greenwood is as much a place for refuge and the re-establishment of political authority as the heath is for Lear. Pastoral is traditionally associated with the spring, but many modern directors, their attention caught by the repeated reminders that 'winter and foul weather' also visit the forest, have set the play – or at least its first half – in the bleak midwinter, a device that also suggests certain aspects of the social condition of an England that was, on occasion, afflicted by famine, grain riots, and internecine strife. Unlike those of the earlier comedies, the play's resolution is not associated with a triumph over death[2] – nor are the gifts of fortune redistributed to the rural poor.

Politics

A Marston or a Jonson would have placed Jaques in the court of Duke Frederick rather than Duke Senior. Yet there is a place for Jaques in Arden, for there Duke Senior's rule, although not irksome, is absolute, a benign version of the malignant and violent tyranny of his usurping brother.[3] (It is significant that, as with the important female figures of *Titus Andronicus*, *A Midsummer Night's Dream*, *Hamlet*, *Othello*, and *King Lear*, there is no mention of Rosalind's mother.) Although Arden may represent a nostalgic dream of the 'antique world' (2.3.57), when Duke Senior is restored to his lands justice may be restored but the state is not reconstituted. (This kind of scepticism has been registered in modern productions in which the parts of the two dukes have been doubled.) In Arden liberty is not defined as a republican ideal, a categorical imperative, or an inalienable right, but, as Jaques recognises, it is something to be bestowed as a 'charter', licensed by the ruler, something that can be measured:

> I must have liberty
> Withal, as large a charter as the wind,
> To blow on whom I please: for so fools have.
> And they that are most gallèd with my folly,
> They most must laugh. (2.7.47–51)

(The cognate meaning of a 'liberty', a delimited area within the confines of a country or city, designated the licensed spaces where the playhouses were situated.) The play had begun with a particular claim for liberty by Orlando, who felt he was entitled to it by virtue of his gentle (noble) birth, without realising that his position as a younger brother had been exacerbated by the principle of primogeniture that served

---

[1] Edgar seems to identify himself with 'Child Roland' (3.4.166), a form of Orlando, when, in his madness, he seems to be plotting revenge upon his father; Louis Adrian Montrose, '"The place of brother" in *As You Like It*: social process and comic form', *SQ* 32 (1981), 28–54; the dark side of the play is well explored in 'For other than for dancing measures', Thomas McFarland, *Shakespeare's Pastoral Comedy*, 1972, pp. 98–121.

[2] Anne Barton, '*As You Like It* and *Twelfth Night*: Shakespeare's "sense of an ending"' [1972], *Essays, Mainly Shakespearean*, 1994, pp. 91–112.

[3] For Duke Senior's role in controlling Rosalind's feelings and her control over Celia (1.3.20–8), see Girard, *Theater of Envy*, pp. 93–4.

to preserve and contain the very gentility he sought. His fortunes are made when, like Bassanio in *The Merchant of Venice*, he secures a wealthy bride and, with her, a 'potent dukedom' (5.4.153). In reality, younger sons were more likely to seek their economic salvation in commerce or the law: the play's resolution would do nothing to mitigate the legal prejudice against younger sons in general. If, as seems obvious, social divisions often derived from conflicts between those who held power by birth and those who gained power through wealth, Shakespeare, unrealistically, proposes the remedy of offering rewards to worth.

Nor does the play accommodate the kind of libertarian reaction against tyrannical forest-laws that helped to keep tales and ballads of Robin Hood in circulation. Shakespeare's contemporary John Stow set out the themes of this poetic corpus:

> In this time [about the year 1190, in the reign of Richard I] were many robbers and outlaws, among the which Robert [*sic*] Hood and Little John, renowned thieves, continued in woods, despoiling and robbing the goods of the rich. They killed none but such as would invade them, or by resistance for their own defence.
>
> The said Robert entertained an hundred tall men and good archers with such spoils and thefts as he got, upon whom four hundred (were they never so strong) durst not give the onset. He suffered no woman to be oppressed, violated, or otherwise molested; poor men's goods he spared, abundantly relieving them with that which by theft he got from abbeys and the houses of rich carls; whom [John] Major [the historian (1469–1550)] blameth for his rapine and theft, but of all the thieves he affirmeth him to be the prince and the most gentle [noble] thief.[1]

A passage in a Robin Hood play of 1598 may give some idea of the content of dramatised versions of the myth. Little John is apprehensive that a performance may not please the king:

> Methinks I see no jests of Robin Hood,
> No merry morrises of Friar Tuck,
> No pleasant skippings up and down the wood,
> No hunting songs, no coursing of the buck.[2]

There may be passing allusions to Robin Hood in the text and a 'hunting song' in 4.2, but the play does not match either of the above in action or tone (see Plate 6).

---

[1] *The Annals of England* (1600), p. 234; see Stephen Knight, *Robin Hood: A Complete Study of the English Outlaw*, 1994, and Stephen Knight (ed.), *Robin Hood: An Anthology of Scholarship and Criticism*, 1999; Eric Hobsbawm categorised the images of the noble robber (*Bandits*, 1969, pp. 35–6); the historical debate over whether Robin was a peasant hero or a figure who appealed to a gentle audience which disliked forest-laws is reviewed in R. H. Hilton (ed.), *Peasants, Knights and Heretics*, 1976; for other forest outlaws, see Margaret Spufford, *Small Books and Pleasant Histories: Popular Fiction and its Readership in Seventeenth-Century England*, 1981, pp. 231–2.

[2] [Chettle and Munday], *The Downfall of Robert Earl of Huntington* (1601), [Act 4], sig. I2ʳ. This play, along with the same authors' *The Death of Robert, Earl of Huntington*, introduced 'chaste Matilda, his fair maid Marian' (title page to *The Death of Robert* (1601)), and was performed by the Admiral's Men at the Rose and at court in 1598; compare Robert Greene's *George a Green* (1590) and Peele's *Edward I* (1591), in which Robin Hood games are inserted; the anonymous 'pastoral comedy' *Robin Hood and Little John* (1594) and Haughton's *Robin Hood's Pennyworths* (1601) which was performed by the Admiral's Men are both lost: see A. H. Thorndike, 'The relation of *As You Like It* to Robin Hood plays', *JEGP* 4 (1902), 59–69, and Lois Potter (ed.), *Playing Robert Hood: The Legend as Performance in Five Centuries*, 1998; see also p. 51.

6   The Horn Dance: production by Mark Brickman, Crucible Theatre, Sheffield, 1991

Although *As You Like It* is far more suffused with nostalgia for a lost Eden than imbued with hope for a New Jerusalem,[1] it has become fashionable to relate the activities of the court in exile to resistance politics, to see Duke Senior and his company as what Eric Hobsbawm called 'social bandits' with whom the dispossessed Orlando feels instinctively at one. (Such a reading was spectacularly enacted in John Caird's 1989 production at Stratford-upon-Avon when, at the beginning of 2.1, the foresters burst their way through stage trapdoors into an Art Deco interior that seemed to have been designed for a play in the tradition of bourgeois realism and which disconcertingly resembled the design at that time of the Royal Shakespeare Theatre foyer.)[2] We might expect banditry to flourish in Arden given that, in the 'forest', enclosure is generating pauperisation.[3] There is, in fact, one reference in the text to the foresters as 'outlaws' (2.7.0 SD): in the earlier *Two Gentlemen of Verona* Valentine meets a band of outlaws,[4] a group of gentlemen banished from Verona and Mantua. Like Jaques they are exiled from their cities for crimes of libertinism and are now engaged in 'an honourable kind of thievery' – and contradicting their Italian origins by swearing 'by the bare scalp of Robin Hood's fat friar' (4.1.39, 36)! But overall in *As You Like It* there is no stress on forest-trespass or on hunting as poaching – and no indication that the foresters are armed. When they might be, as in the deer-killing scene (4.2), the emphasis is on masculinity rather than the violation of any ducal prerogative.[5] When Celia speaks of 'smirching her face' (1.3.102) she cannot be joining the 'Blacks', the hunters in Windsor Forest, as these groups emerged only in the eighteenth century, nor can she be taking the part of Lady Skimington who led anti-enclosure riots, but only in 1626–32.[6] (An Act of 1485 had noted the fact that 'divers persons in great number, some with painted faces, some with visors . . . riotously and in man-of-war arrayed, have . . . hunted, as well by night as by day . . . whereof have ensued in times past great and heinous rebellions, insurrections, riots, robberies, murders, and other inconveniences.')[7] Overall the gentlemen in exile, just like their counterparts in the legends of Robin Hood, are not revolutionaries but remain steadfastly loyal to their prince.

---

[1] For the contrast between Arcadian Edens and utopian New Jerusalems, see W. H. Auden, 'Dingley Dell and the Fleet' [1948], *The Dyer's Hand and Other Essays*, 1962, pp. 407–28.

[2] Smallwood, p. 16; for a Swedish version of this production see Jacqueline Martin, 'Shakespeare and performance practices in Sweden', in Heather Kerr, Robin Eaden, Madge Mitton (eds.), *Shakespeare: World Views*, 1996, pp. 200–13.

[3] Hobsbawm, *Bandits*, pp. 14–19.

[4] There is a similar band of outlaws in Massinger's *The Guardian* (1633).

[5] For other aspects of hunting symbolism and for an argument that the forest court hunts for survival and not just for sport, see A. Stuart Daley, 'The idea of hunting in *As You Like It*', *S.St.* 21 (1993), 72–95.

[6] See Richard Wilson, 'Like the old Robin Hood: *As You Like It* and the enclosure riots', *Will Power*, 1993, pp. 66–87; Wilson drew upon E. P. Thompson, *Whigs and Hunters: The Origin of the Black Act*, 1977; for Skimingtons, see Sharp, *In Contempt of All Authority*, pp. 100–3; for a link between the Blacks and Charles Johnson's adaptation of *AYLI*, *Love in a Forest* (1723), see Stage History, p. 56 n. 4.

[7] 1° Hen. VII., c.7 (*The Statutes of the Realm*, 8 vols., 1816, II, 505).

However, while *As You Like It* was probably being written, plays like Fulke Greville's closet drama *Alaham* (1598–1600) did subject court life to a sharp moral interrogation, as did *Richard II* (1595), the soon-to-be-written *Hamlet* (1600), and Marston's *The Malcontent* (1603). We remember Shakespeare's more absolute exploration of antique liberty in *Julius Caesar*, roughly contemporary with this play.[1] To complaints about court corruption it became common to suggest that rusticity provided a solution. Life in the forest enacts a humanist ideal: as Reginald Pole is reputed to have said, 'Therefore if this be civil life and order (to live in cities and towns with so much vice and misorder), meseem man should not be born thereto but rather to life in the wild forest, there more following the study of virtue, as it is said men did in the golden age wherein man lived according to his natural dignity.'[2] In 1656 James Harrington was to look back in *The Commonwealth of Oceana*:

> For in the way of parliaments, which was the government of this realm, men of country lives have been still entrusted with the greatest affairs and the people have constantly had an aversion from the ways of the court. Ambition, loving to be gay and to fawn, hath been a gallantry looked upon as having something of the livery and husbandry of the country way of life, though of a grosser spinning, as the best stuff of a commonwealth, according unto Aristotle, *agricolarum democratia respublica optima*; such an one being the most obstinate assertress of her liberty and the least subject unto innovation and turbulency.[3]

There is implicit disillusionment with the court of Eliza in the drama of the Queen's final years, as well as the adulation we find in texts like Dekker's *Old Fortunatus* (1599);[4] Shakespeare does not in this play, however, offer his Arden as a political alternative.

Indeed we might conjecture that the 'greenwood' represents a dream of primitivism by the gentlefolk of the play. Such forest-retreats are fantasies, which expose their ennui as well as their irresponsibility and, in come cases, their decadence. Yet, despite their inhabiting a hierarchical order, they may feel that being in touch with nature authenticates their individual identities. The audience are kept alert to the dream-status of the forest, and may recognise a fantasy of the rich in the comparative leisure of the shepherd – as opposed to the labour of the ploughman who served as a spokesman for civil virtue in, say, Langland's *Piers Plowman*. Some literary pastorals could be said to legitimate the hegemony of England's sheep-farming gentry. Sir Philip Sidney had described the didactic function of pastoral, which

---

[1] Many commentators have noticed its anticipation of themes from *AYLI*, for example in Antony's eulogy: 'Pardon me, Julius! Here wast thou bayed, brave hart, / Here didst thou fall, and here thy hunters stand, / Signed, in thy spoil, and crimsoned in thy lethe. / O world! Thou wast the forest to this hart, / And this indeed, O world, the heart of thee. / How like a deer, stroocken by many princes / Dost thou here lie!' (*JC*, 3.1.204–10); conversely *AYLI* remembers *JC*: see 4.2.3–5 and 5.2.24–6.

[2] Thomas Starkey, *A Dialogue between Pole and Lupset* [*c.* 1530], ed. T. F. Mayer, *Camden Fourth Series*, XXXVII, 1989, p. 7.

[3] James Harrington, *'The Commonwealth of Oceana' and 'A System of Politics'*, ed. J. G. A. Pocock, 1992, p. 5.

[4] See Appendix 1, p. 225.

taught 'the misery of people under hard lords or ravening soldiers'. Yet he went on to expunge these radical implications by praising the 'blessedness . . . derived to them that lie lowest from the goodness of them that sit highest'.[1]

Social factors are glanced at in the play, but Duke Senior does not use his banishment to the forest to redress inequality of wealth, or, like Robin Hood, to attack the fat-cats of the church and protect maidenly virtue, even to muster his forces for a counter-coup, but as a time for exploring his vocation,[2] a saintly refashioning of his self that anticipates the conversions at the end of the play. The reasons for his banishment are not spelt out: perhaps it was because, like the Duke in *Measure for Measure* and Prospero in *The Tempest*, Duke Senior was more enamoured of the contemplative life than the world of court intrigue. In the forest he can exercise the Christian virtues of fortitude and patience. Anticipating the pattern of action in *King Lear*, the Duke's first speech tells of escape from both 'painted pomp' and 'the penalty of Adam' to frugality and a search for self-knowledge and for counsellors who, as he proclaims, will 'feelingly persuade me what I am' (2.1.3, 5, 11). Like the Duke in *Measure for Measure*, he presents himself as 'one that, above all other strifes, contended especially to know himself' (*MM* 3.2.232–3). He is not a rebel but a godly man, able to mitigate the 'penalty of Adam' but always aware of original sin, a man of the kind described by Michael Walzer as one for whom 'righteousness was a consolation and a way of organizing the self for survival . . . a bold effort to shape a new personality against the background of social "unsettledness"'.[3] Exile from the court into the discipline of the forest offers a means of restoration through reformation: the banished Duke and his companions, too few to muster an army, are not revolutionaries but men reacting to the violence and corruption of those that banished them. (This is figured in the 'broken music' (1.2.111) of the wrestling at Duke Frederick's court.) Away from libraries and churches, they find 'books in the running brooks, / Sermons in stones, and good in everything' (2.1.16–17). It was a commonplace for the godly to contrast the profanity of plays with the value of hearing sermons in church:[4] with a sneaky irony Shakespeare has his Duke, in a play, claim that 'sermons' are to be

[1] Sidney, *Apology*, p. 116; Ordelle G. Hill, *The Manor, the Plowman, and the Shepherd: Agrarian Themes and Imagery in Late Medieval and Early Renaissance English Literature*, 1993, describes how the transition from the heroic Piers Plowman to the shepherds of Renaissance pastoral reflects the changes in farming methods and agrarian culture at the time.

[2] Daley, 'The dispraise of the country', p. 306 n. 17, finds the notion of vocation central to the play; however, compare George Bernard Shaw: 'And the comfortable old Duke, symbolical of the British villa dweller, who likes to find "sermons in stones and good in everything," and then to have a good dinner! This unvenerable impostor, expanding on his mixed diet of pious twaddle and venison, rouses my worst passions' (*Shaw on Shakespeare*, ed. Edwin Wilson, 1961, p. 25).

[3] Michael Walzer, *The Revolution of the Saints: A Study in the Origins of Radical Politics*, 1966, pp. 309, 312; aspects of Walzer's psycho-sociological models of the 'puritan' mentality are subjected to a radical critique by Patrick Collinson, *The Religion of Protestants: The Church in English Society 1559–1625*, 1982, *passim*, especially pp. 179–81. In contrast, Peter Milward, *The Catholicism of Shakespeare's Plays*, 1997, pp. 22–33 compares the exiled Duke with Catholic exiles.

[4] See, for example, the writings of John Northbrooke (1577) and William Crashaw (1607) in Chambers, IV, 198 and 249; for a possible rebuke to Catholic practices involving church bells, see 2.7.121 n.

found not in churches but in 'stones', in the natural world. (Sir Oliver Martext is presumably what Spenser termed 'a popish priest', unfamiliar with God's word.)[1] In the Duke's company there are no masterless men of the kind that emerged during times of political turmoil. Submitting themselves willingly, as they do, to his patriarchal order, his supporters seek not freedom but 'escape from freedom'.[2] In speaking to Adam, Orlando, victim of a characteristic 'status-anxiety'[3] in that he feels that rusticity takes away his birthright as a gentleman, adheres to the Duke's forest morality by refusing to turn himself into a vagabond or outlaw:

> What, wouldst thou have me go and beg my food,
> Or with a base and boisterous sword enforce
> A thievish living on the common road?
> This I must do or know not what to do;
> Yet this I will not do, do how I can.
> I rather will subject me to the malice
> Of a diverted blood and bloody brother. (2.3.31–7)

He praises the unrewarded industriousness, sobriety, and 'husbandry' of Adam (2.3.65).[4] The language of Jaques, filled with revulsion against 'the foul body of th'infected world' (2.7.60), seems to derive from the pulpit of a fundamentalist preacher: what we might expect from a convert from Italianate libertinism. Self-disdain may explain his ambivalent attitude to Touchstone, whom he admires for his capacity to unmask folly and vice but despises for his cheerless and obdurate pursuit of female flesh. At the end of the play, each gentleman in exile will not be rewarded for his relative virtue but will have his particular feudal status restored by taking up his former estate (5.4.158–9).[5]

This was the liberty that Jaques had abused by taking himself out of the ambience of authority:

> For thou thyself hast been a libertine,
> As sensual as the brutish sting itself,
> And all th'embossèd sores and headed evils
> That thou with *licence* of free foot hast caught
> Wouldst thou disgorge into the general world. (2.7.65–9; emphasis added)

There are also similarities to *Julius Caesar*, another story of usurpation in which the theme of liberty is keenly felt. Its hero Brutus is no revolutionary, more an

---

[1] *The Shepheardes Calender*, Gloss to May, 309; Juliet Dusinberre, 'Topical forest: Kemp and Mar-text in Arden', in Ann Thompson and Gordon McMullan (eds.), *In Arden: Editing Shakespeare. Essays in Honour of Richard Proudfoot*, 2003, pp. 239–51.

[2] The phrase is Erich Fromm's, quoted by Walzer, *Revolution of the Saints*, p. 313.

[3] *Ibid.*, p. 248.

[4] For puritan praises of industriousness, see Max Weber, *The Protestant Ethic and the Spirit of Capitalism*, trans. Talcott Parsons, 1958, pp. 109 ff.; and Walzer, *Revolution of the Saints*, pp. 210–15.

[5] See, however, 5.4.148 n. Moreover, when Celia says 'Now go in we content, / To liberty, and not to banishment' (1.3.127–8), we have to remember again that this forest liberty is not absolute freedom but franchised freedom within a chartered space.

'antique puritan' than a Lenin. As Michael Walzer observed, 'Discipline and not liberty lies at the heart of puritanism.'[1]

'Between you and the women the play may please'

From another perspective the 'forest', or at least that part of it inhabited by Rosalind and Orlando, offers a setting for the studied folly and inflated joyousness of 'holiday humour', of carnival and feasting. Rosalind's first moments in Arden call upon her not only to act weary but to engage in sprightly and sexy cross-talk with Touchstone; Orlando, having escaped from the lean fare that is his portion at Oliver's estate, upon entering the forest stumbles upon a banquet for a Duke.[2] Much of the action, as we have seen, consists of feats of performance, 'sports', songs, and seeming verbal improvisations. In the forest, fools, shepherds, and nobility, disempowered patriarchs and cross-dressed youths, walk along paths of moral re-creation and explore self through the playing-out of ritualised roles.[3]

At the centre of the play's action are those festive sequences in which Rosalind, in man's attire, tutors Orlando in the labours of love.[4] In early modern England cross-dressed men and women, if apprehended, could be pilloried and whipped for transgressing both sexual and theological codes,[5] and yet ritual May-games featured cross-dressing, an index presumably of gender instability enacted within

[1] Walzer, *Revolution of the Saints*, p. 149.
[2] For the meanings of 'banquet', see 2.5.53 n.
[3] For nineteenth-century accounts of the 'morality' of the play, see Russell Jackson, 'Victorian editors of *As You Like It* and the purposes of editing', in Ian Small and Marcus Walsh (eds.), *The Theory and Practice of Text-Editing*, 1991, pp. 142–56.
[4] Since the publication of C. L. Barber's *Shakespeare's Festive Comedy* in 1959 it has become a commonplace to stress this aspect of the play. Barber's paradigm formula for this kind of comedy, 'Through release to clarification', was basically Freudian, treating carnival as a 'safety valve' and concerned with the well-being of the individual rather than of society (compare Sigmund Freud, *Civilization and its Discontents*, in *Civilization, Society and Religion*, ed. James Strachey, The Penguin Freud Library, 1985, XII, pp. 163–4, and *Totem and Taboo*, Essay 4). This Freudian paradigm should be complemented with readings from critics who follow Bakhtin in perceiving the political uses of carnival: 'As opposed to the official feast, one might say that carnival celebrated temporary liberation from the prevailing truth and from the established order; it marked the suspension of all hierarchies, rank, privileges, norms, and prohibitions. Carnival was the true feast of time, the feast of becoming, change, and renewal. It was hostile to all that was immortalized and completed' (Mikhail Bakhtin, *Rabelais and his World*, trans. Hélène Iswolsky, 1984, p. 10). See also, for example, Natalie Z. Davis, *Society and Culture in Early Modern France*, 1975; Peter Stallybrass, '"Drunk with the cup of liberty": Robin Hood, the carnivalesque, and the rhetoric of violence in early modern England', *Semiotica* 54 (1985), 113–45; Julia Kristeva, 'Word, Dialogue and Novel', *The Kristeva Reader*, ed. Toril Moi, 1986, pp. 48–9, 50; Laroque, pp. 232–5.
[5] Michael Shapiro offers a sage evaluation of historical and theoretical accounts of actual and theatrical cross-dressing, and reprints legal records from 1554 to 1604 (*Gender in Play*, pp. 225–340). Aretino's courtesan Nanna habitually dressed in boy's clothing (Pietro Aretino, *The Ragionamenti: The Erotic Lives of Nuns, Wives, and Courtesans* [1534], ed. Peter Stafford, 1971, p. 124). There seems to have been a vogue for this in the second decade of the seventeenth century: see Marjorie Garber, *Vested Interests: Cross-Dressing and Cultural Anxiety*, 1993; Mark Breitenberg, 'Cross-dressing, androgyny, and the anatomical imperative', in *Anxious Masculinity in Early Modern England*, 1996, pp. 150–74; for theologically inspired diatribes, see Laura Levine, *Men in Women's Clothing: Anti-theatricality and Effeminization 1579–1642*, 1994, pp. 22–3.

erotic masquerade, as did carnivalesque practices in the Netherlands and in Italy.[1] The contradiction is caught in *The Faerie Queene* when Britomart, herself disguised as a man, is appalled to witness the 'lothly vncouth sight' of her knight Artegall 'disguiz'd in womanishe attire', and asks 'What May-game hath misfortune made of you?'[2] The allusion is to the habit of having a man in a grotesque garb of Maid Marian taking the place of the May Queen in May Day Robin Hood festivities. Sometimes 'she' cavorted in a Morris Dance, accompanied by a Fool whose stock property was a phallic bladder.[3]

Perhaps Rosalind does have something of the Maid Marian in her: Celia is occasionally embarrassed by her lewd speech, and indeed any woman who passed as a man in early modern England seems to do have done so with some measure of insurrectionary intent. From within that mannered, parodistic, and ludic role of Ganymede, Rosalind can warn Orlando 'that there is a limit to the possession he will have over a wife, a limit set by her desires, her wit, and her tongue'.[4] Yet it is equally possible that the aspect of Maid Marian recalled by Rosalind is her role as '"the loved one" in the May Day games, to whom little presents would be given'.[5] Like all inversion rituals of early modern Europe it is difficult to know whether these licensed sports are tokens of stability and order in a hierarchical society built upon patriarchal gender distinctions or whether they undermined these relationships by disrupting gender difference.[6] As Louis Montrose points out, most of the 'anxieties about womanly independence or dominance are focussed in jokes about cuckoldry' and 'the dependence of the husband's masculine honor upon the feminine honor of his wife simultaneously subordinates and empowers her'.[7] Rather than trying to insist on either the rebellious or the reactionary, we should treat these facets of the play as we should other ambivalent texts. The strangeness of their terms is an index

---

[1] Aretino, *Ragionamenti*, pp. 148–9; Rudolf M. Dekker and Lotte C. van de Pol, *The Tradition of Female Transvestism in Early Modern Europe*, 1989; Sabrina Petra-Rahmet (ed.), *Gender Reversals and Gender Cultures: Anthropological and Historical Perspectives*, 1996; Deanna Shemek, 'Circular definitions: configuring gender in Italian Renaissance festival', *RQ* 48 (1995), 1–40.

[2] *FQ*, v.vii.37, 40.

[3] See *1H4*, 3.3.91–2; John Laneham mentions a 'A lively morris dance according to the ancient manner: six dancers, Maid Marian, and the fool' ('Laneham's Letter' in John Nichols, *Progresses of Queen Elizabeth*, 3 vols., 1823, I, 443; see also Thomas Blount, 'Morisco', *Glossographia* (1656), sig. cc3ᵛ); Henslowe lists 'one green gown for Marian' (p. 317); see also David Wiles, *The Early Plays of Robin Hood*, 1981; Laroque, pp. 124–6; Ann Thompson, in 'Women/"women" and the stage', in Helen Wilcox (ed.), *Women and Literature in Britain 1500–1700*, 1996, pp. 100–16, offers interesting evidence that in fact women may, on occasions, have taken part in 'feats of activity' like this. William Kempe tells how a 'lusty country lass' joined him to tread a mile on his morris dance from London to Norwich: the implication is that Audrey could be the Maid Marian figure rather than Rosalind (see William Kempe, *Kemp's Nine Days' Wonder* (1600), sig. B3ᵛ–B4ʳ.)

[4] Natalie Z. Davis, *Society and Culture*, p. 135.

[5] See [Richard Brathwait?], *The Whimzies* (1631), p. 139, cit. Laroque, p. 125; Wiles, *Robin Hood*, p. 21.

[6] See Natalie Z. Davis, *Society and Culture*, p. 130 for suggestions about the functions of magical transvestism and the ritual inversion of sex roles; see also Stuart Clark, 'Inversion, misrule and the meaning of witchcraft', *Past and Present* 87 (1980), 98–127.

[7] *The Purpose of Playing: Shakespeare and the Cultural Politics of the Elizabethan Theatre*, 1996, p. 120.

not simply of parody but of seriousness and may offer an *understanding* rather than a *critique* of the social order: 'Misrule can have its own rigor and can also decipher king and state.'[1]

Gender

If the carnivalesque creates one of the tones of this multi-coloured play, an examination of gender roles is one of its themes. Just as Shakespeare, by welding elements of pastoral and folk-play onto a comic structure, was able to show how *genre* is both reproduced and appropriated, so, by writing plays for playhouses in which feminine parts were taken by young males, his texts demonstrated the way that *gender* may be as dependent upon social forms and pressures as upon sexual identities. In this Edenic forest the dialogue often reminds us that there at least gender relationships are not representations but fantasies.[2] Indeed, in all of the play's settings, Oliver's estate, the court, and Arden, characters are not born but made, inhabitants of culturally specific language domains and objects of particular defining and expropriating gazes.

Traditionally critics adopted an essentialist model for character, writing about Rosalind, along with other seemingly emancipated feminine characters who played out breeches-parts or otherwise exposed the excesses of masculine behaviour, as if she was a real person, 'pleasingly devious and full-blooded',[3] possessed of a engagingly quick wit and a subversively bold spirit. Dominic Dromgoole places Rosalind among 'the flying consciousnesses, the rasping, rapping mouths exhilarated by the invention of their own minds – the Rosalinds, the Hamlets, the Falstaffs'.[4] The play seemed to set itself against the topics of misogyny that stud so many texts that are ostensibly about love,[5] and also to endorse a romantic-sounding dictum of Marlowe's that is quoted in the text, 'Who ever loved that loved not at first sight?' (3.6.81). Yet Shakespeare had written a comedy around that theme, *A Midsummer Night's Dream*, a text that, from certain perspectives, suggests that being in love is literally a condition of being spell-bound. The earlier play dwells as much on

[1] Natalie Z. Davis, *Society and Culture*, p. 97. 'Marxist critics, such as Walter Benjamin or Mikhail Bakhtin, divined a glimmer of utopia in art and carnival; but for New Historicism, literature, play or transgression were merely pretexts for redoubled oppression' (Richard Wilson and Richard Dutton (eds.), *New Historicism and Renaissance Drama*, 1992, p. 7).

[2] In Eden, Auden writes, 'three kinds of erotic life are possible, though any particular dream of Eden need contain only one. The polymorphous-perverse promiscuous sexuality of childhood, courting couples whose relation is potential, not actual, and the chastity of natural celibates who are without desire' ('Dingley Dell and the Fleet', p. 411).

[3] Gareth Lloyd Evans, *The Upstart Crow*, 1982, p. 171; see also George Bernard Shaw: 'Rosalind is not a complete human being: she is simply an extension into five acts of the most affectionate, fortunate, delightful five minutes in the life of a charming woman' (Wilson ed., *Shaw on Shakespeare*, p. 23); Marilyn French, *Shakespeare's Division of Experience*, 1981, p. 108.

[4] Dominic Dromgoole, *Will and Me: How Shakespeare Took Over My Life*, 2006, p. 93.

[5] For a diatribe in *Rosalind* against the destructiveness and fickleness of women, see Appendix 2, p. 227; see also Michael Hattaway, 'Fleshing his will in the spoil of her honour: desire, misogyny, and the perils of chivalry', *S.Sur.* 46 (1994), 121–36.

the pains of passion as on its pleasures and, in the Titania and Oberon episodes, it registers the struggle for mastery between feminine and masculine principles that continues after marriage is supposed to have made, in Rosalind's terms, 'all even' (5.4.25). This is not surprising, given that the sermon, based on Ephesians 5, ordained for the conclusion of the Church of England's 'Form of Solemnisation of Matrimony' bade wives 'to be in subjection unto their own husbands in all things'.[1] Moreover, when it is realised that, in giving herself in marriage to Orlando, Rosalind loses the mastery she possessed in the forest, and that the forest is a licensed never-never land removed from the obligations of customary life, a feeling may arise that Shakespeare is not indicating how women might create autonomy for themselves but is dramatising the power of patriarchy and masculine persuasiveness.[2] (Dr Johnson wrote tersely: 'I know not how the ladies will approve the facility with which both Rosalind and Celia give away their hearts.')[3] Perhaps Shakespeare was anticipating this kind of response when he had Rosalind say in her Epilogue, 'I charge you, O women, for the love you bear to men, to like as much of this play as please you' (9–10).[4] We realise how the play's title encompasses yet another reading, the evocation of orthodox patriarchal spectators – the way they like it entails surrender of liberty for Rosalind and Celia – set against the tastes of those play-going women who may have liked non-submissive heroines.[5]

It is worthwhile considering the specific making of the theatrical fictions and gender roles we call Shakespeare's women. In fact comparatively little can be known about the acting styles of the boys or young men who played feminine roles in the public playhouses of the 1590s.[6] They inherited verse and prose styles from the youths who acted dramas at court, and presumably had skills of elocution fitted to, for example, the precocity of Phoebe's verse and the antithetical patterns of the debate about Nature and Fortune between Rosalind and Celia. Evidence from Henslowe's *Diary* indicates that large amounts could be spent on rich costumes for women's roles.[7] Inductions to plays by Marston suggest that Hamlet's 'little eyases',

[1] *The First and Second Prayer Books of Edward VI*, 1910, p. 258.

[2] Rosalind, who at times plays the love-sick maid and who faints at the sight of blood, is no more like the figure of the unruly woman represented in plays like Dekker and Middleton's *The Roaring Girl* (1611) than Duke Senior is a social bandit. See Jean Howard, 'Cross-dressing, the theatre, and gender struggle in early modern England', *SQ* 39 (1988), 418–40. In *The Stage and Social Struggle in Early Modern England*, 1993, Howard emphasises the way in which Rosalind's participation in playful masquerade destabilises categories of gender and power (pp. 118–21); see also Leah Marcus, 'Shakespeare's comic heroines, Elizabeth I, and the political uses of androgyny', in Mary Beth Rose (ed.), *Women in the Middle Ages and the Renaissance*, 1985, pp. 135–53.

[3] *Samuel Johnson on Shakespeare*, ed. H. R. Woodhuysen, 1989, p. 180.

[4] See Richard Levin, 'Women in the Renaissance theatre audience', *SQ* 40 (1989), 165–74; Thompson, 'Women/"women"'.

[5] Women, both ladies and citizen's wives, went 'in numbers' to the Globe from 1599 to 1614 (Andrew Gurr, *Playgoing in Shakespeare's London*, 1987, p. 63).

[6] J. B. Streett, 'The durability of boy actors', *NQ* 208 (1973), 461–5, points out that 'boy' actors could often be post-pubertal young men; cf. David Kathman, 'How old were Shakespeare's boy actors?', *S.Sur.* 58 (2005), 220–46.

[7] Henslowe, pp. 291–4, 319–20, 321–3; see also Mark Albert Johnston, 'Playing with the beard: courtly and commercial economies in Richard Edwards's *Damon and Pithias* and John Lyly's *Midas*', *ELH* 72 (2005), 79–103.

the boy players in the private playhouses that were very fashionable at the time *As You Like It* was written, worked within a tradition of parody and pastiche that kept conventions to the fore and invited both sexual suggestiveness and allusions to matter outside the narrative.[1] In such texts, gender, like social rank, was marked out by costume, something to be put on or disowned by its wearer. So presumably was age, and the fact that Rosalind does not wear a false beard would have said something about 'her' masculinity.[2] This tradition presumably generated a kind of demonstrative acting: boy players would have exhibited the behaviour of the witty woman, the cruel woman, the hoyden, the mature or older man, without identifying with these roles.

There is some evidence of saucy boys being associated with homo-eroticism in these private playhouses, which suggests that certain players were exhibiting themselves rather than the parts they played. In Jonson's *Poetaster* performed by the Chapel Boys about 1601, we hear, 'What, shall I have my son a stager now, an ingle [male lover] for players?' (1.2.15–16).[3] There is an intriguing suggestion in Lodge's *Rosalind* that cross-dressing might please because, paradoxically, it exposed the real power of the female. There Aliena claims, '"It is enough for pages to wait on beautiful ladies, and not to be beautiful themselves." "O mistress", quoth Ganymede, "hold you your peace, for you are partial. Who knows not, but that all women have desire to tie sovereignty to their petticoats and ascribe beauty to themselves, where if boys might put on their garments, perhaps they would prove as comely – if not as comely, it may be more courteous."'[4] However, modern experience of some cross-dressed productions where all parts are taken by men reveals that in a play like *As You Like It* sexually suggestive acting styles are inappropriate, that conventions often become 'invisible', and that the effect of the courtship sequences (if not the meaning of the play) may be unproblematic.[5]

Theatre and romance thrive on tales of mistaken identity, particularly mistaken gender, and it is difficult to recover how much Shakespeare's audience would have taken cross-dressed characters for 'real'. Presumably the distinction depended upon whether the players separated or fused the personae that constituted their roles, and whether in performance they sexualised their own bodies or enacted a constant

---

[1] See R. A. Foakes, 'John Marston's fantastical plays: *Antonio and Mellida* and *Antonio's Revenge*', *PQ* 41 (1962), 229–39.

[2] Will Fisher, 'The Renaissance beard: masculinity in early modern England', *RQ* 54 (2001), 155–97: this essay reviews relevant gender theory and also lists theatrical inventories of false beards.

[3] See chap. 1, '"As boys and women are for the most part cattle of this colour": female roles and Elizabethan eroticism', in Lisa Jardine, *Still Harping on Daughters: Women and Drama in the Age of Shakespeare*, 1983, pp. 9–36.

[4] *Rosalind*, pp. 153–4.

[5] Perhaps the convention was made visible not by theatrical convention but by awareness on the part of at least some of the audience that the practice of women's parts being taken by men had engendered a virulent debate based upon biblical authority (see Kathleen McLuskie, *Renaissance Dramatists*, 1989, pp. 111–12.)

single gender.[1] Michael Shapiro puts the case well when he writes, 'Although some dramatic texts were clearly polemical, the disguised-heroine plays . . . usually acted as fields of play, that is, as arenas in which spectators could test or try on imaginary roles or respond to hypothetical situations without having to bear responsibility for their choices.'[2]

Yet theatrical experience always takes place within a cultural context. Antitheatrical writers considered that the theatre was immoral because it effeminized the boy players, adulterated male gender, and thereby demolished the 'real' self. Even in a comedy there can be undercurrents that surface to spread anxiety: Rosalind offers one of the prevalent models for what is now termed homosexuality when she speaks of possessing a woman's heart behind a mannish caparison (1.3.106–12).[3] Phoebe seems to see through to the feminine nature of the disguised Rosalind:

> There was a pretty redness in his lip,
> A little riper and more lusty red
> Than that mixed in his cheek: 'twas just the difference
> Betwixt the constant red and mingled damask. (3.6.119–22)

These lines suggest feelings tilting towards same-sex desire between women[4] – or, if we think of the players, between men dressed as women. However, it has

---

[1] We cannot know whether same-sex affections enacted by Elizabethan boy players in travesty represented androgyny, and whether androgyny figured the ancient quest for a love that transcends sexual division or is an emblem of same-sex desire. For androgyny could be a symbol of both transcendence – as it was in the tradition that derived from Plato's *Symposium* – or, in its physical manifestations, of monstrosity or demonism. Pliny tells of 'children of both sexes whom we call hermaphrodites. In old time they were known by the name of "androgyni"' (*The History of the World*, 7.3, trans. Philemon Holland, 2 vols., 1601, I, 157); Beza wrote of 'These vile and stinking androgynes, that is to say, these men–women, with their curled locks, their crisped and frizzled hair' (Theodore Beza, *Sermons upon the Three First Chapters of the Canticle of Canticles*, trans. John Harmar, 1587, p. 173); [Guillaume de la Perrière] described 'Sardanapalus . . . who painted his face, and . . . [who] burnt himself, by which act he delivered his subjects from a monstrous hermaphrodite who was neither true man nor true woman, being in sex a man and in heart a woman' (*The Mirror of Policy*, trans. anon., 1598, sig. Hij^r); for the topic in Greek texts, see David M. Halperin, 'Why is Diotima a woman?', in *One Hundred Years of Homosexuality and Other Essays on Greek Love*, 1989, 113–51; William Keach notes how Ovid's myth of Hermaphroditus loved by Salmacis (*Metamorphoses*, IV, 352–481) became 'an emblem of bestial transformation' in Renaissance culture (*Elizabethan Erotic Narratives: Irony and Pathos in the Ovidian Poetry of Shakespeare, Marlowe, and their Contemporaries*, 1977, pp. 141 and 191); for affinities between Ganymede and the god Hermaphroditus, see James M. Saslow, *Ganymede in the Renaissance: Homosexuality in Art and Society*, 1986, pp. 77–8.

[2] Shapiro, *Gender in Play*, p. 6.

[3] Saslow, *Ganymede in the Renaissance*, pp. 75–84; compare 3.3.162–3; she also associates herself with hares and hyenas, both thought to be hermaphroditic (see 4.1.124 n. and 4.3.17 n.).

[4] Phoebe's infatuation with 'Ganymede' could be read as a homo-erotic one: relevant is the myth of Iphys, a girl brought up by her mother as a boy, with whom Ianthe falls in love, to Iphys' horror, but who then is transformed by Isis into a man (*Metamorphoses*, IX, 787–937); the imagery of red and white occurs in Donne's homo-erotic heroical epistle, 'Sappho to Philaenis' (see Janel Mueller, 'Troping Utopia: Donne's brief for lesbianism', in James Grantham Turner (ed.), *Sexuality and Gender in Early Modern Europe*, 1993, pp. 182–207; Ilona Bell, 'Gender matters: the women in Donne's poems', *The Cambridge Companion to John Donne*, ed. Achsah Guibbory, 2006, pp. 201–16); for a survey of writings on female homosexuality ('tribadry') in the period see Merry E. Wiesner, *Women and Gender in Early Modern Europe*, 1993, pp. 54–6; see also Stephen Orgel, 'Gendering the crown', in Margreta de Grazia, Maureen Quilligan, and Peter Stallybrass (eds.), *Subject and Object in Renaissance Culture*, 1996, pp. 133–65.

been argued that 'unlike either Lyly or Jonson [in *Epicoene*], Shakespeare refuses to dissolve the difference between the sex of the boy actor and that of the heroine he plays; and he uses his boy heroines' sexual ambiguity not only to complicate his plots but also to resolve them'.[1] Orlando offers no hint of being attracted to a feminised male, and Rosalind, unlike Viola, seems perfectly happy in her disguise. One of the functions of Celia in her role as an on-stage spectator of the wooing games is to remind the audience of the double sexual identity of Ganymede/Rosalind. We can therefore construct a reading of *As You Like It* that insists that Rosalind keeps her masculine and feminine identities separate.[2] This kind of reading would align itself with the mannerist art of Sir Philip Sidney who, when he shows the Princess Philoclea falling in love with Pyrocles disguised as an Amazon, Zelmane, keeps fictitiousness and not passion to the fore.[3]

We may, however, feel less secure with this distinction when we consider that Rosalind's forest name is 'Ganymede', and that Ganymede – 'Jove's own ingle' as Middleton called him in a Paul's play of 1601[4] – a Trojan youth whom Jupiter abducted to become his cup-bearer before turning him into the constellation Aquarius, has featured not only in tales of androgyny or hermaphroditism but, since antiquity, of same-sex, 'homosexual', relations. Rosalind, having announced that she will 'suit herself' like a man to avoid 'thieves' or sexual predators (1.3.100, 106), joyously designates herself as a 'catamite': the Latinate form of the word derived from the name 'Ganymede', and in early modern England the two forms were synonymous. Shakespeare seems to be moving beyond mere transvestism towards a mode where an androgynous figure could be taken as a model for a lover of the same sex. Rosalind's discourse is frequently sexually suggestive, and she delights in her improvised androgyny.[5] (The fact that Shakespeare took over the forest name from Lodge may, however, suggest that we should not place too much emphasis on its erotic connotations.) Orlando had fallen in love with a Rosalind, before whom he is tongue-tied, but, at ease with himself and his partner, plays a wooing game

---

[1] Phyllis Rackin, 'Androgyny, mimesis, and the marriage of the boy heroine', *PMLA* 102 (1987), 29–41; compare the way that, when she was playing Rosalind, Juliet Stevenson was always aware of playing a double character (Rutter *et al.*, *Clamorous Voices*, p. 104).

[2] Peter Erickson, *Patriarchal Structures in Shakespeare's Drama*, 1985, pp. 22–37. Debates over the effects of the appropriation of female parts by boy players are usefully reviewed in Thompson, 'Women/"women"'.

[3] Sir Philip Sidney, *The Countess of Pembroke's Arcadia*, 2.4, ed. Maurice Evans, 1977, pp. 237–40.

[4] Thomas Middleton, *Blurt Master Constable*, 5.2. Virgil's second eclogue tells of the passion the shepherd Corydon felt for his fellow Alexis: translations of the poem had been included in both William Webbe's *A Discourse of English Poetry* (1586) and Abraham Fraunce's *The Lawyer's Logic* (1588). Compare the Ganymede who is an 'open ass [arse]' in 'Satire 3', in Davenport (ed.), *Poems of John Marston*, p. 78 line 37. The speaker of Richard Barnfield's pastoral *The Affectionate Shepherd* (printed in 1594) proclaims his love for a young man called 'Ganymede'; for Ganymede and the blurring of distinctions between hermaphroditism and homosexuality, see Panofsky, pp. 171–230; Curtius, pp. 113–17; Alan Bray, *Homosexuality in Renaissance England*, 1982, pp. 33–4, 65.

[5] Camille Paglia, *Sexual Personae: Art and Decadence from Nefertiti to Emily Dickinson*, 1991, contrasts the 'Dionysian' hermaphroditism of Rosalind with 'formalized, frozen, and emblematic' versions of the theme in Belphoebe and Britomart in *The Faerie Queene* (p. 195); see also Bruce R. Smith, *Homosexual Desire in Shakespeare's England: A Cultural Poetics*, 1994 edn, pp. 144–50.

with a Ganymede. The Italianate libertine Jaques also seems erotically taken with Ganymede (4.1.1–30).[1] In her epilogue to *As You Like It*, 'Rosalind' speaks both as a 'lady' and as a boy player (lines 1 and 13). In *Twelfth Night* Orsino and Olivia discover that both have desired a Ganymede creature, Viola/Cesario, in the case of Orsino a boy playing a young woman playing a young man.

We might read this doubleness of gender in two ways. First, if Orlando was sexually attracted to a masculine figure, this may have been an interim feeling that reveals that his gender identity was not fully established. It is implicitly parallel to the very close and all-absorbing adolescent relationship between Rosalind and Celia at the beginning of the play (1.3.63–6),[2] as well as to Phoebe's infatuation with Ganymede/Rosalind.[3] Alternatively we may remember that, in an age when women were accounted imperfect men, eroticized boys are represented as '*enabling* figures, as a way of getting from women to men'.[4] We note that gender identity is not entirely consolidated by the resolution of Shakespeare's play, and that gender difference, which is the basis of so many people's sense of identity, is thereby dissolved.[5]

Such has been the direction of interpretation in recent years. However, it is worth entering a caveat. Shakespeare may very well have thought of 'Ganymede' as Chapman did who, following neo-platonic tradition, celebrates him as a figure of the beauty of the mind:

> The mind, in that we like, rules every limb,
> Gives hands to bodies, makes them make them trim.
> Why then in that the body doth dislike
> Should not his sword as great a veny [wound] strike?
> The bit and spur that monarch ruleth still
> To further good things and to curb the ill;
> He is the Ganymede, the bird of Jove,

---

[1] Compare how Laxton in Middleton and Dekker's *Roaring Girl* is attracted by the woman–man Moll (2.1.187 ff.); see also Field and Fletcher's *The Honest Man's Fortune* (1613): ' 'twas never good world since our French lords learned of the Neapolitans to make their pages their bedfellows' (Fredson Bowers (ed.), *The Dramatic Works in the Beaumont and Fletcher Canon*, 1996, vol. x, 3.3.219–20).

[2] Bray, *Homosexuality*, 1982, pp. 78–9; for parallel patterns in other Shakespearean texts, see Marjorie Garber, *Coming of Age in Shakespeare*, 1981, pp. 32–6, 145–8.

[3] In the anonymous *The Maid's Metamorphosis* (1599–1600) this coming-of-age rite is the pattern of the love of Apollo who, having inadvertently killed his fifteen-year-old page-boy Hyacinth, finds himself in love with Eurymine (3.1). In anger at his pursuit of her, Eurymine challenges the god to change her into a man – which he does. The pattern is repeated when her true love Ascanio pursues her, knowing she is a man until, urged by a hermit–magician Aramanthus, Apollo bars confusion by transforming her back into woman's shape – and revealing that Aramanthus had been exiled for an 'undeserved crime' (5.2.102) and that Eurymine is the magician's long-lost daughter – the parallels with *As You Like It* are obvious. The play is reprinted in John Lyly, *Complete Works*, ed. R. Warwick Bond, 3 vols., 1902, III.

[4] Stephen Orgel, *Impersonations: The Performance of Gender in Shakespeare's England*, 1996, p. 63; see also Thomas Laqueur, *Making Sex: Body and Gender from the Greeks to Freud*, 1990.

[5] See Levine, *Men in Women's Clothing*, pp. 3–4, 10; Valerie Traub, *Desire and Anxiety: Circulations of Sexuality in Shakespearean Drama*, 1992, argues that cross-dressing liberated desire from the binary oppositions that generally define love; but see Christopher Wixson, 'Cross-dressing and John Lyly's *Gallathea*', *SEL* 41 (2001), 241–56.

Rapt to his sovereign's bosom for his love.
His beauty was it, not the body's pride,
The made him great Aquarius stellified:
And that mind most is beautiful and high
And nearest comes to a divinity
That furthest is from spot of earth's delight,
Pleasures that lose their substance with their sight:
Such one Saturnius ravisheth to love,
And fills the cup of all content to Jove.
                        (*The Shadow of Night* (1594), 'Hymnus in Cynthiam', 456–71)[1]

The problematic gender of 'Ganymede' disappears if, in performance, it is decided to play the wooing scenes in a way that signals that Orlando has seen through Rosalind's masculine disguise.[2] And it is worth recalling here a note about Rosalind from the German director Peter Stein: 'it is impossible to approach these events in a psychological manner, because they cannot be played that way'. With a gesture to Brecht, he suggested that actors would have to find 'something more theatrical, treat it like some kind of sport (e.g. a boxing-match). Each member of the audience will anyway at any given point introduce psychological dimensions for himself.' Stein went on to direct the mock wedding of Orlando and Rosalind conducted by Celia in such an innocent way that there was no question of Orlando falling in love with the 'boy' with whom he stood at the forest altar.[3]

Orlando is a father's-son boy,[4] who moves into manhood through the rites of wrestling.[5] He ventures to fight for food to nurture old Adam (2.6.5–6) who perhaps serves, like Duke Senior, as a substitute father-figure. Orlando 'falls in love' and exercises his virtue in the most conventional Petrarchan manner. Yet he is as happy in the 'male utopia'[6] as he is with Rosalind. His avatars are Robin Hood, who wrestled with Much the Miller's son, and Hercules, another lion killer.[7] But Orlando is made of sighs and tears as well as strength and courage, a devotee of a cult of pity:

[1] Modernised from *Poems*, ed. Phyllis Brooks Bartlett, 1941, p. 41, and see p. 45 n. 25; Chapman derived much of this from Natalis Comes, *Mythologiae* (1568), 'De Ganymede', 9.13.
[2] This was done in Robert Helpmann's 1955 Old Vic production with John Neville as Orlando and Virginia McKenna as Rosalind (see J. C. Trewin, *Going to Shakespeare*, 1978, p. 146 n. 3; Shattuck, p. 64, no. 104); it had to be done in the 1978 BBC television production because of the producer's decision to shoot on location which entailed the adoption of a realistic code throughout the performance (see Stage History, pp. 75–6 and 80–1 below).
[3] Michael Patterson, *Peter Stein: Germany's Leading Theatre Director*, 1981, p. 142.
[4] Orlando is a bit like Hamlet in that his dead father's spirit is within him. Like Hamlet he both admires and resents his father, in his case for leaving him only a thousand crowns.
[5] The anti-theatrical writer John Northbrooke names wrestling as a fit sport for gentlemen (*A Treatise wherein . . . Vain Plays . . . are Reproved* (1577), p. 29) but, by the time of *AYLI*, wrestling was falling out of favour as an aristocratic pastime: see Joseph Strutt, *The Sports and Pastimes of the People of England*, ed. William Hone, 1830, pp. 80–5, and John Stow, *A Survey of London*, 1598, p. 70.
[6] Erickson, *Patriarchal Structures*, p. 28; see also Marjorie Garber, 'The education of Orlando', in A. R. Braunmuller and James C. Bulman (eds.), *Comedy from Shakespeare to Sheridan*, 1986, pp. 113–30.
[7] Laroque, p. 233; Plutarch, in a treatise on temperance, 'That Brute Beasts have Discourse of Reason', notes that Hercules was left behind on the voyage for the Golden Fleece because of 'a young beardless Ganymede whom he loved', *Moralia*, trans. Philemon Holland, 1603, p. 568.

ORLANDO If ever you have looked on better days,
If ever been where bells have knolled to church,
If ever sat at any goodman's feast,
If ever from your eyelids wiped a tear,
And know what 'tis to pity and be pitied,
Let gentleness my strong enforcement be,
In the which hope, I blush, and hide my sword.

To this the Duke offers a gentle rebuke, turning Orlando's self-pity towards piety:

DUKE SENIOR True is it that we have seen better days,
And have with holy bell been knolled to church,
And sat at goodmen's feasts, and wiped our eyes
Of drops that sacred pity hath engendered. (2.7.113–23)

Later, in his courtship lesson with Rosalind, we have the feeling that she is preparing him to be her 'child's father' – the thought had come into her mind as early as 1.3. Unpunctual writers of trite verse are not made for such a role, and Rosalind initiates the therapy her lover seems to require, fashioning him according to her needs as well as her desires. The play had opened in a world where status rules: men play games within rules of hierarchy, women evince solidarity and sisterhood. It is notable that the love between Orlando and Rosalind is initiated by Rosalind's desirous gaze in the wrestling scene, and it is she, emotionally secure by virtue of her friendship with Celia, who reminds Orlando of the dangerous anarchies of desire but then hustles him precipitately towards betrothal, figured in this play by the mock-marriage conducted by Celia.[1]

Like other lovers, Romeo and Lysander for example, Orlando has found a discourse of love that is registered in the Petrarchan poems he hangs on the forest's trees. Rosalind's mind encompasses a much wider range of possibilities: as Juliet Stevenson said, '[Rosalind's] a mental dancer. She's thinking on her feet. And she moves so fast, all he can do is ask the questions.'[2] It is for Rosalind to debunk Orlando and Silvius, to make them both realise that romantic love does not last for ever, that their kind of trite idealising is solipsistic in that it crystallises the object of their love and denies feminine desires. This she does by a radiant invocation of the ways of courtly love and a clamorous parody of its conventions – as well as by reminding Phoebe point-blank of the ordinariness of her attractiveness. (Phoebe demonstrated the absurdities of Silvius' Petrarchan conceits (3.6.8–27), but, infatuated with 'Ganymede', writes to her in the same vein (4.3.39–61).) Moreover, after the wooing is ended, that same desire may not be confinable within marriage – Rosalind's talk of infidelity and cuckoldry is a kind of homeopathy, a mocking but serious indication of independence, a way of pricking Orlando's inflated predilections, and a reminder to the audience that married women serve both as affirmations

[1] See Susanne L. Wofford, '"To you I give myself, for I am yours": erotic performance and theatrical performatives in *As You Like It*', in Russ McDonald (ed.), *Shakespeare Reread: The Texts in New Contexts*, 1994, pp. 147–69.
[2] Rutter *et al.*, *Clamorous Voices*, p. 106.

of male identity and sovereignty and threats to them. As Erickson observes: 'Discussions of androgyny in *As You Like It* usually focus on Rosalind whereas in fact it is the men rather than the women who are the last beneficiaries of androgyny. It is Orlando, not Rosalind, who achieves a synthesis of attributes traditionally labelled masculine and feminine when he combines compassion and aggression in rescuing his brother from the lioness.'[1]

It is, however, impossible and wrong to fix one tone for the performance of much of the dialogue between the lovers. For example, the following might be played to demonstrate that, even after Rosalind's therapy, Orlando is unable to distinguish between poetic conceit and narrative fact:

> ROSALIND O, my dear Orlando, how it grieves me to see thee wear thy heart in a scarf.
> ORLANDO It is my arm.
> ROSALIND I thought thy heart had been wounded with the claws of a lion.
> ORLANDO Wounded it is, but with the eyes of a lady.
> ROSALIND Did your brother tell you how I counterfeited to sound when he showed me your handkerchief?
> ORLANDO Aye, and greater wonders than that.   (5.2.15–23)

But this could equally be played as a game between two lovers who dextrously appropriate familiar styles, perhaps to cover their emotional raggedness at this moment, perhaps to expose the absurdities of romance narratives.

As for Celia, we may begin by likening her relationship with Rosalind to that between Helena and Hermia in *A Midsummer Night's Dream*, concerning whom the text gives us to believe that they must grow apart in order to achieve a necessary maturity. But it is different in *As You Like It*: the emphasis is not upon *growth*, let alone growth under the eye of a dicey male like Oberon, but upon liberation, upon risks and choices. At the beginning of the play, Celia by rank and character is in the ascendancy: as Le Beau points out (1.2.224), she is the 'taller' (more spirited) of the two, and it is she who proposes that the two flee the court. Yet Celia recognises that Rosalind is not going to follow stereotyped patterns or reciprocate her possessive friendship – 'thou lov'st me not with the full weight that I love thee' (1.2.6–7) – and is going to woo and win her man. She, perhaps out of a sense of loss, follows suit, plighting herself to the new Oliver that Fortune and Orlando deliver into the forest, but perhaps confident by virtue of Rosalind's example of how to handle him.[2]

But whatever a director or reader decides about the meaning of the forest scenes, no production is going to succeed unless Arden is a place for *fun*, unless an exploration of political and moral knowledge, of metatheatricality and the inscriptions of gender on the body, leaves space for wit and laughter, even if that laughter is

---

[1] *Patriarchal Structures*, p. 30; compare Froma Zeitlin, who notes that 'theater uses the feminine for the purposes of imagining a fuller model for the masculine self, and "playing the other" opens that self to those often banned emotions of fear and pity' ('Playing the other: theater, theatricality and the feminine in Greek drama', *Representations* 11 (1985), 63–89).

[2] For Oliver's conversion, see Richard Knowles, 'Myth and type in *As You Like It*', *ELH* 33 (1966), 1–22; Cynthia Lewis, 'Horns, the dream-work, and female potency in *As You Like It*', *South Atlantic Review* 66 (2001), 45–69; and Tiffany Stern, *Making Shakespeare*, 2004, p. 107.

the laughter of knowingness. Although Ben Jonson had once, thinking of possible vulgarities in stage representations, opined that 'the moving of laughter is a fault in comedy',[1] he later wrote concerning his *Sad Shepherd* (1637):

> But here's a heresy of late let fall,
> That mirth by no means fits a pastoral.
> Such say so who can make none, he presumes:
> Else there's no scene more properly assumes
> The sock [light shoe worn by comic actors in antiquity]. For
>   whence can sport in kind arise,
> But from the rural routs and families?   (Prologue, 31–6)

Nuptials

The play moves towards marriage, or more strictly a set of betrothals that are cemented by desire and by compact (Phoebe and Silvius). Although we are aware that Rosalind is giving up her liberty by giving up her disguise, ritually giving her 'self' back to her father and then to her husband (5.4.101–2), we recognise that the moment comes immediately after Touchstone's declaration that there is 'much virtue in "if"' (5.4.88). The emphasis of the play's ending is on the provisional: the penultimate sequence of the game between Rosalind and Orlando may be said to end with Orlando's line 'I can live no longer by thinking' (5.2.40). This could be delivered as a 'suddenly impatient and agonised cry',[2] implying naiveté on Orlando's part, or, by a more knowing and suave Orlando, with a degree of suggestiveness. In either case it is a reminder to the audience that the two lovers have only begun to know each other. The play contrasts our hope that sanctified desire might bring people the happiness they crave with our knowledge that marriages are beginnings and not endings. The forest idyll is over, and the responsibilities of the 'working-day' world have yet to be confronted. (Rosalind's saucy epilogue with its avowal that if 'she' were a woman, the men in the audience would be kissed in general may offer some consolation to those who see marriage as no resolution.)

Rosalind had been speaking of conjuring: like Prospero, she blesses the nuptials that are to ensue with a sequence something like a court masque: the god Hymen enters to preside over betrothals and a family reunion. His appearance was disdained by some eighteenth-century editors and often cut from nineteenth-century productions.[3] Yet pastoral and mythological elements were mingled in classical texts,[4] and in drama the pattern of resolution through an appearance of a god goes back to the classical *deus ex machina*. It was used by Jonson in *Cynthia's Revels*, written about the same time as *As You Like It*, whose idle courtiers await the coming of the

---

[1] Ben Jonson, *Timber or Discoveries*, VIII, 643; Jonson was quoting from Heinsius, *Ad Horatii de Plauto et Terentio Judicium, Dissertatio*, 1618.
[2] Richard David, *Shakespeare in the Theatre*, 1978, p. 138.
[3] See Knowles, pp. 292–3; Nigel Playfair, *The Story of the Lyric Theatre, Hammersmith*, 1925, p. 51.
[4] See Arthur Golding's apology for writing 'the heathen names of feignèd gods' in his translation of Ovid's *Metamorphoses*, 1593 edn, 'To the reader', sig. B1^r.

goddess Cynthia, a figure of the Queen. Moreover, by invoking Hymen, the ending presents a subtle combination of magic and human contrivance. There is emphasis on 'wonder', a reaction that is conspicuously not called for in the 'antics' (pageants) that end *Love's Labour's Lost*. However, this may be undercut by a continuing sense of the intractability of people and situations: there is indeed 'much virtue in if':

> ROSALIND You say you'll marry me, *if* I be willing.
> PHOEBE That will I, should I die the hour after.
> ROSALIND But *if* you do refuse to marry me,
>   You'll give yourself to this most faithful shepherd.
> PHOEBE So is the bargain.
> ROSALIND You say that you'll have Phoebe *if* she will.
> SILVIUS Though to have her and death were both one thing.
>
> (5.4.11–17, emphases added)

Rosalind's 'ifs' are echoed by Hymen:

> Here's eight that must take hands
> To join in Hymen's bands,
> *If* truth holds true contents.   (112–14, emphasis added)

The immediate context suggests that we understand 'truth' and 'true' in terms of couples plighting their troth in a condition of emotional honesty. But it may also suggest a conflict between moral truth and unruly life, or an awareness that the 'truth' of theatrical representation is established not by belief but by collusion on the part of the audience with the 'false forgeries'[1] of the poet and players.

In a modern production it is for a director to decide whether the god is a token of concord, cosmic and social, or is an agent of Rosalind,[2] and whether, as the former, having been presumably summoned by Rosalind, he should arrive in miraculous stillness or in a bit of a huff, miffed at being upstaged by Rosalind who seems to have sorted things out fairly adequately herself and who, usurping the patriarchal role, gives herself away in a celebration of joyful resolution ('To you I give myself, for I am yours' (101)):

> Peace, ho: I bar confusion,
> 'Tis I must make conclusion
> Of these most strange events.   (109–11)

The serious reading of the above lines bespeaks an expression of that desire for order that is characteristic of Duke Senior's forest rule – without Hymen all are in danger of finding themselves in the world of *Comus*. The comic reading comes by

---

[1] *Son.* 138.4 (the version that appears in the first edition of *PP*).

[2] 'Rosalind is imagined to be brought by enchantment and is therefore introduced by a supposed aerial being in the character of Hymen' (Johnson, n. to 5.4.93).

the actor playing Hymen stressing the repeated 'I'.[1] If it is decided that the final sequence of a production should be joyful, it may be best to intersperse comedy with moments of seriousness as, in the manner of Shakespeare's later romances, Rosalind is reunited with her father, and Silvius and Phoebe settle for a marriage based upon 'neighbourliness' (3.6.89) rather than passion.

The sense of indeterminacy is compounded by the unexpected appearance of Jacques de Boys, a moment not to the liking of Dr Johnson, who thought Shakespeare had 'lost an opportunity of exhibiting a moral lesson' by not dramatising the encounter between Duke Frederick and the hermit.[2] But Shakespeare was presumably deliberately eschewing the moral in his deference to and exposure of the conventions of romance narrative, at once wondrous and absurd.

After Duke Senior has substituted measures of music for measures of justice, the rustic revelry is interrupted once more by the considered verdicts of Jaques upon the matches, an invocation not of poetic justice but of the conventions imposed by genre. There is, moreover, no metamorphosis of a Jaques: from this last act Jaques may exit in a direction different from that taken by the lovers, to seek not happiness but knowledge in another other world elsewhere, among that second band of 'convertites' (5.4.168), the ones we did not see, Duke Frederick and his entourage.

There may be little substance in the play's last lines, but the rites of dance that at last conclude the action can be performed in many fashions. In 1977 Trevor Nunn's production for the Royal Shakespeare Company ended with a protracted and gracefully exuberant ballet, like the closing number of a Hollywood musical;[3] in 1991 a production by Mark Brickman at the Crucible Theatre in Sheffield ended as it had begun with a sombre version of the play's horn song, suggesting cuckoldry and death.

Sources

Shakespeare's main source was the immensely popular prose narrative *Rosalind or Euphues' Golden Legacy* (1590), written by Thomas Lodge while voyaging to the Canaries.[4] Lodge took the story of an old man with three sons from a

---

[1] It is common in productions for Corin and Hymen to be doubled: a shepherd in fancy dress may suggest a parodic ending – or, equally, a miracle of transformation. Doubling Hymen with Sir Oliver Martext makes a riddling statement about Christian marriage; for the doubling of Hymen and Adam, see Stage History, p. 55.

[2] Woodhuysen (ed.), *Johnson on Shakespeare*, p. 180.

[3] For 'rustic revelry' from 1952 to 2000 at Stratford, see Smallwood, pp. 189–214.

[4] This text, printed eleven times between 1590 and 1642, was dedicated to the Queen's cousin, Henry Carey, Lord Hunsdon, Lord Chamberlain, and patron to Shakespeare's company. The introductions to Thomas Lodge, *Rosalynd*, ed. Brian Nellist, 1995, and *Rosalind*, ed. Donald Beecher, 1997 both offer excellent accounts of the work. See also Bullough, pp. 143–57; Kenneth Muir, *The Sources of Shakespeare's Plays*, 1977, pp. 125–31; Marco Mincoff, 'What Shakespeare did to *Rosalynde*', *Shakespeare Jahrbuch* 96 (1960), 78–89; Knowles, pp. 475–83; Edward I. Berry, 'Rosalynde and Rosalind', *SQ* 31 (1980), 42–52; Gibbons, *Shakespeare and Multiplicity*, pp. 226–7; for the 'masculinity' of Lodge's romance, see Nathaniel Strout, '*As You Like It*, *Rosalynde*, and mutuality', *SEL* 41 (2001), 277–95; David Margolies, 'Shakespeare and Elizabethan popular fiction', in Stuart Gillespie and Neil Rhodes (eds.), *Shakespeare and Elizabethan Popular Culture*, 2006, 112–35.

fourteenth-century poem of some 900 lines, *The Tale of Gamelyn*. Like the Robin
Hood tales, this is a story of 'greenwood' outlaws that centres around the tribulations
of Gamelyn, the youngest son who is driven off his father's estate and, having heard
how a franklin lost two sons killed by the champion wrestler, has many adventures,
including winning the prizes of a ram and a ring at a wrestling match.[1] Lodge
added a narrative of a king (Gerismond) that 'lived as an outlaw in the Forest
of Arden[ne]',[2] the pastoral romance of the love between Rosader (Orlando) and
Rosalind, Saladyne (Oliver) and Alinda (Celia), Montanus (Silvius) and Phoebe
(there are no female characters in *Gamelyn*), and set the story in France.[3] Silvius
and Phoebe come from the eclogue tradition that runs back through Sidney's
Arcadia and Spenser's *Shepheardes Calender* to Theocritus and Virgil. Lodge in fact
calls their verse debates 'eclogues', and also gives Rosader and Rosalind a wooing
eclogue.[4] In Lodge as in Shakespeare we find hostilities both at court and between
the noble brothers, a wrestling match, forest exile, the wooing of Rosalind disguised
as Ganymede,[5] Phoebe's proud disdain for her lover, Rosader's rescue of his brother
from a lion, the marriage of the Oliver and Celia figures, and the restoration of the
exiled king.[6] Shakespeare, however, excises the violence that occurs in Lodge's
narrative: Orlando's wrestling opponent seems to be injured rather than killed,[7]
Celia is not kidnapped and offered to her lecherous father as Alinda is in *Rosalind*,
and the dramatist substitutes a miraculous conversion for the battle in *Rosalind* in
which the usurping duke (Torismond) is killed.

Shakespeare characteristically makes the two dukes brothers, so emphasising the
difficulty of distinguishing between public and private issues, and reminding us
that Arcadian entertainments are also comedies of state. He gives Orlando 'but
poor a thousand crowns' (1.1.2), whereas in *Rosalind* the third and youngest son
Rosader gets more than his brothers from his dying father (Sir John of Bordeaux).[8]
This gives Saladyne (the Oliver figure) the desire for riches rather than, as in
Shakespeare, an unspecified psychological motive for detesting his brother. Adam
is old but hale and helps Rosader to drive his brother away by force. Shakespeare
plays a much more complex game with gender: 'We are never tempted to forget
that Rosalynde is a woman; the Orlando-figure never takes her for anything but a

---

[1] *Gamelyn* is found in many manuscripts of *The Canterbury Tales* and there wrongly attributed to
Chaucer. Bullough, p. 148 summarises the evidence that Shakespeare may have known the poem
(which was not printed until 1721). However, as he admits, the few verbal similarities he lists do not
allow us to come to a settled verdict.

[2] *Rosalind*, p. 108; the names 'Torismond' and 'Gerismond' are taken from Torquato Tasso's play *Il Re
Torismondo* (1587).

[3] His geography is pleasantly vague: like Henry Roberts (see p. 9 n. 5), he implies at several points that
Bordeaux is adjacent to 'Ardenne'.

[4] *Rosalind*, pp. 127–32, 165–8; see Simone Dorangeon, *L'Églogue anglaise de Spenser à Milton*, 1974.

[5] A detail taken ultimately from Italian comedy (see Salingar, *Traditions of Comedy*, p. 190).

[6] It may be that the play's title was suggested by a sentence in Lodge's Epistle to his Gentlemen Readers,
'If you like it, so' (*Rosalind*, p. 26).

[7] See 1.2.172.

[8] *Rosalind*, p. 98.

man. All of Lodge's sexual jokes turn . . . on keeping that distinction clear.'[1] As he added Launce to the sources of *Two Gentlemen of Verona* and Feste to those of *Twelfth Night*, Shakespeare added a set of 'Touchstone' characters whose role is to exemplify wit and folly, as well as to set it off in the main protagonists: Jaques and Touchstone (the forest name of the play's fool), as well as Amiens, William, Audrey, Martext, and Le Beau. Finally, Lodge's moralistic epilogue, addressed to gentlemen, may have generated a retort courteous, in that Rosalind's epilogue is addressed first to the women in the playhouse audience.

Lodge's text is an episodic narrative written in the manner of an earlier and equally popular prose romance, John Lyly's *Euphues: The Anatomy of Wit* (1578). (Some of the situations and structures of Lyly's plays resemble those of *As You Like It*.)[2] The sentences are often built up from symmetrical figures of sense, and the piece is studded with moral maxims and elaborate similes – characteristic of a style that has come to be known as 'euphuistic'. In form *Rosalind* is an assemblage of set pieces: prose narrative is interspersed with verse complaint,[3] characters are given formal meditations and set speeches on moral topics, pairs of characters engage in debates. Here is the beginning of a section Lodge entitled 'Rosalind's Passion':

Unfortunate Rosalind, whose misfortunes are more than thy years, and whose passions are greater than thy patience. The blossoms of thy youth are mixed with the frosts of envy, and the hope of thy ensuing fruits perish in the bud. Thy father is by Torismond banished from the crown, and thou, the unhappy daughter of a king, detained captive, living as disquieted in thy thoughts as thy father discontented in his exile. Ah, Rosalind, what cares wait upon a crown, what griefs are incident to dignity, what sorrows haunt royal palaces. The greatest seas have the sorest storms, the highest birth subject to the most bale, and of all trees the cedars soonest shake with the wind. Small currents are ever calm, low valleys not scorched in any lightnings, nor base men tied to any baleful prejudice. Fortune flies, and if she touch poverty, it is with her heel, rather disdaining their want with a frown, than envying [injuring] their wealth with disparagement [social discredit]. Oh, Rosalind, hadst thou been born low, thou hadst not fallen so high, and yet being great of blood, thine honour is more if thou brookest misfortune with patience.

Suppose I contrary [thwart] Fortune with content, yet Fates, unwilling to have me any way happy, have forced love to set my thoughts on fire with fancy. Love, Rosalind? Becometh it women in distress to think of love? Tush, desire hath no respect of persons. Cupid is blind and shooteth at random, as soon hitting a rag as a robe, and piercing as soon the bosom of a captive as the breast of a libertine. Thou speakest it, poor Rosalind, by experience, for being every way distressed, surcharged with cares, and overgrown with sorrows, yet amidst the heap of all these mishaps Love hath lodged in thy heart the perfection of young Rosader, a man every way absolute as well for his inward life as for his outward lineaments, able to content the eye with beauty, and the ear with the report of his virtue.[4]

This obviously matches little of the tone of Shakespeare's text, and it is likely that in those passages that mock literary conventions, he was writing in a jesting

---

[1] Bruce R. Smith, *Homosexual Desire in Shakespeare's England*, 1991, p. 145.
[2] See Introduction, pp. 13–14.
[3] The text includes a poem in French by Philippe Desportes, pp. 189–90.
[4] *Rosalind*, pp. 115–16.

vein that resembled not so much the style of Thomas Lodge as that of Thomas Nashe.[1] Sir Philip Sidney also laced pastoral romance with wit, and there are marked similarities between Rosalind and Celia and Pamela and Philoclea in his *Old Arcadia*.[2] The similarities between the rhetorical techniques of *As You Like It* and those of these two authors in effect qualify their works as sources.

Shakespeare may well have taken the name for Corin, the third of his overtly pastoral characters, from the anonymous dramatic romance *Syr Clyomon and Clamydes*, printed in 1599 and, according to the title page, acted by the Queen's Men.[3] Neronis, daughter of Patranius, King of the Strange Marshes, loves Sir Clyomon. Having been taken captive by the King of Norway, rival for her love, she escapes in man's apparel into the wilderness and meets a shepherd named Corin with whom she takes service. Unlike Shakespeare's shepherd, this Corin speaks in Mummerset – the West Country dialect used for rustics and clowns[4] – and bears some resemblance to William. Neronis is brought to believe that Clyomon has been killed (in fact he had killed the King of Norway – compare the fainting sequence) and is saved from despair by the descent of Providence from the playhouse 'heavens'. She encounters Sir Clyomon and, both in disguise, they accomplish great adventures until Neronis reveals herself to her lover and they are married. There seem to be no verbal borrowings, and the story is stitched together out of the commonplaces of romance narrative: the play does not really qualify as a 'source' of *As You Like It*. Two Robin Hood plays, Chettle and Munday's *The Downfall of Robert Earl of Huntingdon* and *The Death of Robert Earl of Huntingdon*, performed by the Admiral's Men in 1598 both at the Rose and at court, may have suggested certain details, such as the songs sung by the outlaws.[5]

Date and occasion

Although the assumption that *As You Like It* was originally a Globe play (see below, pp. 52–4, and Appendix 1, pp. 221–6) has been shaken, there is, as yet, no conclusive evidence for either the date of composition or the earliest performance history of *As You Like It*. This is partly because, as is all too often the case with early modern plays, these topics are intimately associated: questions of date, occasion, and venue entail one another in a circular manner. Matters have been complicated by the fact that a poem ('As the dial hand tells o'er'), from a manuscript anthology

---

[1] For parallels between Rosalind's sardonic version of the Hero and Leander story and the version offered in Nashe's *Lenten Stuff*, see Gibbons, *Shakespeare and Multiplicity*, pp. 178–80.
[2] *Ibid.*, pp. 158–66.
[3] Part of the text is reprinted in Bullough, pp. 257–66.
[4] Hattaway, p. 72.
[5] See also p. 51. For parallels between the plot of *AYLI* and the anonymous *The Maid's Metamorphosis*, see Introduction, p. 13 n. 4; for sources or analogues for Touchstone's speech on the degrees of the lie (5.4.78–88), see the works noted by Furness, pp. 275–6; J. J. M. Tobin, 'Nashe and *As You Like It*', *NQ* 223 (1978), 138–9 offers seeming echoes in 2.1 from Nashe's *Pierce Pennilesse*.

put together by Henry Stanford,[1] has been proposed as an epilogue to the play[2] and, partly because of this hypothetical linkage, been attributed to Shakespeare. Working 'backwards' from this authorship problem towards the problem of original venue does not create any greater certainty. There are no positive terms, and it follows that the temptation to construct a single narrative out of the evidence that we have must be resisted.[3]

As You Like It is not included in the list of plays by Shakespeare that appears in Francis Meres' *Palladis Tamia*, which was entered in the Stationers' Register on 7 September 1598.[4] Patterns of publication in the period suggest it was likely to have been written some twenty months before 4 August 1600, the date when it was itself entered in the same Register and probably just after *Palladis Tamia* had appeared. That would have been in late 1598 or early 1599.[5] In the event no quarto edition ever appeared.

There is little evidence for dating within the text. The Pages' song in 5.3, 'It was a lover and his lass', appeared in Thomas Morley's *First Book of Airs* which, although not entered in the Stationers' Register, was printed in 1600/01. Inconveniently, we cannot tell whether Shakespeare wrote or whether he appropriated its words, possibly from a popular song, whether he collaborated with Morley, or even whether the song was originally performed to Morley's tune.[6] We also have to entertain the conjecture that the song may not have been included in the earliest performances, and that, at a later date, it was inserted into the playbook or a manuscript used by the compositor.[7] Since the order of the verses as printed in Morley's song-book is more

---

[1] Cambridge University Library, ms. Dd.5.75, f. 46.

[2] Juliet Dusinberre, 'Pancakes and a date for *As You Like It*', *SQ* 54 (2003), 371–405; compare Appendix 1.

[3] Compare Paul Werstine, 'Narratives about printed Shakespeare texts: "foul papers" and "bad" quartos', in Russ McDonald (ed.), *Shakespeare: An Anthology of Criticism and Theory 1945–2000*, pp. 296–317.

[4] For the possible unreliability of Meres' list – which does not name any of the histories – see E. A. J. Honigmann, *Shakespeare's Impact on his Contemporaries*, 1982, pp. 75–6. The citation at 3.6.81 of a line from Marlowe's *Hero and Leander*, the first extant edition of which dates from 1598, is inconclusive evidence for dating, since the poem may well have been published before that. John Dover Wilson argued for revision of an early version of 1593 (Wilson, pp. 94–108). Putative echoes from other works are reviewed in Chambers, *Shakespeare*, 1, pp. 402–4. Statistical tests on the text, which variously date the play between 1596 and 1600, are summarised in Wells and Taylor, *Textual Companion*, p. 121. There is no external evidence that *As You Like It* was the alternative title of the lost play *Love's Labour's Won* (see Knowles, p. 366; compare David Ormerod, 'Love's Labour's Lost and Won: the case for *As You Like It*', *Cahiers élisabéthains* 44 (1993), 9–21).

[5] This entry, anomalously on a flyleaf of the Register and lacking a record of payment of the normal fee, was a 'staying entry'. It is uncertain whether this designates a desire to prevent surreptitious publication by establishing a right to the text, whether the players had some reason for not wanting the playtext to be available at that time, whether a manuscript was not yet available, or whether the phrase means that the license lacked ecclesiastical authorization (see Knowles, pp. 353–64; Lukas Erne, *Shakespeare as Literary Dramatist*, 2003, pp. 84 and 103; Cyndia Susan Clegg, 'Liberty, license, and authority: press censorship and Shakespeare', in David Scott Kastan (ed.), *A Companion to Shakespeare*, 1999, pp. 464–85.)

[6] Morley says that his songs were 'made this vacation time' (sig. A2[r]), which could refer to the summer of either 1599 or 1600; see Knowles, n. 2546 and pp. 377–8.

[7] For the promiscuous use of songs, see Knowles, p. 377 and Tiffany Stern, 'Re-patching the play', in Peter Holland and Stephen Orgel (eds.), *From Script to Stage in Early Modern England*, 2004, pp. 151–77.

apt for the moment in the play in which they appear, it is tempting to suggest that the Folio's version, the stanzas of which seem to be in the wrong order, was taken from a manuscript text of unknown authorship that was somehow (by copying?) corrupted between an early performance of the play and its printing.[1] At 1.2.70–1 there may be a reference to the burning of satirical books along with Marlowe's translation of Ovid's *Elegies* in June 1599,[2] but this is also uncertain. (Those lines too may well have been an insertion.)

Evidence from performance records is equally inconclusive. It seems that for about ten years the repertories of the Lord Admiral's Men and the Lord Chamberlain's Men were in a kind of dialogue one with the other – from the end of 1594 until the end of the Queen's reign the rival companies played regularly at court at both Christmas and Shrovetide.[3] Philip Henslowe, by that time associated with the Admiral's Men, had lent Henry Chettle 10 shillings on 25 November 1598 for 'mending' a Robin Hood play for court performance, probably at Whitehall at Christmas that year.[4] This is likely to have been either *The Downfall of Robert Earl of Huntingdon* or *The Death of Robert Earl of Huntingdon*, both performed also at the Rose and for which Henslowe had lent Anthony Munday and Henry Chettle £5 each.[5] *As You Like It* too may well have been performed at court: Bullough's inference that 'Shakespeare's play was probably written for the sophisticated Essex circle to excel these crude works' remains suggestive, although it must also remain hypothetical.[6] It implies, however, that the phrase 'As you like it' may have been, if this play was indeed first performed by Shakespeare's company, the Lord Chamberlain's Men, at court, at Christmas 1598 or Shrovetide 1599, a knowingly loaded reference to royal taste, and may account for the Robin Hood motifs and references to hunting festivities that stud the text,[7] as well as for the prominent device of disguising through cross-dressing.[8]

---

[1] Ernest Brennecke, 'Shakespeare's musical collaboration with Morley', *PMLA* 54 (1939), 139–49.

[2] See p. 15 note 3; Knowles, p. 369.

[3] Chambers, IV, 111–16; Andrew Gurr, 'Intertextuality at Windsor', *SQ* 38 (1987), 189–200 and *Playing Companies*, pp. 243–5.

[4] Henslowe, p. 102; Chambers, IV, 111; James Shapiro, *1599: A Year in the Life of William Shakespeare*, 2005, p. 36.

[5] Henslowe, pp. 86–7; Henslowe paid 14 shillings to the Master of the Revels for licensing these on 28 March; his inventory of March 1598 lists various costumes and properties for the plays (pp. 317, 320, 322, 323).

[6] Bullough, p. 143; for elements of the devotional in the Robin Hood tradition, see Sean Field, 'Devotion, discontent, and the Henrician Reformation: the evidence of the Robin Hood stories', *Journal of British Studies* 41 (2002), 6–22, and for the way the play both laments a lost age of hospitality and also deflates its own nostalgia, see Indira Ghose, '"Better days": cultural memory in *As You Like It*', in Graham Bradshaw and Tom Bishop (eds.), *The Shakespearean International Yearbook*, 2008, vol. 8, 204–15.

[7] See 4.2 n. Edward I. Berry, 'Pastoral hunting in *As You Like It*', in *Shakespeare and the Hunt*, 2001, pp. 159–89; Heather Dubrow, 'Fringe benefits: Rosalind and the purlieux of the forest', *NQ* 53 (2006), 67–9; Robert N. Watson, 'As you liken it: simile in the forest', *Back to Nature: The Green and the Real in the Late Renaissance*, 2006, pp. 77–107; Leah S. Marcus, 'Shakespeare and festivity', in Stuart Gillespie and Neil Rhodes (eds.), *Shakespeare and Elizabethan Popular Culture*, 2006, pp. 42–66.

[8] See Scott McMillin, 'The sharer and his boy: rehearsing Shakespeare's women', in Peter Holland and Stephen Orgel (eds.), *From Script to Stage in Early Modern England*, 2004, pp. 231–45; compare the excellent essay by Barbara Hodgdon, 'Sexual disguise and the theatre of gender', in Alexander Leggatt (ed.), *The Cambridge Companion to Shakespearean Comedy*, 2002, pp. 179–97.

Disguise can be more than a plot device and become a means of characterisation or re-creating identity, as Shapiro and, implicitly, Bloom point out.[1] Andrew Gurr has brought this last topic into historical focus by noting that, within the repertory of the Admiral's Men, there is a significant cluster of plays that include this game of disguise, which was to be picked up by Shakespeare and inserted into his pastoral romance. In addition to the Robin Hood plays already mentioned, this cluster includes Munday's *John a Kent* or *The Wise Man of Westchester* (1594), Chapman's *The Blind Beggar of Alexandria* (1596), and the anonymous *Look About You* (1597–9?), imitated in Munday's Robin Hood plays.[2] This last is an intrigue of politics and passion at court, which also features Robin Hood (who disguises himself as a woman), along with a seeming hermit[3] and a ruler in exile (Richard Coeur de Lion). These were followed in due time by Samuel Rowley's *When You See Me You Know Me* (1604) and, within the genre of city comedy, Thomas Middleton's *The Roaring Girl* (1611) and *No Wit, No Help like a Woman's* (1611).[4]

Even if *As You Like It* was first performed at court, it was probably transferred to an amphitheatre playhouse fairly promptly. This had happened with other plays: *The Merry Wives of Windsor* (1597–8) was probably performed before the Queen at the royal palace of Windsor,[5] and the title page of its first quarto (1602) advertises the text by noting that it had been 'diverse times acted by the right honourable my Lord Chamberlain's servants, both before Her Majesty and elsewhere'. The first surviving quarto of *Love's Labour's Lost* (1598) reveals that it 'was presented before Her Highness this last Christmas', while the second quarto (1631) notes that it was 'acted by His Majesty's servants at the Blackfriars and the Globe'.[6]

If, on the other hand, the play opened at a public playhouse, the following factors obtain. It is probable that William Kempe, the company's clown, left the Chamberlain's Men in which he was a sharer in 1599, shortly after signing the lease for the site of the New Globe.[7] He had been associated with the jigs that had customarily ended performances and that had drawn the opprobrium of justices of the peace whose job it was to control the playhouses. In Touchstone *As You Like It* may contain an important part for the reputedly more refined Robert Armin, who almost certainly joined the company in the second half of 1599 and was certainly with the Lord Chamberlain's Men on the day *As You Like It* was entered in the

---

[1] See Susan Baker, 'Personating persons: rethinking Shakespearean disguises', *SQ* 43 (1992), 303–16.

[2] See Fred L. Jones, '*Look about You* and the disguises', *PMLA* 44 (1929), 835–41; Robert Leach, '*As You Like It* – a "Robin Hood" play', *ES* 82 (2001), 393–400.

[3] Compare *AYLI*, 3.3.288–9; there is also a hermit in *John a Kent* and *The Blind Beggar of Alexandria*.

[4] See chap. 2 of Andrew Gurr, *Shakespeare's Opposites: The Admiral's Company 1594–1625*, 2009; see also p. 21 n. 4.

[5] See, however, Wells and Taylor, *Textual Companion*, p. 120.

[6] See *ibid.*, pp. 117 and 270.

[7] Chambers, II, 326; Christopher Sutcliffe, 'Kempe and Armin: the management of change', *Theatre Notebook* 50 (1996), 122–34.

Stationers' Register.[1] Armin had been a goldsmith: that trade may be recalled by the Fool's forest-name 'Touchstone', which designates a piece of quartz or jasper used for testing gold and silver alloys. A good singer, he may have doubled the part of Amiens with that of Touchstone.[2] *As You Like It* could therefore well have been the first play performed at the company's new playhouse, the Globe, which had probably opened between June and September 1599.[3] (As we have seen, though, this could have followed an earlier court performance.)

However, Armin may equally have taken over the part of Touchstone only later: Kempe could well have first performed it both at court and at the Globe.[4] Moreover, in *The Italian Taylor and his Boy* Armin wrote that in his time he had been 'writ down for an ass', indicating that, like Kempe, he had played the part of Dogberry in *Much Ado about Nothing*, written about 1598.[5] Touchstone is designated 'Clown' in speech prefixes, and the fact that Armin took parts that have been traditionally associated with 'clowns' like Kempe as well as those in which he shone as a 'fool' (Feste in *Twelfth Night* and the Fool in *King Lear*, for example) indicates a lack of distinction between these two roles and that this evidence can have little validity for questions of dating.

It happens, moreover, that both Kempe and Armin were associated with the Marprelate controversy. Martinists had inveighed against the stage, alleging its links with Catholicism. Kempe had been named in the *Theses Martiniae* of 1589 and Armin was known as an anti-Marprelate pamphleteer. Perhaps this explains an act of gentle revenge, the mocking of the play's hedge-priest, Sir Oliver Martext.[6] Likewise, it is tempting to conjecture that Jaques' speech about the theatricality of life (2.7.139–66) was a gesture towards the supposed motto of the new playhouse, *Totus mundus agit histrionem* – 'All the world plays the actor.' Tiffany Stern, however, has argued that although Hercules shouldering the globe may have been the playhouse sign, there is no evidence now extant that the motto appeared at the New

[1] Chambers, III, 300; Knowles, pp. 374, 377; Wiles, p. 138; Armin reported at Christmas 1600 that he was to 'rake his journey' to Hackney with the 'good lord, my master whom I serve' (Robert Armin, *Quips upon Question* (1600) sig. Aii^r): this suggests a quick excursion (see *OED* Rake VI) from the City (the Lord Chamberlain lived in the Blackfriars), perhaps for a solo performance, and not that Armin had joined another company (see Gurr, *Playing Companies*, p. 313; compare Knowles, pp. 375–6).

[2] An entrance is marked for Amiens at 5.3.0 SD, a scene in which Touchstone appears, but he is given no dialogue.

[3] See Peter Thomson, *Shakespeare's Theatre*, 1983, pp. 63–4; Wiles, pp. 47–8; Gurr, *Playing Companies*, p. 291. The case that the new playhouse opened with performances of *H5* is summarised in *H5*, ed. Andrew Gurr, 1992, p. 6.

[4] See James Nielson, 'William Kemp at the Globe', *SQ* 44 (1993), 466–8; likewise Richard Dutton argues that Kempe remained in the company long enough to have played in *JC* (*Licensing, Censorship, and Authorship in Early Modern England*, 2000, p. 34).

[5] Robert Armin, *The Italian Taylor, and his Boy* (1609), sig. A3^r; Chambers, II, 300; Wells and Taylor, *Textual Companion*, p. 120.

[6] See Dusinberre, 'Topical forest', pp. 239–51, and Charles S. Felver, *Robert Armin, Shakespeare's Fool*, 1961, pp. 12–13 (cit. Knowles, p. 376); for anti-Martinism on the stage, see Peter Lake and Michael C. Questier, *The Anti-Christ's Lewd Hat: Protestants, Papists and Players in Post-Reformation England*, 2002, pp. 556–63.

Globe.[1] As with conjectured court performances, therefore, no firm inference concerning an exact date of a first public performance between June 1599 and August 1600 can be drawn from any of these facts and conjectural events.

There is a tradition, deriving from a lost letter, that the play was performed for King James I during festivities in 1603 at Wilton House in Wiltshire, home of the Earls of Pembroke. An outbreak of the plague had kept the new monarch away from London for some time, and while at Wilton James almost certainly engaged in his favourite sport of hunting. The Countess of Pembroke is supposed to have written to her son William Herbert, 'We have the man Shakespeare with us,' an unlikely turn of phrase for the period.[2] However, the pastoral setting and hunting sequences of *As You Like It* would have been appropriate for such a rural retreat. A record of a payment from the Chamber accounts confirms that there was such a performance (even if it was not of *As You Like It*):

To John Hemyngs one of his ma[ts] players vppon the Councells warraunte dated at the Courte at Wilton iij° december for the paynes and expences of himselfe and the rest of the Company in coming from mortelacke in the Countie of Surrie vnto the Courte aforesaid and there p[r]senting before his ma[tie] one playe on the second of December laste by way of his ma[ts] rewarde xxx[li]3

This may have been the company's first performance for their new patron: it may have cost the players much more than usual to travel from Mortlake to Wilton (about 86 miles), but the payment for one play is the same as Elizabeth paid for three performances.

Stage history

As we have seen, it is impossible to decide whether the play was first performed by the Lord Chamberlain's Men before the court, possibly in the Palace of Richmond,[4] or in a public playhouse, probably the Globe, in 1600.[5] Moreover, we can know little about these putative early performances beyond making an informed guess about the number of players required. 'Ten men can play twelve principal male roles, and four boys four principal female roles; these fourteen actors speak 96% of the lines . . . Seven men can play nine small speaking parts and six mutes; two boys

---

[1] See 2.7.137–66 n., Knowles, p. 373, and Tiffany Stern, 'Was *Totus mundus agit histrionem* ever the motto of the Globe Theatre?', *Theatre Notebook* 51 (1997), 122–7.

[2] There is some semi-documentary evidence about a garden temple erected to celebrate the event in David Roper, 'By Shakespeare's other Avon', in Richard Malim (ed.), *Great Oxford: Essays on the Life and Work of Edward De Vere, 17th Earl Of Oxford, 1550–1604*, pp. 299–311; for indoor performances in provincial great houses, see John Astington, *English Court Theatre, 1558–1642*, 1999, pp. 73–4.

[3] David Cook and F. P. Wilson (eds.), *Dramatic Records in the Declared Accounts of the Treasurer of the Chamber, 1558–1642*, 1962, p. 38; they also performed for the burgesses of Wilton at about the same time (Park Honan, *Shakespeare: A Life*, p. 302).

[4] See Appendix 1, and for descriptions of the palace hall and great chamber at the Palace of Richmond, see Astington, *Court Theatre*, 1999, pp. 57–63.

[5] See Date and Occasion, p. 52; the story that Shakespeare himself played Adam originates in the eighteenth century (see S. Schoenbaum, *Shakespeare's Lives*, 1991, p. 54); for a repertory of performance details, see A. C. Sprague, *Shakespeare and the Actors*, 1944, pp. 31–40; Knowles, pp. 629–62, offers a concise overview of productions, and there is a much fuller survey in Marshall, pp. 1–93.

play one small speaking part each [the singing pages of 5.3].' This does not suggest
much doubling, since these numbers match almost exactly the average number of
players who, according to the four surviving prompt-books for the King's Men (the
name of Shakespeare's company after the accession of King James in 1603), were
required for the performance of those texts.[1] If doubling was required, as it may
have been if the play was toured in the provinces, smaller groups may have followed
a pattern like the following, which was deployed by the English Touring Theatre's
production of 1994 directed by Stephen Unwin.[2] Sixteen of the smaller roles were
distributed between six actors:

Adam / Corin / Hymen
Duke Frederick / Duke Senior
Charles / 2 Lord / Sir Oliver Martext / William
Oliver / Amiens
Denis / Silvius
Le Beau / 1 Lord / Jacques de Boys

Doubling can add to the play's resonances, as it may do, for example, by associating
the two dukes and Corin and Hymen,[3] and can also disguise the fact that, like the
Fool in *King Lear* who vanishes in 3.6, Adam drops out of sight after Act 2.

Three documents offer hints as to who may have first taken these parts. The list
of signatories for the lease of the new Globe playhouse of 21 February 1599,[4] the
cast list for a performance of *Every Man in his Humour* on 20 September 1598,[5] and
the 'plot' (a manuscript catalogue of the scenes with appropriate players' names) of
the second part of *The Seven Deadly Sins*, a lost play now believed to have belonged
to the Lord Chamberlain's Men and to date from 1597–8,[6] together with lists of
apprentices drawn up by David Kathman,[7] enable us to have a fair idea of the
membership of Shakespeare's company at the end of the sixteenth century. On the
basis of this evidence Juliet Dusinberre generated a hypothetical original cast list for
the play.[8]

After 1603 there are no records of professional performance in the seventeenth
century, although there are two documents that associate the play with the theatre.

[1] T. J. King, *Casting Shakespeare's Plays: London Actors and their Roles, 1590–1642*, 1992, pp. 13, 88;
for doubling for effect, see Giorgio Melchiori, 'Peter, Balthasar, and Shakespeare's art of doubling',
MLR 78 (1983), 777–92'; see also Glynne Wickham, 'Reflections arising from recent productions of
Love's Labour's Lost and *As You Like It*', in Marvin and Ruth Thompson (eds.), *Shakespeare and the
Sense of Performance*, 1989, 210–18; Dusinberre, pp. 355–8.
[2] It is reviewed by Peter Holland, 'Shakespeare performances in England, 1993–1994', *S.Sur.* 48 (1995),
191–226.
[3] This was done by the RSC in 1980: Corin/Hymen entered on a rustic cart, brimming with corn and
decked with flowers, the monarch of a harvest-home festival.
[4] Honan, *Shakespeare*, p. 268.
[5] Chambers, *Shakespeare*, II, 71–2.
[6] See David Kathman, 'Reconsidering *The Seven Deadly Sins*', *Early Theatre* 7 (2004), 13–44.
[7] David Kathman, 'Grocers, goldsmiths, and drapers: freemen and apprentices in the Elizabethan
theater', *SQ* 55 (2004), 1–49; Kathman, 'Shakespeare's boy actors'.
[8] Dusinberre, pp. 361–7.

As You Like It appears in a list made in January 1669 of plays previously performed at the Blackfriars playhouse by the King's Men, which was now 'allowed of' to Thomas Killigrew, Master of the Theatre Royal in Bridges Street.[1] This should not be taken as evidence that it was aimed at an elite audience: productions often switched between the amphitheatre or public playhouses and indoor private playhouses like the Blackfriars. There is also a manuscript transcript of the play that records amateur staging at the seminary in Douai in 1695.[2] The hypothesis has to be entertained that the play may not have been professionally performed before 1740, although the former of these two documents and features of the text make this unlikely.[3]

Charles Johnson adapted the play as *Love in a Forest* for Drury Lane in 1723, a version from which Touchstone, Audrey, Martext, Corin, Phoebe, Silvius, and William – the non-courtiers – were erased. Colley Cibber played Jaques – who, in Act 3, falls in love with Celia and purloins some of Benedick's lines from *Much Ado*. Johnson also imported the mechanicals from *A Midsummer Night's Dream* to perform 'Pyramus and Thisbe' before the restored Duke Senior while Rosalind was changing her costume, and even appropriated lines of Bullingbrook and Norfolk from the first act of *Richard II* for Charles' challenge to Orlando. Perhaps in deference to a genteel audience, he substituted a rapier duel for the wrestling. This adaptation ran for only six performances at Drury Lane.[4] (Another eighteenth-century adaptation is John Carrington's *The Modern Receipt: or, A Cure for Love* of 1739, which not only excludes the base-born but is a text not designed for performance but to be read by polite society.)[5] In non-English-speaking countries the tradition of very loose adaptations, with the text radically revised for cultural reasons, continued into the nineteenth century: Henrik Ibsen was involved in a *comédie-vaudeville* version of the text performed by the Norwegian Theatre in 1855, a version similar to George Sand's *Comme il vous plaira* – which was designed to introduce Shakespearean

---

[1] Knowles, p. 634; for a possible production in 1618, see Bentley, I, 137, 157; II, 347.

[2] See G. Blakemore Evans, 'The Douai manuscript – six Shakespearean transcripts (1694–5)', *PQ* 41 (1962), 158–72; this is fully collated in Dusinberre, pp. 374–87.

[3] See Textual Analysis, pp. 215–18; Gurr, *Playgoing*, argues that lines from a letter concerning a play that Sir John Harington wrote in 1605 contain an allusion to *As You Like It*: 'the world is a stage and we that live in it are stage players . . . I played my child's part happily, the scholar and student's part too negligently, the soldier and courtier faithfully, the husband lovingly, the countryman not basely nor corruptly' (pp. 97–8; the letter is in the Bodleian Library (MS Rawl.B162) and is reprinted in *Nugae Antiquae*, 2 vols., 1804, I, 186–232). Other putative allusions in the anonymous play *The Fair Maid of the Exchange* (1602?) and in John Cotgrave's compilation *The English Treasure of Wit and Language* (1655) may be found in C. M. Ingleby, L. Toulmin Smith, F. J. Furnivall (eds.), *The Shakspere Allusion-Book*, 2 vols., 1909, I, 179; II, 51, 52. It is notable that the number of 'allusions' to *AYLI* in this work is notably smaller than those to comparable comedies. For a coranto of 1623, see Marcus Nevitt, 'An early allusion to *As You Like It?*', *NQ* 53 (2006), 484–6.

[4] Odell, I, 244–7; Emmett L. Avery (ed.), *The London Stage, 1660–1800, Part 2 1700–1729*, 1960, pp. 704–5; Michael Dobson, *The Making of the National Poet*, 1992, pp. 131–2; Katherine West Scheil, 'Early Georgian politics and Shakespeare: the Black Act and Charles Johnson's *Love in a Forest* (1723)', *S.Sur.* 51 (1998), 45–56; Marshall, pp. 7–10.

[5] Dobson, *Making of the National Poet*, pp. 132–3.

comedy to the Comédie-Française.[1] It made Jaques the hero of the play and Celia's successful suitor.

The unadapted text was eventually performed at the Theatre Royal in Drury Lane in 1740–1,[2] possibly because ladies of quality desired to see Shakespeare unadapted and unadulterated, and helped mark the beginning of the appreciation of Shakespeare as a comic dramatist in an age which, before then, had been dominated by David Garrick's performances in the histories and tragedies.[3] The production also enabled some of the first performances of renown by Shakespearean actresses: Hannah Pritchard, much praised for her natural diction, starred as Rosalind, and her friend Kitty Clive played Celia. Charles Macklin took over the role of Touchstone in the many revivals of this production,[4] and Thomas Arne set the songs, which, as in *Love in a Forest*, included 'When daisies pied' with its 'cuckoo' refrain from *Love's Labour's Lost*.[5] The play was interspersed with dances and, as was the custom at the time, followed by a pantomime, *Robin Goodfellow*, in which Macklin originally played the part of Slouch.[6] A few years later Margaret (Peg) Woffington, who had flourished in breeches-parts such as Sylvia in *The Recruiting Officer*, made her last appearance as Rosalind in a performance of May 1757.[7] Then from 1776 to 1817 *As You Like It*[8] was more frequently acted 'than any other Shakespearean play at Drury Lane; it missed but three seasons out of forty-one. Why? Because a succession of great Rosalinds graced the boards of that playhouse: Mrs Barry, Miss Younge, Mrs Jordan – even Mrs Siddons essayed the part.'[9] But Mrs Siddons, according to the production's critics, suffered from her costume: 'her dress was injudicious. The scrupulous prudery of decency produced an ambiguous vestment that seemed neither male nor female'.[10]

---

[1] *Comme il vous plaira, comédie en trois actes et en prose. Tirée de Shakespeare et arrangée par George Sand. Représentée pour la première fois à la Comédie-Française le 12 avril 1856*, 1856; see Inga-Stina Ewbank, 'European cross-currents: Ibsen and Brecht', in Jonathan Bate and Russell Jackson (eds.), *Shakespeare: An Illustrated Stage History*, 1996, pp. 128–38.

[2] For this and following productions, see Marshall, pp. 10–19; Neil Rolf Schroeder, '*As You Like It* in the English theatre, 1740–1955,' unpublished PhD dissertation, Yale, 1962, and Alice Anne Margarida, 'Shakespeare's Rosalind: a survey and checklist of the role in performance, 1740–1980', unpublished PhD dissertation, University of New York, 1982.

[3] Michael Dobson, 'Improving on the original: actresses and adaptations', in Bate and Jackson, *Illustrated Stage History*, pp. 45–68.

[4] Macklin's manuscript part-book is in the Folger Shakespeare Library: only Touchstone's lines appear in full – those of others are abbreviated to cues (compare *MND*, 3.1.80–2). A painting by Francis Hayman in London's Tate Britain Gallery, 'The wrestling scene in *As You Like It*', derives from this production (see Sillars, *Painting Shakespeare*, pp. 64–5).

[5] Odell, I, 228, 260; II, 206; the various ballets that were added to the production can be traced in Arthur H. Scouten (ed.), *The London Stage, Part 3: 1729–1747*, 1961, pp. 875 and *passim*.

[6] Playbills that identify other pantomimes can be found interleaved into a huge two-volume souvenir album in the Folger Shakespeare Library's copy of William Shakespeare, *As You Like It*, 2 vols., New York, Privately printed for Mr Daly, 1890 (Art vol. b23 and b24).

[7] She was taken fatally ill when delivering the Epilogue: see Salgado, *Eyewitnesses*, p. 162.

[8] The text used was that in Bell; cuts and changes made are listed by Odell, II, 21–3.

[9] Odell, II, 20; in Germany, surprisingly, *AYLI* was considered 'unstageable' until 1916: see Wilhelm Hortmann, *Shakespeare on the German Stage: The Twentieth Century*, 1998, pp. 7–8.

[10] Salgado, *Eyewitnesses*, p. 163; see also Linda Kelly, *The Kemble Era*, 1980, p. 54.

7   Mrs Abington as Rosalind, William Shakspere, *Dramatic Writings*, 20 vols., 1788, VII, facing p. 90

Theatre Royal, Drury-Lane,

This prefent FRIDAY FEBRUARY 9, 1798,
Their Majefties Servants will act a Comedy called

AS YOU LIKE IT.

Duke, Mr. A I C K I N,
Frederick, Mr. MADDOCKS, Amiens, Mr. DIGNUM,
Jaques, Mr. W R O U G H T O N,
Le Beau, Mr. R U S S E L L,
Oliver, Mr. C A U L F I E L D,
Jaques de Boys, Mr. H O L L A N D,
Orlando, Mr. B A R R Y M O R E,
Adam, Mr. P A C K E R,
Touchftone, Mr. P A L M E R,
Corin, Mr. HOLLINGSWORTH, Sylvius, Mr. TRUEMAN.
Rofalind, Mrs. J O R D A N,
Celia, Mifs MELLON, Phebe, Mifs HEARD,
Audrey, Mifs P O P E,
In Act V· a Song by Mrs. BLAND.

To which will be added (17th. time) a new Grand Dramatick Romance called

B L U E - B E A R D;

Or, FEMALE CURIOSITY!

The Scenery, Machinery, Dreffes, and Decorations, entirely new.
The Mufick Compofed, and Selected, by Mr. K E L L Y.
Abomelique, *(Blue-Beard)* Mr. P A L M E R,
Ibrahim, Mr. S U E T T,
Selim, Mr. K E L L Y,
Shacabac, Mr, B A N N I S T E R, Jun.
Haffan, Mr. H O L L I N G S W O R T H,
Fatima, Mrs, C R O U C H,
Irene, Mifs D E C A M P,
Beda, Mrs. B L A N D.
SPAHIS. Mr. SEDGWICK, Mr. BANNISTER, Mr. DIGNUM,
Mr. WATHEN, Mr. TRUEMAN, Mr. MADDOCKS, &c. &c.
JANIZARIES. Meffrs. Danby, Wentworth, Brown, Tett, Denman, Atkins,
PEASANTS. Meffrs Grimaldi, Gregfon, Gallow, Aylmer, Potts, Willoughby, &c.
Meffds. Aine, Roffey, Wentworth, Jackfon, Maddocks, Menage, &c.
Principal Dancer
Mademoifelle P A R I S O T.
SLAVES. Meffrs. Roffey, Thompfon. Whitmell, Wells, Male, Garman, W. Banks
Meffes. Brooker, Daniels, Brigg, Haskey, Illingham, Byrne, Willis, Vining.
The Scenes Defigned, and Executed,
by Mr. GREENWOOD, Mr. CHALMERS, and others.
The Machinery, and Decorations, defigned, and under the direction of
Mr. JOHNSTON, and executed by Him. and Mr. UNDERWOOD,
The Dreffes by Mr. JOHNSTON, Mr GAY, and Mifs REIN.
Books of the Songs to be had in the Theatre.
Printed by C. LOWNDES next the Stage-Door   *Vivant Rex et Regina!*

To-morrow, The Comedy of A BOLD STROKE for a WIFE, with (18th.
time) The New Dramatick Romance of BLUE-BEARD; Or, FEMALE
CURIOSITY.
Ladies and Gentlemen who have been difppointed of Places for The new Drama
of The CASTLE-SPECTRE, are refpectfully informed, that the fame will be
repeated for the 26th. time on Monday next.
On Tuefday, The Comedy of TWELFTH NIGHT, with the 19th. night of
The New Dramatick Romance of BLUE-BEARD; Or, FEMALE CURIOSITY.
☞ A New PLAY is in Rehearfal, and will fpeedily be produced

8   Playbill for a revival at the Theatre Royal, Drury Lane, 1798

John Philip Kemble played Jaques in his production of 1806 at Covent Garden,[1] where in 1824 Frederic Reynolds mounted 'operatised' versions (with music by Henry R. Bishop and Thomas Arne) that incorporated songs from other plays and some of Shakespeare's sonnets in melodic settings.[2] The performance ended with a farce, *Children in the Wood*.[3] In 1827 the play opened the new theatre at Stratford-upon-Avon.[4]

William Macready produced the play at Covent Garden in 1837–9 and at Drury Lane in 1842–3, playing Jaques himself, with Ada Nisbett and later Helen Faucit as Rosalind.[5] The playbill advertises that 'The first movement of Beethoven's Pastoral Symphony will be given as an overture to the play, and the entre-acts will be selected from the same work.'[6] The production had an enormous number of 'supers' for the sake of lifelikeness and excised or expurgated fewer than 400 lines. It was praised by many for a set (designed and painted by Charles Marshall) that, among its ten complete settings, offered magnificently realistic trees but did not swamp the performances. Jaques' invective (2.7.35–87) was cut to make him seem more noble and tender. There was 'a kind of rural temple' for the final scene. Charles Hamilton Smith, a retired colonel who was also an antiquarian, designed the 'accurate' costumes in the style of fifteenth-century France.[7]

In 1879, in a production at Stratford, Audrey was given a turnip from Anne Hathaway's garden.[8] Charles Kean directed an even more opulent production of the play with a huge cast at the Princess's Theatre in 1850–1,[9] and John Hare and W. H. Kendal produced a version at the St James's in 1885 with elaborate and 'historically accurate' sets by Lewis Wingfield that included stage grass.[10]

Indeed, most productions in the nineteenth century depended for their success upon their sets, costuming, and settings of the songs, but George Bernard Shaw, who seems to have appreciated 'deep feeling for sylvan and pastoral scenery', on one occasion took exception to what was literally melodrama – 'slow music

---

[1] His part-book is in the Folger Shakespeare Library.

[2] Odell, II, 51, 142–3; Shattuck, p. 44, no. 9.

[3] Birmingham Shakespeare Library, Playbills, *As You Like It*, II, 248.

[4] T. C. Kemp and J. C. Trewin, *The Stratford Festival*, 1953, pp. 4–5.

[5] The prompt-book is in the Folger (Shattuck, p. 46, no. 18). It records no fewer than thirty-two court lords, thirty court ladies, six pages, and twelve attendants for 1.3. For the opening of 2.1, hunters played '*an air on their horns. Attendants are discovered preparing for the chase; others, with hoops of birds* [i.e. falcons] *pass over the stage and exit l* [eft], *while some lead hounds, leashed together, from the cave off r* [ight].' Faucit's rehearsal copy is in the Folger Shakespeare Library; see also Marshall, pp. 23–9 and, for an extract from her essay on the role, Smallwood, p. 6.

[6] Folger Art, vol. b23, p. 49.

[7] Odell, II, 205–6, 229; see Charles H. Shattuck, *Mr Macready Produces 'As You Like It': A Prompt-Book Study*, 1962; Alan S. Downer, *The Eminent Tragedian William Charles Macready*, 1966, pp. 243–4; Shattuck, pp. 45, no. 15, pp. 46–7, nos. 17–24; Carol J. Carlisle, 'Helen Faucit's Rosalind', *S.St.* 12 (1979), 65–94; later nineteenth-century versions can be traced in Donald Mullin (ed.), *Victorian Plays: A Record of Significant Productions on the London Stage, 1837–1901*, 1987, pp. 14–16.

[8] Kemp and Trewin, *Stratford Festival*, p. 18.

[9] Odell, II, 285; Shattuck, pp. 45 no. 16, p. 47, no. 21, p. 49 no. 31; Marshall, pp. 29–30.

[10] Odell, II, 381–2, 435–7; Marshall, pp. 33–5.

9   'What shall he have that killed the deer?': Stratford-upon-Avon, 1879

stealing up from the band at the well-known recitations of Adam, Jaques, and Rosalind'.[1] This production, by Augustin Daly at the Lyceum with a bowdlerised and rearranged text and with the American Ada Rehan as Rosalind, had played in New York in 1889 and London in 1890 (see Plate 10).[2] Oscar Asche went further, using 'a collection of moss-grown logs, two thousand pots of fern, large clumps of bamboo, and leaves by the cartload from the previous autumn'[3] in a production in 1907 at His Majesty's. Asche himself played Jaques, and Lily Brayton Rosalind. In a performance in Manchester a herd of deer appeared on the stage. There was also a vogue for staging the play out of doors, which has continued in this century with

---

[1] George Bernard Shaw, reviewing a production by Augustin Daly (1897) in Wilson (ed.), *Shaw on Shakespeare*, pp. 21, 30; this volume also contains reviews of productions at St James's Theatre by George Alexander with music by Edward German (1896), and of a revival by Mrs Langtry at the St James's in 1890.

[2] Odell, II, 371, 386, 406, 441; Shattuck, pp. 55–6, nos. 58–66; hundreds of MS letters, playbills, engravings, costume designs, illustrations of 'The Seven Ages of Man', reviews, and photographs associated with this and other productions in Britain and the United States can be found interleaved into the Folger Shakespeare Library's *As You Like It* (privately printed for Mr Daly). Part of this is based on a text with a facing performance picture for each page; it also contains introductions by Edward Dowden and William Winter, the latter detailing many productions. For Rehan's performance, see William Winter, *Shadows of the Stage*, 1893, pp. 161–3 and Marshall, pp. 47–51. Productions in New York from 1855 to 1876 can be also tracked through a dossier collected by John Moore, now in the Folger (Folger, AYL 23).

[3] J. C. Trewin, *Shakespeare on the English Stage 1900–1964*, 1964, p. 47; Shattuck, p. 61, no. 86; Marshall, pp. 55–6.

10 Ada Rehan as Rosalind, 1889

productions in the Open Air Theatre in London's Regent's Park and in Central Park New York.[1]

Sir Frank Benson's production of the play at Stratford-upon-Avon was given almost every year from 1910 until 1919. 'Benson's sets consisted of heavy canvas flats festooned with painted ivy, which would quiver and shake when Benson, as Orlando, attempted to nail his verses to them. To convey the Forest of Arden with verisimilitude Benson used to cover the stage ankle-deep with leaves, through which his actors, clad in autumnal russets and greens, tripped and scuffed.'[2] Nigel Playfair's 1919 production of the play at Stratford and then at the Lyric Theatre in London (1920) was important because it broke with this tradition of illusionism: musicians were visible on stage, and its emblematic medieval-cubist sets with the costumes (by Claud Lovat Fraser) in primary colours were virulently attacked by some critics for their 'futuristic' qualities.[3]

The middle of the century saw a number of picturesque productions that incorporated some elements of modernist *mise-en-scène*. On a wintry set Peggy Ashcroft played Rosalind in a production by Harcourt Williams in 1932–3 at the Old Vic with Alistair Sim as Duke Senior;[4] she was to play the role again opposite Richard Johnson as Orlando at Stratford in a production by Glen Byam Shaw in 1951.[5] Edith Evans, wearing a Blue-boy costume out of Thomas Gainsborough, starred as Rosalind with Michael Redgrave as Orlando in a production by Esmé Church at the Old Vic in 1936–7 which was also notable for a Watteauesque rococo set,[6] while in Prague the same year the designer František Tröster used

---

[1] A performance in the orangery of a French country house is described in Théophile Gautier's first novel, *Mademoiselle de Maupin*, 1835; Oscar Wilde reviewed one directed in 1885 by E. W. Godwin, father of Gordon Craig, in which Lady Archibald Campbell played Orlando (Salgado, *Eyewitnesses*, pp. 163–6); Max Reinhardt directed the play at the Summer Riding School in Salzburg; Maria Aitken directed the play for the New Shakespeare Company at the Open Air Theatre at Regent's Park from 17 June 1992, and in the same year Adrian Hall directed it for the New York Shakespeare Festival at the Delacorte Theater in Central Park from 9 July. See Marshall, pp. 57–60; Michael Dobson, 'Shakespeare exposed: outdoor performance and ideology, 1880–1940', in Peter Holland (ed.), *Shakespeare, Memory and Performance*, 2006, pp. 256–77.

[2] Sally Beauman, *The Royal Shakespeare Company: A History of Ten Decades*, 1982, p. 65; Shattuck, p. 59, nos. 76–8; for a survey of Stratford productions from 1946, see Smallwood.

[3] The original designs are in the Bryn Mawr College Library. The production is described in Nigel Playfair, *The Story of the Lyric Theatre*, 1925, pp. 43–57, who also quotes extensively from reviews; Beauman, *Royal Shakespeare Company*, pp. 65–7; Dennis Kennedy, *Looking at Shakespeare*, 1993, pp. 120–1; Playfair jettisoned the moth-eaten stuffed Charlecote stag which had been used in 4.2 at Stratford since 1879 when the original Shakespeare Memorial Theatre was inaugurated (Marshall, pp. 35–6, 56–7).

[4] Trewin, *Shakespeare on the English Stage*, p. 140; Robert Speaight, *Shakespeare on the Stage*, 1973, pp. 150–1; Harcourt Williams, *Four Years at the Old Vic*, 1935, pp. 189–91. Edward Gordon Craig never designed the play for the stage in England but was involved in a production in Copenhagen at the Royal Theatre of Denmark (see Enid Rose, *Gordon Craig and the Theatre*, 1931, pp. 197–8).

[5] Michael Billington, *Peggy Ashcroft*, 1988, pp. 60–1, 160, 170–1.

[6] Trewin recalls how Evans 'burnished the [Epilogue] by turning Rosalind, without pretence, into a Restoration belle and ending the night in a quick blaze of Millamantine sophistication' (J. C. Trewin, *Going to Shakespeare*, 1978, p. 145).

11   Colin Blakely (Touchstone), Rosalind Knight (Celia), Vanessa Redgrave (Rosalind): Stratford-upon-Avon, 1961

expressionist techniques to project leaf patterns for a production by Jiří Frejka: this technique was to reappear at the RSC in the 1960s and 1970s.[1] In 1948 the cinema director Luchino Visconti mounted a fantastical production at the Teatro Eliseo in Rome with designs by Salvador Dalí. 'The combination of a realist director and a surrealist designer who had turned his back on surrealism was to get the worst of both conventions.'[2] Glen Byam Shaw's 1952 production at Stratford with Margaret Leighton as Rosalind and Michael Hordern as Jaques was one of many to use an opening wintry set (designed by Motley),[3] while in Michael Elliot's 1961 production with Vanessa Redgrave as an acclaimed Rosalind (see Plate 11), the

[1] Kennedy, *Looking at Shakespeare*, p. 100; in Warsaw in 1925 Wincenty Drabnik used 'geometric costumes and metaphoric costumes' in a production by Leon Schiller (*ibid.*, p. 104).

[2] Speaight, *Shakespeare on the Stage*, p. 263; it is described by Mario Praz with an illustration, *S.Sur.* 3 (1950), 108.

[3] Kemp and Trewin, *Stratford Festival*, pp. 252–3; Shattuck, p. 64, nos. 102–3. The sets by Bert Kistner for a production by Roberto Ciulli in Cologne in 1974 and by Hans Peter Schubert for an all-male production by Petrica Ionescu in Bochum in 1976, wintry and urban brutalist respectively, made it impossible, according to Wilhelm Hortmann, for the 'transforming power of love' to operate ('Word into image: notes on the scenography of recent German productions', in Dennis Kennedy (ed.), *Foreign Shakespeare: Contemporary Performance*, 1993, pp. 232–53); for a production by John Hirsch in 1983 at Stratford, Ontario that worked in this way, see Roger Warren, 'Shakespeare at Stratford, Ontario: the John Hirsch years', *S.Sur.* 39 (1986), 179–90.

set (by Richard Negri) was dominated by a great oak, leafless at the start, through which patterns could be projected onto the ground.[1]

As You Like It had been the eminent Romanian director Liviu Ciulei's first Shakespeare production, staged in Bucharest, also in 1961. The director ignored the requirements of realism and of socialist realism in particular, thus creating a watershed in Romanian theatre. The representation was no longer centred upon social criticism delivered by Jaques and Touchstone. Socialist representations of the play were supposed to foreground Jaques' 'satire' and his 'progressive ' stance against the shortcomings of the time, whereas the love story was of little importance. Ciulei marginalised Jaques and focussed upon the romantic love story. In his view Jaques was like an English lord walking haughtily in an art exhibition and criticizing this and that painting. His performance therefore no longer conveyed any message that could be appropriated ideologically, an audacious gesture that was not punished – in Romania a short-lived détente had set in. The *mise-en-scène* highlighted theatrical convention as a source for both political iconoclasm and a new theatrical vocabulary, although the eclecticism and poetic qualities of the production meant that there was a risk of its being rejected as 'formalist' or 'aestheticising'. Ciulei attempted a mock re-creation of Elizabethan staging conditions, building an apron stage in front of the proscenium arch. He placed cardboard *trompe l'œil* paintings of Elizabethan spectators in the auditorium next to the real audience and above the stage, suggesting a lord's room. The costumes, however, echoed Botticelli's 'Primavera': Rosalind was Flora (walking barefooted on the stage, which shocked the critics of the time). The Forest of Arden was also designed to echo Botticelli, but what was unexpected was a further deconstruction of the dominant norm of naturalistic representation, in that the forest was created by ballet dancers who waved tree branches around the characters.[2]

Clifford Williams' all-male production for the National Theatre in 1967, revived in 1974, had been influenced by Jan Kott's essay 'Shakespeare's bitter Arcadia'.[3] As well as extracts from that essay, the programme contained a long illustrated section on 'The drag tradition' in pantomime and music-hall, as well as the following by the director:

> the examination of the infinite beauty of Man in love – which lies at the very heart of *As You Like It* – takes place in an atmosphere of spiritual purity which transcends sensuality in the search for poetic sexuality. It is for this reason that I employ a male cast; so that we shall not – entranced by the surface reality – miss the interior truth.

---

[1] Speaight, *Shakespeare on the Stage*, pp. 282–3; Shattuck, p. 65, no. 109; Marshall, pp. 70–2. For details and images of this and many other British productions from about 1961 see http://ahds.ac.uk/performingarts/collections/designing-shakespeare.htm; also Lesley Wade Soule, *'As You Like It': A Guide to the Text and its Theatrical Life*, 2005.

[2] This account was kindly supplied to me by Prof. Nicolaescu privately; see also Ileana Berlogea, *Liviu Ciulei. Regizor pe patru continente*, 1998, p. 60; Mircea Alexandrescu, 'Regie in slujb textului sau demonstratie de regie? cum va place la Teatrul Municpal', *Teatrul* 8 (1961), 74–8; Odette-Irenne Blumenfeld, 'Shakespeare in post-revolutionary Romania: the great directors are back home', in Michael Hattaway, Boika Sokolova, and Derek Roper (eds.), *Shakespeare in the New Europe*, 1994, pp. 230–46.

[3] Jan Kott, *Shakespeare our Contemporary*, trans. Boleslaw Taborski, 1967 edn.

Ronald Pickup played Rosalind, Jeremy Brett Orlando, and Anthony Hopkins Audrey. The production in fact eschewed any engagement with gender issues, although the determination of the actors to avoid the kind of camp behaviour deployed for 'queer' characters on television in those years paradoxically invoked alternative contemporary sexualities. 'It succeeded partly because of Ralph Koltai's design, which transformed Arden into a man-made forest, a dreamspace of modern art . . . in the form of hanging Plexiglass tubes and abstract sheets cut out of a metal screen.'[1] In the same year David Jones' production for the RSC with Dorothy Tutin as Rosalind and Roy Kinnear as Touchstone was again dominated by great trees.[2] (In 1968 Janet Suzman, previously Celia, took over the main female role.)

In the 1970s the play became politicised. A 'modern' version by Buzz Goodbody for the RSC in 1973, with sets by Christopher Morley, again used Plexiglass tubes for the forest settings. Eileen Atkins played Rosalind, Maureen Lipman Celia, and Bernard Lloyd Orlando. (Lloyd was later replaced by David Suchet. See Plate 12.) Richard Pasco was an acidic, Chekhovian Jaques whose fine performance seemed to be fired by his dislike of both Arden and the production, and Derek Smith played Touchstone in the manner of a contemporary television comedian with allusions to music-hall.[3] The production poster set a back view of the boyish, trim-bottomed Atkins in flared jeans against some lines from Martin Luther: 'Men have broad shoulders and narrow hips, and accordingly they possess intelligence. Women have narrow shoulders and broad hips. Women ought to stay at home; the way they were created indicates this, for they have broad hips and a wide fundament to sit upon, keep house and bear and raise children.' The well-meaning polemical endeavour did not liberate the wit of the play. In 1983 a Catalan version, *Al vostre gust*, directed by Lluis Pasqual at the Teatre Lliure in Barcelona, offered an Arden that was 'an ecological, pure, and peaceful forest . . . the frame for the social conflict between an unfair hierarchy and those that suffered from its invasion of individual rights'.[4]

In 1977 there was a spectacular adaptation by Peter Stein at the Schaubühne am Halleschen Ufer in what was then West Berlin. According to Michael Patterson,[5] the production gained resonance from the fact that escape to anything resembling a

[1] Kennedy, *Looking at Shakespeare*, p. 258; it was reviewed by Frank Marcus, 'New approaches', *London Magazine*, December (1967); Irving Wardle, *The Times*, 4 October 1967; see Marshall, pp. 72–6.

[2] See Peter Ansorge, *Plays and Players*, July 1968; Smallwood, p. 13.

[3] Pasco was given the same role in the BBC television version of 1978; the production is described by Richard David, *Shakespeare in the Theatre*, 1978, pp. 135–8 and analysed in Dympna Callaghan, 'Buzz Goodbody: directing for change', in Jean I. Marsden (ed.), *The Appropriation of Shakespeare*, 1991, pp. 163–81; modern-dress productions in the United States are noticed by Sylvan Barnet, '*As You Like It* on stage and screen', Gilman (1998 edn), pp. 200–13.

[4] Rafael Portillo and Manuel Gómez-Lara, 'Shakespeare in the new Spain: or, What you Will', Hattaway *et al.*, *New Europe*, pp. 208–20.

[5] Patterson, *Peter Stein*, pp. 132–49; Kennedy, *Looking at Shakespeare*, pp. 260–5; Hortmann, *Shakespeare on the German Stage*, pp. 272–5.

12   Eileen Atkins (Rosalind), David Suchet (Orlando): Stratford-upon-Avon, 1973

large greenwood was impossible for the play's audiences while the city was encircled by the German Democratic Republic. During the first half of the production the audience stood, while scenes were played on platforms, their cubist forms suggesting the exterior of the evil Duke's palace and arranged with reference to Elizabethan great hall productions, and using a montage technique: 'the players would freeze into a tableau while a passage from another scene was interposed from other players elsewhere in the hall'.[1] The company had been studying not only Elizabethan thought but also the popular sports of the time and, in the first half, as in so many productions, the showpiece was the wrestling match, for which Stein had hired a professional wrestler. Yet this and the surrounding court scenes were played in a deliberately stilted manner in order to set off the wonderland forest in a film studio next door into which the audience promenaded through a labyrinth for the second half. There, different groups – bird-watching lords, hunters shooting their game, and Audrey as a dairymaid – were on stage continuously, while exotic figures – a witch, a hermit, Robin Hood, and Robinson Crusoe – occasionally wandered through Karl-Ernst Herrmann's imposing design. The stylisation of Orlando's wrestling contrasted with two pieces of business inserted by the director: in the deer-killing scene Orlando struggled with a wild horned beast, 'emblematic of his violent masculine nature', while Rosalind and Celia rolled across the stage in a tight embrace, and then he engaged in a life-and-death struggle with a lioness to save his brother. Duke Frederick and his lords invaded the forest, but were magically stunned into defeat.

In the same year Trevor Nunn produced a version for the RSC that, as in the early nineteenth century, 'operatised' the play. It was translated to a Restoration setting (design by John Napier) to match the pastiche Purcell music, with a marked contrast between its spectacular court settings and its harsh, wintry forest. Kate Nelligan played Rosalind. The descent of Hymen used the techniques of theophany from Stuart masques (see Plate 13), and the whole ended with a prolonged celebratory ballet.[2] Another production that was remarkable for its music (by Georges Auric) had been that of Jacques Copeau, whose version enjoyed a long run at the Théâtre de l'Atelier in 1934, with a Touchstone played as a circus clown by Jean-Louis Barrault, the director as Jaques, and Madeleine Lambert as Rosalind. Copeau re-directed the play in 1938 at the Boboli Gardens in Florence.[3]

Adrian Noble's 1985 production presented an Arden 'that didn't have trees or logs. The programme spoke of "within the forest: the forest within": the set created a dream landscape'.[4] 'It had mirrors, a clock that didn't tick – because time

---

[1] Patterson, *Peter Stein*, pp. 134–5.
[2] See Kennedy, *Looking at Shakespeare*, pp. 259–60; Smallwood, pp. 14–15.
[3] See Jean Jacquot, *Revue d'histoire du théâtre*, Jan.-Mar. 1965, 119–37; Speaight, *Shakespeare on the Stage*, pp. 190–3; David, *Shakespeare in the Theatre*, p. 136; for further French productions see Guy Boquet, 'Comme il vous plaira à Paris', in Jean-Paul Débax and Yves Peyré (eds.), *As You Like It: Essais Critiques*, 1998, pp. 187–206.
[4] Marion Lomax, *Stage Images and Traditions: Shakespeare to Ford*, 1987, pp. 112–14.

13   The final scene: Stratford-upon-Avon, 1977

is suspended there – and swags of white silk that could be used in many ways, to create many images. It was a place that allowed for chaos.'[1] Juliet Stevenson was a marvellous, intelligent Rosalind, and Fiona Shaw was Celia (see Plate 14).[2] Geraldine McEwan directed the play in 1988 for the Renaissance Theatre Company, a group that was set up by Kenneth Branagh to allow actors to regain control from directors, in the studio at the Birmingham Repertory and then on a provincial tour. She exploited 'the affinity between [the play's] stylization and Victorian melodrama, set the play in the late nineteenth century, and as in productions of this play during that period, ran the forest scenes together'. Branagh played an 'ebulliently vulgar

[1] Fiona Shaw, 'Rosalind: iconoclast in Arden', in Rutter *et al.*, *Clamorous Voices*, p. 98 – the volume contains perceptive conversations with Juliet Stevenson (Rosalind) and Fiona Shaw (Celia), pp. 97–121; in another essay, 'Celia and Rosalind in *As You Like It*', in Russell Jackson and Robert Smallwood (eds.), *Players of Shakespeare 2*, 1988, pp. 55–71, Fiona Shaw and Juliet Stevenson give useful accounts of the changes made in the production when it opened in London after its Stratford run; see also Fiona Shaw in Carole Woddis (ed.), *Sheer Bloody Magic: Conversations with Actresses*, 1991, p. 135 and Marshall, pp. 82–5; there is a good psychoanalytic account of the production by Helen Golding in Gary Waller (ed.), *Shakespeare's Comedies*, 1991, p. 101.

[2] These actors can be seen in a video made with Patrick Stewart, 'Shakespeare explorations with Patrick Stewart: Rosalind and Celia', distributed by Barr Films, 1991; the production is fully described by Nicholas Shrimpton, 'Shakespeare performances in London and Stratford-upon-Avon 1984–5', *S.Sur.* 39 (1986), 191–206; in his review in *S.Sur.* 40 (1987) Shrimpton compares it unfavourably with a 1986 production by Nicholas Hytner for the Royal Exchange in Manchester with Janet McTeer as Rosalind (p. 174).

14 Colin Douglas (Corin), Juliet Stevenson (Rosalind), Fiona Shaw (Celia): Stratford-upon-Avon, 1985

and cockney bookie of a Touchstone, with hair sleeked back and in Archie Rice costume'.[1]

Cheek by Jowl's all-male production of 1991–5 directed by Declan Donnellan offered a memorable and influential interpretation, its reputation enhanced by being sent on a world tour.[2] The play was set in a canvas box with a plain deal floor. Arden was created by green pennants hanging from the flies – and snatches of jazz played by actors on stage. The actors came on as a company: for the opening all wore black trousers, white shirts, black braces.[3] Token costumes were added to this uniform, a bowler hat for Adam, for example. Later the 'women' wore brightly coloured long

[1] Stanley Wells, 'Shakespeare performances in England, 1987–8', *S.Sur.* 42 (1990), 129–48; the production is described by Sophie Thompson, who played Celia in this production and Rosalind in John Caird's jokey 1989 Stratford production ('Rosalind (and Celia) in *As You Like It*', in Russell Jackson and Robert Smallwood (eds.), *Players of Shakespeare 3*, 1993, pp. 77–86); the latter is discussed by Alan C. Dessen, 'Problems and options in *As You Like It*', *Shakespeare Bulletin* 8 (1990), 18–20, and by Peter Holland, *English Shakespeares*, 1997, pp. 56–8.

[2] Reviews include those by Michael Billington, *Guardian*, 14 October 1991, 34; Mel Gussow, *New York Times*, 26 July 1991, B4; Benedict Nightingale, *The Times*, 5 December 1991, 20; Paul Taylor, *Independent*, 6 December 1991; Peter J. Smith, *Cahiers élisabéthains* 42 (1992), 74–6; Holland, *English Shakespeares*, pp. 91–4; see also Marshall, pp. 88–91.

[3] This recalled the opening of Clifford Williams' brilliant 1962 RSC production of *Err.*

dresses with no padding. The play began with Jaques' 'All the world's a stage' taken as the company made their entrances. Donnellan spoke of the 'despair' at the centre of Jaques – he looked like Dirk Bogarde in Visconti's film of *Death in Venice* – as well as his conviction that there is no such thing as love and his demonstration that all action is acting. The whole company remained on stage for the first sequence, monitoring each other's performances.

Doubling was used extensively and varied as replacement actors joined the group. Most reviewers did not note that Rosalind (Adrian Lester) was not only male but black: 'colour-blind casting' was an index of the way in this production the lovers were of all genders and no gender (see Plate 15).[1] At Duke Frederick's court, a male world of privilege, Rosalind and Celia (Simon Coates) were lovers. The courtiers de-bagged Le Beau (who obviously desired Orlando) for not arranging the circle for the wrestling. Duke Senior's courtiers in Arden, as a contrast, wore working-men's clothes. In Arden Celia fully occupied her disguise: she wore a shapeless dress, cardigan and pearls, a chaperone in love with her charge, perpetually jealous of Orlando. There was a running gag: when the women spoke the word 'man' they spat, and yet Rosalind seemed truly randy throughout the wooing of Orlando. Silvius was a cod rustic, Corin spoke with a pronounced northern accent and with a distinct gap between each word. In 1995 Phoebe was played by a short actor (Wayne Cater) wearing an obvious wig, and speaking with a Welsh accent. Audrey wore a long yellow wig – and yodelled. Below her mini-skirt she got her legs knotted when curtseying to the Duke.

In some ways, unlike the National Theatre's all-male production of 1966, it was an appropriation of the play for a homosexual perspective, although it was far more about 'love' than 'sex': the 1995 programme was topped by a banner headline, 'there is no fear in love'. In its 1995 version at least (when Simon Coates replaced Tom Hollander as Celia) it tilted towards misogyny in that the straight women, Celia and Phoebe, were travesties, naff housewives from television soap opera. (Celia went to strangle Phoebe out of jealousy.) It could be brutal: the refrain of the hunting song, 'Take thou no scorn to wear the horn' (4.2.12) was directed at Jaques who, the unsuccessful wooer of 'Rosalind', had been cuckolded. The *coup de théâtre* came when Orlando could not kiss Rosalind at 'To you I give myself, for I am yours' (5.4.102): he was straight. He went and leant in agony against the proscenium arch. He came back slowly and then, still reluctantly, was drawn into a passionate embrace. It ended with a bizarre Fellini-like carnival accompanied with jazz. Hymen got off with Jaques.[2]

---

[1] Sarah Hemming, 'Taking strides', *Independent*, 15 April 1992, 19, discusses Rosalind with players who have taken the role: Samantha Bond, Cathryn Harrison, Eileen Atkins, Jemma Redgrave, Juliet Stevenson, Emma Croft, and Adrian Lester.

[2] Jonathan Bate singles it out as a representative production for the 1990s: see Bate and Jackson, *Illustrated Stage History*, pp. 5–7; for the theories of reading cross-dressed performances, see James C. Bulman, 'Bringing Cheek by Jowl's *As You Like It* out of the closet: the politics of gay theater', *Shakespeare Bulletin* 22.3 (2004), 31–46. In 1993 at the Schillertheater in Berlin, Katharina Thalbach directed an all-male version 'with Michael Maertens as a beautiful Rosalind both to convey and to mock the whirling emotions' (Hortmann, *Shakespeare on the German Stage*, p. 453).

15   Patrick Toomey (Orlando) and Adrian Lester (Rosalind): Cheek by Jowl, 1991–5

Steven Pimlott's 1996 production for the RSC used an aluminium setting: a sheet metal box for the court, the back wall of which rose to reveal steel cladding which could be lit to suggest the wood of the forest. Steel pillars descended around a mound of RSC dirt, on which were strewn yellow flowers. There were striking directorial interventions in the production: Orlando defeated Charles with a foul kick in the balls; a remarkably robust Adam died of cold on stage and was carried off at the end of the first half. Rosalind (Niamh Cusack) was no 'Ganymede' but remained totally feminine with long blonde hair. Touchstone was young and played his part with a Scottish accent: his parti-coloured costume looked as though Pantaloon had made a surprise appearance at hogmanay. Phoebe was a pert minx, primping her locks as she painfully twisted Silvius' hair during moments of high fantasy. Hymen was played by a middle-aged woman in black, a grandmotherly usher in a trouser suit who looked like the then Speaker of the House of Commons, Betty Boothroyd, and who ascended from the stalls and spoke her lines with the conviction of sincerity.[1]

Lucy Bailey's production for the Red Company opened at Shakespeare's Globe Theatre in London in 1998.[2] It explored the resources of this replica Elizabethan playhouse without being dominated by them. Before a half-curtain strung between the stage pillars, the production began with a dumb-show that accompanied a ballad that described the death of old Sir Roland and explained the legacy to Orlando. The only concession to illusion was a bare tree placed mid-stage with a few apples on it: the central opening looked like a barn door, and the stage hangings were made of white canvas distressed at the bottom to look as though they were muddy. Musicians were placed around the galleries, many entrances and exits took place through the theatre yard, and the wrestling and a mime of the killing of the deer (4.2) spilled into this audience space: both Charles and a frail and long-haired Orlando (Paul Hilton) played dirty. Anastasia Hille, slim and, as Ganymede, a blonde version of Orlando (they wore matching shirts seemingly designed by the Elizabethan miniaturist Nicholas Hilliard) was excited, commanding, sexy, and vulnerable – a performance that matched the play's intelligent exploration of the joy and earnestness of the text (see Plate 16). The forest court were dressed in animal skins, and David Rintoul played both dukes, while Jonathan Cecil offered three character parts, Le Beau, Corin, and Sir Oliver Martext. The audience delighted in the way the director enacted Shakespeare's mockery of his own conventions: Jaques' exposure of the improbability of meeting a fool in a 'forest' (2.7.12) and the palpable contrivances of the dénouement. Touchstone and Audrey stripped for action during 'It was a lover and his lass', but decorum was restored in the final ceremony as a bell tolled from the hut above the stage canopy. Hymen was a gaunt, elderly, almost naked man, played by Leader Hawkins, who had also taken the part

[1] It is reviewed by Russell Jackson, 'Shakespeare in Stratford-upon-Avon: the Royal Shakespeare Company's "half season", April–September 1996', SQ 48 (1997), 208–15.

[2] Marshall, pp. 91–2; it is reviewed by Lois Potter, 'A stage where every man must play a part?', SQ (1999), 74–86.

16 Anastasia Hille (Rosalind): Shakespeare's Globe, 1998

of Adam. Perhaps he was the 'old religious man' whom Rosalind had claimed as an 'uncle'.[1]

SCREEN VERSIONS

In 1935 Paul Czinner directed Laurence Olivier, Elizabeth Bergner, and Felix Aylmer in a film version of the play.[2] The director created a picturesque 'merrie France' inspired by nineteenth-century theatre design for the setting, with a thatched, mushroom-shaped cottage and lots of flocks of real sheep. The acting also recalled a theatricalised language of gesture that derived from Victorian melodrama: its persistence in the new medium of talkies and its incongruity with the necessarily more modulated gestures of film is displayed by Elizabeth Bergner's performance as Rosalind which now looks not like cinematic acting but a record of a bad theatrical performance. Certainly she gave no space to Laurence Olivier, who came out of a more temperate acting tradition.

The BBC's television production of the play in 1978 inaugurated their venture to broadcast versions of all the plays. The notion of filming on location at Glamis Castle in Scotland was that of the series' producer, Cedric Messina, who had won a reputation as a director of television versions of classic naturalist drama. For most viewers the decision to shoot the production (directed by Basil Coleman and with Helen Mirren as Rosalind) outside was very misconceived, a transgression beyond the *ne plus ultra* of nineteenth-century theatrical illusionism:[3] the play, as its very title proclaims, opens not only onto life but onto art, the traditions of comic, pastoral, and morality drama. Filming on location fixes one world for the action: and yet Corin and Silvius are inhabitants of a heterocosm very different from that of William and Audrey. The Scottish midges that swarmed from the long grass of the castle park and that the actors had to swat away could not be turned into a counter-pastoral motif but remained a distraction, a reminder of the moment of shooting which, by a convention appropriate to this kind of realist film, has to be occluded. Christine Edzard's film version (1992) was also shot on location but in a very different mode.[4] It was a bold, but not entirely successful, attempt to locate

---

[1] 5.4.144; compare 3.3.288–9. Good performance photographs and suggestions for teaching the play as performance are found in Kate Clarke, 'Reading *As You Like It*', in W. R. Owens and Lisbeth Goodman (eds.), *Shakespeare, Aphra Behn and the Canon*, 1996, pp. 193–250.

[2] Olivier himself described it as a 'mess' (Laurence Olivier, *On Acting*, 1986, p. 178), and it was disliked by both J. C. Trewin and James Agate: see Trewin, *Shakespeare on the English Stage*, pp. 172–3; see also Donald Spoto, *Laurence Olivier*, 1991, pp. 83–4 and Russell Jackson, 'Remembering Bergner's Rosalind: *As You Like It* on film in 1936', in Holland (ed.), *Shakespeare, Memory and Performance*, pp. 237–55. For early film and television versions, see Marshall, pp. 65–7, 79–80.

[3] The problems of the production are reviewed by Stanley Wells, 'Television Shakespeare', *SQ* 33 (1982), 261–77, and by excerpts from other reviewers gathered in J. C. Bulman and H. R. Coursen (eds.), *Shakespeare on Television*, 1988, pp. 251–2, but in the same volume, J. C. Bulman, '*As You Like It* and the perils of pastoral', pp. 174–9, offers a measured defence of it. The BBC had earlier screened another television version on 22 March 1963.

[4] For reviews see Anon., *Plays and Players* 464 (1992), 27; John Carey, *English Review* 3 (1992), 12–14; Ilona Halberstadt, *Sight and Sound* 2 (1992), 45; Samuel Crowl, *Shakespeare Bulletin* 11 (1993), 41.

'pastoral' in a modern urban setting: the odd sheep in the cityscapes of London's docklands, at that time being re-developed, was a sign of the artificiality of the pastoral convention. The film seemed to be saying, 'The text has a few things to say about social deprivation: let's see if we can bring this home to the audience by playing the game of pastoral not in an Elizabethan wilderness but in a modern wasteland.' Part of the problem came from the over-determination of the setting: having established a strong sense of milieu, the urban devastation that signified the dispossession of a modern underclass, it was impossible to match the heightened speech of the text to the naturalistic milieu. Even Touchstone's prose encounter with Audrey (Griff Rhys Jones as a spiv and Miriam Margolyes as the proprietor of a roadside caravan 'caff') could not work since the actors obviously did not have the confidence to believe that lines like 'sluttishness may come hereafter' (3.4.29–30) is the kind of language to be heard in such places.

Recent critical and stage interpretations

CONTEXTS

The most significant scholarly work during the last decade has focussed on the forms and cultural pressures of the immediate period in which the play seems to have been written,[1] on the repertoires of the Elizabethan theatre companies and on Elizabethan court culture, and on dates for the writing and early performances of the play.[2]

There has been something of a reaction against 'theoretical' criticism: conspicuous in the vanguard was Harold Bloom, who was determined to see the origins of Shakespeare's genius in his 'imagination' rather than in materialist or historicist descriptions of Renaissance or twentieth-century society. In *Shakespeare: The Invention of the Human*, 1998, he worked though the plays at some length, almost always focussing on the moral or personal qualities of their characters. In Rosalind he found a radiant example of one of the types of character he takes to be essentially 'human', possessed of a capacity to change 'their relationship to themselves . . . Sometimes this comes about because they *overhear* themselves talking, whether to themselves or to others.'[3] This may indeed be a useful concept for both readers and players: Rosalind, he continues, follows Falstaff as Shakespeare's second great character, and 'Rosalind's role', he writes, 'was the best preparation for the revised Hamlet of 1600–1601, where wit achieves an apotheosis and becomes a kind of negative transcendence'.[4] 'To see the "how" and "why" of her greatness, the reason she must be the most remarkable and persuasive representation of a woman in all of Western literature [*sic*], is also to apprehend how inadequate nearly

---

[1] James Shapiro, 'Simple truth suppressed', in *1599*, pp. 228–57; Maurice A. Hunt, *Shakespeare's 'As You Like It': Late Elizabethan Culture and Literary Representation*, 2008.
[2] See Date and Occasion (pp. 49–54) and Appendix 1.
[3] Harold Bloom, *Shakespeare: The Invention of the Human*, 1998, p. xvii.
[4] *Ibid.*, p. 206.

every production of *As You Like It* has been to Rosalind.'[1] This circular argument allows Bloom to be uncritically enamoured of his heroine: he claims that, despite a few 'dark traces' in Arden, she is able to create an 'earthly paradise', 'simply the best place to live, anywhere in Shakespeare'.[2] (If so, why did Duke Senior and his daughter not choose to stay there?) It is not surprising that Bloom takes his rhapsodic idealisation of Rosalind as the anti-type of the 'rancid' Touchstone – he wrote his essay with scarce a mention of the duplicities of pastoral – and opines that, while 'the expected transports of tranvestism and transgression' may be stirred up by the play's epilogue, 'such raptures have little to do with Shakespeare's Rosalind and her final words'.[3]

In contrast, Frank Kermode argues that no play of Shakespeare's, 'apart perhaps from *Love's Labour's Lost* . . . requires of the reader more knowledge of Elizabethan culture and especially of its styles of poetry'. He locates it at a time when Shakespeare seems to have been reviewing the dominant genres of the previous few years: pastoral, romance, Petrarchism, pastiche, song, and, in prose, satire and urbane or courtly repartee. 'The first quarter of an hour of the play in performance is in prose – an augury, for prose is the language of criticism.'[4] Allusions render homage to Christopher Marlowe,[5] and the appearance of Jaques the satirist marks a nod to Ben Jonson. The play was, Kermode argues, prepared for the Globe, but his praise is qualified because he considers that the play does not break new ground as did the great run of Shakespeare's tragedies and tragi-comedies (or problem plays) that came immediately after: 'it has too much to say about what was once intimately interesting and now is not'.[6]

Pace Kermode, there is a strong hypothetical case for locating the play's origins in court performance rather than in the Lord Chamberlain's Men's public playhouse repertory, as well as in rivalry between Shakespeare's company and the Admiral's Men (see Date and Occasion, pp. 51–2). The topicality and linguistic self-consciousness noted by Kermode would be well suited to a select audience. Even if this case could be finally proven, however, little light would be shed on the 'meaning' or effect of the play. The text explicitly addresses itself to matters of elite taste, as in Touchstone's dialogue with Corin, which plays court and country cultures against one another. Yet it is typical of Shakespeare that the text seems neither to endorse nor refute the position of either side.

James Shapiro also reads *As You Like It* as marking a cusp in Shakespeare's achievement. He too notes a new complexity in Shakespeare's characterisation, 'achieved through role-playing and the suppression of simple truths'. This 'jolt of realism', as Shapiro terms it, sourced from Lodge's *Rosalind*, which, however, is steeped in nostalgia, may account for the comparatively small amount of attention

[1] *Ibid.*, p. 221.
[2] *Ibid.*, p. 205.
[3] *Ibid.*, p. 225.
[4] Frank Kermode, *Shakespeare's Language*, 2000, pp. 77–8, 81.
[5] 3.4.10, 3.6.80–1, and 4.1.79.
[6] Kermode, *Language*, p. 82.

it drew from contemporaries who were exposed to the more aggressive moder-
nity of Jonson's satirical comedies. Yet it is one of the canon's most frequently
performed plays today.[1] In contrast, Stephen Greenblatt, who reads the play in
the context of records of Shakespeare's life, colours his account with biographical
speculation: 'How could the earnest, decent, slightly dim Orlando ever take in
Rosalind?' Although this couple is joyously embarking on what 'officially promises'
to be a good marriage, a few years later Shakespeare was to write *Measure for Measure*
and *All's Well That Ends Well*, plays that 'bring the latent tensions [in the romantic
comedies] . . . right up to the surface'.[2]

In *Shakespeare the Thinker*, A. D. Nuttall sees Shakespeare moving beyond the
playfulness of *Much Ado About Nothing* into a far more thoughtful mode, galvanised
by the arrival of Armin into his company. Taking as his keynote Touchstone's
line 'the truest poetry is the most feigning' (3.4.14) and moving beyond a simple
distinction between pastoral and anti-pastoral, Nuttall writes:

> Duke Senior's praise of the country life [2.1.1–17] is so radical that we are involved . . . in
> epistemology and ontology, with the questions, 'What do we know?' and 'What is real?' There
> is nothing especially philosophical in his observation that rural life is free from the flattery that
> poisons life at court. It becomes philosophical when it is joined, as here, to a special claim for
> reality status . . . [The Duke] is not content to say that toil makes you tough; he says that rural
> hardship acquaints you with reality . . . The court is a mere tissue of forms . . . eloquence is
> mendacity and style a mere truancy from the real. The cold wind cannot lie, but it can apprise
> him of his bodily humanity, the fundamental truth of his condition.[3]

Although the subtitle of his section on the play is 'Rosalind Triumphans', Nuttall
does not keep company with the love-lorn Bloom but reminds us of 'the central
psychosis of pastoral: it is in art that the artless is celebrated'.[4] If Rosalind, this 'clear-
eyed realist', is 'almost divinized at the end of the play',[5] Shakespeare obviously felt
that only a god (Hymen) could supply the necessary 'intuition of transcendence' and
that heterosexual unions, from which procreation might proceed, had to displace
infertile homosexual relationships.[6]

RECENT STAGE HISTORY

Two excellent book-length studies of the stage history of *As You Like It* have
appeared: R. L. Smallwood's *Shakespeare at Stratford: As You Like It*, 2003, and
an edition of the play by Cynthia Marshall in the *Shakespeare in Production* series
(2004).

In the first year of the new millennium there was another admirable production at
the Crucible Theatre in Sheffield, this time directed by Michael Grandage (it later

---

[1] Shapiro, *1599*, pp. 228–9.
[2] Stephen Greenblatt, *Will in the World: How Shakespeare Became Shakespeare*, 2004, p. 136.
[3] A. D. Nuttall, *Shakespeare the Thinker*, 2007, pp. 230–1.
[4] *Ibid.*, p. 231.
[5] *Ibid.*, p. 237.
[6] *Ibid.*, p. 238.

transferred to London). Victoria Hamilton was uncomfortable in her male attire, giving a performance that Michael Dobson described as 'vulnerable, febrile, dark-haired, small, even birdlike'.[1] 'Lucy Briers and Martin Hutson's Phebe and Silvius are not the usual stock country bumpkins but lovers for whom love and hate are near cousins, and Nicholas Le Prevost's Jaques is a man whose dry, donnish approach to life keeps him at arm's length from humanity.'[2] In 2005 Dominic Cooke directed the play for the RSC in Stratford, the production transferring to London in 2006. Like that of Grandage, his production seems to have centred on character: 'It is high praise that [Lia] Williams, a flaxen-haired tomboy in her guise as Ganymede, reminds you of Hazlitt's perceptive comment that "[Rosalind's] tongue runs the faster to conceal the pressure at her heart. She talks herself out of breath only to get the deeper in love." Williams also conveys well how chancy and hand-to-mouth are her dealings with Orlando. She has no clear game plan, but relies on desperate, spur-of-the-moment inspiration. She's giddy, radiant, playful and passionate.'[3] The deliberative aspect of the play centred on sign-charged costuming:

The idea of court and country as opposing yet dependent worlds is registered with dazzling theatricality: Jonathan Newth's tyrannical Duke and his thuggish apparatchiks simply reverse their costumes to become fur-clad, tree-hugging occupants of a wintry Arden. And Cooke rescues Orlando from his usual role as a muscular dupe by suggesting that he instantly sees through Rosalind's disguise. What follows is a kind of extended foreplay that lends weight to Barnaby Kay's charged delivery of 'I can live no longer by thinking' (5.2.40).[4]

During the epilogue Kay lay on stage, proudly watching his wife to be.

At Sheffield again Sam West directed the play in 2007. Here the set was also semantically highly charged, one of those productions that opened in black and white, and was coloured only after the interval.

The main thrust of the show's visual statement, however, came in the costumes, for it was not only Rosalind who cross-dressed. This idea was only mutely stated at first, but spoke with increasing volume as the show progressed. The 'chain' which Rosalind gave to Orlando was a double string of pearls, and the otherwise conventional suit worn by Jaques (Daniel Weyman) was accessorised with high heels and a small feathered hat. After the interval, a whole crop of hats grew up out of the floor downstage on milliners' display stands, and characters experimented with putting them on themselves and each other, most notably when Phebe signalled her final acceptance of Silvius by choosing a hat for him. It was in this final scene that the cross-dressing motif reached its height, as Orlando gave Rosalind his jacket and himself took her bridal veil, and couple after couple exchanged clothes and so, symbolically, made the journey into mutuality, while Jaques, who had been a crossover figure from the start, looked on.[5]

From innumerable reviews of recent productions in the United States one might single out Patricia Lennox's account of a well-received production by Mark Lamos

---

[1] Michael Dobson, 'Shakespeare performances in England, 2000', *S.Sur.* 54 (2001), 246–82.
[2] Lyn Gardner, *Guardian*, 4 March 2000.
[3] Paul Taylor, *Independent*, 13 March 2006.
[4] Michael Billington, *Guardian*, 19 August 2005.
[5] Lisa Hopkins, 'Review of *As You Like It* at the Crucible Theatre, Sheffield', *Early Modern Literary Studies* 12.3 (2007), 16.3.

17 Alfred Molina (Touchstone), David Oyelowo (Orlando), Bryce Dallas Howard (Rosalind): Kenneth Branagh's screen version, 2007

in the Delacorte Theatre in Central Park, New York in 2005[1] and Nick Walton's account of a production by the American Shakespeare Center at the Blackfriars Playhouse in Staunton Virginia in 2006 – this includes a useful critique of the attempts made for authentic 'original practice' at this replica playhouse.[2]

A SCREEN VERSION

In 2007 Kenneth Branagh's film of the play was belatedly released. The DVD case bears the title '*As You Like It*: Romance or Something Like It'. Branagh chose to set it in an English trading enclave in nineteenth-century Japan (in homage to Akira Kurosawa?). It began with an induction in the 'court' of the Old Duke while the family and retainers were watching a Kabuki play: samurai warriors broke in through the paper screens, and Brian Blessed, who played both Duke Senior and Duke Frederick, found himself confronting his 'other' through the bars of the latter's samurai helmet. The Japanese *mise-en-scène* allowed for some measure of delight – painted fans and prayer flags, sumo wrestling and Touchstone teaching Jaques (Kevin Kline) t'ai chi – but the scenes that followed the entrance into Arden of Rosalind (Bryce Dallas Howard), Celia (Romola Garai), and Touchstone (Alfred Molina), wearing very English kit, were filmed on location at Wakehurst Place in West Sussex (see Plate 17). An English-born Nigerian, David Oyelowo, played

[1] See Patricia Lennox, '*As You Like It*', *Shakespeare Bulletin* 24 (2006), 98–100.
[2] Nick Walton, '*As You Like It*', *Shakespeare Bulletin* 23 (2005), 76–8.

Orlando. There was a formal Japanese garden, raked sand and rocks, in the middle of bluebell-pretty English woodland, but, as the BBC version had demonstrated almost thirty years before, 'real' woods do not suit pastoral.[1] There was, however, a final gesture towards meta-cinema: Howard spoke Rosalind's epilogue as she returned to her trailer while the location crew were packing up.

---

[1] See Kenneth Branagh, '"Shakespeare-san"', *Saturday Telegraph Magazine*, 18 February 2006. It was reviewed by Virginia Heffernan (*New York Times*, 21 August 2007), positively by Peter Bradshaw (*Guardian*, 21 September 2007) and negatively by Philip French (*Observer*, 22 September 2007); see also Sarah Hatchuel, 'Kenneth Branagh's *As You Like It*, or all the world's a film', *Shakespeare* 3 (2007), 365–8 and Samuel Crowl, '*As You Like It*', *Shakespeare Bulletin* 26 (2008), 97–101.

NOTE ON THE TEXT

The principal authoritative text for this play is that provided by the 1623 First Folio (F). The nature and provenance of F – it derives basically from Shakespeare's manuscript – are discussed in the Textual Analysis (pp. 215–20) below. The 'editor' of the Second Folio (F2) made a number of corrections, especially corrections to metre. Some of these have been accepted, although they have no special authority.

The collation in this edition (immediately below each page of text) records all significant departures from F, including variants in lineation, variants in the wording and placing of stage directions as well as in speech headings. It does not record corrections of misprints or modernisations of spellings, except where these may be of some consequence. In the format of the collation, the authority for this edition's reading follows immediately after the quotation from the text. Other readings, if any, follow in chronological order. Readings offered by previous editors are registered only if they must be considered in relationship to recent discussions of the play's textual cruces, or if they offer a challenging alternative where no certainty is possible. When, as is usually the case, the variant or emendation adopted has been used by a previous editor or suggested by a textual commentator, those authorities are cited in abbreviated forms, e.g. *Rowe* and *conj. Vaughan*, respectively. *Subst.* stands for *substantively*, and indicates that only the relevant elements have been transcribed – see pp. ix–xv above for an explanation of the abbreviations and a full list of the editions and commentaries cited. The form *Eds.* is used for insignificant and obvious editorial practices (minor clarifications and expansions of stage directions or modernisations of proper names, for example, which do not need to be ascribed to one originator), and the form *This edn* is used for innovations of my own. Significant additions in the text to the Folio stage directions are enclosed in square brackets. In the commentary an asterisk in the lemma (the key word or phrase printed in bold type) is used to call attention to an emendation in the text; the collation should be consulted for further information.

I have, according to the convention of this edition, regularised and modernised proper names in both the play-text and when citing early modern texts elsewhere. The problem of whether the play is set in England or France[1] causes difficulties with the expansion of F's 'M ˈ'. When a title is attached to Jaques, the text in certain places spells out 'Monsieur', a jibe at the self-regarding traveller who sees himself as a sophisticated, Frenchified gentleman, and I have so expanded when appropriate. When it is used by rustic characters, I have preferred 'Master'. Where past forms of verbs require an accentuation that they would not receive in modern speech,

---

[1] See Introduction, pp. 9–11.

they are marked with a *grave* accent ('forkèd', 'answerèd'). Unmarked '-ed's can be assumed to have been elided.

I have tried to keep punctuation as light as is consistent with the clarification of sense, often removing line-end commas from F's verse, for the reason that a line-ending can itself provide a subtle and flexible pause or a break in the sense. Any significant departure from the F punctuation, however, is recorded in the collation. I have not attempted to purge the text of half-lines, nor automatically to expunge metrical irregularity, believing that players can use these for special emphases or effects.[1] Consistency in this area is both impossible and undesirable: if I have regularised metre, I have done so only when I would have made the decision as an actor. Punctuating Shakespearean prose may pose more problems than does verse for an editor, who has, for example, to clarify antithetical definitions that are embedded in the swing and rhythm of 'natural' speech.

I have not recorded the location of any scenes, as it seems to me that all scenes in the drama of the English Renaissance 'take place' on the stage – not in 'Oliver's orchard', 'An open walk, before the Duke's palace',[2] 'Arden Forest', or, rather desperately, 'Another part of the forest'[3] – and that localisation encourages readers at least to impose expectations appropriate only to naturalist drama.

In the commentary I have preferred to cite entries in works of reference rather than analogous passages in Renaissance texts.

[1] For the neo-Augustan regularising of the Oxford edition, see David Bevington, 'Determining the indeterminate', *SQ* 38 (1987), 501–19.
[2] Theobald's location for 1.2.
[3] Malone's location for 2.6.

As You Like It

LIST OF CHARACTERS

The de Boys household
OLIVER, *oldest son of Sir Roland de Boys*
JACQUES DE BOYS, *second son of Sir Roland*
ORLANDO, *third son of Sir Roland*
ADAM, *servant to the de Boys household*
DENIS, *servant to Oliver*

The court of the usurping Duke
DUKE FREDERICK, *younger brother to Duke Senior*
CELIA, *his daughter*
ROSALIND, *daughter to Duke Senior*
LE BEAU, *a courtier*
CHARLES, *a wrestler*
CLOWN (TOUCHSTONE)

The court in exile
DUKE SENIOR, *older brother to Duke Frederick*
AMIENS, *a lord attendant*
JAQUES, *a melancholic traveller*

The greenwood
CORIN, *a shepherd*
PHOEBE, *a shepherdess*
SILVIUS, *a shepherd*
WILLIAM, *a countryman*
AUDREY, *a country girl*
SIR OLIVER MARTEXT, *a vicar*
HYMEN, *god of marriage*
LORDS, PAGES, FORESTERS, *Attendants*

Notes
F does not supply a list of characters; the first list was offered by Rowe.

OLIVER Saladyne in *Rosalind*. Shakespeare pointedly gives Orlando's estranged brother the name of Roland's boon companion in the chivalric epics (the twelve peers of France aid Gerismond in *Rosalind*, p. 226); he appears in Greene's *Orlando Furioso*. The name 'Oliver' never appears in the dialogue of the play.

JACQUES DE BOYS The second brother is called Fernandyne in *Rosalind*. There was a well-known Leicester De Boys family who held the manor of Weston-in-Arden, although 'De Boys' ('of [the] wood') may have been suggested by the greenwood setting. To avoid confusion with 'the melancholy "Jaques"' (2.1.26), it is best to modernise the name completely, but as Jacques de Boys appears only in 5.4 (where he is designated 'Second Brother') audiences will either not notice imperfect revision (the addition of the role of Jaques?), or

86

will accept a possible wilful eccentricity on Shakespeare's part. Perhaps Shakespeare had simply forgotten that he had named Orlando's brother Jacques in the first couple of lines of the play. (Both names generally appear as *Iaques* in F.)

ORLANDO Rosader in *Rosalind*. The name is the Italian version of Roland (as in Ariosto's *Orlando Furioso*, translated by Sir John Harington in 1591, and in Greene's play *Orlando Furioso* probably written in the same year). The name of their father in *Rosalind* is Sir John of Bordeaux.

ADAM A 'spencer' or steward of this name appears in both *The Tale of Gamelyn* and *Rosalind*. Adam disappears from the play after 2.7. 'This name . . . together with some similarity perceived between . . . the Garden of Eden and the setting of . . . [*Rosalind*], initiated a series of memory associations which constituted an undercurrent of religious reminiscence manifesting itself in the imagery of the play from beginning to end' (Armstrong, pp. 125–6).

DENIS F spells the name 'Dennis', but there is no way of telling if this makes it a surname.

DUKE FREDERICK Torismond, King of France, in *Rosalind*; see 1.2.66 SH n. The two rulers are not brothers in *Rosalind*.

CELIA Alinda in *Rosalind* (in disguise, Aliena); Celia is an important character in *FQ* 1.10.

ROSALIND The name of Lodge's heroine who also becomes Ganymede in exile; the form 'Rosaline' that appears sometimes in F is compositorial (see Textual Analysis, p. 217 n. 6). 'Rosaline' is the name given to a romantic heroine in Marston's *Antonio and Mellida*; 'Rosalinde' is the woman who has broken Colin Clout's heart in the April Eclogue of Spenser's *Shepheardes Calender*.

LE BEAU Spelt 'Le Beu' throughout F, except at 1.2.72 SD.

CHARLES An unnamed 'Norman' in *Rosalind*.

CLOWN (TOUCHSTONE) 2.4.0 SD '*Enter . . . Clowne, alias Touchstone*' indicates that 'Touchstone', like 'Ganymede' and 'Aliena', is just a forest name; the role was probably taken by Robert Armin (Wiles, pp. 144–58); Charles S. Felver, 'Robert Armin, Shakespeare's source for Touchstone', *SQ* 7 (1956), 135–7, believes that the name is an allusion to Armin's training as a goldsmith: a 'touchstone' (made of quartz or jasper) was used to register the quality of gold and silver alloys. There is a character of the same name in Chapman, Jonson, and Marston's play for the Queen's Revels, *Eastward Ho!* (1605). For Armin's acting style and his ugliness and dwarfishness, see Wiles, pp. 146–51.

DUKE SENIOR Gerismond, lawful king of France, in *Rosalind*. Shakespeare may not have given him a name, and the designation 'Senior', which appears in SHs and SDs, may have been supplied by a scribe or book-holder. 'The manuscript at Douai (1694–5) contains a list of characters in which Duke Senior is described as "Ferdinand, Old Duke of Burgundy"' (G. Blakemore Evans, 'The Douai manuscript – six Shakespearean transcripts (1694–5)', *PQ* 41 (1962), 158–72).

AMIENS No equivalent in *Rosalind*. His role resembles that of Balthazar in *Ado*, and the part may have been taken by Jack Wilson, a singer whose name appears in the F text of that play (TLN 868). The role may equally have been doubled with that of Touchstone and taken by Robert Armin who was a counter-tenor (Wiles, p. 157; compare Dusinberre, p. 364).

JAQUES A name affected by 'some Frenchified English' (Camden, *Remaines* (1605), sig. 12), but also possibly derived from St James or St Jacques, whose shrine at Santiago (Compostella) was a great site of pilgrimage (Jaques is a traveller, see 4.1.14–15, Introduction, p. 16 n. 2). Where this name appears in verse, the metre sometimes suggests a disyllable, perhaps with a very lightly sounded second syllable, (see 2.1.26), and it is pronounced thus in various other plays (see Furness, p. 1 n.). However, this pronunciation obscures another connection with Harington (see Orlando note above) and a possible cloacal joke: Sir John Harington's *Metamorphosis of Ajax* (1596) described how to turn a 'jakes' or privy into a water-closet. In the quarto version of *Lear* a 'jakes' (privy) is spelt 'iaques' (sig. E1 ᵛ), and 'Iaques', the spelling used in F for the character in *AYLI*, is a common sixteenth-century spelling for 'jakes' (see *OED* Jaques 1). 'Qu' was historically pronounced 'k' (Cercignani, pp. 365–6). Ajax was the type of the melancholic humour (see *Tro.* 1.2.26–30), or, as Harington described him, 'a perfect malcontent' (Sir John Harington, *The Metamorphosis of Ajax*, ed. Elizabeth Story Donno, 1962, p. 67).

CORIN There is a shepherd of that name in *Syr Clyomon and Clamydes*, printed in 1599. His equivalent in *Rosalind* is Corydon; Corydon is a wise shepherd in Virgil, *Eclogues*, II, 7.

PHOEBE Phoebe also in *Rosalind*; her name is that of the virgin goddess of the moon.

SILVIUS Montanus in *Rosalind*; the name Silvius, which occurs in *Aeneid*, VI, 1008, is appropriate for a 'sylvan', a dweller in a wood (*silvus*), or perhaps someone mad ('wood') for love. Lodge may have taken the name Montanus from that of a love-sick shepherd who appears in the story of Selvagia that ends Book 1 of Jorge de Montemayor's *Diana* (*c.* 1559).

WILLIAM William need not be poor (see 5.1.21–2), but he seems simple. It is conceivable that he derives his name from the clown William Kempe, who left the company about the time that the play was written, and who was replaced by Robert Armin.

AUDREY There is a rustic, 'Audrey Turf', in Jonson's *Tale of a Tub* (1596?).

SIR OLIVER MARTEXT Those clergy who had graduated were given the title 'Dominus', translated as 'Master'. If 'Sir' was used for graduates, it was placed before their surnames and not their Christian names (see *OED* Sir 4 and 5). The surname suggests an illiterate 'hedgepriest' who could not expound upon scripture, and is similar to names that appear in the Marprelate tracts.

HYMEN In Jonson's masque *Hymenaei* (1606), the god of marriage appears '*in a saffron-coloured robe, his under-vestures white, his socks* [shoes] *yellow, a yellow veil of silk on his left arm, his head crowned with roses and marjoram, in his right hand a torch of pine tree*' (42–5); compare Middleton, *Women Beware Women* (1621) where, in the inset masque, appears '*Hymen in yellow, Ganymede in a blue robe powdered with stars*' (5.1.87 SD).

AS YOU LIKE IT

1.1 *Enter* ORLANDO *and* ADAM

ORLANDO As I remember, Adam, it was upon this fashion bequeathed
me by will but poor a thousand crowns and, as thou say'st, charged
my brother, on his blessing, to breed me well: and there begins my
sadness. My brother Jacques he keeps at school, and report speaks
goldenly of his profit. For my part, he keeps me rustically at home   5
or, to speak more properly, stays me here at home unkept – for call
you that 'keeping' for a gentleman of my birth, that differs not from
the stalling of an ox? His horses are bred better for, besides that they
are fair with their feeding, they are taught their manège, and to that
end riders dearly hired. But I, his brother, gain nothing under him   10
but growth – for the which his animals on his dunghills are as much

---

Act 1, Scene 1   1.1] *Eds.; Actus primus. Scœna Prima.* F   1 fashion] F; my father *Warburton;* fashion; my father
Hanmer; fashion he *Dyce³, conj. Ritson*   4 Jacques] *This edn; Iaques* F   9 manège] *Oxford;* mannage F

Title In the epistle dedicatory to 'the gentlemen
readers', Lodge writes 'If you like it, so' (*Rosalind*,
p. 95), and Rosalind may allude to the title in her
epilogue (10). There is no evidence that the phrase
was proverbial.

Act 1, Scene 1
   1.1 The play begins in the middle of a conversation between Orlando and Adam. (In *Rosalind* Lodge
includes the death of the father and the details
of his will.) Orlando's anger leads to dislocated
syntax (unless there is textual corruption – see
collation), and we never learn why he may have
incurred his father's displeasure and a niggardly
inheritance.
   1–2 upon . . . will in this manner left to me in
[my father's] will.
   2 poor a a mere (for the construction, see Abbott
85, *OED* A *art* 1d).
   2 crowns gold coins worth, during the reign of
Elizabeth, five shillings (*Shakespeare's England*, 1,
341).
   2 charged Unless we assume that 'my father'
has disappeared from the text (see collation), or was
elided (Abbott 399), this is an impersonal construction, i.e. 'it was charged'.
   3 my brother i.e. Oliver.
   3 on (1) as a condition of receiving (*OED* sv *prep*

12), (2) upon. The hatred of Oliver for Orlando
recalls the hatred of Esau for Jacob after both had
sought the blessing of their father Isaac in Gen. 27.
   3 breed educate.
   4 Jacques The middle son of Sir Roland appears
only in 5.4 to recount the news of Duke Frederick's
conversion.
   4 keeps at school maintains at university. In
Rosalind, Fernandyne 'hath no mind but on Aristotle' (p. 104).
   4 report rumour, common talk.
   5 profit progress (*OED* sv *sb* 3).
   5 rustically in the manner of a peasant.
   6 properly accurately.
   6 stays detains (*OED* Stay *v¹* 20).
   6 unkept without the money and comforts I
expect.
   7 keeping A possible echo of Gen. 4.9 where
Abel says of Cain, 'Am I my brother's keeper?'.
   8 stalling of stall for.
   9 fair handsome.
   9 *manège paces and conduct (*OED* sv 2a).
   10 riders trainers (*OED* Rider 4a).
   10 dearly at great cost (*OED* sv 4).
   10–11 gain . . . growth under his tutelage remain
poor and uneducated.
   11 the which which (Abbott 270).
   11 animals brutes.

89

bound to him as I. Besides this nothing that he so plentifully gives me, the something that Nature gave me his countenance seems to take from me: he lets me feed with his hinds, bars me the place of a brother, and, as much as in him lies, mines my gentility with my 15 education. This is it, Adam, that grieves me, and the spirit of my father, which I think is within me, begins to mutiny against this servitude. I will no longer endure it, though yet I know no wise remedy how to avoid it.

Enter OLIVER

ADAM Yonder comes my master, your brother. 20

ORLANDO Go apart, Adam, and thou shalt hear how he will shake me up.

[*Adam withdraws*]

OLIVER Now, sir, what make you here?

ORLANDO Nothing: I am not taught to make anything.

OLIVER What mar you then, sir? 25

ORLANDO Marry, sir, I am helping you to mar that which God made, a poor unworthy brother of yours, with idleness.

OLIVER Marry, sir, be better employed, and be naught awhile.

ORLANDO Shall I keep your hogs and eat husks with them? What prodigal portion have I spent that I should come to such penury? 30

OLIVER Know you where you are, sir?

---

22 SD] *Collier subst.; not in* F   28 awhile] *Eds.;* a while F

13 **something . . . me** Orlando in fact means social status.

13 **countenance** (1) behaviour, (2) patronage (*OED* sv *sb* 1 and 8).

14 **hinds** farm-hands.

14 **bars** For the omitted 'from', see Abbott 198.

15 **as much . . . lies** with all the power at his disposal.

15 **mines my gentility** undermines my good birth.

16 **grieves** vexes.

16 **spirit** mettle.

19 **avoid** get rid of (*OED* sv 4c).

21 **Go apart** Stand aside.

21–2 **shake me up** abuse me violently (*OED* Shake *v* 21 f.).

23 **make you** are you doing (*OED* Make *v* 58) – with the implication that Orlando should not be in the orchard; Orlando in the next line deliberately misconstrues 'make' to mean 'fashion', commenting bitterly on his unproductivity.

25 **mar** Generated by the proverb, 'To make and mar' (Tilley M48; see line 23).

26 **Marry** A mild oath, 'by St Mary'.

26 **that . . . made** Compare the proverb, 'He is (is not) a man of God's making' (Tilley M162).

27–8 **idleness . . . employed** Compare the proverb, 'Better to be idle than not well occupied (employed)' (Tilley I7).

28 **be naught awhile** Proverbial (Dent N51.1; *OED* Naught *sb* 1e), meaning something like 'to hell with you'.

29 **husks** scraps, refuse; this is the word used in the Geneva Bible – the Bishops' has 'cods' – in its narrative of the prodigal son.

30 **prodigal** wastefully lavish (*OED* sv *adj* 2), alluding proleptically to the parable of the prodigal son (Matt. 25.14–30, Luke 15.11–32) who would eat the food ('husks') of the swine he was minding.

31–2 **where . . . orchard** The sense of Oliver's question is 'What do you mean?' (Dent W295.1; compare 5.2.24 and *Ham.* 1.5.150) but Orlando chooses to take it literally (compare 23 n.).

ORLANDO O, sir, very well: here in your orchard.

OLIVER Know you before whom, sir?

ORLANDO Aye, better than him I am before knows me: I know you are
my eldest brother, and in the gentle condition of blood you should   35
so know me. The courtesy of nations allows you my better in that
you are the first-born, but the same tradition takes not away my
blood, were there twenty brothers betwixt us. I have as much of my
father in me as you, albeit I confess your coming before me is nearer
to his reverence.   40

OLIVER [*Raising his hand*] What, boy!

ORLANDO [*Seizing his brother*] Come, come, elder brother, you are too
young in this.

OLIVER Wilt thou lay hands on me, villain?

ORLANDO I am no villein: I am the youngest son of Sir Roland de Boys;   45
he was my father, and he is thrice a villain that says such a father
begot villeins. Wert thou not my brother, I would not take this hand
from thy throat till this other had pulled out thy tongue for saying
so: thou hast railed on thyself.

ADAM [*Coming forward*] Sweet masters, be patient, for your father's   50
remembrance, be at accord.

OLIVER Let me go, I say.

ORLANDO I will not till I please. You shall hear me. My father charged
you in his will to give me good education: you have trained me like
a peasant, obscuring and hiding from me all gentleman-like quali-   55

---

41 SD] *This edn; not in* F; *menacing with his hand / Johnson*   42 SD] *This edn; not in* F; *collaring him / Johnson*   **45**
villein] *Oxford;* villaine F   45 Roland] *This edn; Rowland* F   45 Boys] F *subst.;* Bois *Oxford*   47 villeins] *Oxford;*
villaines F   50 SD] *Collier; not in* F

33, 34 **know** acknowledge.

34 **him** he whom (for the usage, see Abbott 208).

35 **in . . . blood** because of our noble breeding.

36 **so know me** know me as a brother.

36 **courtesy of nations** custom (of primogeniture) among civilised peoples.

37 **tradition** surrender (of rank) (*OED* sv 2a).

38 **blood** (1) rank, (2) spirit.

39–40 **coming . . . reverence** earlier birth entitles you to the veneration he received (ironical).

41 **boy** An insult that provokes Orlando to 'manly' behaviour.

42–3 **you . . . this** Compare the proverb, 'He has made a younger brother of him' (Tilley B686), i.e. even though you are older I am stronger.

43 **young** inexperienced, weak.

44 **thou** Oliver's use of the singular pronoun is a calculated insult.

44 **villain** rogue.

45 *****villein** The context indicates that the meaning here is 'fellow of base extraction' (Johnson), although F does not make a distinction between villain/villein (see collation): another example of the way Orlando twists his brother's words.

45 **Roland** As 'Orlando' is the Italian form of this name, it may be that Orlando is claiming the virtues of his father.

46–7 *****such . . . villeins** Compare the proverb, 'Such a father, such a son' (Tilley F92).

49 **railed on** insulted.

50 **be patient** calm yourselves.

50–1 **for your father's remembrance** in memory of your father.

55 **peasant** In the period more a term of abuse than a designation of specific rank.

55 **obscuring** concealing (*OED* Obscure *v* 4b).

55–6 **qualities** accomplishments, manners (*OED* Quality 2b).

ties. The spirit of my father grows strong in me – and I will no
longer endure it. Therefore allow me such exercises as may become
a gentleman or give me the poor allottery my father left me by
testament: with that I will go buy my fortunes.

[He releases Oliver]

OLIVER And what wilt thou do? Beg when that is spent? Well, sir, get   60
you in. I will not long be troubled with you: you shall have some
part of your 'will'; I pray you leave me.

ORLANDO I will no further offend you than becomes me for my good.

OLIVER *[To Adam]* Get you with him, you old dog.

ADAM Is 'old dog' my reward? Most true, I have lost my teeth in your   65
service. God be with my old master: he would not have spoke such
a word.

Exeunt Orlando [and] Adam

OLIVER Is it even so, begin you to grow upon me? I will physic your
rankness, and yet give no thousand crowns neither. – Holla, Denis.

Enter DENIS

DENIS Calls your worship?   70

OLIVER Was not Charles, the Duke's wrestler, here to speak with me?

DENIS So please you, he is here at the door, and importunes access to
you.

---

59 SD] *Collier; not in* F   62 'will'] *Wilson, conj. Furness;* will F   64 SD] *Wilson subst.; not in* F   68 grow] growl *conj.
Collier*   69 Denis] *Oxford; Dennis* F (*throughout*)

56, 59, 63 will have a mind to (*OED* sv v^1 5).

57 exercises acquired skills (*OED* Exercise *sb*
6b).

58 allottery portion; a nonce-word not recorded
in *OED*, and probably a pun on 'lottery'.

59 testament his will.

59 buy my fortunes purchase an office (at
court?).

60 And . . . spent Another allusion to the prodigal son, disdained by his older brother.

60–1 thou . . . you in Orlando used 'you' in the
preceding lines; Oliver's use of 'thou' is the language of a master to a servant (Abbott 232); the
'you' that comes next, following 'sir', is even more
contemptuous.

62 will (1) wishes (see 54, 59), (2) our father's
testament.

63 offend assail (*OED* sv 5).

65–6 'old dog' . . . service In Aesop there is a
fable of an old greyhound who, rebuked by his master when he could not hold a beast he had captured,

responded 'Thou has loved me catching game, thou
has hated me being slow and toothless' (William
Bullokar, *Aesop's Fables in True Orthography* (1585),
sig. D1ʳ).

66 spoke For the form, see Abbott 343.

68 grow upon become troublesome to.

68–9 physic your rankness cure your excessive
exuberance or insolence; 'rankness' is a symptom of
murrain, a disease of cattle, a condition that requires
bloodletting. *OED* Rankness cites Jon Fitzherbert,
A Tract for all Husbandmen (1523), par. 58: 'Murrain
. . . cometh of a rankness of blood' and compare *JC*
3.1.153; there may also be an allusion to pruning a
'rank' or over-luxuriant plant (*OED* Rank *adj* 5).

69 neither either (Abbott 128).

69 Holla Come here (Cotgrave, cited in *OED*).

71 Charles, the Duke's wrestler He may have
been thought of as the Duke's 'champion', as in
Rosalind (p. 107).

72 So please you If it may please you.

72 door Perhaps to a walled garden or orchard.

OLIVER Call him in.

[*Exit Denis*]

'Twill be a good way, and tomorrow the wrestling is.   75

Enter CHARLES

CHARLES Good morrow to your worship.

OLIVER Good Monsieur Charles, what's the new news at the new
court?

CHARLES There's no news at the court, sir, but the old news: that is, the
old Duke is banished by his younger brother, the new Duke, and   80
three or four loving lords have put themselves into voluntary exile
with him, whose lands and revenues enrich the new Duke; therefore
he gives them good leave to wander.

OLIVER Can you tell if Rosalind, the Duke's daughter, be banished
with her father?   85

CHARLES O no; for the Duke's daughter, her cousin, so loves her, being
ever from their cradles bred together, that she would have followed
her exile or have died to stay behind her; she is at the court and no
less beloved of her uncle than his own daughter, and never two
ladies loved as they do.   90

OLIVER Where will the old Duke live?

CHARLES They say he is already in the Forest of Arden, and a many
merry men with him; and there they live like the old Robin Hood of

---

75 SD] *Johnson; not in* F   77 Good] F; Good morrow, *Walker*   77 at the new] F; at the *conj. Furness*   79 at the] F;
at the new *Lettsom*   84 the] F; the old *Hanmer*   86 the] F; the new *Hanmer*   87 she] F3; hee F   88 her] F; their F3

---

75 'Twill . . . is A short soliloquy or aside.

75 way i.e. of killing Orlando.

76 morrow morning.

77–8 new news . . . court Oliver's supercil-
ious pleasantry offers Charles a cue for a passage of
exposition.

77–8 new court It would seem from the reference to Celia's youth at 1.3.61 that Duke Senior had
been in exile for several years.

80 old Duke i.e. Duke Senior.

81 loving loyal (as in the proclamation phrase
'our loving subjects').

82 whose i.e. of the exiled lords.

83 good leave full permission.

86 being they being (Abbott 399).

87 ever always.

87 bred brought up.

88 to stay by staying (for this usage, see Abbott
356).

89 of by (Abbott 170).

90 loved loved each other (*OED* Love *v*¹ 3b).

92–4 Forest . . . England Lodge (*Rosalind*,

p. 108) wrote that the banished Gerismond 'lived
as an outlaw in the Forest of Arden', ostensibly the Forêt des Ardennes in Flanders, although
in his narrative the girls start at Bordeaux and
walk due east. The Forest of Arden was an exten-
sive tract of country north of Shakespeare's birth-
place, Stratford-upon-Avon, although the addition
'of England' implies that the forest of the play is
in France (compare 'the stubbornest young fellow
of France' (1.1.111–12). Shakespeare overlays these
mythical locations with another, the antique greenwood that figures so often in the Robin Hood ballads.

92 a many The indefinite article makes numeral
adjectives less definite (see *OED* A *art* 2).

93 merry The word was often used to designate utopian equality in populist texts of the period;
compare 'it was never merry world in England since
gentlemen came up' (*2H6* 4.2.6–7).

93–4 Robin Hood of England The phrase associates the exiled Duke and his companions with
characters in a popular May-game (see Laroque,
pp. 138–9).

England. They say many young gentlemen flock to him every day,
and fleet the time carelessly as they did in the golden world.   95

OLIVER What, you wrestle tomorrow before the new Duke?

CHARLES Marry, do I, sir; and I came to acquaint you with a matter. I
am given, sir, secretly to understand that your younger brother
Orlando hath a disposition to come in, disguised, against me to try
a fall. Tomorrow, sir, I wrestle for my credit, and he that escapes me   100
without some broken limb shall acquit him well. Your brother is but
young and tender and, for your love, I would be loath to foil him, as
I must for my own honour, if he come in; therefore, out of my love
to you, I came hither to acquaint you withal, that either you might
stay him from his intendment, or brook such disgrace well as he   105
shall run into, in that it is a thing of his own search and altogether
against my will.

OLIVER Charles, I thank thee for thy love to me, which thou shalt find
I will most kindly requite. I had myself notice of my brother's
purpose herein, and have by underhand means laboured to dissuade   110
him from it – but he is resolute. I'll tell thee, Charles, it is the
stubbornest young fellow of France, full of ambition, an envious
emulator of every man's good parts, a secret and villainous contriver

---

97 came] F; come F4

95 fleet while away (*OED* sv *v*¹ 10d – the first
recorded instance of the verb used transitively).

95 carelessly without cares.

95 golden world The first age of the world,
described, for example, in *Metamorphoses*, I, 103–
28. Duke Senior's description of the bracing rigours
of the simple life in 2.1, however, is unlike the
descriptions of care-free existence in classical 'age'
texts.

96 What Oliver's exclamation of impatience may
be generated by Charles' idealising description of the
rival court.

97 Marry Indeed.

97 a a certain (for the article used thus emphati-
cally, see Abbott 81).

99 disposition inclination.

99 disguised It was not becoming for a gentleman to fight with a common wrestler.

100 fall bout (*OED* sv *sb*² 13).

100 credit reputation.

101 shall will have to (Abbott 315).

101 acquit perform.

101 him himself (Abbott 223).

102 tender immature (*OED* sv 4).

102 love sake.

102 foil (1) throw, defeat (*OED* sv *v*¹ 4), (2) vio-
late sexually (?; see *OED* sv *v*¹ 7).

104 withal with this (Abbott 196).

105 intendment intention (*OED* sv 5).

105 brook endure.

106 run into incur.

106 thing of his own search plan of his own
devising.

108 thee . . . thou Oliver changes to the intimate
form of the pronoun.

109 kindly requite appropriately reward.

110 by underhand means unobtrusively.

111 it is he is (*OED* sv 2d).

112 stubbornest fiercest, most ruthless (*OED*
Stubborn 1).

112 of France See 92–4 n., above.

112–13 envious emulator malicious disparager.

113 parts qualities.

113 contriver plotter.

against me, his natural brother. Therefore use thy discretion: I had
as lief thou didst break his neck as his finger. And thou wert best   115
look to't – for if thou dost him any slight disgrace or if he do not
mightily grace himself on thee, he will practise against thee by
poison, entrap thee by some treacherous device, and never leave
thee till he hath ta'en thy life by some indirect means or other. For
I assure thee – and almost with tears I speak it – there is not one so   120
young and so villainous this day living. I speak but brotherly of him,
but should I anatomise him to thee as he is, I must blush and weep,
and thou must look pale and wonder.

CHARLES   I am heartily glad I came hither to you. If he come tomorrow,
I'll give him his payment; if ever he go alone again, I'll never wrestle   125
for prize more – and so God keep your worship.   *Exit*

OLIVER   Farewell, good Charles. – Now will I stir this gamester. I hope
I shall see an end of him, for my soul – yet I know not why – hates
nothing more than he. Yet he's gentle, never schooled and yet
learned, full of noble device, of all sorts enchantingly beloved, and   130
indeed so much in the heart of the world, and especially of my own
people who best know him, that I am altogether misprized. But it
shall not be so long this wrestler shall clear all: nothing remains but
that I kindle the boy thither, which now I'll go about.   *Exit*

---

127 SH] F2; *not in* F

114 natural blood (*OED* sv 13b).

114–15 I . . . finger At this stage in Lodge's narrative Saladyne bribes Charles (*Rosalind*, p. 107): handing the wrestler a purse would be an appropriate piece of stage business here.

115 thou wert best For the construction, see Abbott 230.

116 look to't be careful.

116 disgrace injury of disfigurement.

117 grace himself on thee gain credit at your expense.

117 practise plot.

118 device trick.

121 but brotherly with the reserve of a brother – in the manner of the innumerable hostile brothers in Shakespearean texts.

122 anatomise him lay his character bare.

125 payment punishment (*OED* sv *sb*¹ 3).

125 go alone walk without aid.

126 prize This was often a ram (see Joseph Strutt, *The Sports and Pastimes of the People of England*, ed. William Hone, 1830, p. 80).

127 stir this gamester torment this 'athlete' (see *OED* Gamester 1).

128–9 soul . . . he Like Iago, Oliver finds it difficult to rationalise his jealousy to himself.

129 he him (Abbott 206).

129 gentle well born.

130 learned educated (*OED* sv *ppl adj* 2).

130 device inclinations, thoughts (*OED* sv 4).

130 of all sorts by all ranks.

130 enchantingly as if they were under his spell.

132 people servants.

132 misprized despised.

133 clear all settle matters.

134 kindle incite.

134 boy an insulting designation for a man.

134 go set.

1.2 *Enter* ROSALIND *and* CELIA

CELIA I pray thee, Rosalind, sweet my coz, be merry.

ROSALIND Dear Celia, I show more mirth than I am mistress of, and would you yet were merrier: unless you could teach me to forget a banished father, you must not learn me how to remember any extraordinary pleasure. 5

CELIA Herein, I see, thou lov'st me not with the full weight that I love thee; if my uncle, thy banished father, had banished thy uncle, the Duke my father, so thou hadst been still with me, I could have taught my love to take thy father for mine; so wouldst thou, if the truth of thy love to me were so righteously tempered as mine is to 10 thee.

ROSALIND Well, I will forget the condition of my estate to rejoice in yours.

CELIA You know my father hath no child but I, nor none is like to have; and, truly, when he dies thou shalt be his heir: for what he hath 15 taken away from thy father perforce I will render thee again in affection. By mine honour, I will, and when I break that oath, let me turn monster. Therefore, my sweet Rose, my dear Rose, be merry.

Act 1, Scene 2   1.2] *Eds.; Scæna Secunda.* F   2 of, and] F; of. /   CELIA And *conj. Jourdain (Philological Society Transactions, 1860–1, p. 143)*   3 yet] F; yet I *Rowe³*   6 Herein . . . see,] *Theobald;* Heerein I see F

Act 1, Scene 2

1.2 In Elizabethan amphitheatre playhouses entrances were usually made from doors in the tiring-house at the rear of the stage and it would take some time for players to come forward to the front edge of the stage. This scene could therefore have begun by the players walking forward as though they were in mid-conversation, thus 'quoting' the entrance of Orlando and Adam in 1.1.

1–3 thee . . . you It is notable that Celia generally uses the familiar form of the pronoun, whereas Rosalind employs the more formal 'you' to the daughter of the ruling Duke.

1 sweet my coz For the construction, see Abbott 13.

1 coz Abbreviated form of 'cousin'.

2–3 show . . . merrier am less happy than I seem, and wish that you were more cheerful than that; Rowe's emendation 'yet I were merrier?' has been widely followed.

4 learn teach.

4 remember be mindful of, mention (*OED* sv 3a).

5 extraordinary great (*OED* sv 4).

6 that with which.

8 so provided that (Abbott 133).

8 still constantly (Abbott 69).

9 so wouldst thou you would do likewise.

10 so as (Abbott 275).

10 righteously tempered properly composed.

12 estate condition, situation.

14 I me (Abbott 209).

14 nor none For the double negative, see Abbott 406.

14 like likely.

15 be his heir i.e. inherit his dukedom.

16 perforce by violence.

16 again back.

17 mine The form used before vowels and words beginning with '*h*' (Abbot 237).

18 sweet Rose Either containing the abbreviated form of the name 'Rosalind' or a reference to the Spanish words *rosa linda*, beautiful (sweet) rose, from which 'Rosalind' derives.

ROSALIND From henceforth I will, coz, and devise sports. Let me see, what think you of falling in love?   20

CELIA Marry, I prithee do, to make sport withal: but love no man in good earnest – nor no further in sport neither – than with safety of a pure blush thou mayst in honour come off again.

ROSALIND What shall be our sport then?

CELIA Let us sit and mock the good housewife Fortune from her wheel,   25 that her gifts may henceforth be bestowed equally.

ROSALIND I would we could do so: for her benefits are mightily mis-placed, and the bountiful blindwoman doth most mistake in her gifts to women.

CELIA 'Tis true, for those that she makes fair she scarce makes honest,   30 and those that she makes honest she makes very ill-favouredly.

ROSALIND Nay, now thou goest from Fortune's office to Nature's: Fortune reigns in gifts of the world, not in the lineaments of Nature.

Enter [TOUCHSTONE *the*] *clown*

---

28 blindwoman] *This edn;* blinde woman F   31 ill-favouredly] F *subst.;* ill-favoured *Rowe*³   34 SD TOUCHSTONE]
*Theobald*² *subst.;* Clowne F

21 **make sport** pass the time pleasantly (here with a bawdy sense).

21 **withal** (1) with, (2) with all (men).

22 **with safety of** without damage to (*OED* records this usage, but only from 1619 (Safety 1c)).

23 **pure** shame-free.

23 **come off** retire as from a field of combat; there is a possible reference to orgasm, although *OED* records the usage only from 1650 (Come *v* 17); see, however, 2.4.40–2 n., Dekker, *1 Honest Whore* (1604), 'a wench that will come with a wet finger' (1.2.4), and Middleton and Dekker, *The Roaring Girl* (1611), ed. Paul Mulholland, 1987, 2.1.192.

25–6 Celia proposes a discussion on a set theme.

25 **housewife** (1) mistress of a household, (2) hussy, whore.

25 **Fortune** For the iconology of Fortune and debates between Fortune and Nature, see Frederick Kiefer, *Fortune and Elizabethan Tragedy*, 1983, pp. 277–81; there is a set meditation on Fortune by Adam in *Rosalind*, pp. 141–2 (Appendix 2, pp. 232–3).

25 **wheel** By which Dame Fortune, commonly depicted as wearing a blindfold, raised people into prosperity and happiness and then plunged them down again to misery – with a disparaging pun on a housewife's spinning-wheel (see plate 2).

26 **equally** justly (*OED* sv 3).

27 **benefits** favours, gifts.

27–8 **misplaced** improperly bestowed.

28 **bountiful** (1) liberal, (2) promiscuous (?).

28 **blindwoman** Compare the proverb, 'Fortune is blind' (Tilley F604).

28 **mistake** go astray (*OED* sv 6).

30–2 Compare the proverb, 'Beauty and chastity (honesty) seldom meet' (Tilley B163).

30 **fair** beautiful.

30 **scarce** seldom.

30 **honest** virtuous, chaste.

31 **ill-favouredly** of uncomely appearance; 'ill-favoured' (see collation) improves the balance of the sentence.

32 **office** function.

33 **gifts of the world** material possessions, power.

33–4 **lineaments of Nature** e.g. virtue, wit, beauty.

34 SD *TOUCHSTONE . . . clown* Touchstone's name does not appear in F until 2.4 (see 2.4.0 SD. 2–3 n.); it is also likely that he wears the fool's uniform of motley only in this latter scene (see 2.7.13 n.). His entrance, some lines before he speaks, is either evidence of prompt-book copy, or perhaps it gives him an opportunity silently to upstage his mistress and her friend.

CELIA No? When Nature hath made a fair creature, may she not by   35
Fortune fall into the fire? Though Nature hath given us wit to flout
at Fortune, hath not Fortune sent in this fool to cut off the
argument?

ROSALIND Indeed there is Fortune too hard for Nature, when Fortune
makes Nature's natural the cutter-off of Nature's wit.   40

CELIA Peradventure this is not Fortune's work neither but Nature's
who, perceiving our natural wits too dull to reason of such goddesses, hath sent this natural for our whetstone: for always the
dullness of the fool is the whetstone of the wits. – How now, Wit,
whither wander you?   45

TOUCHSTONE Mistress, you must come away to your father.

CELIA Were you made the messenger?

TOUCHSTONE No, by mine honour, but I was bid to come for you.

ROSALIND Where learned you that oath, fool?

TOUCHSTONE Of a certain knight that swore, by his honour, they were   50
good pancakes, and swore, by his honour, the mustard was naught.
Now, I'll stand to it, the pancakes were naught and the mustard was
good – and yet was not the knight forsworn.

---

35 No?] *Hanmer;* No; F   42 perceiving] F2; perceiueth F   42–3 goddesses] F; goddesses, and *Malone*   46 SH]
Malone subst.; Clown. F *subst.* (*throughout*)

35–6 Nature . . . fire Compare the proverb, 'Shunning the smoke, he fell into the fire' (Tilley S570).

36 Fortune Chance.

36 fall into the fire lose her virtue.

36 wit intelligence.

36–7 flout at rail at, complain about.

38 argument (1) theme, discussion (*OED* sv 6), (2) penis (Williams, pp. 29–30).

39 there in that.

39 too hard more than a match.

40 natural fool, idiot (*OED* sv *sb* 2); compare 3.3.17 where Touchstone puts down Corin by calling him 'a natural philosopher'.

40 Nature's wit the wit Nature has given us; 'wit' may refer here to the sexual organs (see Williams, pp. 340–1).

41 Peradventure Perhaps.

42 *perceiving F2's reading (see collation) improves the sentence structure.

42–4 wits . . . wits Compare the proverbs, 'X is the whetstone of wit' (Dent W298.1) and 'A whetstone cannot itself cut but yet it makes tools cut' (Tilley W299).

42 wits mental faculties.

42 reason discourse, talk.

44 dullness slowness, bluntness.

44–5 Wit . . . you Compare the proverb, addressed to anyone too loquacious, 'Wit, whither wilt thou?' (Tilley W570; *OED* Wit 2e).

46 away along.

47 messenger officer sent to apprehend state prisoners (*OED* sv 3a); compare Prov. 26.6: 'He that sendeth a message by the hand of a fool, is as he that cutteth off the feet and drinketh iniquity.'

49–63 The jest of the man who swears by what he has not is also found in Richard Edwards' *Damon and Pithias* (1565?), 1155–8.

50–1 honour . . . mustard For a link with a jest in Jonson's *Every Man in his Humour*, where a clown buys a coat of arms and the motto 'Not without mustard', a possible reference to Shakespeare's motto *Non sanz droict* ('Not without right'), see Samuel Schoenbaum, *William Shakespeare: A Documentary Life*, 1975, p. 171.

51 pancakes pancake, fritter, or flapjack are alternatives or synonyms.

51 naught bad, unsatisfactory (*OED* sv B1).

52 stand to it insist, swear.

53 forsworn perjured (with a possible allusion to the homily 'Against Swearing and Perjury' (Shaheen, p. 160)).

CELIA How prove you that in the great heap of your knowledge?

ROSALIND Aye, marry, now unmuzzle your wisdom.   55

TOUCHSTONE Stand you both forth now. Stroke your chins and swear,
by your beards, that I am a knave.

CELIA By our beards – if we had them – thou art.

TOUCHSTONE By my knavery – if I had it – then I were. But if you
swear by that that is not you are not forsworn: no more was this   60
knight swearing by his honour, for he never had any; or if he had,
he had sworn it away before ever he saw those pancakes or that
mustard.

CELIA Prithee, who is't that thou mean'st?

TOUCHSTONE One that old Frederick, your father, loves.   65

CELIA My father's love is enough to honour him. Enough! Speak no
more of him; you'll be whipped for taxation one of these days.

TOUCHSTONE The more pity that fools may not speak wisely what wise
men do foolishly.

CELIA By my troth, thou say'st true: for, since the little wit that fools 70
have was silenced, the little foolery that wise men have makes a
great show. – Here comes 'Monsieur the Beau'.

---

65 One that] F; One *Collier*   65 Frederick] F *subst.;* Ferdinand *conj. Capell; Collier²*   66 SH] *Theobald; Ros.* F   66
him. Enough!] *Hanmer subst.;* him enough; F   72 'Monsieur the Beau'] *This edn;* Monsieur the *Beu* F

56 Stand you both forth Both step forward
(*OED* Stand *v* 93a).

58 By (1) In accord with, (2) By reason of.

59 were would be.

59–61 if . . . any Compare the proverb, 'No man
ever lost his honour but he that had it not' (Tilley
M326).

65 The line may well be corrupt (see collation).
As the usurping Frederick was in fact the younger
brother, 'old' might be taken as a jocular and over-
familiar epithet that stings Celia into defending her
father.

65 Frederick It is conceivable that this is a compositorial misreading for 'Ferdinand' (see List of
Characters, n. to Duke Senior, p. 87), in which case
Theobald's emendation of the following SH is unnecessary. Alternatively 'Frederick' may have been the
name of the knight (see collation).

66 SH* Theobald's emendation is justified by the
fact that at 1.2.186 and 5.4.138 we learn that it is
Celia's father who is called Frederick – although
possibly Shakespeare himself made the error. The
line occurs in part of a stint set by Compositor B
who made similar errors with speech headings in
5.1.

66 *him. Enough F's reading meaning 'Even

though my father may not have been an honourable
man himself, his favour confers sufficient honour'
could just stand; however, the two 'enoughs' in the
sentence are awkward, so Hanmer's emendation is
attractive.

67 whipped Even an allowed fool might be
whipped for overstepping the mark.

67 taxation slander (*OED* sv 3); for a pun
on '*tax*', the sound of a whip-stroke, see Hulme,
p. 163.

70 troth faith.

70 wit wisdom.

70–1 since . . . silenced Either a reference to
the decree of June 1599 by the Archbishop of Canterbury and the Bishop of London to the Stationers' Company prohibiting the printing of satires and
epigrams (see Introduction, pp. 15–16); or a general
reference to attempts by the City to put down the
players.

71 was has been (Abbott 347).

72 *'Monsieur the Beau' Celia's designation
may draw attention to his foppish character and the
spellings (see collation) 'Beu' and 'Boon-iour' (72,
76) may mock his affected diction; in F the name
appears in the following SD as '*le Beau*', but in SHS
as *Le Beu*.

Enter LE BEAU

ROSALIND With his mouth full of news.

CELIA Which he will put on us as pigeons feed their young.

ROSALIND Then shall we be news-crammed.   75

CELIA All the better: we shall be the more marketable. – *Bonjour*, Monsieur Le Beau, what's the news?

LE BEAU Fair princess, you have lost much good sport.

CELIA 'Sport': of what colour?

LE BEAU 'What colour', madam? How shall I answer you?   80

ROSALIND As wit and fortune will.

TOUCHSTONE [*Imitating Le Beau*] Or as the destinies decrees.

CELIA Well said: that was laid on with a trowel.

TOUCHSTONE Nay, if I keep not my rank –

ROSALIND Thou loosest thy old smell.   85

LE BEAU You amaze me, ladies! I would have told you of good wrestling which you have lost the sight of.

ROSALIND Yet tell us the manner of the wrestling.

LE BEAU I will tell you the beginning and, if it please your ladyships, you may see the end, for the best is yet to do; and here where you   90 are they are coming to perform it.

CELIA Well, the beginning that is dead and buried.

---

76 *Bonjour*] *Eds.;* Boon–iour F   78 SH] LE BEAU *Eds.;* Le Beu F (*throughout scene*)   78 princess] *Eds.;* Princesse F   79 Sport] F; Spot *Collier*   80 madam] *Eds.;* Madame F   82 SD] *This edn; not in* F   84 rank–] *Rowe;* ranke. F   85 loosest] F; losest *Eds.*

74 put force.

75 crammed stuffed (bawdy?).

76 marketable Like plump pigeons.

78 lost missed.

79 'Sport' It is probable that Le Beau affectedly pronounced the word 'spot' (compare 224 n. below; Cercignani, pp. 108–9); the word could mean 'amorous dalliance'.

79 colour (1) kind, nature; this is the first recorded use of the word in this sense (*OED* sv *sb* 16a), which may explain Le Beau's response in the next line, (2) hue.

81 Compare the proverb, 'Little wit serves unto whom fortune pipes' (Tilley W560).

81 fortune good luck.

82 Touchstone implies that Le Beau is foolish, seldom fated to make a witty response.

82 decrees For the termination, see Abbott 333.

83 laid on with a trowel Like mortar, 'a bit thick', the first recorded use of the phrase (Tilley T539).

84 rank social station or, possibly, fast rate of verbal delivery (see *OED* sv *sb³* 3), or even straight row (of bricks).

84 The unemended line (see collation) could mean that Touchstone fears that Le Beau could deprive him of his job, or, as emended here, means that the fool was going to aver that his gifts as a clown were quite secure.

85 loosest release; Rosalind wilfully construes 'rank' as foul smell, i.e. a fart.

86 amaze confuse, bewilder (*OED* sv 2).

87 lost the sight of missed.

90 the best . . . do Compare the proverb, 'The best is behind' (Tilley B318).

90 to do to be done (Abbott 359).

90–1 and . . . it In 'reality' Rosalind would go to a place for wrestling: the passage celebrates the flexibility of the non-illusionistic stage by telling the audience that the wrestling place is coming to Rosalind.

92 Come, then, tell us what has happened already (the phrase 'dead and buried' occurs in the catechism in the Book of Common Prayer); Celia is construing Le Beau's 'end' (90) to mean 'death'.

LE BEAU There comes an old man and his three sons –

CELIA I could match this beginning with an old tale.

LE BEAU Three proper young men, of excellent growth and presence –   95

ROSALIND With bills on their necks: 'Be it known unto all men by these presents'.

LE BEAU The eldest of the three wrestled with Charles, the Duke's wrestler, which Charles in a moment threw him and broke three of his ribs that there is little hope of life in him. So he served the   100 second and so the third: yonder they lie, the poor old man, their father, making such pitiful dole over them that all the beholders take his part with weeping.

ROSALIND Alas!

TOUCHSTONE But what is the sport, monsieur, that the ladies have   105 lost?

LE BEAU Why, this that I speak of.

TOUCHSTONE Thus men may grow wiser every day. It is the first time that ever I heard breaking of ribs was sport for ladies.

CELIA Or I, I promise thee.   110

ROSALIND But is there any else longs to see this broken music in his sides? Is there yet another dotes upon rib-breaking? Shall we see this wrestling, cousin?

LE BEAU You must if you stay here, for here is the place appointed for the wrestling and they are ready to perform it.   115

CELIA Yonder, sure, they are coming. Let us now stay and see it.

---

93 sons –] *Theobald;* sons. F   95 presence –] *Theobald subst.;* presence. F   95–6 presence –/ ROSALIND . . . necks:] F *subst;* presence, with bills on their necks. ROSALIND *conj. Farmer in Steevens*   111–12 ROSALIND . . . -breaking?] F *subst.;* TOUCHSTONE . . . -breaking? / ROSALIND *Cam., conj. anon*   111 see] F; set *Theobald, conj. Warburton*

93 **comes** For the singular form, see Abbott 335.

93–4 Parents with three children provide a common motif in folk stories – *Rosalind* and the pseudo–Chaucerian *Tale of Gamelyn* are examples. This nameless family is a figure of the de Boys family in which there were also three sons, in their case reunited at the end of the play. The episode of the old man and his sons who are killed by Charles is narrated in *Rosalind* (p. 110) – in Lodge, however, there are only two sons in this inset episode, and Rosader seeks to avenge their deaths.

94 **match** rival.

94 **tale** Celia may be continuing the bawdy puns with a jest on 'tail'.

95 **proper** honest, good–looking.

95 **growth** stature.

96 **bills** papers, writings.

96–7 **Be . . . presents** Many legal documents began '*Noverint universi per praesentes*': 'know all men by these presents' – Rosalind's line is an excuse for a pun on 'presence'.

97 **presents** (1) documents, writings (*OED* Present *sb* 2b), (2) genitals (Rubinstein, p. 203).

99 **which** the which (Abbott 269).

100 **that** so that (Abbott 283).

102 **dole** lamentation.

110 **promise** assure (*OED* sv *v* 5b).

111 **any** anyone (Abbott 244).

111 **see** experience, attend (*OED* sv *v* 5a).

111 **broken music** Music arranged for more than one instrument (*Shakespeare's England* II, 31, 33), but here also referring to the sound of ribs being broken.

112–13 **Shall . . . cousin** The line could express either desire to see the sport or repulsion.

Flourish. Enter DUKE [FREDERICK], *Lords,* ORLANDO,
CHARLES, *and Attendants*

DUKE FREDERICK Come on; since the youth will not be entreated, his
own peril on his forwardness.
ROSALIND Is yonder the man?
LE BEAU Even he, madam.   120
CELIA Alas, he is too young; yet he looks successfully.
DUKE FREDERICK How now, daughter – and cousin: are you crept
hither to see the wrestling?
ROSALIND Aye, my liege, so please you give us leave.
DUKE FREDERICK You will take little delight in it, I can tell you: there   125
is such odds in the man. In pity of the challenger's youth, I would
fain dissuade him, but he will not be entreated. Speak to him, ladies:
see if you can move him.
CELIA Call him hither, good Monsieur Le Beau.
DUKE FREDERICK Do so; I'll not be by.   130
[*The Duke stands aside*]
LE BEAU Monsieur the challenger, the princess calls for you.
ORLANDO I attend them with all respect and duty.
ROSALIND Young man, have you challenged Charles the wrestler?
ORLANDO No, fair princess, he is the general challenger. I come but in
as others do to try with him the strength of my youth.   135
CELIA Young gentleman, your spirits are too bold for your years: you
have seen cruel proof of this man's strength. If you saw yourself

---

116 SD FREDERICK] *Rowe; not in* F   117–18] *As prose, Pope; Duke* . . . intreated / His . . . forwardnesse. F   122–3]
As prose, Pope; Du. Cousin: / Are . . . wrastling? F   125 you:] *Globe subst.;* you F   126 man] F; men *Hanmer*   130
SD] *Theobald subst.; not in* F   131 princess calls] F *subst.;* princesses call *Theobald*   132 them] F; her *Rowe*

116 SD *Flourish* Sounded on trumpets to signify
the presence of authority.
117 **Come on** Approach.
117 **entreated** persuaded (*OED* Entreat *v* 10).
117–18 **his own . . . forwardness** his rashness
has created the danger he is in.
121 **successfully** able to succeed.
122 **cousin** Used indifferently for various relatives including, as here, nieces.
122–3 **are you crept hither** have you sneaked
here (for the use of 'are' for 'have', see Abbott 295).
126 **odds in the man** advantage in Charles (see
OED Odds 4a).
126 **In pity of** Out of compassion for.
131–2 **princess . . . them** The title 'princess'

could be applied to a female member of any ruling family (*OED* Prince 6); grammatically 'princess'
could be an uninflected plural (Abbott 471) and
'calls' a third person plural termination (Abbott
333); if, however, 'princess' was singular, 'them'
meant 'her and her entourage'.
134 **is the general challenger** will take on all
comers (compare Hulme, p. 145).
134 **come but in** merely enter the competition
(*OED* Come 63k).
135 **try** test.
137 **cruel proof** Charles' defeat of the old man's
three sons.
137–8 **If . . . eyes** Compare the proverb, 'The eye
that sees all things else sees not itself' (Tilley E232).

with your eyes or knew yourself with your judgement, the fear of
your adventure would counsel you to a more equal enterprise. We
pray you, for your own sake, to embrace your own safety and give   140
over this attempt.

ROSALIND Do, young sir: your reputation shall not therefore be
misprized. We will make it our suit to the Duke that the wrestling
might not go forward.

ORLANDO I beseech you, punish me not with your hard thoughts,   145
wherein I confess me much guilty to deny so fair and excellent
ladies anything. But let your fair eyes and gentle wishes go with me
to my trial, wherein if I be foiled, there is but one shamed that was
never gracious; if killed, but one dead that is willing to be so. I shall
do my friends no wrong, for I have none to lament me; the world no   150
injury, for in it I have nothing; only in the world I fill up a place,
which may be better supplied when I have made it empty.

ROSALIND The little strength that I have, I would it were with you.

CELIA And mine to eke out hers.

ROSALIND Fare you well: pray heaven I be deceived in you.   155

CELIA Your heart's desires be with you.

CHARLES Come, where is this young gallant that is so desirous to lie
with his mother earth?

ORLANDO Ready, sir, but his will hath in it a more modest working.

138 your . . . your] F; our . . . our *Hanmer*   138 your eyes] F *subst.;* your own *Rowe*²   140 your own safety] F *subst.;*
your safety *conj. Furness*   148 wherein] F; Therein *conj. Johnson*   156 SH] F *subst.; Orla./ Theobald*

138 your eyes . . . your judgement Hanmer's
emendation 'our' is attractive, especially since the
compositor might have caught 'your' from 'your
judgement'. But if the emphasis is placed on 'eyes'
and 'judgement', F's reading can stand.

138 knew yourself The classical injuction 'know
thyself' was often repeated (Tilley K175).

138 fear formidableness (*OED* sv *sb* 5c).

140–1 give over abandon.

142 therefore for that.

143 misprized despised.

143–4 We . . . forward If the request comes from
the women, Orlando's honour will be saved.

144 might may (for irregular tense sequences,
see Abbott 370).

144 go forward proceed.

145 with your hard thoughts by thinking badly
of me.

146 wherein in respect of which (*OED* sv *adv* 3).

146 me myself (Abbott 223).

146 much very (Abbott 51).

146 to deny in denying.

147 fair (1) beautiful, (2) favourable.

148 foiled thrown, defeated.

149 gracious in favour (*OED* sv 1) – politically
or with Fortune.

150 friends kinsfolk (*OED* Friend 3).

151 injury wrong (*OED* sv 1).

151 only merely; in modern usage the word
would come after 'I' (Abbott 420).

152 supplied made good (*OED* Supply *v* 4).

154 eke stretch.

155 be deceived in you underestimate your
strength.

157–8 desirous . . . earth A sneeringly obscene
version of the proverb, 'Earth is the (common
mother of us all' (Dent E28.1). It may also signal an identification with Antaeus, son of Tellus
(Earth), who could renew his strength by lying
on the ground, but who was defeated by Hercules (see 165); for biblical analogues, see Shaheen,
p. 160.

159 will (1) sexual desire, penis (Williams,
pp. 337–9), (2) intention.

159 more modest working humble and less
wanton endeavour.

DUKE FREDERICK You shall try but one fall.   160

CHARLES No, I warrant your grace you shall not entreat him to a
  second, that have so mightily persuaded him from a first.

ORLANDO You mean to mock me after: you should not have mocked me
  before. But come your ways.

ROSALIND Now Hercules be thy speed, young man.   165

CELIA I would I were invisible, to catch the strong fellow by the leg.

[They] wrestle

ROSALIND O excellent young man.

CELIA If I had a thunderbolt in mine eye, I can tell who should down.

[Charles is thrown to the ground.] Shout

DUKE FREDERICK No more, no more!

ORLANDO Yes, I beseech your grace, I am not yet well breathed.   170

DUKE FREDERICK How dost thou, Charles?

LE BEAU He cannot speak, my lord.

DUKE FREDERICK Bear him away.

[Charles is carried out]

  What is thy name, young man?

ORLANDO Orlando, my liege, the youngest son of Sir Roland de Boys.   175

DUKE FREDERICK I would thou hadst been son to some man else;
  The world esteemed thy father honourable
  But I did find him still mine enemy.
  Thou shouldst have better pleased me with this deed
  Hadst thou descended from another house.   180

---

163 You] F; An you *conj.* Theobald   168 SD *Charles . . . ground*] Rowe *subst.; not in* F   173–4] *As prose,* Pope:
Duk. . . . awaie: / What . . . man? F   173 SD] Capell *subst.; not in* F

160 **fall** This 'consisted in either the adversary's
back or one shoulder and the contrary heel touching
the ground' (*Shakespeare's England*, II, 456).

163–4 Compare the proverbs, 'Do not triumph
before the victory' (Tilley V50) and 'He who mocks
shall be mocked' (Tilley M1031).

  164 **come your ways** let's get under way.

  165 **Hercules** See 157–8 n.

  165 **be thy speed** lend you success.

166 SD The wrestling 'is a kind of popular tourna-
ment, a ritual spectacle associated with the ballads
of Robin Hood, the legendary righter of wrongs of
Sherwood Forest' (Laroque, p. 233).

168 **thunderbolt in mine eye** In Petrarchan
verse, the conceit of a woman having the power to
wound with darts shot from her eyes is frequently
found; here Celia craves the might of Jupiter.

168 **down** fall (for the omission of verbs of
motion, see Abbott 405).

170 **breathed** exercised, warmed up.

172 In *Rosalind* the champion is killed by the
heroic Rosader. Le Beau's line may mean that
Charles is dead, although 2.2.14 suggests that
Charles was just 'foiled', i.e. victim of a trick 'in
which a skilful weak man will soon get the overhand
of one that is strong and ignorant' (Carew, *Survey of
Cornwall*, quoted in *Shakespeare's England*, II, 456).

176 The play's first switch to verse registers the
way in which the formalities of power politics are
used to cover the violence of the characters' feelings
and emotions at this point.

  178 **still** always.

  179 **Thou shouldst** You would (Abbott 322).

But fare thee well. Thou art a gallant youth:
I would thou hadst told me of another father.

[*Exeunt Duke Frederick, Le Beau, Touchstone, Lords, and Attendants*]

CELIA Were I my father, coz, would I do this?

ORLANDO I am more proud to be Sir Roland's son –
His youngest son – and would not change that calling   185
To be adopted heir to Frederick.

ROSALIND My father loved Sir Roland as his soul
And all the world was of my father's mind;
Had I before known this young man his son,
I should have given him tears unto entreaties   190
Ere he should thus have ventured.

CELIA   Gentle cousin,
Let us go thank him and encourage him;
My father's rough and envious disposition
Sticks me at heart. – Sir, you have well deserved:
If you do keep your promises in love   195
But justly, as you have exceeded all promise,
Your mistress shall be happy.

ROSALIND [*Giving him a chain from her neck*] Gentleman,
Wear this for me: one out of suits with Fortune,
That could give more, but that her hand lacks means. –
Shall we go, coz?

CELIA   Aye. – Fare you well, fair gentleman.   200

---

182 thou hadst] F thou'dst *conj. this edn*   182 SD] *Theobald subst.; Exit Duke* F   194 deserved:] *Hanmer;* deseru'd,
F   195 love] *Hanmer;* loue; F   196 justly,] *Hanmer;* justly F   196 exceeded all] F; exceeded *Hanmer;* exceeded
here *conj.* Oxford   197 SD] *Theobald (after* coz *in* 200); *not in* F   198 Fortune,] F3; fortune F   199 could] F; would
Hanmer

182 *SD In many productions Touchstone is
given Le Beau's line at 172 and exits with Charles.
183 That Rosalind does not respond to Celia's
rhetorical question suggests that she may be reflecting not only on Orlando's person but on the similarities between his fortunes and her own.
185 change exchange.
185 calling name, vocation, station in life (*OED*
sv 4, 9a, 10).
190 given him tears unto entreaties wept as
well as begged.
191 ventured put his person at risk.
191 Gentle Noble.
193 envious malicious (*OED* sv 2).
194 Sticks me at Wounds me to the (for the
omission of the definite article in adverbial phrases,
see Abbot 90).

194 have well deserved are worthy of good
reward.
196 But justly Exactly (*OED* Justly 5).
197 Your mistress Celia probably means
Rosalind specifically.
197 shall will surely (Abbott 305).
197 *SD 3.3.151 indicates that it was a chain that
Rosalind gave Orlando.
198 out of suits with Fortune no longer wearing Fortune's livery, i.e. enjoying success and happiness (see *OED* Suit *sb* 13d), although the phrase
could possibly have to do with losing at cards as Dr
Johnson thought.
199 could would.
199 hand (1) power (*OED sb* 2), (2) possibly a
'hand' of cards, although this usage is recorded only
from 1630 (*OED* sv *sb* 23).

[*They turn to go*]

ORLANDO [*Aside*] Can I not say, 'I thank you'? My better parts
 Are all thrown down, and that which here stands up
 Is but a quintain, a mere lifeless block.

ROSALIND [*To Celia*] He calls us back. My pride fell with my fortunes,
 I'll ask him what he would. – Did you call, sir?   205
 Sir, you have wrestled well and overthrown
 More than your enemies.

       [*They gaze upon each other*]

CELIA   Will you go, coz?

ROSALIND Have with you. – Fare you well.

          Exeunt [*Rosalind and Celia*]

ORLANDO What passion hangs these weights upon my tongue?
 I cannot speak to her, yet she urged conference.   210

       Enter LE BEAU

 O poor Orlando! thou art overthrown:
 Or Charles or something weaker masters thee.

LE BEAU Good sir, I do in friendship counsel you
 To leave this place. Albeit you have deserved
 High commendation, true applause, and love,   215
 Yet such is now the Duke's condition
 That he misconsters all that you have done.
 The Duke is humorous: what he is indeed
 More suits you to conceive than I to speak of.

---

200 SD] *This edn; not in* F 201 SD] *Oxford; not in* F 204 SD] *Oxford; not in* F 207 SD] *Wilson; not in* F 208 SD]
Eds.; Exit F 211 overthrown:] *Rowe³ subst.;* ouerthrowne F

201 better parts spirits.

203 quintain A butt used as a target by those riding at tilt, sometimes carved in the likeness of a Saracen or Turk (see Joseph Strutt, *The Sports and Pastimes of the People of England*, ed. William Hone, 1830, pp. 112–22).

203 mere complete.

204 He calls us back Rosalind's overhearing of Orlando's aside constitutes a kind of theatrical joke – or is evidence of her infatuation.

207 Will A subtle variation on Rosalind's question at 205.

208 Have with you I'm coming.

209 passion strong feeling.

210 conference conversation, a rendezvous (*OED* sv 4b).

212 Or Either.

212 something weaker (1) a woman (the 'weaker vessel' (1 Pet. 3.7)), (2) the feminine part of my nature.

214 deserved acquired (*OED* Deserve 1).

216 condition mood (four syllables: Cercignani, p. 309).

217 misconsters misconstrues (the spelling indicates the stress on the second syllable).

218 humorous ill-humoured (*OED* sv 3b); headstrong (Furness).

218 indeed in reality.

219 conceive understand.

219 I i.e. I choose (for the construction, see Abbott 216).

ORLANDO I thank you, sir; and pray you tell me this: 220
     Which of the two was daughter of the Duke,
     That here was at the wrestling?
LE BEAU Neither his daughter, if we judge by manners,
     But yet indeed the taller is his daughter;
     The other is daughter to the banished Duke   225
     And here detained by her usurping uncle
     To keep his daughter company, whose loves
     Are dearer than the natural bond of sisters.
     But I can tell you that of late this Duke
     Hath ta'en displeasure 'gainst his gentle niece,   230
     Grounded upon no other argument
     But that the people praise her for her virtues
     And pity her for her good father's sake;
     And, on my life, his malice 'gainst the lady
     Will suddenly break forth. Sir, fare you well,   235
     Hereafter, in a better world than this,
     I shall desire more love and knowledge of you.
ORLANDO I rest much bounden to you: fare you well.

                          [Exit Le Beau]

     Thus must I from the smoke into the smother,
     From tyrant duke unto a tyrant brother.   240
     But heavenly Rosalind!   *Exit*

---

224 taller] F; shorter *Rowe*³; smaller *Malone*; less taller *Keightley*   225 other is] F; other's *Pope*   238 SD] *Rowe; not in* F   241 Rosalind] *Rowe; Rosaline* F (*this spelling also at* 1.3.0 SD, 1.3.1, 80, 86, 2.4.0 SD)

222 was The subject is 'two', treated as a collective noun.

223 manners moral behaviour (*OED* Manner *sb*¹ 4a).

224 taller more spirited or handsome (*OED* Tall 2b, 3 which cites John Dickenson, *Greene in Conceit New Raised from his Grave* (1598): 'With her tongue she was as tall a warrioress as any of her sex'). Editorial tradition detected error, with the word bearing its modern sense: Rosalind describes herself as tall (1.3.105), and at 4.3.82 Celia is described as being 'low'. F's reading could, it was argued, be either an authorial carelessness, or a compositorial error, possibly for 'smaller' (i.e. 'more slender'), or 'shorter' which would give Le Beau a prissy rhyme with 'daughter' (see 79 n.); alternatively it could be evidence that the text was revised to match the heights of a new set of boy players (see Greg, *The*

Shakespeare First Folio, 1955, p. 297). It is apparent from the text of *MND* that Helena and Hermia were played by one tall and one 'low' boy.

227 whose Referring to both Celia and Rosalind.

230 gentle well born.

231 argument basis.

235 suddenly immediately.

236 world times.

237 knowledge friendship, intimacy (*OED* sv 6a).

238 bounden indebted.

239 Compare the proverb, 'Shunning the smoke, he fell into the fire' (Tilley s570).

239 smother smouldering or slow-burning fire (*OED* sv *sb* 1b).

241 *Rosalind F's 'Rosaline' is a compositorial idiosyncrasy (see Textual Analysis, p. 217 n. 6).

1.3 *Enter* CELIA *and* ROSALIND

CELIA Why, cousin; why, Rosalind – Cupid have mercy, not a word?

ROSALIND Not one to throw at a dog.

CELIA No, thy words are too precious to be cast away upon curs: throw some of them at me. Come, lame me with reasons.

ROSALIND Then there were two cousins laid up, when the one should   5
be lamed with reasons, and the other mad without any.

CELIA But is all this for your father?

ROSALIND No, some of it is for my child's father – O how full of briars is this working-day world!

CELIA They are but burs, cousin, thrown upon thee in holy-day foolery: 10
if we walk not in the trodden paths, our very petticoats will catch them.

ROSALIND I could shake them off my coat: these burs are in my heart.

CELIA Hem them away.

ROSALIND I would try, if I could cry 'hem' and have him.   15

CELIA Come, come, wrestle with thy affections.

ROSALIND O they take the part of a better wrestler than myself.

CELIA O, a good wish upon you: you will try in time in despite of a fall.
But turning these jests out of service, let us talk in good earnest. Is

---

Act 1, Scene 3   1.3] *Eds.; Scena Tertius.* F   8 child's father] F *subst.;* father's child *Rowe*³   10 holy-day] *Malone subst.;* holiday F   18 try] F *subst.;* cry *Sisson, 'New Readings', 1, 147*

Act 1, Scene 3

1 Cupid have mercy A literary variation upon 'God have mercy'.

2 Compare the proverb, 'He has not a word to cast at a dog' (Tilley w762).

4 reasons observations, remarks (*OED* Reason *sb* 3).

5 Then there were If I did that there would be.

6 mad without any infatuated, melancholy because she loves without reason.

8 child's father Orlando (by whom I hope to have a child); the expression seemed indelicate to earlier generations, who accepted Rowe's emendation 'father's child', i.e. 'myself'.

8–9 O . . . world Compare the proverb, 'To be in the briars' (Tilley B673), i.e. to encounter difficulties or changes of fortune.

9 working-day (1) work-day, (2) work-a-day (i.e. ordinary or 'fallen').

10 burs sticky or prickly seed-heads of various plants, including burdock; compare the proverb, 'To stick like burs' (Tilley B724).

10 in . . . foolery as a festive ritual (responding to 'working-day world').

13 coat petticoat, skirt (*OED* sv 2a).

14 Hem (1) Tuck, (2) Cough (with a pun on 'Bur in the throat', i.e. 'anything that appears to stick in the throat or that produces a choking sensation' (*OED* Bur *sb* 4).

15 cry . . . him Probably proverbial (see Dent H413.1).

15 cry 'hem' attract [Orlando's attention] with a cough; utter the bawd's warning if somebody comes by during sexual activity (Williams, p. 156; compare *Oth.* 4.2.29).

16 affections emotions.

17 take . . . of support (*OED* Part *sb* 23c).

18 a . . . upon (1) bless, (2) may Orlando mount.

18 will are determined to (*OED* sv *v*¹ B10b).

18 try . . . fall chance a bout even though you may lose (by succumbing physically to Orlando); compare the Nurse to Juliet: 'Thou wilt fall backward when thou hast more wit' (*Rom.* 1.3.42).

19 service (1) the condition of being a servant (including the chivalric service of adoring a lady by a knight in a romance), (2) sexual intercourse (Williams, p. 274).

it possible, on such a sudden, you should fall into so strong a liking   20
  with old Sir Roland's youngest son?
ROSALIND The Duke my father loved his father dearly.
CELIA Doth it therefore ensue that you should love his son dearly? By
  this kind of chase I should hate him for my father hated his father
  dearly; yet I hate not Orlando.   25
ROSALIND No, faith, hate him not, for my sake.
CELIA Why should I not? Doth he not deserve well?

Enter DUKE [FREDERICK] *with Lords*

ROSALIND Let me love him for that, and do you love him because I do.
  Look, here comes the Duke.
CELIA With his eyes full of anger.   30
DUKE FREDERICK Mistress, dispatch you with your safest haste
        And get you from our court.
ROSALIND   Me, uncle?
DUKE FREDERICK   You, cousin.
        Within these ten days if that thou be'st found
        So near our public court as twenty miles,
        Thou diest for it.
ROSALIND   I do beseech your grace   35
        Let me the knowledge of my fault bear with me:
        If with myself I hold intelligence,
        Or have acquaintance with mine own desires,

20 strong] F; strange F3   24 him for] *This edn;* him, for F   26 not,] *Eds.;* not F   27 I not?] F; I? *Theobald;* I hate
conj. Theobald; not I not *conj. this edn*   28–9] *As prose, Pope;* Ros. . . . him / Because . . . Duke. F   31 safest] F;
fastest *Collier*

20 **on such a sudden** so suddenly.
22 This line may imply that F3's 'strange' for F's
'strong' in 20 is correct.
23 **ensue** follow as a logical conclusion (*OED* sv
7).
24 **kind of chase** course of argument; perhaps
the metaphor was generated by 'dearly' ('deerly').
24 **for** because.
25 **dearly** keenly (*OED* sv 3c).
26 **faith** in truth.
27 **Why should I not** Why should I not not hate
him (i.e. love him).
27 **deserve well** merit my hate (according to this
line of reasoning).
28 **that** his virtues (Rosalind ignores Celia's
sophistry).
30 In *Rosalind* Torismond fears that one of his
peers 'who were enamoured of her beauty' might

marry her, 'and then in his wife's right attempt the
kingdom' (p. 118).
31 **Mistress** Used with contempt and anger,
although *OED* records this usage only from 1883
(13b).
31 **dispatch you** get away quickly.
31–3 **you . . . thou** The change to the singular
pronoun indicates increasing disdain.
31 **safest** Proleptic: if Rosalind were to tarry, her
life would be in danger (compare *OED* Safe *adj* 9b).
32 **cousin** Used of any near relative.
33, 39 **if that** if (Abbott 287).
34 **public** general, common.
36 **fault** offence (*OED* sv 5).
37 **hold intelligence** communicate (as between
spies).
38 **acquaintance** With a sexual connotation as
'quaint' meant female genitals (Williams, p. 252).

If that I do not dream or be not frantic
(As I do trust I am not) then, dear uncle,   40
Never so much as in a thought unborn,
Did I offend your highness.

DUKE FREDERICK   Thus do all traitors:
If their purgation did consist in words,
They are as innocent as grace itself.
Let it suffice thee that I trust thee not.   45

ROSALIND Yet your mistrust cannot make me a traitor;
Tell me whereon the likelihoods depends?

DUKE FREDERICK Thou art thy father's daughter, there's enough.

ROSALIND So was I when your highness took his dukedom,
So was I when your highness banished him;   50
Treason is not inherited, my lord,
Or if we did derive it from our friends,
What's that to me? My father was no traitor.
Then, good my liege, mistake me not so much
To think my poverty is treacherous.   55

CELIA Dear sovereign, hear me speak.

DUKE FREDERICK Aye, Celia, we stayed her for your sake,
Else had she with her father ranged along.

CELIA I did not then entreat to have her stay,
It was your pleasure – and your own remorse   60
I was too young that time to value her,

---

47 likelihoods] F; likelihood F2

39 frantic insane.

40 dear noble (*OED* sv *adj* 1a).

41–2 Never . . . highness Treason had been defined in 1350–1 by Act 25 Edw. III, Stat. 5, c. 2, as compassing or imagining the king's death (see Penry Williams, *The Tudor Regime*, 1979, pp. 375–80).

42 offend sin against, wrong (*OED* sv 3).

42 traitors (1) renegades, (2) 'traders' or whores (Rubinstein, p. 280).

43 purgation action of clearing themselves (*OED* sv 4).

43 in words 'Vulgar purgation' was performed by ordeals of fire or water, whereas 'canonical purgation' merely entailed an oath (compare 5.4.42); see William Blackstone, *Commentaries on the Laws of England*, 4 vols., 1768, IV.xxvii, 336.

44 innocent as grace Proverbial, although Tilley (T560) cites only this instance of this particular form. 'Grace' means someone in a state of grace or, possibly, the rank of duke.

47 whereon on what.

47 likelihoods indications (*OED* Likelihood 3).

47 depends For the singular termination, see Abbott 333.

48 Compare 1.2.182 where the Duke reveals his hatred of Roland for being the enemy of his son.

48 there's that's (*OED* There *adv* 3c).

52 friends relatives (*OED* Friend 3).

54 mistake misunderstand (*OED* sv *v* 4b).

55 To As to (Abbott 281).

57 stayed kept.

58 ranged roamed.

60 pleasure will, choice (*OED* sv *sb* 2).

60 remorse compassion (*OED* sv 3); although Celia may be implying that Duke Frederick was attempting to assuage his guilt for the usurpation.

61 young immature (compare 1.1.43 n.).

61 that time For the omission of 'at', see Abbott 202.

But now I know her: if she be a traitor,
Why so am I. We still have slept together,
Rose at an instant, learned, played, eat together,
And wheresoe'er we went, like Juno's swans,   65
Still we went coupled and inseparable.

DUKE FREDERICK She is too subtle for thee, and her smoothness,
Her very silence, and her patience
Speak to the people and they pity her.
Thou art a fool: she robs thee of thy name   70
And thou wilt show more bright and seem more virtuous
When she is gone.

> [*Celia starts to speak*]

Then open not thy lips!
Firm and irrevocable is my doom
Which I have passed upon her: she is banished.

CELIA Pronounce that sentence then on me, my liege,   75
I cannot live out of her company.

DUKE FREDERICK You are a fool. – You, niece, provide yourself:
If you outstay the time, upon mine honour
And in the greatness of my word, you die.

> *Exeunt Duke and Lords*

CELIA O my poor Rosalind, whither wilt thou go?   80
Wilt thou change fathers? I will give thee mine!
I charge thee be not thou more grieved than I am.

ROSALIND I have more cause.

CELIA   Thou hast not, cousin:
Prithee be cheerful. Know'st thou not the Duke
Hath banished me, his daughter?

---

66 inseparable] F; inseparate F2 *Collier*   68 her] F2; per F   71 seem] F; shine *Warburton*   72 SD] *This edn; not in*
F   72 lips!] *This edn;* lips F   79 SD] *Eds.;* Exit Duke, *&c.* F   80 whither] *Eds.;* whether F; whe'er *Pope subst.*

63 **still** always.

64 **at an instant** at the same time.

64 **eat** eaten (see Abbott 343).

65 **Juno's swans** In most mythologies it was Venus whose chariot was drawn by swans (see, for example, *Metamorphoses*, x, 831, 841): Celia may, however, have been invoking the women's capacity for virtue rather than passionate love. Brissenden cites Edgar Wind, *Pagan Mysteries in the Renaissance*, 1967, pp. 196–200, who shows that the gods sometimes partook of one another's qualities, as well as Kyd's reference to 'Juno's goodly swans', *Soliman and Perseda* (1590?), 4.1.70.

67 **subtle** sly, cunning.

67 **smoothness** plausibility (*OED* sv 3).

68 **patience** three syllables (Cercignani, p. 309).

70 **name** reputation.

71 **show** appear.

71 **virtuous** endowed with good qualities.

73 **doom** sentence.

77 **provide** prepare (*OED* sv 7b).

79 **greatness** power.

80 **whither** Probably a monosyllable (whe'er).

81 **change** exchange.

ROSALIND   That he hath not.   85

CELIA No? 'Hath not'? Rosalind lacks then the love
    Which teacheth thee that thou and I am one;
    Shall we be sundered, shall we part, sweet girl?
    No, let my father seek another heir!
    Therefore devise with me how we may fly,   90
    Whither to go, and what to bear with us;
    And do not seek to take your change upon you,
    To bear your griefs yourself and leave me out:
    For, by this heaven, now at our sorrows pale,
    Say what thou canst, I'll go along with thee.   95

ROSALIND Why, whither shall we go?

CELIA To seek my uncle in the Forest of Arden.

ROSALIND Alas, what danger will it be to us
    (Maids as we are) to travel forth so far?
    Beauty provoketh thieves sooner than gold.   100

CELIA I'll put myself in poor and mean attire
    And with a kind of umber smirch my face;
    The like do you. So shall we pass along
    And never stir assailants.

ROSALIND   Were it not better,
    Because that I am more than common tall,   105
    That I did suit me all points like a man,

---

86 No? 'Hath not'?] *Rowe*[3] *subst.;* No, hath not? F   86 Rosalind . . . then] F *subst.;* Rosalind, lacks thou then
Oxford   87 thee] F; me *Theobald*   91 Whither] F2; Whether F   92 your] F; the *Singer*   92 change] F; charge
F2   94 at] F; as *conj. this edn*   94 pale,] pale; F   104 Were it] F; Were't *Pope*

87 Compare the proverb, 'A friend is one's
second self' (Tilley F696).

87 **thee** Theobald's substitution, 'me', has been
widely followed, but F's reading could mean
'Rosalind, you are eschewing the love that instructs
you . . .'.

87 **am** The verb agrees with the nearer subject.

88 **sundered** Probably an echo of the marriage
service: 'Those whom God hath joined together, let
no man put asunder' (compare Matt. 19.6).

92–3 Compare the proverb, 'Grief is lessened
when imparted to others' (Tilley G447).

92 **change** change of fortune, although F2's
'charge' (burden) may be correct.

94 **at our sorrows pale** dimmed in sympathy
with our grief; however, if 'pale' is read as a noun,
it could mean 'at the extremity of our grief' (*OED*
Pale *sb*[1] 2c); if we were to read 'as' for 'at', the sense
would be 'as our griefs infest us'.

101 **mean** lowly.

102 **umber** brown pigment from Umbria; here
needed to conceal the pale complexions of these two
gentlewomen, which would have made them conspicuous among the country-folk.

102 **smirch** stain, smear.

104 **stir** arouse sexually (Williams, pp. 290–1).

104 **Were it not** Would it not be.

105 Compare *Rosalind*: 'I, thou seest, am of a tall
stature, and would very well become the person and
apparel of a page' (p. 123), although 'tall' could mean
'valiant' (see 1.2.224 n.).

105 **common** usually.

106 **suit me** clothe myself.

106 **all points** For the omission of 'in', see
Abbott 202.

A gallant curtal-axe upon my thigh,
A boar-spear in my hand, and in my heart
Lie there what hidden woman's fear there will.
We'll have a swashing and a martial outside   110
As many other mannish cowards have
That do outface it with their semblances.

CELIA What shall I call thee when thou art a man?

ROSALIND I'll have no worse a name than Jove's own page,
And therefore look you call me 'Ganymede'.   115
But what will you be called?

CELIA Something that hath a reference to my state:
No longer 'Celia' but 'Aliena'.

ROSALIND But, cousin, what if we assayed to steal
The clownish fool out of your father's court: 120
Would he not be a comfort to our travail?

CELIA He'll go along o'er the wide world with me:
Leave me alone to woo him. Let's away
And get our jewels and our wealth together,
Devise the fittest time and safest way   125
To hide us from pursuit that will be made

---

109 will.] *Oxford;* will, F   **116** be] F2; by F   **121** travail] F *subst.;* travell F3

107 gallant fine.

107 curtal-axe cutlass or heavy slashing sword; nineteenth-century illustrations of Rosalind generally portray her carrying a little axe.

107–8 For the sword and spear as tokens of virility, see Jones, pp. 197–8.

107 upon my thigh Changed to 'by my side' in acting editions prepared by those who thought F's original was provocative (see Knowles, p. 62).

108 boar-spear Furnished with a broad and strong blade with a cross-bar to prevent it piercing the animal completely; Spenser's Belphoebe carries the same weapon (*FQ* 2.3.29), in her case for killing the boar of lust.

109 will may (arise).

110 swashing blustering.

110 outside outer garments (Hulme, p. 336).

111 mannish pertaining to a grown man (*OED* sv *adj* 3).

112 outface it brazen things out (Abbott 226).

112 semblances false appearances.

114 Jove's own page This detail is not found in Lodge: perhaps Shakespeare wished to foreground the gender implications.

115 Ganymede A beautiful youth who, while hunting, was seized by Jupiter in the form of an eagle and became the god's cup-bearer; see *Aeneid*, v, 251–7 and *Metamorphoses*, x, 157–67. The name was used to designate a catamite (*OED* sv 2); for contemporary homo-erotic connotations, see Introduction, pp. 36–7. The word seems to have been pronounced with a short 'e' – see Christopher Marlowe, *Edward II*, ed. W. D. Briggs, 1914, p. 126.

117 state new (common) rank (*OED* sv *sb* 15).

118 Aliena The 'other' or the stranger. A Latinate pronunciation would suggest that the word should be stressed on the third syllable, although the metre here (the only occurrence of the name in a verse line) would create a stress on the second syllable.

119 assayed attempted (*OED* Assay *v* 17).

121 travail (1) labour, (2) wearisome journey.

123 Leave me alone Let me (*OED* Leave v^1 13a).

123 woo coax.

124 jewels precious ornaments.

124 wealth wordly goods.

After my flight. Now go in we content,
To liberty, and not to banishment.

Exeunt

2.1 *Enter* DUKE SENIOR, AMIENS, *and two or three* LORDS *dressed as foresters*

DUKE SENIOR Now, my co-mates and brothers in exile,
Hath not old custom made this life more sweet
Than that of painted pomp? Are not these woods
More free from peril than the envious court?
Here feel we not the penalty of Adam,   5
The seasons' difference, as the icy fang
And churlish chiding of the winter's wind –
Which when it bites and blows upon my body
Even till I shrink with cold, I smile and say,

---

127 in we] F; we in F2   **Act 2, Scene 1**   2.1] *Eds.; Actus Secundus. Scœna Prima.* F   0 SD. I AMIENS] *Eds.; Amyens* F   0 SD.1–2 dressed as] *Oxford; like* F   **5** not] F; *but Theobald*   **5** Adam,] F *subst.;* Adam; *Furness*   **6** seasons'] *Theobald subst.;* seasons F   **7** wind –] *Hudson subst.;* wind, F *subst.*   **8** bites] F; baits F3   **9** Even] F *subst.;* E'en *Yale*

127 in we F2's reversal of these words has been widely followed, but F neatly suggests both a return to their chambers and, for the actors, an exit through the tiring-house doors.

127 content contentedly.

128 liberty Possibly a metatheatrical reference to the 'liberties' on the outskirts of the City of London where the playhouses were situated.

Act 2, Scene 1

0 SD.2 foresters forest-dwellers (*OED* Forester 3); in *Rosalind* the word is used frequently to designate characters in a pastoral or 'forest' tale. Their presence rather than any scenic device establishes the setting.

1 exile Accented on the second syllable (Cercignani, p. 38).

2–3 Compare the proverb, 'Custom makes all things easy' (Tilley C933).

2 old custom (1) habitual (or good, hallowed) practice (*OED* Old *adj* 6; Custom *sb* 1), (2) the ways of this long-established pastoral culture.

3 painted pomp false and boastful show.

4 free from peril Forests could in fact be dangerous places in early modern England.

4 envious malicious; Envy is the Prologue to Jonson's court play *Poetaster* (1601).

5 Theobald's emendation (see collation) is attractive, but we can retain F's reading by either construing this line as part of a rhetorical question, or understanding 'feel we not' as 'are not bothered by' rather than 'do not experience'. 'The penalty of Adam' is less likely to be simply 'the loss of Eden' than 'God's curse upon the earth and the toil of cultivation' (see Gen. 3.17–23). The Duke may therefore mean that Arden provides game in such numbers that there is no need to labour to eat. In the Epistle to Leicester, Ovid's translator, Arthur Golding, equates the Golden Age with Paradise, and notes how, after the fall, 'both heat and cold did vex [Adam] sore' (*Metamorphoses*, Epistle, 474); compare *Paradise Lost*, x, 201–8 and x, 678–9 where Milton describes the loss of 'spring Perpetual', one of the attributes of the Golden Age in antiquity which disappeared with the imposition of the Silver Age (*Metamorphoses*, 1, 122–40). The Duke and his fellows do not experience any sense of loss after explusion from their 'Eden', the court.

6 difference (1) change, (2) contention.

6 as namely (Abbott 113).

7 churlish rude, violent.

7 chiding angry noise.

8 Which As to which (Abbott 272).

'This is no flattery' – these are counsellors   10
That feelingly persuade me what I am.
Sweet are the uses of adversity
Which like the toad, ugly and venomous,
Wears yet a precious jewel in his head,
And this our life exempt from public haunt   15
Finds tongues in trees, books in the running brooks,
Sermons in stones, and good in everything.
AMIENS I would not change it; happy is your grace
That can translate the stubbornness of Fortune
Into so quiet and so sweet a style.   20
DUKE SENIOR Come, shall we go and kill us venison?
And yet it irks me the poor dappled fools,
Being native burghers of this desert city,
Should, in their own confines, with forkèd heads
Have their round haunches gored.
I LORD   Indeed, my lord.   25

---

10 flattery –] *Hudson subst.;* flattery: F   18] F *subst.;* I . . . it. / AMIENS Happy . . . grace *White*

11 **feelingly** (1) by experience, (2) intensely.

11 **persuade** impress upon (*OED* sv *v* 3).

12 Compare Ecclus. 2.5: 'For as gold and silver are tried in the fire, even so are men acceptable in the furnace of adversity', and the proverb, 'Adversity makes men wise' (Tilley A42).

13 **toad . . . venomous** Toads were proverbially poisonous (Tilley T360); the notion goes back to Pliny, *Natural History*, xxv.

14 **yet** nevertheless, always.

14 **jewel** For this fabled 'toadstone' which was reputed to serve as an antidote to the toad's venom, see *OED* Toad 1, and Brewer, pp. 1232–3.

15 **exempt** free (*OED* sv *adj* 6).

15 **haunt** resort (*OED* sv *sb* 2).

16–17 For Richard Hooker on the necessity of books of God, sermons ('keys to the kingdom of heaven'), and the way that divine knowledge revealed through the works of nature does not constitute a saving wisdom, see *Laws of Ecclesiastical Polity* (1592–7), v.21–2.

16 **tongues** discourses, languages, with a possible reference to speaking with tongues (1 Cor. 12.30).

16 **tongues in trees** For this commonplace, see Curtius, p. 337.

18 See collation; if the first part of the line is reassigned to the Duke, Amiens appears as only a reluctant co-mate in exile.

18 **change** (1) alter, (2) exchange.

19 **translate** (1) transform, (2) rewrite.

19 **stubbornness** obstinate harshness.

20 **style** (1) manner of expression, (2) way of life (*OED* sv *sb* 19b).

21–5 **Come . . . gored** King James regarded the use of guns and bows as opposed to running hounds 'a thievish form of hunting' (King James, *Political Writings*, ed. Johann P. Sommerville, 1994, p. 56).

21 **venison** Any beast of the chase, taken only by permission of the king (John Manwood, *A Treatise of the Laws of the Forest* (1592), f.29^{r-v}).

22 **fools** simple creatures (regarded with endearment – see *OED* Fool *sb* 1c).

23 **burghers** inhabitants.

23 **desert** uninhabited.

24 **confines** territory (accented on the second syllable (Cercignani, p. 38)).

24 **forkèd heads** (1) arrow-heads with 'points stretching forwards' (R. Ascham, *Toxophilus* (1545), *English Works*, ed. W. A. Wright, 1904, p. 93), (2) the horns of a cuckold.

25 SH There is evidence in many acting versions that, following Charles Johnson's *Love in a Forest* (1723), the lines of this character were, with necessary emendations, in performance reassigned to Jaques (Odell, I, 245; II, 23).

The melancholy 'Jacques' grieves at that,
And in that kind swears you do more usurp
Than doth your brother that hath banished you.
Today my lord of Amiens and myself
Did steal behind him as he lay along   30
Under an oak, whose antique root peeps out
Upon the brook that brawls along this wood,
To the which place a poor sequestered stag,
That from the hunter's aim had ta'en a hurt,
Did come to languish; and indeed, my lord,   35
The wretched animal heaved forth such groans
That their discharge did stretch his leathern coat
Almost to bursting, and the big round tears
Coursed one another down his innocent nose
In piteous chase; and thus the hairy fool,   40
Much markèd of the melancholy Jaques,
Stood on th'extremest verge of the swift brook,
Augmenting it with tears.

DUKE SENIOR   But what said Jaques?
Did he not moralise this spectacle?

---

26 'Jacques'] *This edn;* Jacques *Eds.;* Iaques F (*throughout*)   31 antique] *Pope;* anticke F   34 hunter's] *Pope;* Hunters F

---

26 melancholy afflicted by an excess of the humour of black bile; melancholy was a fashionable affectation at the time of the play's composition; compare the association of melancholy with a privy in Jonson's *Every Man in his Humour* (1616) where Stephen asks for 'a stool . . . to be melancholy upon' (3.1.100), a scabrous gesture towards the traditional pose of Melancholy in illustrations of the period (see R. Klibansky, E. Panofsky, and F. Saxl, *Saturn and Melancholy*, 1964, pp. 286–9).

26 *Jacques' The metre indicates that here the First Lord pronounces the name as a disyllable, perhaps mockingly (see List of Characters, pp. 71–2 n.); at 41, 43, 54 the name is monosyllabic.

26 grieves (1) laments, (2) grows angry (*OED* Grieve 7).

27 in that kind accordingly.

30 along at full length; a fashionable pose by a melancholic (see Roy Strong, 'The Elizabethan Malady', in *The English Icon: Elizabethan and Jacobean Portraiture*, 1969, pp. 352–3).

31 antique (1) ancient, (2) grotesquely shaped ('antic'), accented on the first syllable (Cercignani, p. 34).

32 brawls runs noisily or, possibly, waveringly (*OED* Brawl v^2).

33–5 Compare the proverb, 'As the stricken deer withdraws himself to die' (Tilley D189).

33 sequestered separated.

33 stag five-year-old male deer.

35 languish sink and pine away (Schmidt).

38 and the big round tears The detail of the tears falling into the brook may be taken from the tale of Actaeon, who died after being transformed into a stag, having seen Diana bathing (*Metamorphoses*, III, 207–304); for other figures of Actaeon, see Leo Salingar, *Shakespeare and the Traditions of Comedy*, 1974, p. 236.

38 tears 'The hart weepeth at his dying, his tears are held to be precious in medicine' (Drayton, *Polyolbion*, Thirteenth Song, marginal note).

39 Coursed Chased.

40 fool (1) dupe, (2) a term of endearment (see 22 n. above).

41 markèd of noted by.

41 Jaques See 26 n.

42 extremest furthest, i.e. closest to the stream.

44 moralise this spectacle read the sight as a moral emblem; see Claus Uhlig, '"The sobbing deer": *As You Like It*, II.i.21–66 and the historical context', *Ren. Drama* n.s. 3 (1970), 79–110, for the relationship between this passage, emblem books,

1 LORD O yes, into a thousand similes.   45
            First, for his weeping in the needless stream:
            'Poor deer', quoth he, 'thou mak'st a testament
            As worldlings do, giving thy sum of more
            To that which hath too much.' Then, being there alone,
            Left and abandoned of his velvet friend: 50
            ''Tis right', quoth he, 'thus misery doth part
            The flux of company.' Anon a careless herd,
            Full of the pasture, jumps along by him
            And never stays to greet him. 'Aye', quoth Jaques,
            'Sweep on you fat and greasy citizens,   55
            'Tis just the fashion. Wherefore do you look
            Upon that poor and broken bankrupt there?'
            Thus most invectively he pierceth through
            The body of country, city, court,
            Yea, and of this our life, swearing that we   60

---

46 in] *Pope;* into F   49 hath] *Collier;* had F   49 much] F2; must F   49 being there] F; being F2   50 friend] F; friends *Rowe*   51 thus] F; this *Reed*   56 do] F; should *Oxford; conj. Proudfoot*   59 of] F; of the F2   60 and of] F; and F3

and hunting as usurpation; also E. Michael Thron, 'Jaques: emblems and morals', *SQ* 30 (1979), 84–9; for anti-hunting sentiments in the period, see Keith Thomas, *Man and the Natural World*, 1983, pp. 161–3; see also Michael Bath, 'Weeping stags and melancholy lovers . . . ', *Emblematica* 1 (1986), 13–52.

45 similes comparisons.

46 for his as concerning the deer's.

46 *in into (Abbott 159); Pope's emendation may be justified by conjecturing that the compositor caught 'into' from the previous line.

46 needless not in need (for adjectives used with both an active and passive sense, see Abbott 3).

47–9 On 19 March 1601 John Manningham saw a scutcheon at the Shield Gallery in Whitehall, aspects of which resemble this part of Jaques' moralisation: 'A stag, having cast his head [horns] and standing amazedly, weeping over them; the word over, *Inermis et deformis* [Unarmed and unsightly]; under, *Cur dolent habentes* [Why those that have grieve]' (*The Diary of John Manningham*, ed. Robert Parker Sorlien, 1976, p. 33).

47 testament will; P. J. Frankis, *Neuphilologische Mitteilungen* 59 (1958), 65–8, traces the commonplace of the will-making deer back to certain medieval texts.

48 worldlings people who are devoted to things material; bequeathing wealth to others more wealthy in the hope that they would reciprocate (and then

die first) is one of the tricks deployed by Jonson's Volpone.

48 sum of more superabundance.

49 *hath too much The emendations of Collier and F2 (see collation) are supported by a similar passage in *3H6*: 'With tearful eyes . . . give more strength to that which hath too much' (5.4.8–9).

50 of by (Abbott 170).

50 velvet (1) carrying the 'velvet' of new antlers, (2) richly dressed (like wealthy burghers).

50 friend Although Rowe's emendation (see collation) has been widely followed, the 'friend' could be the stag's heir, described in 48–9.

51–2 misery . . . company Compare the proverb, 'Poverty parts good company' (Tilley P529); for biblical analogues, see Shaheen, p. 161.

52 flux continuous stream (*OED* sv 5b).

52 careless (1) carefree, (2) uncaring.

54 stays pauses, stops.

55 greasy (1) prime and ready for killing – compare the hunting term 'in grease' (*OED* Grease *sb* 1b), (2) opulent.

55 citizens In *Britannia's Pastorals* (1613–16), William Browne describes wild beasts as 'this forest's citizens' (1.1.510).

56–7 look Upon detach yourselves from (compare *Tro.* 5.6.10); alternatively, 'Wherefore do' could mean 'Why should'.

57 broken (1) injured, (2) ruined.

58 most invectively in the most bitter terms.

Are mere usurpers, tyrants, and what's worse,
To fright the animals and to kill them up
In their assigned and native dwelling-place.

DUKE SENIOR And did you leave him in this contemplation?

2 LORD We did, my lord, weeping and commenting   65
Upon the sobbing deer.

DUKE SENIOR   Show me the place;
I love to cope him in these sullen fits,
For then he's full of matter.

1 LORD   I'll bring you to him straight.

Exeunt

2.2 *Enter* DUKE [FREDERICK] *with* LORDS

DUKE FREDERICK Can it be possible that no man saw them?
It cannot be: some villeins of my court
Are of consent and sufferance in this.

1 LORD I cannot hear of any that did see her;
The ladies, her attendants of her chamber,   5
Saw her abed and, in the morning early,
They found the bed untreasured of their mistress.

2 LORD My lord, the roinish clown, at whom so oft
Your grace was wont to laugh, is also missing.
Hisperia, the princess' gentlewoman,   10
Confesses that she secretly o'erheard

---

62 and to] F; and *Capell*   65 SH] F *subst.*; AMIENS *Capell*; 1 *Lord.* / *Rann*   68 SH] F *subst.*; 2 *Lor.* F3   Act 2,
Scene 2   2.2] *Eds.*; *Scena Secunda.* F   2 villeins] *This edn*; villaines F

61 **mere** absolute.
61 **tyrants** usurpers (*OED* Tyrant 1): a figure for
the political usurpation by Duke Frederick.
61 **what's worse** whatever is worse than these.
62 **To** In that we.
62 **kill them up** exterminate (*OED* Kill *v* 4).
63 **assigned** legally owned.
65 **commenting** meditating (*OED* Comment *v*
5).
67 **cope** meet, debate with.
67 **sullen** dark, gloomy.
68 **matter** good sense (*OED* sv *sb*¹ 11b).
68 **straight** immediately.

Act 2, Scene 2
2 **villeins** (1) servants, retainers (*OED* Villein
1b), (2) evil-doers.

3 **Are accessories** (*OED* Consent *sb* 1b) and have
allowed this to happen.
5 **her attendants of her chamber** For the construction, see Abbott 423.
7 **untreasured** robbed.
8 **roinish** covered with scale or scurf, hence
scurvy, base.
8 **clown** jester (here contemptuous).
10 **Hisperia** As in *Lear* there is no mention
of the mothers of Rosalind and Celia, and this
character is the only named court lady; in many
productions an unwilling and contrite Hisperia is
dragged on stage.

Your daughter and her cousin much commend
The parts and graces of the wrestler
That did but lately foil the sinewy Charles;
And she believes, wherever they are gone,   15
That youth is surely in their company.
DUKE FREDERICK Send to his brother: 'Fetch that gallant hither.'
If he be absent, bring his brother to me –
I'll make him find him. Do this suddenly,
And let not search and inquisition quail   20
To bring again these foolish runaways.

Exeunt

2.3 *Enter* ORLANDO

ORLANDO Who's there?

[*Enter* ADAM]

ADAM What, my young master! O my gentle master,
O my sweet master, O you memory
Of old Sir Roland, why, what make you here?
Why are you virtuous? Why do people love you?   5
And wherefore are you gentle, strong, and valiant?
Why would you be so fond to overcome

---

17 brother:] *This edn, conj. Andrews;* brother, F; brother's, *Capell*   Act 2, Scene 3 2.3] *Eds.; Scena Tertia.* F   0
SD] *This edn; Enter Orlando and Adam* F   1 SD] *This edn; not in* F

13 **parts and graces** good qualities and behaviour.

13 **wrestler** Trisyllabic (Abbott 477).

14 **foil** throw (*OED sv v* 4).

14 **sinewy** well-developed, strong.

17 The elliptical syntax has made Capell's emendation attractive to editors.

17 **gallant** i.e. Orlando.

18 **brother** i.e. Oliver, although this could conceivably be a reference to Jacques de Boys, the second brother.

19 **suddenly** immediately.

20 **inquisition** investigation; the word may have reminded Elizabethan audiences of the Papal 'Holy Office' or Inquisition, set up in the thirteenth century for the suppression of heresy.

20 **quail** fail.

21 **again** back.

21 **foolish runaways** i.e. Celia and Rosalind, half-forgiven by Duke Frederick in his anxiety to capture Orlando.

Act 2, Scene 3

0 *SD, 1 *SD Adjusting the stage directions in this way (see collation) obviates the need for a door; alternatively Orlando could enter by one door onto the stage and knock at the other (see Hattaway, pp. 25–6).

1 **Who's there?** Who is within?

2 **What** Expresses excitement (*OED sv int* B3).

2 **gentle** noble.

3 **memory** likeness, reminder.

4 **make you** are you doing.

4 **here** i.e. at the family estate.

7 **fond** imprudent, foolish.

The bonny prizer of the humorous Duke?
Your praise is come too swiftly home before you.
Know you not, master, to some kind of men   10
Their graces serve them but as enemies?
No more do yours: your virtues, gentle master,
Are sanctified and holy traitors to you.
O what a world is this when what is comely
Envenoms him that bears it!   15

ORLANDO Why, what's the matter?

ADAM   O unhappy youth,
Come not within these doors: within this roof
The enemy of all your graces lives
Your brother – no, no brother – yet the son –
Yet not the son, I will not call him son   20
Of him I was about to call his father –
Hath heard your praises, and this night he means
To burn the lodging where you use to lie
And you within it. If he fail of that,
He will have other means to cut you off: 25
I overheard him and his practices.
This is no place, this house is but a butchery:
Abhor it, fear it, do not enter it.

---

8 bonny] F *subst.;* bony *Warburton subst.*   10 some] F2*;* seeme F   16 SH] ORLANDO F2 *subst; not in* F   17 within]
F*;* beneath *conj. Capell*   18 lives] F*;* lives, *Eds.*

8 **bonny** stout, strapping (*OED* 2a).
8 **prizer** one who fights in a 'prize' or match.
8 **humorous** capricious (*OED* 3a).
9 **praise** merit, reputation.
10 **kind of men** For the construction, see Abbott 410.
11 **graces** virtues.
11 **them** A redundant object (Abbott 414).
12 **No more do yours** Yours do no less.
12–13 **your . . . you** Compare Ps. 37.32: 'The wicked watcheth the righteous, and seeketh to slay him.'
13 **sanctified** sanctimonious (*OED* sv 2).
14 **what a world is this** Proverbial (Dent w889.1).
14 **comely** becoming.
14–15 **when . . . it** A possible reference to the shirt given by Nessus, a centaur wounded by Hercules, to Deïanira the betrayed wife of the hero, and which, smeared with poison from the blood of the Hydra, clung to Hercules' skin and caused him great pain (*Metamorphoses*, IX, 121 ff.).
15 **Envenoms** Poisons.

17 **within this** Capell's conjecture 'beneath this' is attractive, given that the compositor may have caught 'within' from earlier in the line. However, 'roof' is readily taken as a synecdoche for 'dwelling' (*OED* Roof 1c).
18 **graces** virtues, fortunes.
18 **lives** lives as (*OED* Live *v* 7).
19–21 Adam is loath to admit that Oliver can be brother to Orlando or son to Sir Roland.
22 **your praises** the praise of you.
23 **lodging** dwelling-place.
23 **use** are accustomed (*OED* sv *v* 20).
24 **fail of** fails to do; for the construction, see Abbott 177.
25 **cut you off** kill you.
26 **practices** plotting (*OED* Practice 6c).
27 **place** (1) fit place (*OED* sv *sb*[1] 12a), (2) dwelling, mansion (?) (*OED* sv *sb*[1] 5b).
27 **butchery** slaughter-house.
28 **Abhor** Loathe (possibly with the etymological sense of 'shrinking back from with shuddering' (*OED* sv 1)).

ORLANDO Why whither, Adam, wouldst thou have me go?

ADAM No matter whither, so you come not here.   30

ORLANDO What, wouldst thou have me go and beg my food,
       Or with a base and boisterous sword enforce
       A thievish living on the common road?
       This I must do or know not what to do;
       Yet this I will not do, do how I can.   35
       I rather will subject me to the malice
       Of a diverted blood and bloody brother.

ADAM But do not so: I have five hundred crowns,
       The thrifty hire I saved under your father,
       Which I did store to be my foster-nurse   40
       When service should in my old limbs lie lame
       And unregarded age in corners thrown;
       Take that, and He that doth the ravens feed,
       Yea providently caters for the sparrow,
       Be comfort to my age. Here is the gold: 45
       All this I give you; let me be your servant –
       Though I look old, yet I am strong and lusty;
       For in my youth I never did apply
       Hot and rebellious liquors in my blood,
       Nor did not with unbashful forehead woo   50

---

29 SH] F2 *subst; Ad.* F   37 blood] F*; proud* Collier

30 **so** as long as.

32 **base** mean (*OED* sv *adj* 13).

32 **boisterous** massive, cumbrous (*OED* sv 3).

33 **common** public.

35 **do how I can** whatever may befall me.

36 **malice** harmfulness, hatred (*OED* sv 2, 4).

37 **diverted blood** 'blood turned out of the course of nature' (Johnson).

37 **bloody** blood-thirsty, cruel (*OED* sv 6).

38 **five hundred crowns** There were four crowns to a pound; the sum is rhetorical and the level of Adam's savings unlikely, given that wages for a serving-man seem to have been about £2 per annum (D. M. Palliser, *The Age of Elizabeth: England under the Later Tudors, 1547–1603*, 1983, p. 151). However, if Adam was, like his original in *Rosalind*, a steward, he may have earned twice that amount.

39 **thrifty hire** wages saved by my thrift.

41 **service** my ability to act as a servant.

42 **thrown** should be thrown (Abbott 403).

43 **that** i.e. the five hundred crowns.

43 **doth the ravens feed** Compare Ps. 147.9, 'Which giveth to beasts their food and to the young ravens that cry'; other references to God feeding ravens are in Luke 12.24 and Job 39.3.

44 Compare Luke 12.6, 'Are not five sparrows bought for two farthings, and yet not one of them is forgotten before God?', and *Ham.* 5.2.219–20: 'There is special providence in the fall of a sparrow.'

44 **providently** providentially (*OED* sv 2).

47 **strong ... lusty** The phrase inverts the order and meaning of Ps. 73.4, 'For there are no bands in their death, but they are lusty and strong.'

47 **lusty** vigorous.

48–9 **apply ... in** make use of (as a medicine).

49 **rebellious** causing the flesh to rebel (against the faculty of reason), a transferred epithet (*OED* sv 1c).

50 **Nor ... not** This double negative does not, as often in Shakespeare, generate a positive sense (see Abbott 406).

50 **unbashful forehead** shameless countenance; compare the proverb, 'To have an impudent forehead' (Dent F590.1).

The means of weakness and debility;
Therefore my age is as a lusty winter,
Frosty but kindly. Let me go with you:
I'll do the service of a younger man
In all your business and necessities.   55

ORLANDO O good old man, how well in thee appears
The constant service of the antique world,
When service sweat for duty not for meed.
Thou art not for the fashion of these times
Where none will sweat but for promotion   60
And, having that, do choke their service up
Even with the having. It is not so with thee;
But, poor old man, thou prun'st a rotten tree
That cannot so much as a blossom yield,
In lieu of all thy pains and husbandry.   65
But come thy ways: we'll go along together
And, ere we have thy youthful wages spent,
We'll light upon some settled low content.

ADAM Master, go on, and I will follow thee
To the last gasp with truth and loyalty.   70
From seventeen years till now almost fourscore
Here lived I, but now live here no more.
At seventeen years many their fortunes seek,
But at fourscore it is too late a week;

---

57 service] F; favour *Collier*² ; fashion *Keightley*   58 service] F; labour *conj. this edn*   71 seventeen] *Rowe;* seauentie F

51 Womankind; it was commonly argued that ejaculation weakened a man – see Michael Hattaway, 'Fleshing his will in the spoil of her honour . . .', *S.Sur.*, 46 (1994), 121–36. Adam ascribes his vigour in old age to teetotalism and chastity.

52 lusty bracing.

53 Frosty Adam may be referring to a white beard or hair.

53 kindly genial, pleasant (*OED* sv 5b, 6).

57 constant (1) unchanging, (2) faithful.

57–8 service . . . service The repetition suggests possible compositorial corruption (see collation).

57 antique ancient, former (see 2.1.31 n.).

58 service servants (see *OED* sv *sb*¹ 3a and b).

58 sweat worked (for the form, see Abbott 341).

58 meed reward dishonestly offered or accepted (*OED* sv *sb* 2).

60 promotion Pronounced with four syllables (Cercignani, p. 308).

61–2 having . . . having 'Even with the promotion gained by service is service extinguished' (Johnson); compare the garden metaphors in Matt. 7.17: 'So every good tree bringeth forth good fruit, and a corrupt tree bringeth forth evil fruit', and Matt. 13.22: 'the care of this world and the deceitfulness of riches choke the word'.

65 lieu of return for (*OED* Lieu 1).

67 youthful earned in youth.

68 low content humble way of life (see *OED* Content *sb*² 3).

69 thee After speaking to Adam in such a kindly manner, Orlando is addressed by his servant in the familiar form.

71 *seventeen Rowe's emendation is justified by 73.

74 too late a week far too late (*OED* Week 6b: the only example in this sense, so probably a nonce-use for the rhyme).

Yet Fortune cannot recompense me better   75
Than to die well and not my master's debtor.

Exeunt

2.4 *Enter* ROSALIND [*in man's attire as*] GANYMEDE, CELIA [*as a
shepherdess*] ALIENA, *and* [*the*] *clown* TOUCHSTONE [*in the costume
of a retainer*]

ROSALIND O Jupiter, how merry are my spirits!
TOUCHSTONE I care not for my spirits, if my legs were not weary.
ROSALIND [*Aside*] I could find in my heart to disgrace my man's apparel
      and to cry like a woman; but I must comfort the weaker vessel, as
      doublet and hose ought to show itself courageous to petticoat;   5
      therefore – courage, good Aliena!
CELIA I pray you bear with me, I cannot go no further.
TOUCHSTONE For my part, I had rather bear with you than bear you;
      yet I should bear no cross if I did bear you, for I think you have no
      money in your purse.   10
ROSALIND Well, this is the Forest of Arden.

Act 2, Scene 4   2.4] *Eds.; Scena Quarta.* F   0 SD.1–2] *This edn; Enter Rosaline for Ganimed, Celia for Aliena, and
Clowne, alias* Touchstone. F   1 merry] F*; weary Theobald*   3 SD] *This edn; not in* F   5 to petticoat] F *subst.; to a
F3*   6 therefore –] *Furness;* therefore F   7 cannot] F*; can F2*

76 die . . . debtor Compare the proverb, 'I will
not die your debtor' (Tilley D165): Adam does not
wish to die owing his master anything.

Act 2, Scene 4

0 SD.2–3 *in . . . retainer* F's '*alias*' (see collation)
suggests that 'Touchstone' is a forest name; moreover, the fact that he is not recognised by the rustics
as a professional suggests that he did *not* wear motley in Arden (compare 2.7.13 n.) – Jaques refers to
him as 'motley-minded' (5.4.39). Henslowe, in an
inventory of 1598, lists as well as 'one fool's coat,
cap, and bauble', 'one yellow leather doublet for a
clown' (p. 318).
1 Jupiter Jupiter, to whom Ganymede was cup-
bearer, was renowned for his sanguine temperament which engendered a cheerful (Jovial) disposition, the opposite of Jaques' melancholy (Saturnine)
disposition.
1 merry Theobald's emendation 'weary' is
tempting, but F's reading can stand if we assume
that Rosalind is rejoicing in adversity – or being
ironic.

3 *SD] Instead of taking these lines as an aside,
Rosalind might direct them to Touchstone.
3 disgrace shame (*OED* sv *v* 2).
4 weaker vessel The phrase occurs in 1 Pet. 3.7
('Likewise, ye husbands, dwell with them as men of
knowledge, giving honour unto the woman, as unto
the weaker vessel') and became proverbial (Tilley
W655).
5 doublet and hose Typical male attire; a doublet was a close-fitting garment for the body, hose
were long stockings or close-fitting breeches.
5 petticoat representative female attire (*OED* 4),
worn either under a skirt or, if decorated, above.
7 cannot . . . no For the double negative, see
Abbott 406.
8 bear With a sexually suggestive secondary
meaning (Williams, p. 39).
9 cross (1) burden, (2) affront, (3) silver coin
marked with a cross; compare Luke 14.27: 'And
whosoever beareth not his cross, and cometh after
me, cannot be my disciple.'
11 As Elizabethan playhouses were not designed
for scenic illusion, this stands as a theatrical joke.

TOUCHSTONE Aye, now am I in Arden, the more fool I! When I was at
home I was in a better place; but travellers must be content.

Enter CORIN *and* SILVIUS

ROSALIND Aye, be so, good Touchstone. Look you who comes here:
    A young man and an old in solemn talk.   15
CORIN That is the way to make her scorn you still.
SILVIUS O Corin, that thou knew'st how I do love her.
CORIN I partly guess, for I have loved ere now.
SILVIUS No, Corin, being old, thou canst not guess,
    Though in thy youth thou wast as true a lover   20
    As ever sighed upon a midnight pillow.
    But if thy love were ever like to mine –
    As sure I think did never man love so –
    How many actions most ridiculous
    Hast thou been drawn to by thy fantasy?   25
CORIN Into a thousand that I have forgotten.
SILVIUS O thou didst then never love so heartily.
    If thou remembrest not the slightest folly
    That ever love did make thee run into,
    Thou hast not loved.   30
    Or if thou hast not sat as I do now,
    Wearing thy hearer in thy mistress' praise,
    Thou hast not loved.
    Or if thou hast not broke from company
    Abruptly as my passion now makes me,   35

14–15] *As verse, Capell; prose* F   **14 here:**] *This edn;* here, F; here? *Capell*   **28 slightest**] F; slighted *Rowe*   **32**
Wearing] F; Wearying F2

12 Arden Punning on 'a den', here meaning a
hole or vagina: compare 'MERCUTIO God ye good
den [evening], fair gentlewoman. / NURSE Is it good
den? / MERCUTIO 'Tis no less, I tell ye, for the
bawdy hand of the dial is now upon the prick of
noon' (*Rom.* 2.4.110–13). Alternatively there is a
pun on 'harden', 'a coarse fabric made from the
hards of flax or hemp' (*OED* sv *sb*).

12 the more fool I Proverbial (Dent F505.1).

13 travellers Possibly with a pun on 'travailers',
labourers: both senses generate a bawdy meaning of
visiting or toiling in strange places.

16 The dialogue that follows between Corin and
Silvius is like the discourse between Thenot and
Cuddy in the February Eclogue of Spenser's *Shep-
heardes Calender* (1579).

22 were The subjunctive form in a conditional
clause.

23 As For to be (*OED* As *conj* 8d).

25 fantasy (1) imagination (*OED* sv 4), (2)
desire, liking (*OED* sv 7).

32 Wearing Exhausting (*OED* Wear *v* 10a); this
may, however, be a spelling of 'wearying' (see
Hulme, p. 319).

32 in with (*OED prep* 13).

34 broke escaped (for the dropped '-en' inflection, see Abbott 343).

35 Abruptly Interruptedly, with sudden breaks
(*OED* sv 2, although the usage is recorded only from
1607).

35 passion pain in love.

Thou hast not loved.

O Phoebe, Phoebe, Phoebe!   *Exit*

ROSALIND Alas, poor shepherd, searching of thy wound,
I have by hard adventure found mine own.

TOUCHSTONE And I mine: I remember when I was in love, I broke my   40
sword upon a stone and bid him take that for coming a-night to Jane
Smile; and I remember the kissing of her batler and the cow's dugs
that her pretty chapped hands had milked; and I remember the
wooing of a peasecod instead of her, from whom I took two cods
and, giving her them again, said with weeping tears, 'Wear these for   45
my sake.' We that are true lovers run into strange capers; but as all
is mortal in Nature, so is all nature in love mortal in folly.

ROSALIND Thou speak'st wiser than thou art ware of.

TOUCHSTONE Nay, I shall ne'er be ware of mine own wit till I break my
shins against it.   50

36–7] F *subst.; one line, Capell subst.*   38 thy wound] *Rowe;* they would F; their wound F2   42 batler] F; batlet
F2   43 chapped] *Eds.;* chopt F   44 cods] F; peas *Johnson*

37 Phoebe The name is an epithet for the moon-goddess Artemis (or Diana) (*Metamorphoses*, 1, 575; *MND* 1.1.209), who was associated with hunting and virginity.

38 searching of probing.

38 of For the construction (which reveals that 'searching' was taken as a verbal noun), see Abbott 178.

38 *thy wound Rowe's emendation completes a partial correction in F2 of an obvious error (see collation: a compositorial misreading of woūde?).

39 hard adventure bad fortune.

39 mine own For 'wound' meaning vagina, the meaning Touchstone picks up, see Partridge, pp. 221–2.

40–2 I . . . Smile A smutty anecdote that involves punishment of Touchstone's penis either for leading him nightly to his mistress or for ejaculating in her presence (for 'come' in this sense, see 1.2.23 n., Williams, p. 75).

41 him Either Touchstone's sword or the stone: if the latter, there is a continuation of the bawdy since 'stone' was colloquial for testicle. This may also be a reference to the tavern fool, John Stone (Chambers, III, 369), a rival for the love of Jane Smile.

41 a-night at night (Abbott 24).

42 batler wooden paddle or beetle used for washing clothes (see *OED* Battle *v*⁴) or, if small, for making butter – and 'batler', like milking, had bawdy

connotations; F2's 'batlet' may be a Warwickshire form used by Shakespeare (see Knowles, p. 93).

43 *chapped F's 'chopt' is an obsolete form (*OED* Chopped *ppl adj*¹).

44 peasecod pea-pod, here a synecdoche for 'pea-plant' (a sense not recorded in *OED*); for the association of peas with fertility and their use in wooing rituals, see Brewer, p. 954 and Brand, II, 99; given the mention of the 'two cods' in the next line, there is implicit play here on the reversed form 'cod-piece' (Williams, p. 231).

44 whom the pea-plant.

44 cods (1) husks, pods, (2) testicles (*OED* Cod *sb*¹ 4).

45 weeping tears abundant weeping (*OED* Weeping *ppl adj* 3a).

46 capers frolicsome leaps, fantastic situations, acts of copulation (Williams, pp. 62–3; with a pun on *caper* Latin for 'goat', proverbially lecherous).

46–7 all . . . folly all that lives must die, so all those who love are bound to do foolish things.

48 Compare the proverb, 'There is more in it than you are ware of' (Tilley M1158).

48 thou art ware of you know.

49–50 Compare the proverb, 'Fools set stools for wise men to break their shins' (Tilley F543) and the saying, 'To break one's shins' (Dent S342.1) which, given that 'wit' means wisdom and penis (Williams, p. 341), suggests a 'sexual mishap' (Williams, p. 52).

49 ware (1) apprehensive, (2) aware.

ROSALIND Jove, Jove, this shepherd's passion
   Is much upon my fashion.
TOUCHSTONE And mine, but it grows something stale with me.
CELIA I pray you, one of you question yond man
   If he for gold will give us any food: 55
   I faint almost to death.
TOUCHSTONE Holla, you, clown!
ROSALIND Peace, fool; he's not thy kinsman.
CORIN Who calls?
TOUCHSTONE Your betters, sir.   60
CORIN Else are they very wretched.
ROSALIND [*To Touchstone*] Peace, I say. – Good even to you, friend.
CORIN And to you, gentle sir, and to you all.
ROSALIND I prithee, shepherd, if that love or gold
   Can in this desert place buy entertainment,   65
   Bring us where we may rest ourselves and feed.
   Here's a young maid with travel much oppressed
   And faints for succour.
CORIN   Fair sir, I pity her
   And wish, for her sake more than for mine own,
   My fortunes were more able to relieve her;   70
   But I am shepherd to another man,
   And do not shear the fleeces that I graze.

51–2] F *subst.; As prose, Pope* 62 SD] *Oxford; not in* F 62 you, friend] F2*;* your friend F 67 travel] F3 *subst.;* trauaile
F 72 shear] *Eds.;* sheere F*;* share *Johnson²*

51–2 Pope may have been right to regard this as prose; the rhyme, however, may indicate a whimsical couplet.

51 passion love.

52 upon after.

53 something somewhat (Abbott 68).

53 stale A possible pun on 'stale' meaning 'whore'.

57 Holla Hello.

57 clown country bumpkin, here ironical, given that Touchstone himself is a court fool or clown.

61 Else If not.

62 Good even The expression was used at any time after noon (compare 12 n. above).

63 gentle noble.

64 if that If (Abbott 287).

64 love or gold Proverbial (Dent L479.1).

65 desert lonely.

65 entertainment food and accommodation (*OED* sv 11b).

67 maid i.e. maid who is; Rosalind refers to Celia but also, cryptically, to herself.

68 faints is becoming weak (*OED* Faint *v* 2).

68 for for want of.

71–2 Complaints against enclosure (the appropriation of private as well as common land) are common (see Introduction, pp. 23–4); compare the lament of Arden in Drayton's *Polyolbion*: 'For, when the world found out the fitness of my soil, / The gripple wretch began immediately to spoil [despoil] / My tall and goodly woods, and did my grounds enclose: / By which, in little time my bounds I came to lose' (XIII, 21–4).

My master is of churlish disposition
And little recks to find the way to heaven
By doing deeds of hospitality.   75
Besides, his cot, his flocks, and bounds of feed
Are now on sale, and at our sheepcote now
By reason of his absence there is nothing
That you will feed on. But what is, come see,
And in my voice most welcome shall you be.   80
ROSALIND What is he that shall buy his flock and pasture?
CORIN That young swain that you saw here but erewhile,
       That little cares for buying anything.
ROSALIND I pray thee, if it stand with honesty,
       Buy thou the cottage, pasture, and the flock,   85
       And thou shalt have to pay for it of us.
CELIA And we will mend thy wages. I like this place
       And willingly could waste my time in it.
CORIN Assuredly the thing is to be sold.
       Go with me. If you like upon report   90
       The soil, the profit, and this kind of life,
       I will your very faithful feeder be,
       And buy it with your gold right suddenly.

                                                   Exeunt

---

76 cot] *Eds.;* Coate F   87–8] *Capell subst.;* Cel . . . wages: / I . . . could / Waste . . . it. F

73 **churlish** miserly (*OED* sv 3); compare Nabal of the House of Caleb who 'did shear his sheep' but who was of 'churlish and of shrewd conditions' and refused hospitality to David and his followers (1 Sam. 25).

74 **recks** cares.

75 **hospitality** The expansive 'hospitality' of the very rich gradually went out of fashion after the mid-sixteenth century, so that there were fewer left-overs to distribute. On 6 July 1597 a proclamation against 'inordinate excess in apparel' noted that 'in the present difficulties . . . [cold weather leading to crop failures in 1596–8] the decay and lack of hospitality appears in the better sort of all counties' (Paul L. Hughes and James F. Larkin (eds.), *Tudor Royal Proclamations*, 3 vols., 1969, III, 175).

76 **cot** cottage (*OED* sv *sb*¹); F's 'Coate' represents the obsolete form 'cote'.

76 **bounds of feed** range of pasture (*OED* Feed *sb* 2b).

77 **sheepcote** Strictly a building for sheltering sheep (where Corin may have been forced to dwell), but probably a shepherd's cottage as at 4.3.72.

79 **That you will feed on** Suitable for your refined tastes.

80 **in my voice** as far as I am concerned or have influence (see *OED* Voice *sb* 2b).

81 **What** Of what condition (Abbott 254).

82 **but erewhile** just now.

83 Corin is too love-struck to be concerned with things material.

84 **stand** be consistent (*OED* sv *v* 79e).

84 **honesty** honour (*OED* sv 1c).

86 **have** i.e. have the money.

86 **of** from.

87 **mend** increase.

88 **waste** spend (*OED* sv *v* 8).

88 **time** life (*OED* 7a).

90 **upon report** in response to your enquiries.

92 **feeder** dependant, servant (*OED* sv 2b).

93 **right suddenly** without delay.

2.5 *Enter* AMIENS, JAQUES, *and others* [*: Lords dressed as foresters*]

Song

AMIENS Under the greenwood tree,
    Who loves to lie with me
    And turn his merry note
    Unto the sweet bird's throat:

    Come hither, come hither, come hither: 5
      Here shall he see
      No enemy
    But winter and rough weather.

JAQUES More, more, I prithee more.
AMIENS It will make you melancholy, Monsieur Jaques.   10
JAQUES I thank it. More, I prithee more: I can suck melancholy out of
    a song as a weasel sucks eggs. More, I prithee more.
AMIENS My voice is ragged: I know I cannot please you.
JAQUES I do not desire you to please me, I do desire you to sing. Come,
    more, another stanzo – call you 'em 'stanzos'?   15
AMIENS What you will, Monsieur Jaques.

Act 2, Scene 5   **2.5**] *Eds.; Scena Quinta.* F   **0** SD *others . . . foresters*] *This edn; others* F   **1** SH] *Capell; not in* F   **3**
turn] F *subst.; tune Rowe³*   **6–7**] *Pope subst.; Heere . . . enemie,* F   **11–12**] *As prose, Pope subst.; Iaq . . . more, / I . . .*
song, / As . . . More F   **14–15**] *As prose, Pope subst.; Iaq . . . me, / I . . . sing: / Come . . . stanzo's?* F

Act 2, Scene 5

0 *SD The dialogue indicates that during this
scene preparations are made to set out the meal
which is interrupted by the entrance of Orlando and
Adam in 2.7. 'Banquet[s]' (53), following Plato's
Symposium, were associated with formal debates.

1 This phrase is common in love-songs and Robin
Hood ballads of the period: see Claude M. Simpson, *The British Broadside Ballad and its Music*, 1966,
p. 726 and Seng, pp. 70–3.

1 greenwood 'A wood or forest when in leaf'
(*OED* sv 1); the word was traditionally associated
with those who had been banished the court or
turned outlaw.

1 tree It is possible but not necessary that a
property tree appeared at this moment (see Werner
Habicht, 'Tree properties and tree scenes in Elizabethan theater', *Ren. Drama* n.s. 4 (1971), 69–
92. One of the pillars supporting the canopy
over the stage could have been used (see
Hattaway, pp. 31, 37).

2 Who Whoever.

3 turn tune, frame (*OED* Turn *v* 5b).

3 note tune.

4 throat voice (*OED* sv 3b).

5–8 These lines might have been sung as a
chorus.

5 Come Let him come.

10 melancholy For connections between music
and melancholy, see R. Klibansky, E. Panofsky, and
F. Saxl, *Saturn and Melancholy*, 1964, pp. 231, 291,
and plate 70; compare *TN* 1.1.1–15 for an evocation
of the bitter-sweet mood induced by music.

12 as as readily as.

12 weasel known for its ferocity (see
Shakespeare's England, 1, 481).

13 ragged harsh, rough (*OED adj¹* 3b).

14 please me gratify me sexually (Williams,
p. 239).

15 stanzo stanza; 'stanza', 'stanze', and 'stanzo'
are all found in sixteenth-century texts (*OED* sv 1a
and b); the first recorded use of the word in *OED*
comes from *LLL*: 'Let me hear a staff, a stanze'
(4.2.104) – the word was obviously new-fangled.

JAQUES Nay, I care not for their names; they owe me nothing. Will you
     sing?

AMIENS More at your request than to please myself.

JAQUES Well then, if ever I thank any man, I'll thank you; but that they   20
     call 'compliment' is like th'encounter of two dog-apes. And when a
     man thanks me heartily, methinks I have given him a penny and he
     renders me the beggarly thanks. Come, sing; and you that will not,
     hold your tongues.

AMIENS Well, I'll end the song. – Sirs, cover the while; the Duke will   25
     drink under this tree. – He hath been all this day to look you.

JAQUES And I have been all this day to avoid him: he is too disputable
     for my company: I think of as many matters as he, but I give heaven
     thanks and make no boast of them. Come, warble, come.

Song. All together here

Who doth ambition shun   30
And loves to live i'th'sun;
Seeking the food he eats
And pleased with what he gets:

---

21 compliment] *Pope;* complement F   23 not,] F2; not F   27–9] *As prose, Pope subst.; Iaq* .... him: / He ...
companie: / I ... giue / Heauen ... them. / Come ... come. F   29 SD *All together*] *Eds.; Altogether* F

17 I ... nothing There is no need to make me a
list of possible names – unlike a list of debtors which
would be useful.
  20 that that which.
  21 compliment politeness.
  21 encounter (1) affected bowing and scraping,
an aping of court practice, (2) copulation (Williams,
p. 113).
  21 dog-apes dog-faced baboons (*cynocephali*);
the 'bavian' or baboon in *TNK* 3.5 is a figure of
lust; see Laroque, p. 126, Jones, pp. 192–3.
  21–3 when ... thanks the thanks of polite society
resemble in their insincerity the extravagant thanks
of a beggar.
  25 end complete (*OED* sv *v*[1] 1a).
  25 cover the while meanwhile, lay out a cloth
for our repast (either on the stage itself or on a table
brought out for the purpose); see *OED* Cover *v*[1] 2d.
If it is decided not to prepare a banquet on stage in
this scene (see 53 n. below and 2.6 n.) it may be con-
venient for a couple of lords to exit here. This line
and line 53 indicate that the 'banquet' remained on-
stage, unused and 'unseen' by Orlando and Adam
in 2.6, their first appearance in Arden: the stage

simultaneously represented two places. For this convention see Hattaway, pp. 37–40, and for the ways
in which modern editors and directors have confronted what they took to be a problem, see Alan C.
Dessen, *Elizabethan Stage Conventions and Modern
Interpreters*, 1984, pp. 101–3.
  26 drink spend some time drinking.
  26 look look for (Abbott 200).
  27 disputable disputatious: the Duke loves to
'cope him in [his] sullen fits' (2.1.67).
  28 matters topics, disciplines.
  28–9 I ... them Proverbial (Dent B487.1).
  29 warble sing sweetly (*OED* sv *v* 2a).
  29 SD *All together here* This may be a book-
holder's note (see Textual Analysis, p. 218), possibly
displaced from 33 where the chorus begins, or it may
suggest that the attendant lords join in the singing
to support Amiens from Jaques' bitter taunts.
  31 i'th'sun (1) a care-free life (compare *Ham.*
1.2.67), (2) in the rough (compare the proverb, 'Out
of God's blessing into the warm sun' (Tilley G272)).
  32–3 eats ... gets The words used to rhyme
(Cercignani, p. 168).

Come hither, come hither, come hither:
    Here shall he see   35
    No enemy
    But winter and rough weather.

JAQUES I'll give you a verse to this note that I made yesterday in despite
    of my invention.
AMIENS And I'll sing it.   40
JAQUES Thus it goes:
    If it do come to pass
    That any man turn ass,
    Leaving his wealth and ease,
    A stubborn will to please,   45

    Ducdame, ducdame, ducdame:
      Here shall he see
      Gross fools as he,
    And if he will come to me.
AMIENS What's that 'ducdame'?   50
JAQUES 'Tis a Greek invocation to call fools into a circle. I'll go sleep if
    I can: if I cannot, I'll rail against all the first-born of Egypt.

35–7 Here . . . weather] *Eds.; Heere shall he see. &c.* F   **38–9**] *As prose, Pope subst.; Iaq . . . note, / That . . . Inuention.*
F   **41** SH] F2 *subst.; Amy.* F; *Gives a paper / Sisson, 'New Readings',* I, 151   **42–3**] F3 *subst.; If . . . Asse:* F   **46**
Ducdame] F *subst.; Duc ad me / Hanmer*   **47–8**] *Pope subst.; Heere . . . he,* F

38 note tune.
38–9 in despite of notwithstanding.
39 invention A technical term in rhetoric for the
assembling of material to be used in a text; Jaques
means that high rhetorical skill was not necessary to
pen the nonsense that follows.
41 *SH F2 offers what might be a correction to
F's '*Amy.*'. However, it could be that a piece of
business, Jaques' handing Amiens a paper with the
words of the third verse to the song at 39, could be
unrecorded. It has become common in productions
for Jaques to speak his verse, part of the parody
of pastoral built into the play, but there is no real
authority for this.
42–9 Jaques' cod stanza aligns itself with Touchstone's counter-pastoral discourse: see Introduction,
pp. 20–1.
46 Ducdame Probably to be pronounced with
three syllables to match the metre of 'Come hither':
Hanmer emended to '*Duc ad me*', a dog-Latin translation (literally 'lead [him] to me') of these words. It
may be an attempt to render the Welsh '*Dewch da
mi*', 'Come with (or to) me', the French *duc damné*
or *duc d'ânes* (duke of asses), the Romany *dukrà me*,
'I tell fortunes'; it may be 'Duke-dame', a gender

insult, or – which makes the best jest – it is simply nonsense. Directors often have the lords gather
round Jaques during this stanza so that they are
gulled by his wit at 51. In the Cheek by Jowl production the lords, in puzzlement, pronounced the
word as though it was Latin; Jaques triumphed by
correcting the pronunciation as 'Duke damn me.'
48 Gross Palpable.
49 And if If indeed (Abbott 105).
51 Greek Nonsense, gibberish (*OED sv sb* 8
records the usage only from 1600, although the first
use of the proverb 'It is Greek to me' recorded by
Tilley is 1573).
51 invocation incantation to conjure a devil
(*OED sv* 2).
51 circle Like the magic circles with which con-
jurers surrounded themselves, but Jaques may be
thinking of the drawing power of the greenwood,
making a sexual jest (Williams, p. 70), or taking
the opportunity for a metatheatrical statement and
gesturing towards the audience of the 'wooden O'
(*H5* 1 Chorus 13) of the Globe playhouse (compare
3.4.38 n. and Epilogue 8 n.).
52 first-born of Egypt Moses prophesied that
they would die (Ex. 11.5; Shaheen, pp. 163–4): the

AMIENS And I'll go seek the Duke: his banquet is prepared.

Exeunt

2.6 *Enter* ORLANDO *and* ADAM

ADAM Dear master, I can go no further. O, I die for food. Here lie I
down and measure out my grave. Farewell, kind master.

ORLANDO Why, how now, Adam, no greater heart in thee? Live a little,
comfort a little, cheer thyself a little. If this uncouth forest yield
anything savage, I will either be food for it or bring it for food to   5
thee. Thy conceit is nearer death than thy powers. For my sake be
comfortable; hold death a while at the arm's end. I will here be with
thee presently, and if I bring thee not something to eat, I will give
thee leave to die; but if thou diest before I come, thou art a mocker
of my labour. Well said, thou look'st cheerly, and I'll be with thee   10
quickly. Yet thou liest in the bleak air. Come, I will bear thee to
some shelter, and thou shalt not die for lack of a dinner if there live
anything in this desert. Cheerly, good Adam.

Exeunt

53] *As prose, Pope subst.; Amy* . . . . Duke, / His . . . prepar'd. F **Act 2, Scene 6   2.6**] *Eds.; Scena Sexta.* F   1–13]
as prose, Pope subst.; Adam . . . further: / O . . . downe, / And . . . master. / *Orl.* . . . thee: / Liue . . . little. / If . . .
sauage, / I . . . thee: / Thy . . . powers. / For . . . while / At . . . presently, / And . . . eate, / I . . . diest / Before . . .
labor. / Wel . . . cheerely, / And . . . liest / In . . . thee / To . . . die / For . . . dinner, / If . . . Desert. / Cheerely . . .
Adam. F   **7** here be] F *subst.;* be here *Rowe*

phrase designated the high-born, although there
may be oblique references to Oliver and Duke Senior
or to the 'great cry' in the night that announced the
slaughter (Ex. 12.30), the kind of noise that would
prevent sleep.

53 banquet slight repast of fruit (see 2.7.99)
or sweetmeats taken between meals; the line does
not necessarily indicate that the banquet has been
prepared on stage during the scene.

Act 2, Scene 6
2.6 On the grounds that it is unlikely that
Orlando and Adam would profess their hunger in
sight of the banquet which may have been laid out
in the previous scene, it has been argued that the
scene was displaced from the end of 2.4 (Long,
p. 145). However, see 2.5.53 n.

*1–13 Compositor B (see Textual Analysis, p.
217) set all of this scene in blank verse, possibly to
avoid beginning the next scene at the bottom of a
right-hand column.

3 heart courage.
4 comfort take comfort (*OED v* 7e, although no
other example is quoted).
4, 8 If . . . if The conditionals create a kind of
theatrical irony, given that the Duke's banquet may
be visible on the stage (see 2.5.25 n.).
4 uncouth strange, wild.
5 anything savage any wild animal.
6 Thy . . . powers You are imagining yourself
weaker and nearer death than in fact you are.
7 comfortable cheerful (*OED sv* 9).
7 at the arm's end Proverbial (Tilley A317).
8 presently immediately.
10 labour task.
10 Well said This either means 'Well done',
or indicates that Adam makes some inarticulate
response.
11 bleak cold (*OED* Bleak *adj* 3).
12 dinner meal in the middle of the day.
13 Cheerly Cheerily (*OED sv* B1).

2.7 *Enter* DUKE SENIOR, [AMIENS,] *and Lords like outlaws [who set out a banquet]*

DUKE SENIOR I think he be transformed into a beast,
    For I can nowhere find him like a man.
AMIENS My lord, he is but even now gone hence;
    Here was he merry, hearing of a song.
DUKE SENIOR If he, compact of jars, grow musical,   5
    We shall have shortly discord in the spheres.
    Go seek him; tell him I would speak with him.

Enter JAQUES

AMIENS He saves my labour by his own approach.
DUKE SENIOR Why, how now, monsieur, what a life is this
    That your poor friends must woo your company?   10
    What, you look merrily?
JAQUES A fool, a fool: I met a fool i'th'forest,
    A motley fool – a miserable world –

Act 2, Scene 7   2.7] *Eds.; Scena Septima.* F   0 SD.1 AMIENS] *Capell; not in* F   0 SD.1 Lords] *Rowe subst.; Lord* F
0 SD.1–2 *who . . . banquet] Rowe subst.; not in* F   3 SH] *Capell; 1. Lord* F (*throughout the scene*)   10 company?] *Eds.;*
companie, F   13 fool . . . world –] *This edn;* Foole (a miserable world:) F   13 a miserable] F; ah miserable *conj. Wilson*
13 world] F; varlet *Hanmer*

Act 2, Scene 7

0 SD. 1, 3 SH *AMIENS Editors since Capell have
assigned F's 'Lord'; or '1 Lord' to Amiens who disappears from F after 2.5 where he sang to Jaques. In
this scene the actor is again called upon to sing at
174.

0 SD.1 *outlaws* individuals 'put outside the law
and deprived of its benefits and protection; . . .
under sentence of outlawry' (*OED* Outlaw *sb* 1;
compare 4.2.0 SD.1 n.). They may have worn the
Lincoln green of Robin Hood and his merry men
who are customarily called 'outlaws' in the ballads
(see Thomas Percy (ed.), *Percy's Reliques of Ancient
English Poetry*, 2 vols., Everyman, n.d., I, 116).

1 he i.e. Jaques (see 2.5.27).

1 be For the form, see Abbott 299.

2 like a man in the shape of a man.

3 but even only (Abbott 38).

5 compact of jars made up of discords; Plato
argued that music served to harmonise the soul
(*Timaeus*, 47d).

6 discord in the spheres According to Pythagoras, the heavenly spheres generated perfect har-
monies as they rotated: the idea became an
important Renaissance commonplace (see Robin
Headlam Wells, *Elizabethan Mythologies*, 1994,

pp. 92–3). The Duke jokes that discord in the heavens is more likely than the emergence of a musical
talent in Jaques.

9 what a life is this Compare the proverb,
'What a world is this' (Dent w889.1).

13 Jaques may be thinking of the proverb, 'The
world is full of fools' (Tilley w896).

13 motley the parti-coloured costume of a professional jester – although the word could mean
speckled rather than chequered and hence designate a worsted material; the costume could consist
of a hooded coat and breeches with legs of different
colours or a long gown. In fact, since Touchstone
seems to have cast off his court uniform (see 2.4.0
SD.2–3 n.), it would seem that Jaques recognises the
man the rustics take for a gentleman for what he is
(see Wiles, pp. 186–7). Alternatively, the word may
mean 'varying in character or mood' (*OED* sv 3)
as in the first line of Donne's first satire, 'Away,
thou fondling motley humourist.' Jaques would
be drawn to Touchstone by virtue of a common
temperament.

13 world Hulme (p. 208) argues that we should
read 'word' (meaning 'name'), but the subtext could
be a belated reply to the Duke's rhetorical question
at 9–11.

As I do live by food, I met a fool
Who laid him down and basked him in the sun   15
And railed on Lady Fortune in good terms,
In good set terms, and yet a motley fool.
'Good morrow, fool', quoth I. 'No, sir', quoth he,
'Call me not fool till heaven hath sent me fortune.'
And then he drew a dial from his poke   20
And looking on it, with lack-lustre eye,
Says, very wisely, 'It is ten o'clock.
Thus we may see', quoth he, 'how the world wags:
'Tis but an hour ago since it was nine,
And after one hour more 'twill be eleven;   25
And so, from hour to hour, we ripe and ripe,
And then, from hour to hour, we rot and rot,
And thereby hangs a tale.' When I did hear
The motley fool thus moral on the time,
My lungs began to crow like Chanticleer   30

---

16 Perhaps because, proverbially, Fortune customarily favoured fools (Tilley F600).

17 In … terms Roundly (*OED* Set *ppl adj* 3b).

19 Compare the proverb, 'God sends fortune to fools' (Tilley G220).

20–8 Reflections upon mutability are common in early modern literature; classical analogues include *Metamorphoses*, xv, 196–260, to which this passage may be indebted, and the notion is illustrated by an emblem, 'The fruit that soonest ripes, doth soonest fade away' in Geoffrey Whitney, *A Choice of Emblems* (1586), p. 173.

20 dial (1) timepiece – a pocket sun-dial or a watch (*OED* Dial *sb*[1] 3); Touchstone, by carrying a timepiece, reveals how he is not at home in a forest where there are no clocks (see 3.3.254–5), (2) prick, penis (compare *1H4* 1.2.8–9 'dials the signs of leaping-houses'; Partridge, p. 93).

20 poke More likely to have been a bag or small sack (*OED* sv *sb*[1] 1a) carried by the clown than a 'pocket' which is how *OED* glosses the word (Poke *sb*[1] 1c); John Scottowe's portrait of Richard Tarlton (1588) shows him with 'coat of russet', 'startups' (high leather shoes), and a wallet at his waist (Hattaway, plate 11); it is less likely to have been the sleeve of a longer gown (*OED* sv *sb*[1] 3; Wiles, p. 187). Given the proximity of 'dial', it also here designates a codpiece (see Jenijoy La Belle, 'Touchstone's dial: horology or urology', *ELN* 24 (1987), 19–25).

21 lack-lustre The word was coined by Shakespeare (see *OED* sv).

23 the world wags affairs are going (*OED* Wag *v* 7c), with the connotations of staggering or shaking; compare the proverb, 'Let the world wag' (Tilley w879); a 'wagtail' was a prostitute, so 'wags' also means 'flaunts its wantonness' (*Tit.* 5.2.88; Williams, p. 214).

25 eleven Since 'noon' designated an erection as in *Son.* 7.12 and Sidney's 'But lo, while I do speak, it groweth noon with me' (*Astrophil and Stella*, 76.9), so 'eleven' designates tumescence.

26–7 Compare the proverb, 'Soon ripe, soon rotten' (Tilley R133), and *Rosalind*: 'many men have done amiss in proving soon ripe and soon rotten', and 'The joys of man, as they are few, so are they … scarce ripe before they are rotten' (pp. 201 and 141).

26 ripe (1) mature, (2) grope, investigate, search into (*OED* sv *v*[2] 2, 4).

27 hour Possibly pronounced similarly to 'whore' (although Cercignani, p. 194, is doubtful).

27 rot (1) decay, (2) suffer the effects of venereal diseases or are washed out by constant copulation, (3) a semi-pun on 'rut' = copulate (?).

28 thereby hangs a tale Proverbial (Tilley T48), here with a pun on 'tail' = (syphilitic) penis (or possibly a dog's tail, picking up the 'wags' from 23).

29 moral moralise (the first recorded use of the form in *OED*).

30 crow make a delighted sound (*OED* sv *v*[1] 3).

30 Chanticleer A traditional name for a cock, as in *Reynard the Fox* and Chaucer's 'Nun's Priest's Tale'.

That fools should be so deep-contemplative;
And I did laugh, sans intermission,
An hour by his dial. O noble fool,
O worthy fool: motley's the only wear.

DUKE SENIOR What fool is this? 35

JAQUES A worthy fool: one that hath been a courtier
And says, 'If ladies be but young and fair,
They have the gift to know it'; and in his brain,
Which is as dry as the remainder biscuit
After a voyage, he hath strange places crammed 40
With observation, the which he vents
In mangled forms. O that I were a fool!
I am ambitious for a motley coat.

DUKE SENIOR Thou shalt have one.

JAQUES   It is my only suit,
Provided that you weed your better judgements 45
Of all opinion that grows rank in them

---

31 deep-contemplative] *Malone;* deepe contemplatiue F   34 O] *Wilson; Cam., conj. anon;* A F   36 A] *Wilson; Cam.,*
conj. anon; O F   38 know it] F; know't *Dyce²*   38 brain F2; braiue F

31 **deep** (1) deeply (Abbott 2), (2) concerned with
sexual matters – compare the proverb, 'The deeper
the sweeter' (Tilley D188).

32 **sans intermission** without cease; 'sans' is a
French affectation typical of the traveller Jaques;
'intermission' was pronounced with five syllables
(Cercignani, p. 308).

34, 36 *****O, A** Reversal of F's initial letters is justified on the grounds of probable compositorial error.

34 **motley's the only wear** (1) the raiment of a
fool (see 13 n. above) should be worn by all the world,
(2) everyone's genitals are discoloured by venereal
disease (with a pun on 'ware' = genitals (*OED* Ware
sb³ 4c).

36–42 **one . . . fool** Jaques' savage anatomy of
Touchstone's laboured wit recalls Asper's indict-
ment of affected critics in the Induction to Jonson's
Every Man out of his Humour (1599).

38 **gift to know it** (1) wit to recognise their sexual attractiveness, (2) payment for their beauty to be
carnally known.

38–9 **brain . . . dry** A dry brain was the sign
of slowness of apprehension but retentiveness of
memory (see Bartholomaeus Anglicus, *Batman upon*
Bartholome (1582), fo. 37ᵛ); Robert Burton: 'Saturn and Mercury, the patrons of learning, are both
dry planets' (*The Anatomy of Melancholy* (1621), ed.
Floyd Bell and Paul Jordan-Smith, 1948, I.ii. iii. xv,
p. 260).

39 **dry . . . biscuit** Proverbial (Tilley B404).

39 **remainder** left over.

39 **biscuit** ship's bread or, as it came to be known
in the nineteenth century, 'hard-tack'; this was very
dry.

40 **strange** singular.

40 **places** A technical term meaning 'subjects' or
'topics' from rhetorical invention. Bacon writes, in
connection with 'suggestion', of 'marks, or places,
which may excite our mind to return and produce
such knowledge as it hath formerly collected' (*The*
Advancement of Learning, II.13.9).

41 **observation** knowledge, experience (possibly
pronounced with five syllables).

41 **vents** utters (*OED* Vent *v²*, 5).

42 **In mangled forms** Professional fools concealed their satirical barbs as nonsense to avoid punishment.

43 **ambitious for** desirous of (*OED* Ambitious
2).

44 **Thou** The Duke's use of the form used for
a servant (compare 10–11) indicates his impatience
with Jaques.

44 **suit** (1) dress, (2) petition, (3) branch (the
word was pronounced 'shoot', which links the quibble to the following line (Cercignani, p. 203).

45 **weed** Punning on 'weeds' meaning 'clothing'.

46 **opinion** vulgar belief (*OED* sv *sb* 1c).

46 **rank** excessively, coarsely.

That I am wise. I must have liberty
Withal, as large a charter as the wind,
To blow on whom I please: for so fools have.
And they that are most gallèd with my folly,   50
They most must laugh. And why, sir, must they so?
The why is plain as way to parish church:
He that a fool doth very wisely hit,
Doth very foolishly, although he smart,
If he seem senseless of the bob. If not,   55
The wise man's folly is anatomised
Even by the squand'ring glances of the fool.
Invest me in my motley; give me leave
To speak my mind, and I will through and through
Cleanse the foul body of th'infected world,   60
If they will patiently receive my medicine.

DUKE SENIOR Fie on thee! I can tell what thou wouldst do.

JAQUES What, for a counter, would I do but good?

DUKE SENIOR Most mischievous foul sin in chiding sin:

---

55 If he seem] *This edn; Seeme* F; *Not to seem Theobald; Seem aught but Oxford*   57 Even] F; *E'en Yale*   58 my] F; *the* F3

47–9 **liberty . . . please** i.e. licence to criticise whom I will.

48 **as large . . . wind** Compare the proverb, 'As free as the air' (Tilley A88), the metaphor in John 3.8 for the Holy Spirit: 'The wind bloweth where it listeth', and *H5* 1.1.47–8: 'when he speaks, / The air, a charter'd libertine, is still.'

48 **charter** document granting particular privileges.

50 **gallèd with** hurt, annoyed by (for the preposition, see Abbott 193).

52 **why** reason.

52 **as way** For the omission of the article, see Abbott 83.

53 **that** whom.

53 **wisely** heedfully (*OED* sv *adv* 3).

55 *****If he** This addition (see collation) is justified by the metre. The sense of the passage is that a man who does not show that he has recognised the wit of a fool, even if it is hurtful, shows himself to be foolish. Johnson, following Theobald, offers a contrary meaning: 'Unless men have the prudence not to appear touched with the sarcasms of a jester, they subject themselves to his power, and the wise man will have his folly anatomised, that is dissected and laid open by the squandering glances or random shots of a fool.'

55 **senseless of the bob** unaware of the jest (see *OED* Bob *sb*³ 2).

56 **wise man's folly** the foolish utterances that even a wise man will make – although 'folly' could also mean 'lewdness' (*OED* sv 3a).

56 **anatomised** laid bare.

57 **squand'ring** straying (*OED* sv *ppl adj* 2).

57 **glances** satirical hits.

58 **Invest** Array.

58 **leave** liberty (see 47).

58–61 **give . . . medicine** The metaphors of the world's disease and its cure by what Asper in Jonson's *Every Man out of his Humour* (1599) calls 'physic of the mind' or 'pills to purge' (Induction, 132, 175) recall the savage satirical recipes offered by that author as well as John Marston and Joseph Hall.

60 **Cleanse** Purge (*OED* sv 6).

60 **world** society.

63 **for a counter** Jaques' mock wager dismisses the Duke's rebuke – a counter was a (merchant's) token, object of no value (*OED* sv *sb*³ 1a) – although 'counter' could equally mean 'counter-answer'.

64 Compare the proverb, 'He finds fault with others and does worse himself' (Tilley F107).

For thou thyself hast been a libertine,   65
As sensual as the brutish sting itself,
And all th'embossèd sores and headed evils
That thou with licence of free foot hast caught
Wouldst thou disgorge into the general world.

JAQUES   Why, who cries out on pride   70
That can therein tax any private party?
Doth it not flow as hugely as the sea
Till that the weary very means do ebb?
What woman in the city do I name
When that I say the city-woman bears   75
The cost of princes on unworthy shoulders?
Who can come in and say that I mean her,
When such a one as she, such is her neighbour?
Or what is he of basest function
That says his bravery is not on my cost,   80

---

73 weary] F *subst.;* very *Pope;* wearer's *Singer*²   75 city-woman] *This edn;* City woman F

65 libertine one who follows his own (licentious) inclinations; Jaques, who has 'swam in a gondola' (4.1.29–30), has many of the attributes of the Italianate Englishman (see Introduction, p. 16) and is therefore likely to be treated with suspicion by the puritanically minded Duke.

66 sensual lecherous, unchaste (*OED* sv 4b); Kökeritz suggests that the first syllable of the word was pronounced 'sins' (p. 85).

66 brutish sting animal lust (Williams, p. 290).

67 embossèd swollen (*OED* sv *ppl adj*¹ 4).

67 sores symptoms of venereal disease; the Duke may, of course, be speaking figuratively.

67 headed that have come to a head like a boil.

67 evils afflictions, diseases (*OED* Evil *sb* B7a).

68 licence of free foot utter freedom, invoking the meaning of '*foutre*' (Fr. 'to copulate': Williams, pp. 130–1) for 'foot'.

69 disgorge vomit.

69 general whole.

70–3 Jaques artfully deflects the Duke's charges by pretending he has been accused of social as well as sexual excess, of offending individuals rather than exposing the vices to which society as a whole was prey.

70 cries out on denounces.

70 pride (1) sexual desire (Williams, p. 246), (2) arrogance, (3) magnificence in dress (*OED* sv *sb*¹ 7).

71 tax any private party censure any lecher or particular person; for the issues involved, see A. Kernan, *The Cankered Muse*, 1959.

72–3 Compare the proverb, 'To ebb and flow like the sea' (Dent S182.1).

73 weary very means do ebb (1) the object of desire is worn out by physical activity, (2) wealth that generates ostentation exhausts itself; the phrase is, however, obscure, and has attracted emendations (see collation).

73 means Possibly pronounced 'mains' (Cercignani, p. 235), creating a pun that links to the sea imagery in the previous line.

75–6 Compare the proverb, 'He wears a whole lordship on his back' (Dent L452); Thomas Platter, who visited London in 1599, noted the extravagant fashions worn by women in the city of London (*Thomas Platter's Travels in England, 1599*, trans. Clare Williams, 1937, p. 182); such extravagance was a violation of the often enacted but poorly enforced sumptuary laws (see N. B. Harte, 'State control of dress and social change in pre-industrial England', in D. C. Coleman and A. H. John (eds.), *Trade, Government and Economy in Pre-Industrial England*, 1976, pp. 132–65).

76 cost wealth, expenditure (*OED* sv *sb*² 1b).

77 in forward (as before a magistrate); or possibly 'come in' means intervene or interrupt (*OED* Come 63k).

79–84 It was a commonplace for a satirist to disclaim an intention to pillory individuals: see O. J. Campbell, 'Jaques', *HLQ* 7 (1935), 71–102.

79 basest function meanest bearing or office.

80 bravery is not on my cost finery is not paid for by me (and therefore is none of my business).

Thinking that I mean him, but therein suits
His folly to the mettle of my speech?
There then! How then? What then? Let me see wherein
My tongue hath wronged him. If it do him right,
Then he hath wronged himself; if he be free,   85
Why then my taxing like a wild goose flies
Unclaimed of any man. But who come here?

Enter ORLANDO [*with sword drawn*]

ORLANDO Forbear, and eat no more!
JAQUES Why, I have eat none yet.
ORLANDO Nor shalt not, till necessity be served.   90
JAQUES Of what kind should this cock come of?
DUKE SENIOR Art thou thus boldened, man, by thy distress,
          Or else a rude despiser of good manners
          That in civility thou seem'st so empty?
ORLANDO You touched my vein at first: the thorny point   95
          Of bare distress hath ta'en from me the show
          Of smooth civility; yet am I inland bred
          And know some nurture. But forbear, I say;
          He dies that touches any of this fruit
          Till I and my affairs are answerèd.   100

---

83 There] F; Where *Hudson²*, *conj. Malone*   87 any . . . But] *Eds.*; any. man But F   87 come] F; comes F2   87 SD
with . . . drawn] *Theobald*; *not in* F   88–9] F *subst.; As verse, Steevens³*   90 not] F; thou *Theobald²*   96 ta'en] F *subst.*;
torn *conj. Johnson*

81 **suits** (1) matches, (2) adorns.
82 **mettle** quality, nature.
84 **right** justice.
85 **free** guiltless (*OED adj* 7).
86 **taxing** censure.
87 **Unclaimed** The first recorded use of the word in *OED*.
87 **come** Jaques assumes that Orlando is leading on a band of men.
87 ***SD** Theobald's emendation is justified by 119.
90 An allusion to the proverb, 'Necessity hath no law' (Tilley N76), which was cited in justification of food riots in the 1590s: see Buchanan Sharp, *In Contempt of All Authority*, 1980, p. 34.
90–2 **shalt . . . thou** The use of the singular form was characteristic of those addressing strangers with contempt (Abbott 231).
91 **Of . . . of** For the repeated preposition, see Abbott 407.
91 **kind** breed.
91 **cock** (1) fighting cock, (2) one who arouses

slumberers, a watchman of the night (*OED sv sb¹* 6), (3) 'prick' (Jones, p. 206).
92 **boldened** encouraged.
92 **distress** pangs of hunger (*OED sb* 1b).
93 **else** Here redundant.
93 **rude** rustic, uncivilised.
94 **civility** civilised behaviour.
95 **You . . . first** Your first supposition is correct ('vein' means here 'temporary state of mind' (*OED sv sb* 14b).
96 **bare** absolute (*OED sv adj* 12).
96 **distress** pressure caused by hunger (*OED sv sb* 1b).
97 **am I inland bred** I was raised in civilised society, as at 3.3.289, and see 102 (although *OED* Inland svc appears to allow its modern meaning). Richard Wilson, *Will Power*, 1993, p. 77, detects a reference here to the Midland rioters.
98 **nurture** education, breeding (*OED sb* 1).
100 **answerèd** provided for.

JAQUES And you will not be answerèd with reason, I must die.

DUKE SENIOR What would you have? Your gentleness shall force
More than your force move us to gentleness.

ORLANDO I almost die for food, and let me have it.

DUKE SENIOR Sit down and feed, and welcome to our table.   105

ORLANDO Speak you so gently? Pardon me, I pray you:
I thought that all things had been savage here
And therefore put I on the countenance
Of stern commandment. But whate'er you are
That in this desert inaccessible,   110
Under the shade of melancholy boughs,
Lose and neglect the creeping hours of time –
If ever you have looked on better days,
If ever been where bells have knolled to church,
If ever sat at any goodman's feast,   115
If ever from your eyelids wiped a tear,
And know what 'tis to pity and be pitied,
Let gentleness my strong enforcement be,
In the which hope, I blush, and hide my sword.

DUKE SENIOR True is it that we have seen better days,   120
And have with holy bell been knolled to church,

101] F *subst.;* JAQUES . . . not / Be . . . die. *Pope subst.*   **102–3**] *Pope subst.; Du. Sen* . . . . haue? / Your . . . force / Moue . . . gentlenesse. F; DUKE SENIOR What . . . have your . . . force, / More . . . gentlenes. *conj. this edn*   **109** commandment] *Eds.;* command'ment F   **112** time –] time: F   **115** goodman's] *This edn;* good mans F

101 **And** If.

101 **reason** The word may have been pronounced as 'raisin', meaning a fresh grape or bunch of grapes (*OED sv sb* 1; Cercignani, p. 235; compare *1H4* 2.4.239); it is common in productions for Jaques to offer Orlando some of the grapes he is eating at this point.

102 **gentleness** good breeding (*OED sv* 2).

102 **force** prevail.

103 **gentleness** courtesy, kindliness (*OED sv* 3).

104 **for** for lack of.

104 **and** This may have the meaning of 'and I pray you' (Abbott 100).

105 The Duke displays the traditional virtue of hospitality so lacking in Corin's master (see 2.4.73–5).

106 **gently** politely.

107 **had been** would have been.

109 **commandment** authority (*OED sv* 5); pronounced with four syllables (Cercignani, p. 293 – see collation).

110 **desert** remote and empty place.

111 **melancholy** dismal (*OED adj* 4).

112 **Lose** Forget.

112 **creeping** stealthy.

114 **knolled** rung (*OED* Knoll *v* 2).

115 ***goodman** host; F's 'good mans' implies that Orlando is sceptical of the virtue of those he encounters in the forest.

117 **know** known (Abbott 343).

118 **enforcement** constraint (*OED sv* 5).

119 **hide** i.e. sheathe.

121, 123 **holy, sacred** The Duke's adjectives inserted into the liturgical repetition of Orlando's lines may be a gentle rebuke to Orlando's self-pity.

121 **holy bell** In pre-Reformation England bells were regularly consecrated, a practice decried by the Protestant John Foxe and others, who abjured in particular the ringing of the 'holy bell' to help the soul of one recently dead out of purgatory (Thomas, pp. 59, 60, 65, 722); it is conceivable that the phrase aligns itself with Reformation opinion on this matter (see Introduction, p. 31).

121 **knolled** summoned (*OED* Knoll *v* 3).

And sat at goodmen's feasts, and wiped our eyes
Of drops that sacred pity hath engendered:
And therefore sit you down in gentleness
And take upon command what help we have   125
That to your wanting may be ministered.
ORLANDO Then but forbear your food a little while
Whiles, like a doe, I go to find my fawn
And give it food: there is an old poor man
Who after me hath many a weary step   130
Limped in pure love. Till he be first sufficed,
Oppressed with two weak evils, age and hunger,
I will not touch a bit.
DUKE SENIOR   Go find him out,
And we will nothing waste till you return.
ORLANDO I thank ye, and be blest for your good comfort.   [*Exit*] 135
DUKE SENIOR Thou see'st we are not all alone unhappy:
This wide and universal theatre

---

122 goodmen's] *This edn;* good mens F   123 hath] F; had *Warburton*   125 command] F; demand *Johnson*   127
while] F; space *conj. this edn*   135 SD] *Rowe; not in* F

122 **feasts** religious festivals (*OED* Feast *sb* 1).
123 **pity** (1) image of piety (*OED* sv *sb* 6b), (2)
repentance, remorse (*OED* sv 5).
124 **in gentleness** courteously.
125 **upon command** as you wish.
126 **wanting** need.
128 **Whiles** Until (*OED* sv 5).
131 **sufficed** satisfied (*OED* Satisfy 5).
132 **weak** weakening (transferred epithet).
133 **bit** mouthful (*OED* sv *sb²* 1).
134 **waste** consume.
135 **ye** A sign of Orlando's new reverence for the
Duke (Abbott 236).
136–9 **Thou . . . in** This may contain a reference to a specific 'woeful pageant', the words used
to describe Richard II's deposition (*R2* 4.1.321).
136 **unhappy** unfortunate.
137–66 The sequence provides an interlude while
Orlando fetches Adam. For the commonplace about
the theatricality of life, see Curtius, pp. 138–44,
P. Skrine, *The Baroque: Literature and Culture in
Seventeenth-Century Europe*, 1978, pp. 1–24, and, for
proverbial versions, Tilley w882. It was Hippocrates
who divided man's life into seven divisions and
Shakespeare combines the notion with his conceit of
the divisions of a play: see Samuel C. Chew, 'This
strange eventful history', in James G. McManaway
et al. (eds.), *Joseph Quincy Adams Memorial Stud-*

ies, 1948, pp. 157–82. The ages were often matched
to the seven planets (see F. Boll, 'Die Lebensalter',
Neue Jahrbücher für das klassische Altertum 16 (1913),
113–48), and it may be significant that Jaques misses
out the age when man is in his prime, endowed
with reason and governed by the sun: see Alan
Taylor Bradford, 'Jaques' distortion of the seven-
ages paradigm,' *SQ* 27 (1976), 171–6; Michael J. B.
Allen, 'Jaques against the seven ages of the Proclan
man,' *MLQ* 42 (1981), 331–46. Jaques also, significantly, makes no mention of the good life of the
country-dweller. The sign of the Globe playhouse
was supposed to be a figure of Hercules supporting
either a celestial or terrestrial globe with the motto
Totus mundus agit histrionem – 'All the world plays
the actor': see Richard Dutton, '*Hamlet, An Apology for Actors*, and the sign of the Globe', *S.Sur.*
41 (1988), 35–43. The fact that the planets are not
mentioned, however, means that the significance
for most auditors will lie in the vignettes of common life, chosen to illustrate Jaques' sardonicism.
Sources and analogues are reviewed by J. E. Hank-
ins, *Shakespeare's Derived Imagery*, 1953, pp. 15–28.
D. S. Hutchinson, 'The cynicism of Jaques: a new
source in Spenser's *Axiochus*?', *NQ* 39 (1992), 328–
30, suggests that Spenser's translation of Plato's
Axiochus is Shakespeare's source for the speech
(2.7.139–66).

Presents more woeful pageants than the scene
Wherein we play in.

JAQUES   All the world's a stage
And all the men and women merely players: 140
They have their exits and their entrances
And one man in his time plays many parts,
His acts being seven ages. At first the infant,
Mewling and puking in the nurse's arms;
Then the whining schoolboy with his satchel   145
And shining morning face, creeping like snail
Unwillingly to school; and then the lover,
Sighing like furnace, with a woeful ballad
Made to his mistress' eyebrow; then a soldier,
Full of strange oaths and bearded like the pard,   150
Jealous in honour, sudden, and quick in quarrel,
Seeking the bubble 'reputation'
Even in the cannon's mouth; and then the justice,
In fair round belly with good capon lined,
With eyes severe and beard of formal cut,   155
Full of wise saws and modern instances –
And so he plays his part; the sixth age shifts

---

139 Wherein . . . in] F; Wherein we play *Rowe*   143 At] F; As *Dyce²*, *conj. Capell*   145 Then] *Eds.*; Then, F; And then *Rowe³*   149 a] F; the *Dyce²*   151 sudden,] F *subst.*; sudden *Rowe*   153 Even] F *subst.*; E'en *Yale*

138 **pageants** parts, performances (*OED* Pageant 1b).
138 **scene** dramatic representation (*OED* sv 3a).
139 **Wherein . . . in** For the double preposition, see Abbott 407.
140 **merely** actually (*OED adv²* 2b).
143 **acts** (1) actions, (2) parts of a play.
144 **Mewling and puking** Whimpering and vomiting – both words are the earliest examples cited in *OED*.
146 **snail** Proverbial for slowness (Tilley S579); for the omission of the indefinite article, see Abbott 83.
148 **ballad** song.
149 **to his mistress' eyebrow** As in the excesses of Petrarchan love poetry.
150 **Full of strange oaths** Jonson's Captain Bobadill in *Every Man in his Humour* spices his discourse with such: 'By the foot of Pharaoh', 'Body o' Caesar', etc.
150 **strange** foreign.
150 **bearded like the pard** with tufts of facial hair like the whiskers of a leopard or panther.
151 **Jealous** Suspiciously careful.

151 **sudden** (1) impetuous, (2) lustful (Rubinstein, p. 263), (3) looking stewed with drink or marked with venereal disease (see Williams, 'sodden', p. 281). F's comma after the word is significant: Rowe's emendation (see collation) is unnecessary, and would turn the meaning to 'hasty'.
151 **quarrel** quarrelling (*OED* sv *sb³* 4b).
152 **bubble 'reputation'** Compare the proverb, 'Honour (reputation) is a bubble' (Dent B691.1); reputation was probably pronounced with five syllables.
153 **cannon** Andrews suggests a 'cannon'/'canon' quibble here, the latter referring to laws against duelling (compare *Ham.* 1.2.132).
154 **capon** emasculated cock, bred for the table; the phrase 'capon-justice' records the practice of bribing judges with capons (see *OED*).
155 **formal** appropriate to his office (*OED* sv 6b).
156 **saws** sayings.
156 **modern** commonplace (*OED* sv 4).
156 **instances** cases 'adduced in objection to or disproof of a universal assertion' (*OED* sv *sb* 5).
157 **shifts** changes – as in scenic entertainments at court (see *OED* Scene 4).

Into the lean and slippered pantaloon,
With spectacles on nose and pouch on side,
His youthful hose well saved – a world too wide   160
For his shrunk shank – and his big manly voice,
Turning again toward childish treble, pipes
And whistles in his sound; last scene of all
That ends this strange eventful history
Is second childishness and mere oblivion,   165
Sans teeth, sans eyes, sans taste, sans everything.

Enter ORLANDO *with* ADAM [*on his back*]

DUKE SENIOR Welcome. Set down your venerable burden,
    And let him feed.
ORLANDO   I thank you most for him.
ADAM So had you need: I scarce can speak
    To thank you for myself.   170
DUKE SENIOR Welcome; fall to: I will not trouble you
    As yet to question you about your fortunes. –
    Give us some music, and, good cousin, sing.

Song

AMIENS Blow, blow, thou winter wind,
    Thou art not so unkind   175

---

160 wide] F3; wide, F   162 treble,] *Theobald;* trebble F   166 SD on . . . back] *This edn; not in* F   167–70] *Rowe*[3]
subst.; Du Sen. . . . feede. / Orl. . . . him. / Ad. . . . neede, / I . . . selfe. F   174 SH] *Johnson; not in* F   175–8] *Pope*
subst.; Thou . . . ingratitude / Thy . . . seene, F

---

158 pantaloon Pantalone, the ridiculous old merchant from *commedia dell'arte*; see Allardyce Nicoll, *The World of Harlequin*, 1963.
  159 pouch purse.
  160 hose breeches, leggings.
  160 a world far.
  161 shank calf, leg.
  163 his its (Abbott 228).
  164 eventful The first recorded use in *OED*.
  164 history history play (*OED* 6).
  165 second childishness Compare the proverb, 'Old men are twice children' (Tilley M570).
  165 mere oblivion utter forgetfulness.
  166 Compare Montaigne, '. . . the souls of the gods, sans tongues, sans eyes, and sans ears, have each one in themselves a feeling of that which the other feel' (*The Essayes of Michael Lord of Montaigne*, trans. John Florio, 3 vols., 1910, II, 236).
  166 *SD Neither Orlando nor Adam conforms to the stereotypes offered by Jaques, and so this entrance gives the lie to his melancholy or cynicism.

Instead the moment may recall Aeneas bearing on his back his aged father Anchises away from the flames of Troy (see *Aeneid*, II, 705ff., *Metamorphoses*, XIII, 746–53).
  168 And let him feed These words might be effectively addressed to Jaques.
  168 for him on his behalf.
  171 fall to start eating.
  172 to question by questioning.
  173 music This indicates that Amiens' song was accompanied, probably on a lute, although a consort of viols or other stringed instruments may have been used (Hattaway, p. 62).
  173 cousin Used by a prince to address a lord (*OED* 5a).
  174–97 Christmas songs of the holly that contrasted with songs in praise of ivy celebrated masculinity and male bonding (see C. L. Barber, *Shakespeare's Festive Comedy*, 1959, pp. 114–15).
  175 unkind (1) unnatural, (2) ungenerous.

As man's ingratitude;
Thy tooth is not so keen,
Because thou art not seen,
Although thy breath be rude.
  Hey-ho, sing hey-ho   180
  Unto the green holly,
  Most friendship is feigning,
  Most loving mere folly.
  The hey-ho, the holly,
  This life is most jolly.   185

Freeze, freeze, thou bitter sky,
That dost not bite so nigh
As benefits forgot;
Though thou the waters warp,
Thy sting is not so sharp   190
As friend remembered not.
  Hey-ho, sing hey-ho
  Unto the green holly,
  Most friendship is feigning,
  Most loving mere folly.   195
  The hey-ho, the holly,
  This life is most jolly.

DUKE SENIOR If that you were the good Sir Roland's son,

---

178 seen] F *subst.;* sheen *Warburton*   180 Hey-ho] *Wilson;* Heigh ho F   180–1] *Eds.;* Heigh . . . holly, F   182 feigning] *Rowe; fayning* F   182–3] *Eds; Most . . . folly:* F   184 The] F; Then *Rowe*   186–7] *Pope subst.; Freize . . . nigh* F   189–90] *Pope subst.; Though . . . sharpe* F   191 remembered] F *subst.;* rememb'ring *Hanmer*   192–7 hey-ho . . . jolly] *Eds.; &c.* F   198, 199 were] F; are *conj. Dyce*

177 keen sharp.

178 seen Warburton's emendation 'sheen' (beautiful, shining – as in *MND* 2.1.28) is attractive, the idea being that the wind's bite is not as painful as that of the smiling courtier.

179 rude (1) raw, uncivilised, (2) violent.

180 *Hey-ho OED* distinguishes this interjection, which may have a nautical origin and which is often found in the bourdon of songs (see 4.2.11 n.), from 'Heigh-ho' which was associated with sighing or melancholy (as at 4.3.161).

181 holly From ancient times associated with winter festivities: 'the pagan Romans used to send to their friends holly-sprigs, during the Saturnalia, with wishes for their health and well-being' (Brewer).

182 *feigning fictitious, with a pun on 'faining' (desiring); Sir Thomas Smith, *De Recta . . . Anglicae Scriptione Dialogus* (1568), sig. 15ᵛ–16ʳ, comments

on the way 'dainty women . . . and those who wish to sound polite, use *ei* even in words spelt with *ai*' (Cercignani, p. 231).

183 mere complete.

183 folly (1) foolishness, infatuation (2) lewdness (*OED* sv 3a).

187 That For this form of the relative after a vocative, see Abbott 261.

187 nigh deeply.

188 benefits forgot favours ignored or unregistered; compare the proverb, 'Benefits are soon forgotten' (Tilley B309).

189 warp shrink, shrivel, corrugate (*OED* sv *v* 15a).

191 friend remembered not '"who is not remembered by his friend", as well as "who has no remembrance of his friend"' (Capell).

198–9 were . . . were The past tense is used because Sir Roland is dead.

As you have whispered faithfully you were,
And as mine eye doth his effigies witness   200
Most truly limned and living in your face,
Be truly welcome hither. I am the Duke
That loved your father. The residue of your fortune
Go to my cave and tell me. – Good old man,
Thou art right welcome as thy master is. –   205
[*To Orlando*] Support him by the arm. [*To Adam*] Give me
    your hand,
And let me all your fortunes understand.

                                                Exeunt

3.1 *Enter* DUKE [FREDERICK], *Lords, and* OLIVER

DUKE FREDERICK 'Not see him since'? Sir, sir, that cannot be!
    But were I not the better part made mercy,
    I should not seek an absent argument
    Of my revenge, thou present. But look to it:
    Find out thy brother, wheresoe'er he is;   5
    Seek him with candle; bring him dead or living
    Within this twelvemonth, or turn thou no more
    To seek a living in our territory.
    Thy lands and all things that thou dost call thine
    Worth seizure, do we seize into our hands   10

---

205 master] F2; masters F   206 SDD] *This edn; not in* F   **Act 3, Scene 1** 3.1] *Eds.; Actus Tertius. Scena Prima.* F   1 'Not . . . since'] *This edn;* Not . . . since F   1 see] F; seen *Collier*

199 whispered communicated (*OED* Whisper *v* 4b).

199 faithfully confidently, convincingly (*OED* sv 4a).

200 effigies The Latin word for 'likeness', the first recorded use in *OED*; it was accented on the second syllable (Cercignani, p. 42).

201 limned colourfully depicted.

204 cave Traditionally associated with wise hermits: it is notable that the act is never set within the cave.

205 Thou The form of address to a servant.

Act 3, Scene 1

2–4 the better . . . present so inclined to mercy, I would not seek out an absent object for my revenge but, since you are here, visit it upon you ('better' means 'greater' (*OED* sv *adj* 3b)).

2 made mercy For the omitted preposition, see Abbott 202.

4 thou present For the absolute construction, see Abbott 376.

6 with candle assiduously (possibly alluding to the parable of the woman in Luke 15.8 who, 'having ten pieces of silver, if she lose one piece doth . . . light a candle and sweep the house and seek diligently till she find it').

7 turn return.

8 To seek a With the expectation of (*OED* Living *ppl sb* 1).

10 seizure legal confiscation (*OED* sv 1).

Till thou canst quit thee by thy brother's mouth
Of what we think against thee.

OLIVER O that your highness knew my heart in this:
I never loved my brother in my life.

DUKE FREDERICK More villain thou. [*To Lords*] Well, push him out of
    doors   15
And let my officers of such a nature
Make an extent upon his house and lands.
Do this expediently and turn him going.

Exeunt [*severally*]

3.2 *Enter* ORLANDO [*with a paper*]

ORLANDO Hang there, my verse, in witness of my love;
    And thou, thrice-crownèd queen of night, survey
    With thy chaste eye, from thy pale sphere above,
    Thy huntress' name that my full life doth sway.
    O Rosalind, these trees shall be my books,   5
    And in their barks my thoughts I'll character

---

15 SD] *Eds.; not in* F   15 Well,] F2; *Well* F   18 SD *severally*] Oxford; *not in* F   **Act 3, Scene 2** 3.2] *Eds.; Scena Secunda.* F   0 SD *with a paper*] Capell; *not in* F

11 quit thee acquit yourself.

11 mouth testimony.

14 More villain thou Ironic, given that Duke Frederick had usurped his own brother's dukedom.

16 of such a nature appropriate.

17 Make an extent upon Draw up a writ and seize (*OED* sv *sb* 2b).

18 expediently expeditiously (*OED* sv 2, the only example quoted).

18 turn him going send him packing.

Act 3, Scene 2

1 Orlando, like Lodge's Rosader and Montanus, carves his lover's name on the bark of trees and hangs his verses on them – the ritual is imitated by the evil Sacripant in Greene's *Orlando Furioso* (1591); the habit may be traced back to the description of hanging lovers' vows on Ceres' sacred oak (*Metamorphoses*, VIII, 930–1; compare Lyly, *Love's Metamorphosis*, 1.1–2).

1 there Orlando might have hung his verses on one of the stage columns or on a property tree.

1 witness testimony.

2 thrice-crownèd queen of night In Ovid Medea invokes 'three-headed Hecate' (*Metamor-*

phoses, VII, 261) who ruled as Cynthia or Phoebe in the heavens, Diana or Artemis on earth, Hecate or Proserpina in the underworld; compare *MND* 5.1.362 and George Chapman's poem, 'Hymnus in Cynthiam' (1594).

2 survey see, perceive (in Orlando's verses; *OED* sv *v* 4c).

3 thy pale sphere that of the moon (which, like the planets, was supposed to be carried around the earth by a transparent sphere).

4 Thy huntress' name i.e. Rosalind, whom Orlando casts in the role of one of the huntress Diana's votarists: this signifies both her chastity and her role as a huntress in the game of love. In 'Hymnus in Cynthiam' Chapman, taking his cue from Hesiod's *Theogonia*, celebrates Diana who 'rules the fates of all' (206).

4 full entire.

4 sway control (*OED* sv *v* 9b).

6–10 Compare Lodge: '[Orlando] engraved with his knife on the bark of a myrtle tree this pretty estimate of his mistress' perfection' (*Rosalind*, p. 148).

6 character inscribe.

That every eye which in this forest looks
Shall see thy virtue witnessed everywhere.
Run, run, Orlando, carve on every tree
The fair, the chaste, and unexpressive she.   *Exit*   10

3.3 *Enter* CORIN *and* TOUCHSTONE

CORIN And how like you this shepherd's life, Master Touchstone?
TOUCHSTONE Truly, shepherd, in respect of itself, it is a good life; but
in respect that it is a shepherd's life, it is naught. In respect that it
is solitary, I like it very well; but in respect that it is private, it is a
very vile life. Now in respect it is in the fields, it pleaseth me well;   5
but in respect it is not in the court, it is tedious. As it is a spare life,
look you, it fits my humour well; but as there is no more plenty in
it, it goes much against my stomach. Hast any philosophy in thee,
shepherd?
CORIN No more but that I know the more one sickens, the worse at ease   10
he is; and that he that wants money, means, and content is without
three good friends; that the property of rain is to wet and fire to
burn; that good pasture makes fat sheep; and that a great cause of

Act 3, Scene 3 3.3] *Pope subst.; not in* F   1 Master] *Eds.;* Mʳ F; Monsieur *conj. this edn*   5 vile] *Eds.;* vild F

7 That So that.
8 virtue witnessed power and excellent qualities attested to.
10 unexpressive inexpressible (*OED* Inexpres-
sive 1); for the form of the adjective, see Abbott
3.
    10 she woman (Abbott 224).

Act 3, Scene 3
***3.3** F does not mark a new scene here, but
Orlando's exit leaves the stage empty, and his address to the moon suggests a short night interlude.
    1 *Master Corin may well address Touchstone
as 'Monsieur' as an (ironic) admission of his social
superiority.
    1–8 you . . . thee Corin uses the respectful form
of the pronoun, while Touchstone, the 'gentleman',
addresses the shepherd with the familiar form.
    2 in respect of with regard to (*OED* Respect *sb*
4a).
    3 in respect that considering (*OED* Respect *sb*
4c).
    3 naught worthless, useless.

4 private lonely, with a possible quibble on 'pri-
vates' (genitals).
    5 *vile F's 'vild', a variant of 'vile', is a form
'extremely common from *c.* 1580 to 1650' (*OED*).
    6 spare frugal.
    7 humour disposition.
    8 goes much against my stomach Proverbial
(Tilley s874).
    8 stomach (1) belly, appetite, (2) inclination.
    8 Hast For the omission of the subject, see
Abbott 401.
    8 philosophy practical wisdom (*OED* sv 1b).
    10–56 'It is the vocation of the true labourer that
Corin eloquently summarizes for Touchstone and
not, as some have taught us, the joys of country life'
(A. Stuart Daley, 'The dispraise of the country in
As You Like It', *SQ* 36 (1985), 300–14).
    10 but than (*OED* But *conj* 5).
    11 wants lacks.
    13–14 great . . . sun A commonplace: see *The
Poems of John Marston*, ed. Arnold Davenport, 1961,
p. 310.

the night is lack of the sun; that he that hath learned no wit by
nature nor art may complain of good breeding, or comes of a very   15
dull kindred.

TOUCHSTONE Such a one is a natural philosopher. – Wast ever in
court, shepherd?

CORIN No, truly.

TOUCHSTONE Then thou art damned.   20

CORIN Nay, I hope.

TOUCHSTONE Truly thou art damned: like an ill-roasted egg, all on one
side.

CORIN For not being at court? Your reason.

TOUCHSTONE Why, if thou never wast at court, thou never saw'st good   25
manners; if thou never saw'st good manners, then thy manners
must be wicked, and wickedness is sin, and sin is damnation. Thou
art in a parlous state, shepherd.

CORIN Not a whit, Touchstone: those that are good manners at the
court are as ridiculous in the country as the behaviour of the coun-   30
try is most mockable at the court. You told me you salute not at the
court but you kiss your hands: that courtesy would be uncleanly if
courtiers were shepherds.

TOUCHSTONE Instance, briefly; come, instance.

CORIN Why, we are still handling our ewes, and their fells, you know,   35
are greasy.

---

15 complain] F; complain of want *conj. Oxford*   15 good] F; bad *Hanmer;* gross *Warburton*   17–18] *As prose, Pope;*
Clo. . . . Philosopher: / Was't . . . Shepheard? F   21 hope.] F; hope – *Rowe*   29 whit,] F *subst.;* whit, Master *Dyce²*

14 **wit** knowledge.

15 **nature nor art** birth or education; Corin
would seem to have confused the attributes of nurture ('good breeding') and nature ('dull kindred').

15 **complain of good breeding** *OED* offers no
examples of the meaning customarily offered by editors, 'complain of the lack of good breeding' (see
collation): there is no reason why Corin should not
be satirising the wisdom of his 'betters'.

15 **breeding** education (*OED* sv 3).

16 **dull kindred** obtuse family.

17 **Such . . . philosopher** This could be an aside
at Corin's expense, or a description of the individual
Corin has just described.

17 **natural philosopher** (1) student of science,
(2) fool.

21 **Nay, I hope** (1) I hope not, (2) No, I am full
of hope of salvation.

22–3 **like . . . side** as an egg is irretrievably spoiled
by being exposed to heat without being turned –
eggs were roasted in hot ashes; Touchstone may be

invoking the proverb, 'Set a fool to roast eggs and
a wise man to eat them' (Tilley F504), as a jibe at
Corin whose 'natural' virtues need complementing
by courtly ones.

25–7 **Why . . . damnation** Such chop-logic was
popular in the humanist period; Touchstone is playing with two meanings of 'good': (1) courtly, (2)
morally correct.

26 **thy manners** (1) your morals (*OED* Manner
sb¹ 4a), (2) your behaviour (*ibid.* 4c).

28 **parlous** perilous, dangerous.

29 **Touchstone** Corin has dropped the respect-
ful 'Master' (see 1 n.).

31 **salute not** do not greet one another.

32 **but you kiss** without kissing (Abbott 125).

32 **courtesy** usage.

34 **Instance** Either a noun (meaning 'an example
adduced for proof' (*OED* sv *sb* 6)) or a verb.

35 **still** continually.

35 **fells** fleeces; the first recorded use in *OED*
(Fell *sb¹* 3).

TOUCHSTONE Why, do not your courtier's hands sweat, and is not the grease of a mutton as wholesome as the sweat of a man? Shallow, shallow! A better instance, I say – come.

CORIN Besides, our hands are hard.   40

TOUCHSTONE Your lips will feel them the sooner. Shallow again: a more sounder instance, come.

CORIN And they are often tarred over with the surgery of our sheep, and would you have us kiss tar? The courtiers' hands are perfumed with civet.   45

TOUCHSTONE Most shallow man! Thou worms' meat in respect of a good piece of flesh, indeed! Learn of the wise and perpend: civet is of a baser birth than tar, the very uncleanly flux of a cat. Mend the instance, shepherd.

CORIN You have too courtly a wit for me; I'll rest.   50

TOUCHSTONE Wilt thou rest damned? God help thee, shallow man. God make incision in thee, thou art raw.

CORIN Sir, I am a true labourer: I earn that I eat, get that I wear, owe no man hate, envy no man's happiness, glad of other men's good, content with my harm; and the greatest of my pride is to see my   55 ewes graze and my lambs suck.

TOUCHSTONE That is another simple sin in you: to bring the ewes and the rams together and to offer to get your living by the copulation of

---

37 courtier's] *Capell;* Courtiers F; Courtiers' *Theobald*³   46 shallow] F; shallow, *Rowe*   46 man!] *Theobald;* man: F   47 flesh,] *Eds.;* flesh F   52 incision] F; insition *conj. Wilson*   54 good,] F2; good F

37 your Meaning vaguely 'that that you know of' (Abbott 221).

38 grease sweat (it was thought that fat was exuded through the pores as sweat).

38 mutton sheep (*OED* sv 2).

42 more sounder For double comparatives, see Abbott 11.

43 tarred Tar was used to stop the bleeding of cuts made by shearers.

45 civet perfume derived from glands in the anal pouch of civet cats (*OED* sv *sb*¹ 2).

46 worms' meat (1) food for worms or maggots (*OED* Worm *sb* 5a), i.e. a piece of fly-blown flesh, (2) corpse (*OED* Worm *sb* 6c); compare the proverb, 'A man is nothing but worm's meat' (Tilley M253, and see Shaheen, p. 164).

46 respect of comparison with.

47 good piece of flesh fine human being (*OED* Flesh *sb* 8).

47 perpend ponder.

48 flux discharge, secretion (see 45 n.).

48–9 Mend the instance Improve your argument (*OED* Mend *v* 11).

50 rest cease (*OED* sv *v* 2e).

52 God make incision in thee i.e. in order to let blood, a possible cure for madness; compare the proverb, 'To be cut for (of) the simples' (Tilley S463) meaning to be cured of folly; however, the form 'incision' was often used improperly in the period for 'insition' or 'graft' (*OED* Incision 5), a meaning which fits the context perfectly.

52 raw (1) afflicted as with a 'raw' wound, (2) uncultivated, immature (*OED* sv *adj* 3c and 4a).

53 true labourer trustworthy worker, with a possible reference to the sober and labouring brethren of 1 Thess. 5.6 and 12.

53 earn that work for what.

53 get earn.

55 content with my harm resigned to any affliction (*OED* Harm *sb* 2).

55 pride honest pride, as opposed to the vanity of the courtier.

57 simple stupid (*OED* sv *adj* 11) – by virtue of your breeding.

58 offer presume.

cattle; to be bawd to a bell-wether and to betray a she-lamb of a
twelvemonth to a crooked-pated old cuckoldly ram out of all rea-   60
sonable match. If thou be'st not damned for this, the devil himself
will have no shepherds. I cannot see else how thou shouldst 'scape.

CORIN Here comes young Monsieur Ganymede, my new mistress's
brother.

Enter ROSALIND [*as* GANYMEDE]

ROSALIND [*Reading from a paper*]
        'From the East to Western Inde   65
          No jewel is like Rosalind;
        Her worth, being mounted on the wind,
          Through all the world bears Rosalind;
        All the pictures fairest lined
          Are but black to Rosalind;   70
        Let no face be kept in mind
          But the fair of Rosalind.'

TOUCHSTONE I'll rhyme you so eight years together, dinners and sup-
pers and sleeping-hours excepted. It is the right butter-women's
rank to market.   75

---

64 SD *as* GANYMEDE] *Eds.; not in* F   65 SD] *Rowe subst.; not in* F   69 lined] F *subst.;* limn'd *Johnson*   70 black] F
subst; blank *conj. this edn*   72 fair] F *subst.;* face *Walker*   73 SH] F *subst.;* TOUCHSTONE [*Coming forward*] / *conj. this
edn.*   74 sleeping-hours] *Eds.;* sleeping hours F   74 butter-women's] F *subst.;* butter-woman's *Johnson*   74 rank] F
subst.; rate *conj. Hanmer;* rack *White²*, *conj. Cam.*

---

59 **cattle** (1) beasts, (2) whores (*OED* sv 7b).

59 **bawd** procurer, pander (Williams, p. 37).

59 **bell-wether** leading sheep of a flock, bearing
a bell around its neck ('wether' often designated a
castrated ram, but obviously not here).

60 **crooked-pated** with a deformed head.

60 **cuckoldly** possessed of an unfaithful wife and
therefore, like a ram, horned.

60–1 **out of all reasonable match** in defiance
of anything that might be called proper.

61–2 **the . . . shepherds** it is because even the
devil refuses to admit shepherds to hell.

62 **else** otherwise.

62 **'scape** escape.

65 *SD It is not clear whether Rosalind is ignorant
of the presence of Corin and Touchstone, and, if so,
whether she enters to find the poem Orlando pinned
up at the beginning of the scene or has picked up
another paper elsewhere.

65–72 For the equivalent poem in *Rosalind*, see
Appendix 2, p. 233.

65 Compare the proverb, 'From the east to the
west' (Dent E43.1); the East Indies designated India
and the islands of the Malay archipelago and, after

the voyages of Columbus, were distinguished from
the West Indies, the islands off the east coast of
America. Both places were associated with wealth
and gems. 'Inde' was pronounced to rhyme with
'mind' (Cercignani, pp. 24–5).

67 **worth** merit, reputation.

69 **lined** sketched, delineated (*OED* Line *v²* 4,
quoting this as its first example).

70 **black** foul (*OED* sv *a* 9).

70 **to** compared with.

72 **fair** beauty (*OED* sv *sb²* B4a; compare *Son.*
18.7).

73 **you** An ethical dative.

73 **together** without intermission (*OED* sv *adv*
5).

74 **sleeping-hours** (1) hours of rest (prescribed
by a statute of 1563), (2) hours for sex (?).

74–5 **the . . . market** 'i.e. precisely like dairy-
women riding along one behind another at the
same pace on their way to market' (Riverside; see
OED sv *sb¹* 2c, although this is the only instance
offered). White's emendation 'rack' (see collation)
would designate 'a horse's gait in which the two
feet on each side are lifted almost simultaneously,

ROSALIND Out, fool!

TOUCHSTONE For a taste:

> If a hart do lack a hind,
>   Let him seek out Rosalind;
> If the cat will after kind,   80
>   So be sure will Rosalind;
> Wintered garments must be lined,
>   So must slender Rosalind;
> They that reap must sheaf and bind,
>   Then to cart with Rosalind;   85
> Sweetest nut hath sourest rind,
>   Such a nut is Rosalind;
> He that sweetest rose will find,
>   Must find love's prick – and Rosalind.

This is the very false gallop of verses: why do you infect yourself   90
with them?

ROSALIND Peace, you dull fool. I found them on a tree.

TOUCHSTONE Truly, the tree yields bad fruit.

ROSALIND I'll graft it with you, and then I shall graft it with a medlar;

---

82 Wintered] F *subst.;* Winter F3   94 graft *Eds.;* graffe F

and the body is left entirely without support between
the lifting of one pair and the landing of the other'
(*OED* sv *sb*⁶) – Touchstone, as he does below (90),
is berating the jog-trot rhythm of Orlando's verse.

74 right true.

74 butter-women's Part of a generalised insult
(see 85 n.), but with a sexual edge since both 'butter-
quean' and 'butter-whore' (a scolding butter-woman
– *OED* Butter *sb* 5) were current (see Gary Taylor, 'Touchstone's butterwomen', *RES* n.s. 32
(1981)); compare Dekker, Ford, and Rowley, *The
Witch of Edmonton* (1621); 'I took my wife and a
servingman . . . thrashing in my barn together such
corn as country wenches carry to market' (4.1.5–7).

78–89 The two most famous clowns of Shakespeare's times, Richard Tarlton and Robert Armin
(Wiles, pp. 14, 138) were celebrated for their ability
to improvise rhyming verse of this kind; in *Love in
a Forest* (see Stage History, p. 56) the poem is given
to Celia.

78 hart, hind full-grown male and the female
respectively of the red deer.

80 Compare the proverb, 'Cat after kind' (Tilley
C135); 'doing the deed of kind' was a euphemism for
copulation (see *MV* 1.3.85).

82 Wintered Old (*OED* sv 1), rather than
'adapted for or used in winter' (*OED* sv 3).

82 lined In the context a *double entendre*, 'covered
or mounted' as by a dog (see *OED* Line *v*³).

83 slender i.e. before she becomes pregnant.

84 reap Pronounced 'rape' (Cercignani, p. 165).

84 sheaf gather into sheaves.

85 to cart (1) as corn is carried, (2) as a harlot
was whipped at the tail of a cart (see *OED* Cart *v* 2).

86 Compare the proverb, 'Sweet is the nut but
bitter is the shell' (Tilley N360).

86 nut Here the vulva to be opened for its kernel
(Williams, p. 220).

88–9 Compare the proverb, 'No rose without a
prickle' (Tilley R182).

88–9 rose, prick female and male genitals (Jones,
pp. 211–12; Williams, pp. 262–3, 245–6).

89 find suffer (*OED* sv *v* 7a).

90 false gallop canter; proverbial for unmetrical
verse (Dent G14.1).

90 infect stain, poison (*OED* sv *v* 1).

93 Compare Matt. 7.18: 'A good tree cannot yield
evil fruits' (Rheims version; see Shaheen, p. 164).

94 graft The process of inserting a shoot from
one tree into the stock of another was sexually suggestive (Williams, p. 145).

94 you punning on 'yew'.

94–6 Compare the proverb, 'Fools will be meddling' (Tilley F 546, from Prov. 20.3, 'every fool will
be meddling'); 'meddle' meant 'have sexual intercourse with' (*OED* sv 5).

94 medlar (1) species of apple which is eaten
only when over-ripe, (2) someone who interferes,

then it will be the earliest fruit i'th'country, for you'll be rotten ere 95
you be half ripe, and that's the right virtue of the medlar.

TOUCHSTONE You have said – but whether wisely or no, let the forest
judge.

Enter CELIA [*as* ALIENA] *with a writing*

ROSALIND Peace, here comes my sister, reading. Stand aside.

CELIA   'Why should this a desert be? 100
For it is unpeopled? No:
Tongues I'll hang on every tree,
That shall civil sayings show:
Some how brief the life of man
Runs his erring pilgrimage 105
That the stretching of a span
Buckles in his sum of age;
Some of violated vows
'Twixt the souls of friend and friend;
But upon the fairest boughs 110
Or at every sentence end
Will I "Rosalinda" write,
Teaching all that read to know
The quintessence of every sprite

---

98 SD *as* ALIENA] *Eds.; not in* F   100 this a] *Rowe;* this F   100 be?] *Rowe; bee.* F   101 unpeopled?] F *subst.;* unpeopled.
Rowe

(3) a general term of sexual abuse ('open-arse' was a
dialect name for a medlar).
    95 fruit fruit-tree (*OED* sv *sb* 3).
    95 country (1) vicinity, (2) genital area (Partridge, pp. 97–8).
    95–6 rotten . . . ripe Compare the proverbs,
'Medlars are never good till they be rotten' and
'Soon ripe soon rotten' (Tilley M863 and R133).
    95 rotten infected with venereal disease
(Williams, 'rot', pp. 263–4).
    96 ripe sexually mature (Williams, p. 260).
    96 right virtue true quality.
    97 You have said That's what you say; proverbial (Dent S118.1).
    100 *a desert an uninhabited place, including
forest-land (*OED* sv *sb²* 1); Rowe's emendation (see
collation) improves the metre.
    101 For Because (Abbott 151).
    102 Tongues The sheets of verse could appear
like tongues or, in the light of 125 below, perhaps a
reference to the tongues that appeared to the apostles at Pentecost (Acts 2.3).

103 civil civilised, sophisticated.
    104–5 Compare the proverb, 'Life is a pilgrimage'
(Tilley L249).
    105 erring (1) wandering, (2) sinful.
    106 That So that.
    106 stretching of a span fully extended hand;
compare the proverb, 'Life is a span' (Tilley L251)
which derives from Ps. 39.5.
    107 Buckles in Encompasses, limits.
    107 sum of age life-time.
    111 sentence pithy saying or *sententia*: grammatically a possessive (Abbott 217).
    114 quintessence The 'fifth essence' or that
which surpassed the four elements of the terrestrial world, and out of which alchemists and others
considered the heavenly bodies to be composed; it
was thought to be latent in all natural things and
might be extracted by distillation. The word was
stressed on the first and third syllables (Cercignani,
p. 40).
    114 sprite spirit, animating principle.

Heaven would in little show.   115
Therefore Heaven Nature charged
That one body should be filled
With all graces wide-enlarged;
Nature presently distilled
Helen's cheek but not her heart,   120
    Cleopatra's majesty,
Atalanta's better part,
    Sad Lucretia's modesty.
Thus Rosalind of many parts
By heavenly synod was devised,   125
Of many faces, eyes, and hearts,
To have the touches dearest prized.
Heaven would that she these gifts should have,
And I to live and die her slave.'

---

120 her] *Rowe; his* F   123 Lucretia's] F4; Lucrecia's F

115 in little in miniature (as in a painting – see *OED* Little 10), i.e. in the microcosm.

116–27 Shakespeare may have remembered that Pliny relates how the painter Zeuxis demanded to see naked all the maidens of Agrigentum in order that he might choose the fairest parts of five of them in order to make a picture (*The History of the World*, chapter XXXV, 9).

116 Nature In Ovid, Nature worked in partnership with God to impose harmony upon the chaotic substance of the world (*Metamorphoses*, I, 20); for developments of the idea see Curtius, pp. 106–27.

117–18 Compare *Temp.*: 'you, / So perfect and so peerless, are created / Of every creature's best' (3.1.46–8).

118 wide-enlarged spread widely through a multitude of women.

119 presently immediately.

120 The beauty but not the falseness of Helen of Troy.

120 *her F's 'his' (see collation) may derive from authorial or compositorial awareness that Rosalind's part was taken by a boy.

122 Atalanta's better part Atalanta refused to take as husband any man who could not defeat her in a foot-race; Ovid wrote of this great virgin huntress who 'lived in the shady woods . . . hard it is to tell Thee whether she did in footmanship or beauty more excel' (*Metamorphoses*, X, 658, 650–1); Golding uses the phrase 'better part of me' to mean 'my soul' at the end of the poem (XV, 989). Here 'better

part' would seem to refer to beauty as opposed to her cruelty, although it could be an oblique reference to her androgyne beauty or even her vagina (*OED* Part *sb* 3): Ovid writes of her naked body 'the which was like to mine, / Or rather (if that thou wert made a woman) like to thine' (674–5). However, the reference may well be to another Atalanta, daughter of Iasos, who helped Meleager kill the Calydonian boar (*Metamorphoses*, VIII, 359 ff.) Like Rosalind, this Atalanta was also androgynous: 'Her countenance and her grace / Was such as in a boy might well be called a wench's face, / And in a wench a boy's. The Prince of Calydon [Meleager] / No sooner cast his eye on her but being caught anon / In love, he wished her to his wife. But unto this desire / God Cupid gave not his consent' (VIII, 434–9).

123 Sad Grave, serious.

123 Lucretia's modesty The chastity of the Roman matron who killed herself after being raped by Sextus, son of Tarquinius Superbus.

125 heavenly synod assembly of divinities, although 'synod' could mean 'a conjunction of two planets or heavenly bodies' (*OED* 3), one of the meanings of the Greek word from which it derives.

127 touches features, characteristics (*OED* Touch *sb* 18).

128 would willed (Abbot 329).

129 And I to And that I should.

129 live and die The phrase recalls the variations on penile erection and detumescence played out in *Son.* 151.

ROSALIND [*Coming forward*] O most gentle Jupiter, what tedious 130
homily of love have you wearied your parishioners withal, and never
cried, 'Have patience, good people!'

CELIA How now? Backfriends! – Shepherd, go off a little. – Go with
him, sirrah.

TOUCHSTONE Come, shepherd, let us make an honourable retreat, 135
though not with bag and baggage, yet with scrip and scrippage.

Exeunt Touchstone and Corin

CELIA Didst thou hear these verses?

ROSALIND O yes, I heard them all, and more too, for some of them had
in them more feet than the verses would bear.

CELIA That's no matter: the feet might bear the verses. 140

ROSALIND Aye, but the feet were lame and could not bear themselves
without the verse, and therefore stood lamely in the verse.

CELIA But didst thou hear without wondering how thy name should be
hanged and carved upon these trees?

ROSALIND I was seven of the nine days out of the wonder before you 145
came, for look here what I found on a palm-tree. I was never so

---

130 SD] *This edn; not in* F   130 Jupiter] F *subst.;* Juniper *Warburton;* pulpiter *Cam., conj. Spedding*   133 How . . .
Backfriends!] *Theobald subst.;* How now backe friends: F*;* How now? back, friends *Collier*   136 SD] *Rowe subst.; Exit* F

---

130 Jupiter Spedding's emendation 'pulpiter'
(preacher) is attractive (see collation): it forms part
of a conceit with 'homily' and 'parishioners', and F
does not print 'Iupiter' in italics as is normal for
a proper name; *OED*, however, does not record
the word (pulpiteer) before 1642. As Jupiter was
Ganymede's lover, however, Rosalind's oath may be
appropriate – she had invoked him at 2.4.1.

131 you The switch from 'thou' to the more
formal pronoun suggests an element of tetchiness
between the two women.

133 *Backfriends False friends, traitors (compare *Err.* 4.2.37); Theobald's emendation (see collation) is justified by the situation in which Rosalind
and her companions are spying on Celia who comes
not just to mock Orlando's verse but to reveal that
he too is in the forest.

134 sirrah A form of address sometimes expressing contempt.

136 bag and baggage all the equipment of an
army; hence a retreat with 'bag and baggage' was an
honourable retreat (*OED* Bag *sb* 20; Dent BB1); the
phrase was probably meant to be insulting, as 'bag'
designated the scrotum and 'baggage' was slang for
a strumpet or slut (Williams, pp. 33–4).

136 scrip (1) bag worn by a pilgrim, shepherd,
or beggar; (2) the word may designate 'script' as in

MND 1.2.3, implying that Touchstone carried off
the paper bearing the verse; (3) a scornful grimace
(Hulme, p. 36).

136 scrippage A nonce-word coined by Touchstone by analogy with 'baggage', meaning '"contents
of wallet", "what is written" and "mockery"'
(Hulme, p. 37).

137 verses lines of poetry (*OED* Verse *sb* 1).

138–9 some . . . feet Line 128 is indeed unmetrical, unless 'Heaven' is elided to 'Heav'n'.

139 bear tolerate.

140 bear carry.

142 without outside.

143 should be Commonly used in reported
speech for 'was' (Abbott 328), but also expressing
doubt on the part of the speaker (*OED* Shall *v* 15).

145 was . . . out had already experienced a great
deal: the phrase 'a wonder lasts but nine days' was
proverbial (Tilley W728).

146 palm-tree willow (*OED* Palm *sb*¹ 4); the
boughs were used in Palm Sunday processions
(Henry John Feasey, *Ancient English Holy Week Ritual* (1897), pp. 53–62). Alternatively an exotic detail
out of the fantasy landscapes of antiquity (Curtius,
p. 185; compare the 'olive-trees' of 4.3.72), the Bible
(Ex. 15.27 etc.), or medieval representations of the
Garden of Eden.

berhymed since Pythagoras' time that I was an Irish rat – which I can hardly remember.

CELIA Trow you who hath done this?

ROSALIND Is it a man?   150

CELIA And a chain that you once wore about his neck? Change you colour?

ROSALIND I prithee, who?

CELIA O Lord, Lord, it is a hard matter for friends to meet, but mountains may be removed with earthquakes and so encounter.   155

ROSALIND Nay, but who is it?

CELIA Is it possible?

ROSALIND Nay, I prithee now, with most petitionary vehemence, tell me who it is.

CELIA O wonderful, wonderful, and most wonderful wonderful, and yet   160
again wonderful, and after that out of all hooping.

ROSALIND Good my complexion, dost thou think, though I am caparisoned like a man, I have a doublet and hose in my disposition? One inch of delay more is a South Sea of discovery. I prithee tell me

---

151 neck?] *Collier;* neck: F   **162** Good] F; Od's, *Theobald subst.*   **162** complexion] *Eds.;* complection F; complector *conj. this edn*   **164** of] F; off *Theobald*

---

147 berhymed . . . rat Compare the proverb, 'To rhyme to death, as they do rats in Ireland' (Tilley D158), and see Sir Philip Sidney, *An Apology for Poetry*, ed. G. Shepherd, 1965, p. 237, 26 n.; Katherine Duncan-Jones, 'A note on Irish poets and the Sidneys', *ES* 49 (1968), 424–5; Philip Edwards, *Threshold of a Nation*, 1979, pp. 11–12.

147 Pythagoras The Greek philosopher, born about 580 BC, whose teachings included injunctions against killing for food and the notion of the transmigration of the spirit from humans to beasts (see *Metamorphoses*, XV, 84–103, 176–92).

147 that when (Abbott 284).

147 which which thing (Abbott 271)

149 Trow you Can you tell; Celia's switch to 'you' from 'thou' may express some mockery of Rosalind's role as Orlando's courtly mistress.

151–2 Change you colour ? Do you blush?

154–5 hard . . . encounter An inversion of the proverb, 'Friends may meet, but mountains never greet' (Tilley F738); compare Matt. 20.5: 'If ye have faith . . . ye shall say unto this mountain, "Remove hence to yonder place", and it shall remove'; 'hard' is a probable sexual pun (Williams, p. 151).

155 with by means of (Abbott 193).

155 encounter come together in an amatory embrace (Williams, p. 113).

158 with most petitionary vehemence I urgently entreat you.

161 out of all hooping Proverbial (Dent C871.1 'Out of all cry'); literally 'out of earshot', but with a pun on 'hooping' meaning 'embracing' (*OED* Hoop *v* 2).

162 Good my complexion 'By my disposition': an oath possibly coined for the occasion and probably an admission that she is blushing. It is conceivable (see collation) that the compositor mistook 'complexion' for a nonce-word, 'complector', referring to Celia, who could be embracing Rosalind at this moment; Theobald's emendation 'Od's', a minced form of 'God's', is a possibility.

163 caparisoned dressed, decked out.

163 doublet and hose See 2.4.5 n.

164 One . . . discovery Any more delay would seem as long as a voyage of exploration in the South Seas, or, possibly, if you delay your answers any longer I shall inundate you with further questions – or even reveal (discover) my true identity.

164 inch 'iota'.

164 South Sea The South Pacific Ocean (*OED* South Sea 2).

who is it – quickly, and speak apace. I would thou couldst stammer   165
that thou might'st pour this concealed man out of thy mouth as
wine comes out of a narrow-mouthed bottle: either too much at
once or none at all. I prithee take the cork out of thy mouth that I
may drink thy tidings.

CELIA So you may put a man in your belly.   170

ROSALIND Is he of God's making? What manner of man? Is his head
worth a hat or his chin worth a beard?

CELIA Nay, he hath but a little beard.

ROSALIND Why, God will send more if the man will be thankful. Let
me stay the growth of his beard, if thou delay me not the knowledge 175
of his chin.

CELIA It is young Orlando, that tripped up the wrestler's heels and your
heart both in an instant.

ROSALIND Nay, but the devil take mocking! Speak sad brow and true
maid.   180

CELIA I'faith, coz, 'tis he.

ROSALIND Orlando?

CELIA Orlando.

ROSALIND Alas the day, what shall I do with my doublet and hose?
What did he when thou saw'st him? What said he? How looked he?   185
Wherein went he? What makes he here? Did he ask for me? Where
remains he? How parted he with thee? And when shalt thou see him
again? Answer me in one word.

CELIA You must borrow me Gargantua's mouth first: 'tis a word too

---

165 it –] *This edn; it* F; *it,* Rowe

165 apace fast.

167 wine Here means also 'semen' (Rubinstein, p. 305).

170 Brissenden compares Middleton, *A Chaste Maid in Cheapside*, 2.1.15–16: 'Life, every year a child, and some years two; / Besides drinkings abroad, that's never reckoned' to indicate the bawdy construction Celia places upon 'drink' (168).

170 So Thus.

171 of God's making Proverbial for a normal human being (Tilley M162); but compare 'Nature disclaims in thee: a tailor made thee', *Lear* 2.2.54–5.

172 worth equal to.

173 Compare Lodge's Rosader: 'casting up his hand, he felt hair on his face, and, perceiving his beard to bud . . . began to blush' (*Rosalind*, p. 105).

174 be thankful acknowledge God's blessing.

175 stay wait for.

175–6 if . . . chin provided you tell me upon whose chin it grows.

179 mocking teasing.

179–80 sad brow and true maid seriously and honestly (compare the construction of *Oth.* 2.3.279: 'Drunk? and speak parrot?').

184 Alas the day For biblical analogues, see Shaheen, pp. 165–6.

186 Wherein went he ? How was he dressed? (*OED* Wherein *adv* 1).

186 makes does.

187 remains dwells (*OED* Remain *v* 4b).

187 with from (Abbott 194).

189 Gargantua A giant; Rabelais, who celebrated the voracious appetite of this giant, was fully translated only in 1693–4 but was known in England in the 1590s (see Huntingdon Brown, *Rabelais in English Literature*, 1933, pp. 31–70); however, Gargantua also figured in chapbooks of the period.

great for any mouth of this age's size. To say 'aye' and 'no' to these   190
particulars is more than to answer in a catechism.

ROSALIND But doth he know that I am in this forest and in man's
apparel? Looks he as freshly as he did the day he wrestled?

CELIA It is as easy to count atomies as to resolve the propositions of a
lover; but take a taste of my finding him and relish it with good   195
observance. I found him under a tree like a dropped acorn.

ROSALIND [*Aside*] It may well be called Jove's tree when it drops forth
such fruit.

CELIA Give me audience, good madam.

ROSALIND Proceed.   200

CELIA There lay he stretched along like a wounded knight.

ROSALIND Though it be pity to see such a sight, it well becomes the
ground.

CELIA Cry 'holla' to thy tongue, I prithee: it curvets unseasonably. He
was furnished like a hunter.   205

ROSALIND O ominous: he comes to kill my heart.

CELIA I would sing my song without a burden; thou bring'st me out of
tune.

---

197 SD] *This edn; not in* F   197–8 forth such] F2; forth F; such *Capell*   204 thy] *Rowe;* the F   206 heart] *Rowe;* Hart
F   207 burden] *Eds.;* burthen F

190–1 To . . . catechism These questions do not
admit of simple answers as do those in the catechism;
compare Matt. 5.37, 'Let your communication be,
yea, yea; nay, nay.'

191 particulars details.

191 catechism catechesis, or instruction by
word of mouth (*OED* sv 1), as in the set of questions and answers set out in the Book of Common
Prayer.

193 freshly (1) healthy, (2) shamelessly (Partridge, p. 111).

194 atomies atoms, motes.

194 resolve answer (*OED* sv *v* 11a).

194 propositions questions.

195 my finding how I found.

195 relish taste (*OED* sv *v*¹ 2).

196 observance attention (*OED* sv 5).

196 acorn For the phallic connotations, see
Jones, pp. 214–15 and Rubinstein, p. 4.

197 Jove's tree the oak, sacred to Jupiter; in the
Golden Age men lived off wild fruit and 'the acorns
dropped on ground from Jove's broad tree in field'
(*Metamorphoses*, 1, 121; see also 93 n. and 130 n.
above and compare Virgil, *Georgics*, III, 332).

197–8 *forth such F2 probably restores a missing word (see collation), although F's 'forth' could
equally have been a misreading of 'such'; Shake-

speare used 'drop forth such' at 4.3.33, where there
are connotations of child-bearing.

199 Give me audience Hear me.

201 along at length; the pose of a melancholic,
fashionable in portraiture (see Roy Strong, *The
English Icon: Elizabethan and Jacobean Portraiture*,
1969, p. 353).

201 wounded knight Possibly, as in Petrarch,
wounded by Cupid's arrows.

202–3 becomes the ground possibly 'suits the
background', as in a tapestry or picture (*OED*
Ground *sb* 6a and b), although 'becomes' may mean
simply 'adorn' (*OED* Become 9c).

204 holla whoa (stop), as to a horse.

204 *thy Rowe's emendation (see collation)
probably corrects a compositorial error.

204 curvets prances (accented on the second syllable (*OED*)).

204 unseasonably in an ill-timed manner,
indecorously.

205 furnished dressed.

206 *heart a heart/hart pun.

207 would should like to (Abbott 329).

207 *burden 'bourdon' or bass, continuous
undersong (*OED* Burden *sb* 9): Celia means that
Rosalind keeps interrupting her.

207 bring'st put (*OED* Bring 21a).

ROSALIND Do you not know I am a woman? When I think, I must
speak. Sweet, say on.   210

Enter ORLANDO *and* JAQUES

CELIA You bring me out. – Soft, comes he not here?
ROSALIND 'Tis he. Slink by, and note him.
[Rosalind and Celia stand aside]
JAQUES I thank you for your company, but, good faith, I had as lief have
been myself alone.
ORLANDO And so had I. But yet, for fashion sake, I thank you too for   215
your society.
JAQUES God buy you. Let's meet as little as we can.
ORLANDO I do desire we may be better strangers.
JAQUES I pray you mar no more trees with writing love-songs in their
barks.   220
ORLANDO I pray you mar no mo of my verses with reading them ill-
favouredly.
JAQUES 'Rosalind' is your love's name?
ORLANDO Yes, just.
JAQUES I do not like her name.   225
ORLANDO There was no thought of pleasing you when she was
christened.
JAQUES What stature is she of?
ORLANDO Just as high as my heart.
JAQUES You are full of pretty answers: have you not been acquainted   230
with goldsmiths' wives and conned them out of rings?

---

211 here] F *subst.;* neere F2   212 SD] *Theobald subst.; not in* F   213–16] *As prose, Pope; Iaq* . . . faith / I . . . alone. /
Orl. . . . sake / I . . . societie. F   219 more] F; moe *Sisson*

209–10 When . . . speak Compare the proverb,
'What the heart thinks the tongue speaks' (Tilley
H334).

210 say on speak further (compare *2H4* 4.1.29).

211 bring me out make me forget my words, a
petulant repetition of 207–8; compare 'They do not
mark me, and that brings me out' (*LLL* 5.2.173).

211 Soft Hush.

214 myself by myself (Abbott 20 n.).

215 for fashion sake Tilley, from 1721, records
'For fashion's sake, as dogs go to the market'
(F76), but Dent offers further examples from Shake-
speare's time; the words serve as a polite insult. (For
the uninflected possessive form, see the quotation in
OED Fashion *sb* 7.)

216 society company.

217 God buy you Good-bye, derived, via the

present form, from 'God be with you' (see *OED*
Good-bye).

221 mo more (used of greater quantities rather
than larger amounts: see *OED* Mo *adj* 2), but compare 'more' in 219.

221–2 ill-favouredly in an unbecoming
manner.

224 just exactly.

230 pretty clever (*OED* sv 2b).

230–3 Jaques charges Orlando with memoris-
ing the 'posies' or mottoes inscribed within rings
(with lewd overtones, as 'quaint' and '*con*' (Fr.)
were names for the vulva, and 'ring' both designated this organ and served as a symbol of honour –
as in *AWW* 4.2.45–51; Williams, pp. 78 and 260). In
return Orlando accuses Jaques of taking his utterances from the 'sentences' on painted wall-hangings

ORLANDO Not so; but I answer you right painted cloth, from whence
   you have studied your questions.

JAQUES You have a nimble wit; I think 'twas made of Atalanta's heels.
   Will you sit down with me, and we two will rail against our mistress   235
   the world and all our misery.

ORLANDO I will chide no breather in the world but myself, against
   whom I know most faults.

JAQUES The worst fault you have is to be in love.

ORLANDO 'Tis a fault I will not change for your best virtue: I am weary   240
   of you.

JAQUES By my troth, I was seeking for a fool, when I found you.

ORLANDO He is drowned in the brook: look but in, and you shall see
   him.

JAQUES There I shall see mine own figure.   245

ORLANDO Which I take to be either a fool or a cipher.

JAQUES I'll tarry no longer with you. Farewell, good Signor Love.

ORLANDO I am glad of your departure. Adieu, good Monsieur
   Melancholy.

                                                              [*Exit Jaques*]

ROSALIND I will speak to him like a saucy lackey, and under that habit   250
   play the knave with him. [*To Orlando*] Do you hear, forester?

ORLANDO Very well. What would you?

ROSALIND I pray you, what is't o'clock?

---

238 most] F; no F2   249 SD] *Rowe; not in* F   251 SD] *Theobald subst.; not in* F

(cheap substitutes for tapestry which seem to have
been hung not only in domestic houses but on
tiring-house façades in playhouses and which often
depicted scriptural subjects); a set is described in
William Bullein's *Dialogue against the Fever Pesti-
lence* (1564).
   232 **answer** respond to, retort to.
   233 **questions** topics for debate (*quaestiones*).
   234 **Atalanta** See 122 n.
   235 **Will you** If it please you.
   235 **rail** exclaim, complain.
   235–6 **mistress the world** The phrase occurs
in the Epistle to the satirist George Wither's *The
Shepherds Hunting* (1615), a piece of invective in the
style affected by Jaques.
   237 **breather** living creature.
   237–8 **against . . . faults** Orlando claims the
classical and Christian virtue of self-knowledge.
   238 **faults** deficiencies (*OED* Fault *sb* 1).
   240 **change** exchange.
   242 **a fool** Touchstone, although Jaques implies
that Orlando fits the bill.

243–4 Referring to the myth of Narcissus, who
fell in love with his own reflected image (*Metamorphoses*, III, 431–642).
   245 **figure** likeness, image, i.e. not a fool.
   246 **cipher** zero, in the context of the pun on
'figures', a nonentity; compare the proverb, 'He is a
cipher among numbers' (Tilley C391).
   247 **Signor** Sir (with mock reverence).
   250 **saucy lackey** (1) impertinent footman, (2)
wanton rogue or gamester.
   250 **under that habit** in that guise.
   251 **play the knave** (1) pretend to be a boy
servant, (2) put him down, as in a game of cards
(compare Harington, *Epigrams* (1612), 'A saucy
knave, to trump both king and queen' (cit. *OED*
Knave 4)).
   251 **forester** (1) forest-dweller, (2) huntsman (as
in romantic poetry).
   253 Possibly implying that Orlando has not the
wit to know (compare *1H4* 1.2.1).

ORLANDO You should ask me what time o'day: there's no clock in the forest. 255

ROSALIND Then there is no true lover in the forest, else sighing every minute and groaning every hour would detect the lazy foot of Time as well as a clock.

ORLANDO And why not the swift foot of Time? Had not that been as proper? 260

ROSALIND By no means, sir. Time travels in diverse paces with diverse persons. I'll tell you who Time ambles withal, who Time trots withal, who Time gallops withal, and who he stands still withal.

ORLANDO I prithee, who doth he trot withal?

ROSALIND Marry, he trots hard with a young maid between the con- 265 tract of her marriage and the day it is solemnised. If the interim be but a sennight, Time's pace is so hard that it seems the length of seven year.

ORLANDO Who ambles Time withal?

ROSALIND With a priest that lacks Latin, and a rich man that hath not 270 the gout; for the one sleeps easily because he cannot study, and the other lives merrily because he feels no pain; the one lacking the burden of lean and wasteful learning, the other knowing no burden of heavy tedious penury. These Time ambles withal.

ORLANDO Who doth he gallop withal? 275

ROSALIND With a thief to the gallows; for though he go as softly as foot can fall, he thinks himself too soon there.

ORLANDO Who stays it still withal?

254 o'day as measured by the sun.

254–5 there's . . . forest Before the invention of the pendulum in 1657, time-keeping was inaccurate and much more apparent in towns than in the country (see Thomas, p. 744, Laroque, pp. 30–1, and, for a general survey, Gerhard Dohrn-van Rossum, *History of the Hour*, trans. Thomas Dunlap, 1998). In Chapman's 'Hymnus in Cynthiam', Cynthia (to whom Orlando made obeisance in 3.2.2–4) is invoked as having beauty strong enough to 'scorch the wings of Time, / That fluttering he may fall before thine eyes, / And beat himself to death before he rise' (George Chapman, *Poems*, ed. Phyllis Brooks Bartlett, 1941, p. 31, 18–20).

256–80 Rosalind's repartee resembles the crosstalk of a stage jester.

257 detect reveal (*OED* sv *v* 2b).

259 swift foot of Time Time was figured in engravings and proverbs as wing-footed (Tilley T327).

261 diverse different.

262 who whom (Abbott 274).

262 ambles moves at an easy pace (of a horse).

265 hard violently, at an uncomfortable pace (*OED* sv *adv* 2b).

265–6 between . . . solemnised i.e. during her betrothal.

267 sennight week (seven nights).

268 seven year Proverbial for a long time (Tilley Y25); 'year' is a plural.

270 lacks is ignorant of.

273 lean unremunerative (*OED* sv 2a).

273 wasteful causing him to waste away (*OED* sv 6).

274 tedious irksome, painful (*OED* sv 2).

276 softly leisurely (*OED* sv *adv* 3b).

276–7 as . . . fall Proverbial (Tilley F560).

ROSALIND With lawyers in the vacation; for they sleep between term
and term, and then they perceive not how Time moves.   280

ORLANDO Where dwell you, pretty youth?

ROSALIND With this shepherdess, my sister, here in the skirts of the
forest, like fringe upon a petticoat.

ORLANDO Are you native of this place?

ROSALIND As the cony that you see dwell where she is kindled.   285

ORLANDO Your accent is something finer than you could purchase in so
removed a dwelling.

ROSALIND I have been told so of many; but indeed an old religious
uncle of mine taught me to speak, who was in his youth an inland
man, one that knew courtship too well, for there he fell in love. I   290
have heard him read many lectures against it, and I thank God I am
not a woman to be touched with so many giddy offences as he hath
generally taxed their whole sex withal.

ORLANDO Can you remember any of the principal evils that he laid to
the charge of women?   295

ROSALIND There were none principal; they were all like one another as
halfpence are, every one fault seeming monstrous till his fellow-
fault came to match it.

ORLANDO I prithee recount some of them.

ROSALIND No. I will not cast away my physic but on those that are sick. 300
There is a man haunts the forest that abuses our young plants with
carving 'Rosalind' on their barks; hangs odes upon hawthorns and

---

291 lectures] F2 *subst.;* Lectors F

279 **vacation** period during which the London
law-courts did not sit.

279 **term** period of court session.

282 **skirts** border.

284 **Are you native of** Were you born in.

285 **cony** adult rabbit; rabbits were notoriously
lascivious (Partridge, p. 125).

285 **kindled** (1) born, (2) made ardent with passion (*OED* Kindle v^1 and v^2).

286 **purchase** acquire (*OED* sv *v* 4a).

287 **removed** remote.

288 **of** by (Abbott 170).

288 **religious** either monastic (*OED* sv *adj* 2a)
or scrupulous (*OED* 4a; compare 'a most devout
coward, religious in it' *TN* 3.4.389–90).

289 **inland** living near a metropolis (compare
2.7.97 n.).

290 **courtship** (1) courtly manners (*OED* sv 1),
(2) wooing.

290 **there** at court.

291 ***lectures** admonitory speeches (*OED*
Lecture *sb* 6).

292 **touched** tainted, infected.

292 **giddy** (1) fickle, frivolous (*OED* sv 3a), (2)
lecherous (cf. 4.1.122; Rubinstein, p. 110).

293 **generally** collectively.

296–8 'No halfpence were coined in Elizabeth's
reign till 1582–3 . . . They all had the portcullis with
a mint mark . . . so that, in comparison with the
great variety of coins of other denominations then
in circulation, there was a propriety in saying "as
like as one another as halfpence are"' (Wright).

297 **monstrous** absurd (*OED* sv 5).

297 **his** its.

300 **I . . . sick** See Matt. 9.12: 'They that be
whole need not a physician, but they that are sick'
(compare Mark 2.17): the sentence became proverbial (Tilley P271). Rosalind implies that Orlando is
free from the misogyny of her uncle.

300 **physic** medicine.

elegies on brambles; all, forsooth, defying the name of Rosalind. If
I could meet that fancy-monger, I would give him some good
counsel, for he seems to have the quotidian of love upon him.   305

ORLANDO I am he that is so love-shaked. I pray you tell me your
remedy.

ROSALIND There is none of my uncle's marks upon you. He taught me
how to know a man in love, in which cage of rushes I am sure you
are not prisoner.   310

ORLANDO What were his marks?

ROSALIND A lean cheek, which you have not; a blue eye and sunken,
which you have not; an unquestionable spirit, which you have not;
a beard neglected, which you have not – but I pardon you for that,
for, simply, your having in beard is a younger brother's revenue.   315
Then your hose should be ungartered, your bonnet unbanded, your
sleeve unbuttoned, your shoe untied, and everything about you
demonstrating a careless desolation. But you are no such man; you
are rather point-device in your accoutrements, as loving yourself
than seeming the lover of any other.   320

ORLANDO Fair youth, I would I could make thee believe I love.

ROSALIND Me believe it? You may as soon make her that you love
believe it, which I warrant she is apter to do than to confess she
does. That is one of the points in the which women still give the lie

---

303 defying] F; deifying F2   310 arc] F2; art F   315 in] F; no F2

303 **elegies** love poems (especially those that
used the elegiac metre: see *OED* Elegy 2).
   303 **brambles** blackberry bushes.
   303 **defying** setting at nought, demeaning (*OED*
Defy *v*¹ 4), although F2's 'deifying' (see collation)
may be correct.
   304 **fancy-monger** purveyor of fantasies.
   305 **counsel** As with any word containing 'con'
or 'coun' there is a secondary sexually equivalent
meaning (Williams, p. 83).
   305 **quotidian** a fever that recurs every day.
   306 **love-shaked** trembling as with a fever of
love (nonce-word).
   308 **is** For the singular before a plural predicate,
see Abbott 335.
   308 **marks** symptoms.
   309 **cage of rushes** flimsy prison; 'Rosalind is
probably alluding to the custom of country lovers
exchanging rings woven of rushes' (Andrews).
   312 **blue** with dark circles from grief (*OED* Blue
eye).
   313 **unquestionable** taciturn, impatient (*OED*
sv 3a).
   315 **simply** in truth.

315 **your having in** what you have of a.
   315 **younger brother's revenue** small amount
(although Rosalind may be hinting that she knows
more than 'Ganymede' would).
   316–17 **your hose . . . untied** Signs of a melancholic disposition: compare *Ham.* 2.1.79–81.
   316 **bonnet** hat without a brim.
   316 **unbanded** Hat-bands of rich materials were
fashionable (see A. B. Grosart (ed.), *The Non-
Dramatic Writings of Thomas Dekker*, 5 vols., 1884–
6, III, 330); Stubbes comments on 'a new fashion to
wear them [hats?] without bands' (*Anatomy of Abuses*
(1583), ed. F. J. Furnivall, 2 vols., 1879, I, 51.
   318 **demonstrating** exhibiting.
   318 **careless** uncared for.
   319 **rather** instead.
   319 **point-device in your accoutrements**
extremely precise in your dress; F's spelling 'accous-
trements' may indicate that Rosalind was mocking
Frenchified affectation in her imaginary lover.
   319 **as loving** suggesting that you love.
   323 **apter** more prone.
   324 **still** always.

to their consciences. But, in good sooth, are you he that hangs the   325
verses on the trees wherein Rosalind is so admired?

ORLANDO I swear to thee, youth, by the white hand of Rosalind, I am
that he, that unfortunate he.

ROSALIND But are you so much in love as your rhymes speak?

ORLANDO Neither rhyme nor reason can express how much.   330

ROSALIND Love is merely a madness and, I tell you, deserves as well a
dark-house and a whip as madmen do; and the reason why they are
not so punished and cured is that the lunacy is so ordinary that the
whippers are in love too. Yet I profess curing it by counsel.

ORLANDO Did you ever cure any so?   335

ROSALIND Yes, one, and in this manner. He was to imagine me his love,
his mistress, and I set him every day to woo me. At which time
would I, being but a moonish youth, grieve, be effeminate, changeable, longing and liking, proud, fantastical, apish, shallow, inconstant, full of tears, full of smiles; for every passion something, and   340
for no passion truly anything, as boys and women are, for the most
part, cattle of this colour; would now like him, now loathe him; then
entertain him, then forswear him; now weep for him, then spit at
him; that I drave my suitor from his mad humour of love to a living

---

344 living] F *subst.;* loving *conj. Johnson*

325 **consciences** (1) inward thoughts, (2) sex-ual desires ('any word with *con* in it seems to have invited Shakespeare and his contemporaries to play on the commonest name for the female sex organ', *Shakespeare's Sonnets*, ed. Stephen Booth, 1977, p. 526), see 3.3.305 n.

325 **sooth** truth.

326 **admired** held up as an object for wonder.

330 **Neither rhyme nor reason** Proverbial (Tilley R98).

331 **Love is merely a madness** Proverbial (Dent L505.2); for the genealogy of the idea from Plato through Ficino and Castiglione, see Panofsky, pp. 140–8.

331, 346 **merely** entirely.

332 **dark-house and a whip** Conventional ther-apies for the insane: see *TN* 4.2 (*OED* Dark *adj* 1b), and Michael MacDonald, *Mystical Bedlam: Mad-ness, Anxiety and Healing in Seventeenth-Century England*, 1981, pp. 196–7; 'dark-house' in this con-text also suggests a place of assignation.

333 **ordinary** customary.

334 **profess** am expert in.

334 **counsel** (1) advice, (2) love-making (com-pare *Oth.* 4.2.91–6).

337–46 **At . . . monastic** Rosalind offers a version of the cruel and fickle Petrarchan mistress.

338 **moonish** changeable, fickle, possibly hinting at her own menstrual cycle.

338 **effeminate** (1) gentle, (2) voluptuous, (3) like a homosexual (Williams, p. 110); see Seneca, *Epistolae*, CXV, 6–18 translated by Jonson, 'De mol-libus et effoeminatis', *Timber or Discoveries, Works*, VIII, 607, lines 1415–36.

339 **liking** agreeable.

339 **fantastical** capricious.

339 **apish** fantastically foolish.

341 **as** even as (*OED* sv *conj* 8d).

341 **boys and women** The eroticising of boys is both a joky reference to the convention of theatri-cal cross-dressing and an evocation of the veins of homo-eroticism that run beneath the surface of the play.

342 **cattle of this colour** Compare the proverb, 'A horse of that colour' (Tilley H665); 'cattle' can mean whores (*OED* sv 7b).

342 **colour** kind.

343 **entertain** converse with (*OED* sv *v* 7).

344, 348 **that** so that.

344 **drave** this archaic northern form continued to be used in biblical texts.

344–6 **mad humour . . . living** humour whim-sical affected love to a true affliction; Johnson's emendation (see collation), however, is attractive.

humour of madness, which was to forswear the full stream of the 345
world and to live in a nook, merely monastic. And thus I cured him,
and this way will I take upon me to wash your liver as clean as a
sound sheep's heart, that there shall not be one spot of love in't.

ORLANDO I would not be cured, youth.

ROSALIND I would cure you if you would but call me Rosalind and 350
come every day to my cot and woo me.

ORLANDO Now, by the faith of my love, I will. Tell me where it is.

ROSALIND Go with me to it and I'll show it you; and by the way you
shall tell me where in the forest you live. Will you go?

ORLANDO With all my heart, good youth. 355

ROSALIND Nay, you must call me 'Rosalind'. – Come, sister, will you
go?

Exeunt

3.4 *Enter* TOUCHSTONE, AUDREY, *with* JAQUES [*behind, watching them*]

TOUCHSTONE Come apace, good Audrey; I will fetch up your goats,
Audrey. And how, Audrey, am I the man yet? Doth my simple
feature content you?

---

346 nook,] *Collier;* nooke F   347 clean] F; cleare F2   Act 3, Scene 4 3.4] *Pope subst.; Scæna Tertia.* F   0 SD
with . . . them] *This edn; & Iaques.* F

346 **nook** inlet, creek – continuing the conceit of
the 'full stream'.
346 **monastic** in religious seclusion.
347 **take upon me** undertake.
347 **liver** The supposed seat of love and violent
passion (*OED* sv 2a); the liver of a lover was supposed to be diseased (compare Webster who, in *The
Duchess of Malfi*, speaks of the way the livers of the
'luxurious' 'are more spotted than Laban's sheep'
(1.1.298–9)).
348 **sound sheep's heart** Rosalind's simile, of
a heart rinsed of blood before it is cooked, fits her
supposed pastoral occupation; compare *Ado* 3.2.12:
'He hath a heart as sound as a bell.'
351 **cot** small detached house.
352 **faith** truth, obligation.
353 **by** along.
355–6 In production Orlando often gives
'Ganymede' a hearty slap on the shoulder at this
point, which provokes Rosalind's somewhat pointed
reply. Alternatively, we could take Rosalind's praise
of Orlando's kissing at 3.5.11–12 as an indication

that here, or at some other suitable point in the
scene, the couple embrace, perhaps to Celia's
surprise.

Act 3, Scene 4
0 SD It is for a director to decide whether Jaques
enters to listen in on the dialogue between the lovers,
another version of pastoral wooing to contrast with
what has gone before, or whether Touchstone plays
up to this choric listener.
1 **apace** swiftly.
1 **fetch up** arouse, bring up (*OED* Fetch *v* 21a).
1 **goats** In pastoral and Christian traditions, goats
and goatherds are decidedly inferior to sheep and
shepherds.
2 **how** ho (*OED* sv *int* 1).
2 **am I the man** A variant on the saying 'You
are *ipse* (the man)' (Tilley 188), and compare 5.1.39.
2 **yet** still.
2 **simple** honest.
3 **feature** (1) appearance, (2) penis (?).
3 **content** satisfy.

AUDREY Your features, Lord warrant us – what features?

TOUCHSTONE I am here with thee and thy goats as the most capricious   5
   poet honest Ovid was among the Goths.

JAQUES O knowledge ill-inhabited, worse than Jove in a thatched house!

TOUCHSTONE When a man's verses cannot be understood, nor a man's
   good wit seconded with the forward child, understanding, it strikes
   a man more dead than a great reckoning in a little room. Truly, I   10
   would the gods had made thee poetical.

AUDREY I do not know what 'poetical' is. Is it honest in deed and word?
   Is it a true thing?

TOUCHSTONE No, truly; for the truest poetry is the most feigning, and
   lovers are given to poetry; and what they swear in poetry it may be   15
   said, as lovers, they do feign.

---

10 reckoning] F; reeking *Hanmer*   14 feigning] *Eds.;* faining F   15 poetry it] *Collier, conj. Mason;* Poetrie F

4 features face; Audrey possibly misunder-
stands, thinking Touchstone had spoken of 'faitors'
(traitors) which was pronounced similarly (Cercignani, p. 263, however, thinks this homonym 'highly
dubious').

4 warrant protect (*OED* Warrant *v* 1a; compare
4.1.62).

5 thee . . . thy Touchstone turns from 'you'
and 'your' to archaic and high poetic forms of
the pronoun (Abbott 231) suitable to the pastiche
euphuisms with which he dazzles Audrey.

5 capricious fantastical, 'conceited', punning on
Latin *caper* (goat) – goats were fabled for their
lasciviousness; as in *LLL* punning is an index of
the courtly and the urbane.

6 honest chaste – Ovid was, of course, regarded
as a purveyor of erotica.

6 Goths Pronounced 'goats' (Cercignani, pp.
106, 117); Ovid was banished to Tomis on the Black
Sea, among the Getae, probably for writing the *Ars
Amatoria*.

7 It is impossible to tell whether Jaques is lament-
ing the plight of Ovid or Touchstone.

7 ill-inhabited meanly lodged (inhabited =
'made to inhabit' (Abbott 294).

7 worse . . . house Ovid tells the story (*Metamorphoses*, VIII, 801ff.) of how Jove and his son Mercury,
disguised as mortals, were turned away by a thousand householders until they were kindly received
by Philemon and his wife Baucis in their cottage
'thatchèd all with straw and fennish reed' (807).
The story became an exemplum of the simple life,
although here there may be a bawdy invocation of
the vagina (Hulme, p. 150).

8–9 When . . . understanding Ovid complained that his verses were not understood by the
Getae among whom he spent his years in exile (see

Ex Ponto, 4.2.15–38, *Tristia*, 3.14.33–52, 5.12.53–4,
etc.).

9 wit (1) knowledge; compare Sir John Davies,
Nosce Teipsum (1599): 'Wit doth reap the fruits of
sense' (Robert Krueger (ed.), *The Poems of Sir John
Davies*, 1975, p. 45, line 1233), (2) sexual organ (see
Williams, pp. 340–1).

9 seconded with (1) accompanied by, (2) followed by.

9 forward precocious (*OED* sv 7).

9 understanding the rational faculty or intellect
(*OED* sv 1c).

10 great . . . room large bill in a small chamber:
Touchstone compares the deadening effect of a mis-
understood joke with the sobering effect of a large
account for a convivial meal. For summaries of those
who take the line to refer to the mysterious death
of Christopher Marlowe at Deptford, see Knowles,
pp. 188–90.

11 poetical (1) endowed with the faculties of
a poet, (2) worthy of being celebrated in verse
(although *OED* sv 5 and Poetic 5 record this meaning only from 1742).

12 honest respectable.

13 true honest (*OED* sv *adj* 2).

14 *feigning (1) imaginative (*OED* sv 1), (2)
deceiving (*OED* sv 2), (3) expressive of desire
('faining'); see 2.7.182 n.

15–16 what . . . feign For the treatment of
the ancient topos that poetry is the mother of
lies, see Sir Philip Sidney, *An Apology for Poetry*,
ed. Geoffrey Shepherd, 1973, pp. 197–8; Ben
Jonson, however, when he wrote that 'A poet
is . . . a maker, or a feigner' was using the notion
of feigning to mean imitation (*Timber or Discoveries*,
Jonson, VIII, 635, lines 2346–7).

16 feign (1) pretend, (2) desire.

AUDREY Do you wish then that the gods had made me poetical?

TOUCHSTONE I do, truly; for thou swear'st to me thou art honest. Now
 if thou wert a poet, I might have some hope thou didst feign.

AUDREY Would you not have me honest?   20

TOUCHSTONE No, truly, unless thou wert hard-favoured: for honesty
 coupled to beauty is to have honey a sauce to sugar.

JAQUES A material fool.

AUDREY Well, I am not fair, and therefore I pray the gods make me
 honest.   25

TOUCHSTONE Truly, and to cast away honesty upon a foul slut were to
 put good meat into an unclean dish.

AUDREY I am not a slut, though I thank the gods I am foul.

TOUCHSTONE Well, praised be the gods for thy foulness: sluttishness
 may come hereafter. But be it as it may be, I will marry thee, and to   30
 that end I have been with Sir Oliver Martext, the vicar of the next
 village, who hath promised to meet me in this place of the forest and
 to couple us.

JAQUES I would fain see this meeting.

AUDREY Well, the gods give us joy.   35

TOUCHSTONE Amen. A man may, if he were of a fearful heart, stagger
 in this attempt; for here we have no temple but the wood, no

---

17 the gods Audrey's reference to pagan gods is
a pastoral convention.

19 feign lie.

20 have me (1) like me to be, (2) take me sexually
(Williams, p. 153).

20 honest chaste.

21–7 honesty . . . dish Compare the proverb,
'Beauty and honesty seldom meet' (Tilley B163).

21 hard-favoured ugly.

21 honesty (1) chastity, (2) veracity.

22 to have . . . sugar too much of a good thing;
compare the proverb, 'Sweet meat [food] must have
sour sauce' (Tilley M839); there is a bawdy implication as 'saucy' could mean lascivious (*OED* sv 2b).

23 material (1) full of matter or sense (*OED* sv
6), (2) gross (*OED* sv *adj* 4b).

24 fair (1) beautiful (the customary antithesis of
'foul' (26)), (2) virtuous (*OED* sv *adj* 9): Audrey
may be hoping that her character will be redeemed
by marriage.

26–7 Touchstone would rather that Audrey's
virtue be restored by miracle than by his marrying
her.

26 slut (1) slattern, (2) whore.

27 good . . . dish Compare the proverb, 'Put not
thy meat [food] in an unclean dish' (Tilley M834).

27 dish (1) vessel, (2) woman (*OED* sv 2a).

28 slut whore.

28 foul ugly, plain (*OED* sv 11a), perhaps with
implications of homeliness: Audrey has absorbed
Touchstone's sophistical proof that beauty and
chastity do not accord together.

30 be . . . be Compare the proverb, 'Be as be may'
(Tilley B65).

31 been with called upon (*OED* With *prep* 22b).

31 Sir Oliver 'Sir' was the title given to a priest
who had not graduated from a university.

31 Martext Presumably an ignorant 'priest that
lacks Latin' (3.3.270); the name recalls nonce-words
from the Marprelate tracts of the 1580s like 'Mar-
priest', 'Mar-church', and 'Mar-religion' (see *OED*
Mar- *stem*).

31 next nearest.

32 place 'town-square' (?).

33 couple join in wedlock (*OED v* 3a), although
the word has more lascivious connotations.

34 meeting (1) encounter, (2) copulation.

35 give us joy A customary formula pronounced
at weddings.

36 fearful anxious (*OED* sv 3c).

36 stagger waver, hesitate.

37 temple church; woodland areas were outside
of the parochial system (see Christopher Hill, *The
World Turned Upside Down*, 1975, p. 46.)

assembly but horn-beasts. But what though? Courage! As horns are
odious, they are necessary. It is said, 'Many a man knows no end of
his goods.' Right: many a man has good horns and knows no end of   40
them. Well, that is the dowry of his wife, 'tis none of his own
getting. Horns? Even so. Poor men alone? No, no: the noblest deer
hath them as huge as the rascal. Is the single man therefore blessed?
No: as a walled town is more worthier than a village, so is the
forehead of a married man more honourable than the bare brow of   45
a bachelor. And, by how much defence is better than no skill, by so
much is a horn more precious than to want.

Enter SIR OLIVER MARTEXT

Here comes Sir Oliver. – Sir Oliver Martext, you are well met. Will
you dispatch us here under this tree, or shall we go with you to your
chapel?   50
MARTEXT Is there none here to give the woman?
TOUCHSTONE I will not take her on gift of any man.

---

42 Horns? . . . no:] *Keightley subst.;* hornes, euen so poore men alone: No, no, F   51 SH] *Eds.; Ol.* F (*throughout*)

38 **assembly** (1) congregation (*OED* sv 6a: the
first recorded use in this sense), (2) coition (*OED* sv
2).

38 **horn-beasts** (1) Audrey's goats, oxen, or
deer, (2) cuckolds (Touchstone often gestures in
performance towards the theatre audience). Shakespeare implies that the device of horns arose from
the story of Jove taking the form of a white bull to
seduce Europa. (*Tro.* 5.1.53–5; compare *Metamorphoses*, II, 1058 ff.).

38 **though** then.

38–9 **horns . . . necessary** Compare the proverb,
'Cuckolds come by destiny' (Tilley c889).

39 **necessary** inevitable (*OED* sv 5a).

39–40 **knows . . . goods** Proverbial for immensely
wealthy (Tilley E122); 'goods', in this context, could
also mean 'wife' (compare *Shr.* 3.2.230), with the
implication that a cuckold cannot know his wife
carnally.

40 **horns** (1) beasts or articles made out of horn,
(2) penile erections (compare *Shr.* 4.1.26–8), (3)
cuckold's horns.

40 **knows no end of** (1) is over-supplied with,
(2) can obtain no sexual relief from.

41 **the dowry of** brought about by.

42–3 ***Horns . . . rascal** The necessity to emend
the punctuation (see collation) may indicate that the
compositor missed a word or line.

42 **Poor men** (1) Those whose only wealth
was their wives' 'dowries', (2) Pitiable males, (3)
Wretched humankind.

42 **alone** only.

43 **rascal** (1) lean or inferior deer of a herd (*OED*
sv 4), but possibly endowed with great antlers (see
Shakespeare's England, II, 339 n.), (2) a castrated or
impotent man (Rubinstein, p. 214).

44–5 **walled . . . man** The conceit may allude to
'hornwork' which meant both a species of fortifica-
tion and cuckoldry, although *OED* cites the relevant
meanings only from 1641 and 1738 respectively.

44 **more worthier** For the double comparative,
see Abbott 11.

45 **bare brow** unfurnished with horns.

46 **defence** the art of self-defence in fencing or
boxing (*OED* sv 4).

47 **horn** (1) cornucopia, (2) emblem of a cuckold.

47 **want** (1) be lacking in fighting skills, (2) be
unsatisfied sexually.

48 **you are well met** welcome.

49 **dispatch us** conclude the business.

49 **tree** Possibly a Gospel Oak where marriages
could take place: see K. M. Briggs, *The Folklore of
the Cotswolds*, 1974, p. 122.

50 **chapel** (1) church, (2) privy (*OED* sv 11,
although no citations are given). The jest may
explain why Sir Oliver ignores Touchstone's question.

51 **give the woman** give away the bride; compare the marriage service: 'Who giveth this woman
to be married to this man?'.

52 Touchstone does not want 'second-hand
goods'.

MARTEXT Truly, she must be given, or the marriage is not lawful.

JAQUES [*Coming forward*] Proceed, proceed: I'll give her.

TOUCHSTONE Good-even, good Monsieur What-Ye-Call't. How do   55
you, sir? You are very well met. God'ild you for your last company;
I am very glad to see you. Even a toy in hand here, sir.

[*Jaques removes his hat*]

Nay, pray be covered.

JAQUES Will you be married, Motley?

TOUCHSTONE As the ox hath his bow, sir, the horse his curb, and the   60
falcon her bells, so man hath his desires, and as pigeons bill, so
wedlock would be nibbling.

JAQUES And will you, being a man of your breeding, be married under
a bush like a beggar? Get you to church, and have a good priest that
can tell you what marriage is. This fellow will but join you together   65
as they join wainscot; then one of you will prove a shrunk panel and,
like green timber, warp, warp.

54 SD] *Malone subst.; not in* F   55 Monsieur] *Oxford;* M^r F; Master *Rowe³*   56 God'ild] *Theobald;* goddild F   57 SD]
Oxford; not in F   61 so man] F; so a man *conj. this edn*

55 *Monsieur What-Ye-Call't Either Touchstone feigns decorousness by eschewing the mention
of the name of 'Jaques' (privy; see 50 n.), or he cannot remember Jaques' name (see 2.1.26 n.)

56 God'ild Thank you (literally 'God yield'
(meaning 'repay': see *OED* Yield *v* 1).

56 last company fellowship when we last met.

57 Even a toy in hand Indeed a trifling ceremony is taking place (with a pun on 'toy' which designates (1) Audrey, Touchstone's pet or plaything
(*OED* sv 9), whom he is holding by the hand, (2)
possibly, his fool's bauble, (3) his penis (Williams,
pp. 311–12)).

58 Touchstone addresses Jaques as though the
latter had removed his hat in deference to him rather
than for the wedding ceremony, although he may be
enjoining Audrey to cover her head in the forest
church (see 2 Cor. 11.4–6).

60 ox hath his bow Compare the proverb, 'In
time the ox will bear the yoke' (Tilley T303) which
derives ultimately from Ovid, *Tristia*, IV, 6, 1–2
(Knowles).

60 bow Curved wood that went under the ox's
neck and was fitted into the yoke.

60 curb Strap passing under the lower jaw of a
horse and fastened to the bit.

61 falcon The female of the tercel which was
smaller and less suited to the chase.

61 bells Worn both to terrify the game and so
that the bird could be found and retrieved (*Shakespeare's England*, II, 357).

61 bill stroke beak against beak.

62 wedlock marriage, although the word could
mean a wife (*OED* sv 3; see collation 61).

62 nibbling (1) taking small amorous bites or
fornicating (Williams, p. 215), (2) pilfering, i.e. cap-
turing good men? (see *OED* Nibble *v* 4).

63 breeding (1) 'noble' blood, (2) education.

63–4 under . . . beggar a 'beggar's-bush', designated a place of shelter for the indigent.

65 tell you what marriage is (1) understand
the marriage service, (2) instruct you in your mari-
tal duties.

65 join you together The phrase occurs several
times in the marriage service.

66 wainscot imported oak used for fine pan-
elling.

66 shrunk detached (*OED* Shrink *v* 5b).

66 panel (1) board, (2) harlot (see *OED* Parnel,
and Hulme, pp. 104–6).

67 green unseasoned.

67 warp (1) become distorted, (2) leave the
straight and narrow (*OED* sv *v* 16).

TOUCHSTONE I am not in the mind; but I were better to be married of
him than of another, for he is not like to marry me well and, not
being well married, it will be a good excuse for me hereafter to leave   70
my wife.

JAQUES Go thou with me and let me counsel thee.

TOUCHSTONE Come, sweet Audrey, we must be married or we must
live in bawdry. – Farewell, good Master Oliver. Not

[*Sings*]   O sweet Oliver,   75

   O brave Oliver,

  Leave me not behind thee;

but [*Sings*]

   Wind away,

   Begone, I say,   80

  I will not to wedding with thee.

MARTEXT [*Aside*] 'Tis no matter; ne'er a fantastical knave of them all
shall flout me out of my calling.

                  Exeunt

68 SH] F *subst.;* TOUCHSTONE [*aside*] *Capell subst.*   68 mind;] *Sisson;* minde, F   72] *As prose, Pope; Iaq . . . mee, /
And . . . thee.* F   73–4 TOUCHSTONE . . . bawdry.] *As prose, Pope; Ol. . . . Audrey, /* We . . . baudrey: F   73 SH] F2
subst.; Ol. F*; Clo.* [*they whisper*] *Johnson subst., conj. Rann*   74 Master] *Eds.;* M^r F   75 SD, 78 SD] *Capell subst.; not in*
F   74–5 Not . . . O] *Malone subst.;* Not O F   75–81] *As verse, Capell; As prose in* F   77–9 thee. . . . Wind] *Malone
subst.;* thee: But winde F   80 Begone] *Eds.;* bee gone F   81 thee.] F*;* thee. *Exeunt Jaques, Clown, and Audrey /* Capell
subst.   82 SD] *This edn, conj. Knowles; not in* F   83 SD] F*; Exit /* Capell

68–71 There is no need to follow Capell (see collation) and make this an aside: rather it is Touchstone's response to Jaques' bantering catechism.
 68 mind i.e. to be married.
 68 I were better it would be best to be.
 69 like likely.
 69 well (1) legally, (2) happily, (3) wealthily.
 72 thou . . . thee Jaques' resort to the familiar form of the pronoun signifies benign superiority
(Abbott 231).
 72 counsel instruct you in (1) the responsibilities
of marriage, (2) carnality (see 3.3.334 n.).
 73 *SH F's reading could just stand (see collation)
if Sir Oliver were to speak to Audrey in a school-
masterly fashion, but it is more likely to be a compositorial error for 'Clo[*wn*].'
 74 bawdry unchastity, fornication (*OED* sv sb^1
2).
 75–81 A lost ballad, 'O sweet Oliver Leave me not
behind thee', was entered in the Stationers' Regis-

ter on 6 August 1584, and a 'reply', 'The answer
of O sweet Oliver', a fortnight later (Arber, II, 434,
435). It was probably set to the tune of 'The hunt
is up' (see Claude M. Simpson, *The British Broadside Ballad and its Music*, 1966, pp. 323–7). The two
songs may have formed the basis of a players' jig:
see Charles Read Baskervill, *The Elizabethan Jig and
Related Song Drama*, 1929, pp. 181–3. Touchstone
will not endorse the romantic plea of the maiden but
the cynical response of her lover.
 75 A proverbial figure (Tilley O40).
 76 brave fine, good.
 79 Wind Go quickly (*OED* sv v^1 2).
 81 will not to wedding For the omission of the
verb of motion, see Abbott 405.
 82 ne'er not (Abbott 52).
 82 fantastical (1) foppish, capricious (*OED*
Fantastic 4b), (2) love-sick (*OED* sv 3b).
 83 flout mock, jeer.
 83 calling (1) name, (2) vocation.

3.5 *Enter* ROSALIND [*as* GANYMEDE] *and* CELIA [*as* ALIENA]

ROSALIND Never talk to me; I will weep.

CELIA Do, I prithee; but yet have the grace to consider that tears do not
become a man.

ROSALIND But have I not cause to weep?

CELIA As good cause as one would desire: therefore weep.   5

ROSALIND His very hair is of the dissembling colour.

CELIA Something browner than Judas's: marry, his kisses are Judas's
own children.

ROSALIND I'faith, his hair is of a good colour.

CELIA An excellent colour: your chestnut was ever the only colour.   10

ROSALIND And his kissing is as full of sanctity as the touch of holy
bread.

CELIA He hath bought a pair of cast lips of Diana. A nun of winter's
sisterhood kisses not more religiously: the very ice of chastity is in
them.   15

ROSALIND But why did he swear he would come this morning and
comes not?

CELIA Nay, certainly, there is no truth in him.

ROSALIND Do you think so?

Act 3, Scene 5 3.5] *Pope subst.; Scæna Quarta.* F   1–12] *As prose, Pope;* Ros. . . . weepe. / Cel. . . . consider, /
that . . . man. / Ros. . . . weepe? / Cel. . . . desire, / Therefore weepe. / Ros. . . . haire / Is . . . colour. / Cel. . . .
Iudasses: / Marrie . . . children. / Ros. . . . colour. / Cel. . . . colour: / Your . . . colour: / Ros. . . . sanctitie, / As . . .
bread. F   10 colour.] colour: F   13 cast] F; chast F2; chaste *Rowe*   13 winter's] F *subst.;* Winifred's *conj. Theobald*

Act 3, Scene 5

**1–12 Compositor B set this as verse to eke out
copy at the foot of his stint.

  1 **Never** Do not.

  1 **will** intend to (Abbott 316).

  2 **grace** sense of propriety (*OED* sv *sb* 13b).

  6 **dissembling** false, hypocritical.

  6–9 'There is much of nature in this petty per-
verseness of Rosalind: she finds faults in her lover in
hope to be contradicted, and when Celia in sportive
malice too readily seconds her accusations, she con-
tradicts herself rather than suffer her favourite to
want a vindication' (Johnson).

  7 **Something** Somewhat (Abbott 68).

  7 **browner than Judas's** Judas, the betrayer of
Christ (Matt. 26.48–9), traditionally had a red beard
and black hair (Tilley B143) and was so depicted in
tapestries and paintings.

  7–8 **kisses . . . children** Judas' perfidious kissing
of Christ was proverbial (Luke 22.47–8; Tilley J92).

  10 **your** that (*OED* sv 5b).

  11–12 See 3.3.355–6 n.

  11–12 **holy bread** Provided for the Eucharist in
post-Reformation England (*OED* Holy bread); the
line was censored by William Sankey S.J. from the
copy of F provided for students in the English College at Valladolid in Spain (Roland Mushat Frye,
Shakespeare and Christian Doctrine, 1963, p. 276)
and from the Douai manuscript (see Stage History,
p. 56 n. 2).

  13 **cast** cast-off (compare *H8* 1.3.48); although
the word could be a Latinate spelling of 'chaste'
(from *castus*).

  13 **Diana** Here a figure of virginity.

  13–14 **nun of winter's sisterhood** 'one devoted
to cold and barren chastity' (Schmidt).

  14 **ice of chastity** Compare the proverb, 'As
chaste as ice' (Tilley I1).

CELIA Yes, I think he is not a pickpurse nor a horse-stealer but, for his   20
verity in love, I do think him as concave as a covered goblet or a
worm-eaten nut.

ROSALIND Not true in love?

CELIA Yes, when he is in; but I think he is not in.

ROSALIND You have heard him swear downright he was.   25

CELIA 'Was' is not 'is'; besides, the oath of a lover is no stronger than
the word of a tapster: they are both the confirmers of false reckonings. He attends here in the forest on the Duke your father.

ROSALIND I met the Duke yesterday and had much question with him;
he asked me of what parentage I was. I told him of as good as he: so   30
he laughed and let me go. But what talk we of fathers when there is
such a man as Orlando?

CELIA O that's a brave man: he writes brave verses, speaks brave words,
swears brave oaths, and breaks them bravely, quite traverse, athwart
the heart of his lover as a puny tilter that spurs his horse but on one   35
side, breaks his staff like a noble goose. But all's brave that youth
mounts and folly guides. – Who comes here?

Enter CORIN

CORIN Mistress and master, you have oft enquired
After the shepherd that complained of love
Who you saw sitting by me on the turf,   40
Praising the proud disdainful shepherdess
That was his mistress.

CELIA   Well, and what of him?

---

26 of a] F2; of F   27 confirmers] *Pope;* confirmer F   35 puny] *Eds.;* puisny F

21 **verity** honesty, constancy.

21 **concave** hollow (*OED* sv *adj* 1), i.e. insincere.

24–5 **in . . . downright** With sexual innuendoes (Williams, p. 104).

26 **'Was' is not 'is'** Compare the proverb, 'Then was then and now is now' (Dent T98.1).

27 **tapster** tavern-keeper.

27 ***confirmers** maintainers (*OED* Confirm *v* 8).

27–8 **reckonings** (1) tavern bills, (2) accounts of themselves.

29–31 **I . . . go** Rosalind's failure to acknowledge herself to the father she set out to meet may be an index of the degree to which she is under the spell of Orlando, or simply another move by 'Ganymede' in a game of supposes.

29 **question** conversation (*OED* sv *sb* 2a).

31 **what** why (Abbott 253).

33 **brave** fine, showy.

34–6 **quite . . . goose** The imagery comes from the aristocratic sport of running at tilt, a combat on horseback with spears.

34 **traverse** transversely; 'In tilting, when the tilter by unsteadiness or awkwardness suffered his spear to be . . . broken across the body of his adversary, instead of by the push of the point' (Robert Nares, *A Glossary*, cited in *OED* Break *v* 49).

34 **athwart** across.

35 **lover** mistress.

35 **puny** small, novice.

35–6 **spurs . . . side** i.e. so that it does not charge in a straight line.

36 **noble** notable (*OED* sv *adj* 8b).

36 **goose** (1) simpleton, (2) a 'Winchester goose' or client of a Bankside brothel (Williams, pp. 339–40).

39 **of** against (*OED* Complain *v* 4b).

40 **Who** Whom (Abbott 274).

CORIN If you will see a pageant truly played
    Between the pale complexion of true love
    And the red glow of scorn and proud disdain,   45
    Go hence a little, and I shall conduct you
    If you will mark it.
ROSALIND   O come, let us remove,
    The sight of lovers feedeth those in love. –
    Bring us to this sight and you shall say
    I'll prove a busy actor in their play.   50

                 Exeunt

3.6 *Enter* SILVIUS *and* PHOEBE

SILVIUS Sweet Phoebe, do not scorn me, do not, Phoebe.
    Say that you love me not, but say not so
    In bitterness. The common executioner,
    Whose heart th'accustomed sight of death makes hard,
    Falls not the axe upon the humbled neck   5
    But first begs pardon. Will you sterner be
    Than he that dies and lives by bloody drops?

    Enter ROSALIND [*as* GANYMEDE], CELIA [*as* ALIENA],
      and CORIN [*; they stand aside*]

PHOEBE I would not be thy executioner;
    I fly thee for I would not injure thee.
    Thou tell'st me there is murder in mine eye: 10

Act 3, Scene 6 3.6] *Pope subst.; Scena Quinta.* F   1 not,] F3; *not* F   7 dies] F; *deals Theobald, conj. Warburton* 7
SD.2 *they . . . aside*] *Capell subst.; not in* F   10 eye] F; *eyes Rowe*

43 **pageant** scene.
44 **pale complexion** The sighs of lovers were supposed to take blood from the heart (compare *MND* 3.2.96–7).
45 **red glow** Produced by the hot and dry choleric humour.
47 **remove** depart.
50 **Rosalind** in fact has initiated action and indulged in impersonation well before this: the metaphor is typical of the metatheatrical dimension of Shakespearean comedy.
50 SD Directors have often left Rosalind, Celia, and Corin on stage to overhear the beginning of the next scene.

Act 3, Scene 6
5 **Falls** Drops (*OED* Fall *v* 49; Abbott 291).
6 **But first begs** Without begging.
7 **he** i.e. the executioner.
7 **dies and lives** We should say 'lives and dies'.
8–27 **I . . . hurt** Phoebe's retort is not just directed to Silvius but constitutes a critique of the Petrarchisms that inform his discourse.
9 **for** because.
10 **murder in mine eye** A Petrarchan commonplace; compare *Son.* 139.10–12.

'Tis pretty, sure, and very probable
That eyes, that are the frail'st and softest things,
Who shut their coward gates on atomies,
Should be called tyrants, butchers, murderers!
Now I do frown on thee with all my heart;   15
And if mine eyes can wound, now let them kill thee.
Now counterfeit to swoon, why, now fall down
Or, if thou canst not, O for shame, for shame,
Lie not to say mine eyes are murderers.
Now show the wound mine eye hath made in thee.   20
Scratch thee but with a pin, and there remains
Some scar of it; lean upon a rush,
The cicatrice and capable impressure
Thy palm some moment keeps. But now mine eyes,
Which I have darted at thee, hurt thee not,   25
Nor I am sure there is no force in eyes
That can do hurt.
SILVIUS   O dear Phoebe,
If ever – as that 'ever' may be near –
You meet in some fresh cheek the power of fancy,
Then shall you know the wounds invisible   30
That love's keen arrows make.
PHOEBE   But till that time
Come not thou near me; and, when that time comes,
Afflict me with thy mocks, pity me not,
As till that time I shall not pity thee.
ROSALIND [*Coming forward*] And why, I pray you? Who might be your
          mother   35

---

11 pretty,] *Theobald;* pretty F   12 eyes, that] *Eds.;* eyes that F   17 swoon] *Eds.;* swound F   20 eye] F; Eyes *Rowe*³   22
lean] F *subst.;* Leane but F2   24 moment] F; moments *Johnson*   27 O] F; O my *Hanmer*   34 SD] *Capell subst.; not in* F

11 **sure** certainly (*OED* sv B2).
13 **Who** That (Abbott 264).
13 **coward gates** eyelids.
13 **atomies** motes, specks.
15 **with all my heart** in complete earnestness
(*OED* Heart 39a).
16 A Petrarchan conceit taken to extremity.
16 **And if** If.
17 **counterfeit** pretend.
19 **to say** by saying.
23 **cicatrice** scar-like mark (*OED* sv 1b, although
this is the only example cited).
23 **capable** hollow (*OED* sv 1a).

23 **impressure** impression.
24 **some** a (Abbott 21).
25 **darted** shot (like a short arrow).
26 **Nor . . . no** The double negative is for emphasis and does not generate a positive statement
(Abbott 406).
28 **as . . . near** may the time be soon.
29 **the power of fancy** that which generates
desire.
31 **keen** sharp.
33 **mocks** ridicule.
35 **might be your mother** do you think you are.

That you insult, exult, and all at once
Over the wretched? What though you have no beauty,
As, by my faith, I see no more in you
Than without candle may go dark to bed,
Must you be therefore proud and pitiless?   40
Why, what means this? Why do you look on me?
I see no more in you than in the ordinary
Of Nature's sale-work – Od's my little life,
I think she means to tangle my eyes too. –
No, faith, proud mistress, hope not after it;   45
'Tis not your inky brows, your black silk hair,
Your bugle eyeballs, nor your cheek of cream
That can entame my spirits to your worship. –
You, foolish shepherd, wherefore do you follow her
Like foggy South, puffing with wind and rain?   50
You are a thousand times a properer man
Than she a woman. 'Tis such fools as you
That makes the world full of ill-favoured children.
'Tis not her glass but you that flatters her,
And out of you she sees herself more proper   55
Than any of her lineaments can show her. –
But, mistress, know yourself. Down on your knees,
                    [*Phoebe kneels to Rosalind*]

36 all] F; rail *Theobald, conj. Warburton*   37 What] F; What, *Eds.*   37 have no] F; have *Theobald*   44 my] F; mine
F2   52 woman.] F *subst.*; woman: *Capell*   57 SD] *Wilson; not in* F

36 **insult** boast (*OED* 1b).
36 **all at once** and all the rest (Schmidt 'Once').
37 **What** Even.
39 Who, even by night, have no attractiveness; compare the proverbs, 'When candles be out all cats be grey' (Tilley C50), and 'Joan is as good as my lady in the dark' (Tilley J57).
43 **sale-work** ready-made goods, not of the highest quality.
43 **Od's** 'Od' was a 'minced form of God, which came into vogue about 1600, when, to avoid the overt profanation of sacred names, many minced and disguised equivalents became prevalent' (*OED* Od¹); 'Od's' perhaps here means 'God save'; this oath may be an attempt to seem manly (compare 4.1.151, 4.3.16).
44 **tangle** ensnare with her beauty.
45 **after** for.
46 **inky brows** Black brows are a sign of simple rustic beauty – compare *LLL* 4.3.254 and *WT* 2.1.8.

47 **bugle** bead of black glass (*OED* sv *sb*³).
48 **entame** subdue.
48 **your worship** the worship of you.
50 **South** the south wind (*OED* sv 5a).
50 **wind and rain** i.e. sighs and tears.
51 **properer** more handsome.
52–3 **'Tis . . . children** F's punctuation allows for these words to be directed at Phoebe.
53 **makes** For the singular inflection in a relative clause, see Abbott 247.
53 **full . . . children** i.e. by marrying ugly women.
53 **ill-favoured** ugly.
54 **glass . . . flatters** For the commonplace of the flattering mirror, see Dent G132.1.
55 **out of** on account of (*OED* Out of *prep* 5b).
55 **proper** beautiful.
56 **lineaments** facial features.
57 **know yourself** The classical injunction *nosce teipsum*, often repeated (see Tilley K175).

And thank heaven, fasting, for a good man's love;
For I must tell you friendly in your ear,
Sell when you can: you are not for all markets.   60
Cry the man mercy, love him, take his offer,
Foul is most foul, being foul to be a scoffer. –
So take her to thee, shepherd; fare you well.

PHOEBE   Sweet youth, I pray you chide a year together;
I had rather hear you chide than this man woo.   65

ROSALIND He's fallen in love with your foulness – [*To Silvius*] and
she'll fall in love with my anger. If it be so, as fast as she answers
thee with frowning looks, I'll sauce her with bitter words. – Why
look you so upon me?

PHOEBE   For no ill will I bear you.   70

ROSALIND I pray you do not fall in love with me
For I am falser than vows made in wine;
Besides, I like you not. – [*To Silvius*] If you will know my
    house,
'Tis at the tuft of olives, here hard by. –
Will you go, sister? – Shepherd, ply her hard. –   75
Come, sister. – Shepherdess, look on him better
And be not proud, though all the world could see,
None could be so abused in sight as he. –
Come, to our flock.

                                    Exit [with Celia and Corin]

---

60 when] F; what *Rowe*   62 being foul] F *subst.*; being found *Warburton*   66–9] *As prose, Pope; Ros. . . . shee'll /
Fall . . . fast / As . . . sauce / Her . . . me?* F   66 He's] F *subst.; Aside* He's *Johnson*   66 your] F; her *Hanmer*   66
foulness . . . and] *Singer² subst.*; foulnesse, & F   66 SD] *Singer²; not in* F   68 words. –] *Johnson;* words: F   73 SD]
Eds.; not in F   79 SD] *Eds.; Exit.* F

59 **friendly** as a friend.
60 Compare the proverb, 'As the market goes
wives must sell' (Tilley M670).
61 **Cry** Beg (*OED* sv *v* 1).
62 Your evil appearance will be a sign of a most
evil nature if you are shameless enough to mock
[Silvius], or 'foulness is most foul when its foulness
consists in being scornful' (Abbott 356). The word
'foul' has a spectrum of meanings including 'ugly',
'wicked', and 'shameful'. Warburton's emendation
(see collation) is attractive.
63 **take her to thee** take charge of her (*OED*
Take *v* 74a).
64 **chide** scold.
64 **together** without intermission (*OED* sv *adv*
5).
*66–8 Singer's emendation (see collation) deftly

clarifies the mixture of second and third person pro-
nouns in these lines.
68 **sauce** pepper (Schmidt), rebuke.
72 **in wine** when intoxicated.
73 *SD It would seem odd for Rosalind to tell
Phoebe, whom she has just abused, where she lives,
and so I suggest the following words be addressed
to Silvius. He, however, later (105–7) reveals that
he knows already where Rosalind dwells.
74 **tuft** clump.
74 **olives** See Curtius, p. 184, for further
instances of olive-trees in northern settings; for
olives as 'ensigns of peace and quietness', see
Spenser, *The Shepheardes Calender*, gloss to April
124.
78 **abused in sight** deceived by what he sees.

PHOEBE Dead shepherd, now I find thy saw of might: 80
           'Who ever loved that loved not at first sight?'

SILVIUS Sweet Phoebe, –

PHOEBE   Ha, what say'st thou, Silvius?

SILVIUS Sweet Phoebe, pity me.

PHOEBE Why I am sorry for thee, gentle Silvius.

SILVIUS Wherever sorrow is, relief would be. 85
           If you do sorrow at my grief in love,
           By giving love your sorrow and my grief
           Were both extermined.

PHOEBE Thou hast my love: is not that neighbourly?

SILVIUS I would have you.

PHOEBE   Why, that were covetousness. 90
           Silvius, the time was that I hated thee,
           And yet it is not that I bear thee love;
           But since that thou canst talk of love so well,
           Thy company, which erst was irksome to me,
           I will endure – and I'll employ thee too. 95
           But do not look for further recompense
           Than thine own gladness that thou art employed.

SILVIUS So holy and so perfect is my love,
           And I in such a poverty of grace
           That I shall think it a most plenteous crop 100
           To glean the broken ears after the man

---

82 Phoebe, –] *Capell; Phebe.* F **91** thee,] *Cam.;* thee; F **92** love;] *Cam.;* loue, F

80–1 Phoebe's quotation inverts the proverb, 'Love not at the first look' (Tilley L426), and is taken from Marlowe's *Hero and Leander*, 1, 176, a poem with strong homo-erotic elements. Marlowe's lyric, 'The Passionate Shepherd to his Love', was well known and drew a number of verse replies including versions by Ralegh and Donne. Anne Righter conjectures that the reference to Marlowe as a shepherd represents a 'purely private rite of memory' on Shakespeare's part (*Shakespeare and the Idea of the Play*, 1967, p. 139); see also Charles Nicholl, *The Reckoning: The Murder of Christopher Marlowe*, 1992.

80 saw maxim.
80 might power, virtue (*OED* sv *sb* 1c).
84 gentle noble.
85 sorrow mourning, tears (*OED* sv 4).
86 grief suffering (*OED* sv 1).
88 Would both be destroyed.
89 neighbourly 'friendly but not cordial' (*OED*

sv 1b), or a possible reference to the text, 'Love thy neighbour as thyself' (Lev. 19.18; Matt. 19.19).

90 were covetousness would be greedy: Phoebe may be invoking the tenth commandment: 'Thou shalt not covet thy neighbour's house, neither shalt thou covet thy neighbour's wife' (Ex. 20.17).

92 it is not the time has not yet come.
93 that For this conjunctional affix, see Abbott 287.
94 erst formerly.
99 poverty of grace lack of good fortune (*OED* Grace *sb* 10).
100–2 That . . . reaps Compare Lev. 23.22: 'And when ye reap the harvest of your land, thou shalt not rid clean the corners of thy field when thou reapest, neither shalt thou make any after-gathering of thy harvest: thou shalt leave them unto the poor, and to the stranger.'
101 glean gather.
101 broken ears fallen ears of corn.

That the main harvest reaps. Loose now and then
A scattered smile, and that I'll live upon.

PHOEBE Know'st thou the youth that spoke to me erewhile?

SILVIUS Not very well; but I have met him oft   105
And he hath bought the cottage and the bounds
That the old carlot once was master of.

PHOEBE Think not I love him, though I ask for him;
'Tis but a peevish boy – yet he talks well.
But what care I for words? Yet words do well   110
When he that speaks them pleases those that hear.
It is a pretty youth – not very pretty;
But sure he's proud – and yet his pride becomes him;
He'll make a proper man. The best thing in him
Is his complexion; and faster than his tongue   115
Did make offence, his eye did heal it up;
He is not very tall, yet for his years he's tall;
His leg is but so-so, and yet 'tis well;
There was a pretty redness in his lip,
A little riper and more lusty red   120
Than that mixed in his cheek: 'twas just the difference
Betwixt the constant red and mingled damask.
There be some women, Silvius, had they marked him
In parcels as I did, would have gone near
To fall in love with him: but, for my part,   125
I love him not nor hate him not – and yet

---

102 Loose] F *subst.*; lose F4   104 erewhile] *Eds.*; yerewhile F   107 carlot] *Steevens²*; *Carlot* F   118 so-so] *Eds.*; so so F

102 Loose Set free.

103 scattered dropped (continuing the gleaning metaphor from 100–2; *OED* sv 3b).

104 erewhile a little time ago.

106 bounds tracts of land.

107 *carlot carl, peasant (perhaps a nonce-word as this is the only example cited in *OED*). It is derived from 'carl' and cognate with 'churlish', the word used to describe the absent landlord at 2.4.73. It may even be a proper name – it is printed in F in italics and with a capital C.

109 'Tis The neuter pronoun is used humorously.

109 peevish silly, childish, perverse (*OED* sv 1, 4).

114 proper handsome, well-proportioned.

115 complexion face, appearance (*OED* sv 4c, 5).

116 make offence cause a hurt.

117 not very tall i.e. for a man, although, as a woman, Rosalind is 'more than common tall' (1.3.105).

120 lusty luxuriant.

121 difference Pronounced with two syllables (Cercignani, p. 274).

122 constant red uniform red rose.

122 damask The colour of a red and white damask rose, originally supposed to have come from Damascus; compare *Son.* 130.5, and Ovid's description of Hermaphroditus (*Metamorphoses*, IV, 406–9). It stands for perishable beauty in *TN* 2.4.112.

123 be For this use after 'there', see Abbott 300.

124 parcels parts, items.

124–5 gone near To fall been on the point of falling.

Have more cause to hate him than to love him.
For what had he to do to chide at me?
He said mine eyes were black, and my hair black,
And, now I am remembered, scorned at me.   130
I marvel why I answered not again;
But that's all one. Omittance is no quittance.
I'll write to him a very taunting letter
And thou shalt bear it – wilt thou, Silvius?

SILVIUS Phoebe, with all my heart.

PHOEBE   I'll write it straight: 135
The matter's in my head and in my heart;
I will be bitter with him and passing short.
Go with me, Silvius.

Exeunt

4.1 *Enter* ROSALIND [*as* GANYMEDE], *and* CELIA [*as* ALIENA],
and JAQUES

JAQUES I prithee, pretty youth, let me be better acquainted with thee.

ROSALIND They say you are a melancholy fellow.

JAQUES I am so: I do love it better than laughing.

ROSALIND Those that are in extremity of either are abominable
fellows, and betray themselves to every modern censure worse than   5
drunkards.

---

127 Have] F *subst.*; I have F2; Have I *Oxford, conj. Maxwell*   135 straight] *Eds.*; strait F   **Act 4, Scene 1** 4.1] *Eds.*;
Actus Quartus. Scena Prima. F   1 me be] F2; me F

---

128 had he to do cause had he.

129 black The opposite of 'fair', and therefore,
according to the conventions of Petrarchan verse,
not beautiful.

130 remembered reminded (Abbott 291).

130 scorned at mocked.

131 answered not again did not retort (see *OED*
Again 2).

132 Omittance is no quittance That I did not
respond does not mean that I shall not; 'quittance'
is a legal term, meaning release from a debt or
obligation; proverbial (Tilley F584, 'Forbearance is
no quittance').

135 straight immediately.

136 matter's contents are.

136–7 Phoebe may be imagining being cruel to
Rosalind in order to ease her own pangs of love –
the lines could be taken as an aside.

137 bitter cruel (*OED* sv *adj* 5a).

137 passing short exceedingly curt; 'short' may
have rhymed with 'heart' (Cercignani, p. 114).

Act 4, Scene 1

4 in extremity of either either deeply melancholic or boisterously mirthful.

4 abominable The context here generates a
meaning, not recorded in *OED*, of 'unnatural' or
'inhuman' rather than merely odious or execrable.
The word was spelt in the period 'abhominable',
reflecting a false etymology from '*ab homine*', 'away
from man, beastly'; see *LLL* 5.1.24–6.

5 betray expose (*OED* sv 1b).

5 modern ordinary, trite (*OED* sv 4).

5 censure opinion (*OED* sv 3).

JAQUES Why, 'tis good to be sad and say nothing.

ROSALIND Why then, 'tis good to be a post.

JAQUES I have neither the scholar's melancholy, which is emulation;
nor the musician's, which is fantastical; nor the courtier's, which is   10
proud; nor the soldier's, which is ambitious; nor the lawyer's, which
is politic; nor the lady's, which is nice; nor the lover's, which is all
these; but it is a melancholy of mine own, compounded of many
simples, extracted from many objects, and indeed the sundry contemplation of my travels, in which my often rumination wraps me   15
in a most humorous sadness.

ROSALIND A traveller! By my faith, you have great reason to be sad. I
fear you have sold your own lands to see other men's. Then to have
seen much and to have nothing is to have rich eyes and poor hands.

JAQUES Yes, I have gained my experience.   20

Enter ORLANDO

ROSALIND And your experience makes you sad. I had rather have a fool
to make me merry than experience to make me sad – and to travel
for it too!

ORLANDO Good day, and happiness, dear Rosalind.

---

15 in which my] F2; in which by F; and which, by *conj. Malone;* which by *Malone²;* which, by *Collier*   **16** in] F; is
Steevens   **22** travel] F3 *subst.;* trauaile F

7 **sad** serious (*OED* sv 4d).

8 **post** Compare the proverb, 'As deaf (dumb) as
a post' (Tilley P490); Rosalind possibly invokes the
meaning 'heavy' for 'sad' (*OED* sv 7a).

9 **emulation** envy (*OED* sv 3).

10 **fantastical** imaginative, capricious, or perhaps generative of musical fantasias, 'that is when a
musician taketh a point at his pleasure, and wresteth
and turneth it as he list' (Thomas Morley, *A Plain
and Easy Introduction to Practical Music* (1597),
p. 180).

11 **proud** The pride of courtiers generates unsatisfied ambition.

11 **lawyer's** lawmaker's (*OED* Lawyer 2b).

12 **politic** artful, cunning.

12 **nice** It is difficult to know which of the
many contemporary meanings of the word Shakespeare intended here, perhaps 'wanton' (*OED* 2b),
or 'capricious' (Schmidt).

14 **simples** ingredients (*OED* Simple *sb* 7a).

14 **objects** sights (*OED* Object *sb* 3a).

14–20 **and . . . experience** For other 'voyager'
characters in Shakespeare, see John Gillies, *Shakespeare and the Geography of Difference*, 1994, pp. 3–4.

14 **indeed** as a matter of fact.

14 **sundry** composed of many elements (*OED* sv
4b).

15 **in** within.

15 **which** Its antecedent is 'melancholy'.

15 ***my** F2's substitution for F's 'by' (see collation) improves the sense here.

15 **often** frequent.

16 **humorous** fantastic, capricious (*OED* sv 3).

16 **sadness** seriousness (*OED* sv 2); see L. Babb,
The Elizabethan Malady, 1957, p. 74: 'The Italianate
traveller . . . was the principal . . . cause of the melancholia in English life and literature.'

19 **rich eyes and poor hands** It is conceivable
that there is a sexual jibe here, 'eye' often desig-
nating the vagina, and 'hand' the penis (Williams,
pp. 118 and 150–1).

20 **Yes** Yes, but (*OED* sv *adv* 2b).

20 **experience** (1) knowledge (*OED* sv 7a), (2)
sexual skill (Williams, p. 118).

22 **travel** Punning on 'travail', work.

JAQUES Nay then, God buy you, and you talk in blank verse!   25

ROSALIND Farewell, Monsieur Traveller. Look you lisp and wear
strange suits; disable all the benefits of your own country; be out of
love with your nativity, and almost chide God for making you that
countenance you are, or I will scarce think you have swam in a
gondola.   30

[Exit Jaques]

Why, how now, Orlando, where have you been all this while? You
a lover? And you serve me such another trick, never come in my
sight more.

ORLANDO My fair Rosalind, I come within an hour of my promise.

ROSALIND Break an hour's promise in love? He that will divide a   35
minute into a thousand parts and break but a part of the thousand
part of a minute in the affairs of love, it may be said of him that
Cupid hath clapped him o'th'shoulder; but I'll warrant him heart-
whole.

ORLANDO Pardon me, dear Rosalind.   40

ROSALIND Nay, and you be so tardy, come no more in my sight – I had
as lief be wooed of a snail.

ORLANDO Of a snail?

ROSALIND Aye, of a snail; for though he comes slowly, he carries his

---

25 verse!] F *subst.;* verse. *Exit* F2   30 gondola] *Pope;* Gundello F   30 SD] *Hudson; not in* F

25 buy See 3.3.217n.

25 and if.

26–30 Satiric portraits of the affectations of travellers returned from Italy were common: see, for example, Roger Ascham, *The Schoolmaster* (1570), in *English Works*, ed. W. A. Wright, 1904, pp. 234–6, and see Mario Praz, *The Flaming Heart*, 1958, *passim.*

26 lisp As an affectation of speech, perhaps acquired abroad; compare *Rom.* 2.4.28.

27 strange foreign.

27 disable disparage.

27 benefits natural advantages (*OED* sv *sb* 3b).

28 nativity nationality (*OED* sv 5a).

29 countenance dignity, estate (*OED* sv 10).

29 swam floated, been conveyed (*OED* Swim *v* 3b).

30 gondola Venice was the most notorious city in Europe at the time: see the Sir Politic Would-be sequences in Jonson's *Volpone.*

30 *SD F2 supplies an exit for Jaques at 25, and directors might like to have Rosalind throw her jibes

at his departing back while keeping her lover in suspense.

32 trick (1) action, (2) sexual act (Williams, p. 313).

35 hour's A possible pun on 'whore's' (Cercignani, p. 194).

35–8 He . . . shoulder Any lover who is the slightest bit tardy has merely caught Cupid's attention but not fallen under his power; the image in 38 may be of an officer making an arrest; compare a 'shoulder-clapper' (*Err.* 4.2.37); alternatively 'clapped' may mean 'wounded with an arrow' (*OED* sv *v* 10c), or 'winged'.

36 the thousand the thousandth (*OED* sv 4).

38–9 heart-whole unwounded in the heart (*OED* sv 1).

42 of by (Abbott 170).

42 snail Proverbial for slowness (Tilley s579); for the sexual connotations of this 'boneless member', see Jones, pp. 207–8.

44–5 he . . . head Compare the proverb, 'Like a snail, he keeps his house on his head' (Tilley s58).

house on his head; a better jointure, I think, than you make a   45
woman. Besides, he brings his destiny with him.

ORLANDO What's that?

ROSALIND Why, horns; which such as you are fain to be beholden to
your wives for. But he comes armed in his fortune and prevents the
slander of his wife.   50

ORLANDO Virtue is no horn-maker, and my Rosalind is virtuous.

ROSALIND And I am your Rosalind.

CELIA It pleases him to call you so, but he hath a Rosalind of a better
leer than you.

ROSALIND Come, woo me, woo me; for now I am in a holiday humour   55
and like enough to consent. What would you say to me now and I
were your very, very Rosalind?

ORLANDO I would kiss before I spoke.

ROSALIND Nay, you were better speak first, and when you were gravelled for lack of matter you might take occasion to kiss. Very good   60
orators when they are out, they will spit, and for lovers, lacking –
God warrant us – matter, the cleanliest shift is to kiss.

ORLANDO How if the kiss be denied?

ROSALIND Then she puts you to entreaty, and there begins new matter.

ORLANDO Who could be out, being before his beloved mistress?   65

ROSALIND Marry, that should you if I were your mistress, or I should
think my honesty ranker than my wit.

---

48 beholden] *Pope;* beholding F   62 warrant] *Cam., conj. anon;* warne F

45 **jointure** estate settled on a woman in case of
her husband's death.

45 **you make** is settled upon.

46 **he . . . him** Compare the proverb, 'Cuckolds
come by destiny' (Tilley c89).

48 **horns** The customary badge of a cuckold.

48 **fain** obliged (*OED* sv 2b): the implication is
that men like Orlando are so feckless that they can
earn nothing but horns.

48 ***beholden** F's 'beholding' (see collation) is
the only form used by Shakespeare.

49 **comes armed in his fortune** is armed with
the instruments which would be his by destiny.

49 **prevents** precedes, forestalls (*OED* Prevent *v*
1c).

50 **slander** scandal, disgrace (*OED* sv 3).

53 **It . . . so** Compare the proverb, 'It pleases you
to say so' (Dent P407.1).

54 **leer** (1) face, complexion (*OED* sv *sb*²), (2)
cattle-colour (Hulme, p. 121), (3) loin (*OED* sv *sb*⁴).

55 **holiday humour** festive mood.

57 **very** true, real.

59–60 **gravelled** nonplussed (*OED* Gravel *v* 4a):

the image may be of a ship run aground (*OED* sv
2b), or of a horse lamed by gravel stuck between its
hoof and its shoe (*OED* Gravel *v* 5).

60 **lack of matter** want of anything purposeful
to say.

61 **are out** have forgotten their speech.

62 ***warrant** F's 'warne' may be a misprint,
meaning 'protect' (*OED* Warn *v*³, although the last
recorded use there is 1449), or be a dialect form of
'warrant', also meaning 'protect' (as at 3.4.4).

62 **matter** (1) small-talk, (2) semen (Williams,
p. 203).

62 **shift** tactic.

65 **out** (1) nonplussed, (2) astray, lost (*OED* sv
adj 20b).

67 **honesty** (appearance of) chastity; Rosalind
construes Orlando's 'out' to mean sexually excited
(Williams, p. 223).

67 **ranker** (1) greater, more luxuriant, (2) more
corrupt.

67 **wit** (1) intelligence, (2) sexual attractiveness
(see 3.4.9 n.).

ORLANDO What, of my suit?

ROSALIND Not out of your apparel, and yet out of your suit. Am not I
your Rosalind?   70

ORLANDO I take some joy to say you are, because I would be talking of
her.

ROSALIND Well, in her person, I say I will not have you.

ORLANDO Then, in mine own person, I die.

ROSALIND No, faith, die by attorney. The poor world is almost six   75
thousand years old and in all this time there was not any man died
in his own person, videlicet, in a love-cause. Troilus had his brains
dashed out with a Grecian club, yet he did what he could to die
before, and he is one of the patterns of love; Leander, he would have
lived many a fair year though Hero had turned nun, if it had not   80
been for a hot midsummer night, for, good youth, he went but forth
to wash him in the Hellespont and, being taken with the cramp, was
drowned, and the foolish chroniclers of that age found it was Hero
of Sestos. But these are all lies: men have died from time to time –
and worms have eaten them – but not for love.   85

68 What,] F; What, out *Collier*   **69–70**] *As prose, Pope; Ros. . . . suite: / Am . . . Rosalind?* F   **83** chroniclers] F *subst.;*
coroners *Hanmer*   **84** Sestos] F2; Cestos F

68 **of my suit** Continuing the play on 'out' from
65; suit = (1), wooing, (2) apparel.

75 **by attorney** by proxy, the opposite of 'in person' (*OED* Attorney 2).

75 **poor** Writings about the decay of the world in
the period were common: see George Williamson,
'Mutability, decay, and seventeenth-century melancholy', *ELH* 2 (1935), 121–51.

75–6 **six thousand years old** At the end of the
Geneva Bible we read that 'the whole sum of years
from the beginning of the world unto this present
year of our Lord God 1560 are just 5534, 6 months,
and the said odd ten days' (sig. LLliiiᵛ); see also Shaheen, pp. 168–9.

76 **there was not** there has not been.

76–7 **died in his own person** who died in real
life.

77 **videlicet** namely.

77 **love-cause** love-affair or a legal 'case of love'.

77–8 **Troilus . . . club** Chaucer narrates perfunc-
torily that Troilus (son of Priam and abandoned
by his love Cressida for Diomedes) was slain by
'the fierse Achille' (*Troilus and Criseyde*, V.1806),
and Benoît de Sainte-Maure tells how Achilles cut
off Troilus' head with his sword (*Le Roman de

Troie): Shakespeare may therefore have invented the
(phallic?) club as a burlesque detail.

78 **die** experience detumescence after sexual
orgasm (Williams, p. 98).

79 **one . . . love** Compare 'As true as Troilus'
(*Tro.* 3.2.182).

79 **patterns** archetypes.

79 **Leander** A young man of Abydos, who was
devoted to Hero, a priestess of Aphrodite at Sestos
on the other side of the Hellespont, and who was
drowned while swimming to see her in the middle of a tempest; the story is told by Musaeus, a
Greek poet of the fourth or fifth century AD and was
retold by Marlowe in his unfinished poem, 'Hero
and Leander'.

79 **he** For the insertion of the pronoun, see
Abbott 243.

80 **though** even if.

83 **found** discovered from the records (*OED*
Find *v* 1c); Hanmer's emendation of F's 'Chron-
oclers' to 'coroners' (see collation) is unnecessary,
deriving as it does from the assumption that the
meaning of 'found' is a legal one, 'declared' (*OED*
Find *v* 17b).

83 **it was** his death was caused by.

ORLANDO I would not have my right Rosalind of this mind, for I
  protest her frown might kill me.

ROSALIND By this hand, it will not kill a fly. But come, now I will be
  your Rosalind in a more coming-on disposition and, ask me what
  you will, I will grant it.   90

ORLANDO Then love me, Rosalind.

ROSALIND Yes, faith, will I, Fridays and Saturdays and all.

ORLANDO And wilt thou have me?

ROSALIND Aye, and twenty such.

ORLANDO What sayest thou?   95

ROSALIND Are you not good?

ORLANDO I hope so.

ROSALIND Why then, can one desire too much of a good thing? –
  Come, sister, you shall be the priest and marry us. – Give me your
  hand, Orlando. – What do you say, sister?   100

ORLANDO Pray thee, marry us.

CELIA I cannot say the words.

ROSALIND You must begin: 'Will you, Orlando –'

CELIA Go to. – Will you, Orlando, have to wife this Rosalind?

ORLANDO I will.   105

ROSALIND Aye, but when?

ORLANDO Why, now, as fast as she can marry us.

ROSALIND Then you must say, 'I take thee, Rosalind, for wife.'

ORLANDO I take thee, Rosalind, for wife.

ROSALIND I might ask you for your commission, but I do take thee, 110

---

106 SH] F *subst.;* CELIA *conj. this edn*   **108** SH] F *subst.;* ROSALIND [*Aside to Orlando*] / *conj. this edn*   **110** commission, but] *Pope subst.;* Commission, / But F; commission – [*to Orlando*] but *conj. this edn*

86 right true.

87 protest proclaim.

87 frown The mortal frown of a loved one was a Petrarchan commonplace, see *Son.* 25.8, 117.11, etc.

89 coming-on forward; becoming, comely (*OED* Come *v* 26).

92 Fridays and Saturdays Like Friday for most Christians, Saturday was a day of fast for sabbatarians.

98 can . . . thing Compare the proverbs, 'The more common a good thing is the better' and 'Too much of one thing is good for nothing' (Tilley T142 and T158).

98 good thing (1) something pleasing, (2) erect penis.

99–100 Give me your hand Rosalind seems to be enacting a 'handfast' (a betrothal contract) or

even, since Celia is there to witness the little ceremony, a '*verba de praesenti*' marriage.

102 Possibly because she is laughing so much, or because she is shocked by Rosalind's shamelessness.

103 The question addressed to the bride and groom at the marriage ceremony is 'Wilt thou have this man [or this woman] to thy wedded husband [or wedded wife]?'

104 Go to That's enough.

107 fast (1) quickly, (2) firmly bound.

108 The words from the service are 'I, *N.*, take thee, *N.*, to my wedded wife'; in the text 'for' means 'as the equivalent of' (*OED* For *prep* 19a).

110 commission warrant, authority; this could apply to Celia as well as Orlando, and so it may be that 108 should be reassigned to Celia (see collation), particularly in view of the change in pronoun from 'you' to 'thee'.

Orlando, for my husband. There's a girl goes before the priest, and
certainly a woman's thought runs before her actions.

ORLANDO So do all thoughts: they are winged.

ROSALIND Now, tell me how long you would have her after you have
possessed her?   115

ORLANDO For ever and a day.

ROSALIND Say a day without the 'ever'. No, no, Orlando: men are April
when they woo, December when they wed; maids are May when
they are maids, but the sky changes when they are wives. I will be
more jealous of thee than a Barbary cock-pigeon over his hen; more   120
clamorous than a parrot against rain, more new-fangled than an ape;
more giddy in my desires than a monkey. I will weep for nothing,
like Diana in the fountain, and I will do that when you are disposed
to be merry. I will laugh like a hyena, and that when thou art
inclined to sleep.   125

ORLANDO But will my Rosalind do so?

ROSALIND By my life, she will do as I do.

ORLANDO O, but she is wise.

---

114 have] F *subst.;* love *Hanmer*   124 hyena] *Eds.;* Hyen F   125 sleep] F *subst.;* weep *conj. Theobald*

111 There's . . . priest Rosalind has not waited
for Celia to say, 'Will you, Rosalind, have to husband
this Orlando'; the line suggests that she is imagining that she might give herself sexually to Orlando
before marriage.

111 girl girl who (Abbott 244).

113 Compare the proverb, 'As swift as thought'
(Tilley T240).

115 possessed her (1) made her your own by
marriage, (2) known her carnally (*OED* Possess *v*
3b).

116 Proverbial (Tilley D74).

117–19 April . . . maids Perhaps a reference to a
rainy month when lovers are 'all made of sighs and
tears' (5.2.68) and to a time of cold and darkness;
an 'April-gentleman' was a newly married husband
(*OED*); May was associated with merry-making.

118–19 maids . . . wives Compare the proverb,
'Maidens should be meek till they be married'
(Tilley M44) and *LLL* 4.3.100 'Love, whose month
is ever May'.

120 more . . . hen Pliny, *Natural History*, x, 52,
notes that 'the cock-pigeon is suspicious of adultery although not himself given to the practice'; a
'barb' (*OED* sv *sb³* 2) was a 'fancy variety of pigeon,
of black or dun colour, originally introduced from
Barbary' (the Saracen lands of North Africa).

121 parrot against rain Compare the proverb,
'The hoarse crow croaks before the rain' (Tilley
c854).

121 against before (*OED* sv *prep* 18).

121 new-fangled fond of novelty (*OED* sv 1).

122 giddy See 3.3.292 n.

123 like Diana in the fountain A reference
either to the fountain in West Cheap that in 1595
had been restored with a statue of Diana (John
Stow, *The Survey of London*, 1633 edn) or to the
heroine of Jorge de Montemayor's romance *Diana*
(c. 1559), translated into English by Bartholomew
Young in 1598; see Paul Reyher, 'Alfred de Vigny,
Shakespeare et Georges de Montemayor', *Revue
de l'enseignement des langues vivantes* 37 (1920),
1–4.

124–5 I . . . sleep Compare the proverb, 'When
the husband is merry the wife will be sad' (Tilley
H839).

124 *hyena Proverbial for its laughing sound
(Tilley H844) but also renowned for its ability
to counterfeit and, like the hare, thought to be
hermaphroditic (see Marta Powell Harley, 'Rosalind, the hare, and the hyena . . .', *SQ* 36 (1985),
335–7 (compare 4.3.17 n.)); F's 'hyen' is probably a
mistake, although it could be an obsolete form.

128 wise prudent.

ROSALIND Or else she could not have the wit to do this: the wiser, the waywarder. Make the doors upon a woman's wit, and it will out at the casement; shut that, and 'twill out at the keyhole; stop that, 'twill fly with the smoke out at the chimney. 130

ORLANDO A man that had a wife with such a wit, he might say, 'Wit, whither wilt?'

ROSALIND Nay, you might keep that check for it till you met your wife's wit going to your neighbour's bed. 135

ORLANDO And what wit could wit have to excuse that?

ROSALIND Marry, to say she came to seek you there: you shall never take her without her answer unless you take her without her tongue. O, that woman that cannot make her fault her husband's occasion, let her never nurse her child herself for she will breed it like a fool. 140

ORLANDO For these two hours, Rosalind, I will leave thee.

ROSALIND Alas, dear love, I cannot lack thee two hours.

ORLANDO I must attend the Duke at dinner; by two o'clock I will be with thee again. 145

ROSALIND Aye, go your ways, go your ways. I knew what you would prove – my friends told me as much, and I thought no less. That flattering tongue of yours won me. 'Tis but one cast away, and so come, Death! Two o'clock is your hour?

ORLANDO Aye, sweet Rosalind. 150

---

134 wilt] F3; wil't F   135 met] F; meet *Johnson²*

129–30 the wiser, the waywarder Seemingly a proverb for the nonce.

129 wiser more sexually experienced.

130 waywarder (1) more wilful or perverse, (2) more able to control her destiny (compare the spelling 'weyward' in Acts 1 and 2 of *Mac.*).

130 Make Bar, make fast (*OED* sv v^1 37).

131 casement hinged window.

133–4 Wit, whither wilt A proverbial saying (Tilley W570), i.e. where are your senses? (*OED* Wit *sb* 2e).

135 check rebuke.

136 wit sexual organs (see 3.4.9 n.).

137 wit could wit have ingenious excuse could wantonness use.

139 answer Possibly the genitalia (compare *AWW* 2.2.13–14).

139 you . . . tongue Compare the proverb, 'A woman's answer is never to seek' (Tilley W670).

139 take (1) catch, detect, (2) possess sexually (Williams, p. 301).

139 tongue With genital connotations (Williams, pp. 309–10).

140 that cannot . . . occasion Compare the proverb, 'Some complain to prevent complaint' (Tilley C579).

140 fault (1) offence, (2) deficiency, fissure, and hence vagina (Williams, p. 128).

140 husband's occasion 'a "handle" against' (*OED* Occasion sb^1 3d) her spouse.

141 breed raise, educate.

141 like (1) as, (2) in the manner of.

141 It is common for acting editions from 1740 to indicate that the spring song of the cuckoo from the end of *LLL* was introduced at this point (see Knowles).

142 Productions have often inserted a call sounded on a hunting horn at this point, perhaps to indicate that even in a forest without clocks there are social obligations.

143 lack do without (*OED* v^1 2b).

144 dinner the chief mid-day meal.

146 go your ways away with you.

148 cast away more woman deserted.

ROSALIND By my troth, and in good earnest, and so God mend me, and
by all pretty oaths that are not dangerous, if you break one jot of
your promise or come one minute behind your hour, I will think
you the most pathetical break-promise, and the most hollow lover,
and the most unworthy of her you call Rosalind that may be chosen   155
out of the gross band of the unfaithful. Therefore beware my censure, and keep your promise.

ORLANDO With no less religion than if thou wert indeed my Rosalind.
So adieu.

ROSALIND Well, Time is the old justice that examines all such offend-   160
ers, and let Time try. Adieu.

Exit [Orlando]

CELIA You have simply misused our sex in your love-prate. We must
have your doublet and hose plucked over your head, and show the
world what the bird hath done to her own nest.

ROSALIND O coz, coz, coz, my pretty little coz, that thou didst know   165
how many fathom deep I am in love! But it cannot be sounded: my
affection hath an unknown bottom like the Bay of Portugal.

CELIA Or rather bottomless, that as fast as you pour affection in, it runs
out.

ROSALIND No, that same wicked bastard of Venus that was begot of   170

---

154 pathetical] F *subst.*; atheistical *Warburton*   161 try] F; try you *Collier*   161 SD *Orlando*] *Rowe; not in* F   168 in,
it] F2; in, in F

151 **so God mend me** Proverbial (Dent G173.1).

151 **mend** improve (*OED* sv *v* 12b).

152 **by . . . dangerous** see Matt. 5.34: 'Swear
not at all, neither by heaven, for it is the throne of
God'; reformers were inveighing against blasphemy
and profane oaths well before the Statute to Restrain
Abuses of the Players of 1606: see Chambers, I, 244–
5; IV, 192–248, 338–9.

152 **jot** The word derives from 'iota', the Greek
'i' or the smallest letter of the alphabet.

153 **will** Expresses intention.

154 **pathetical** pitiable; shocking (Schmidt); the
primary meaning for the word in the period was
'producing an effect upon the emotions' (*OED*
sv 1): the modern meaning of 'ludicrous' is not
appropriate.

156 **gross** entire.

156–7 **censure** condemnation (*OED* sv 1).

158 **religion** devotion, faithfulness (*OED* sv 6).

160–1 **Time . . . offenders** Compare the proverb,
'Time tries all things' (Tilley T336).

161 **let Time try** Proverbial (Dent T308.2).

162 **simply misused** completely abused, reviled
(*OED* Misuse *v* 4), with, according to Rubinstein
(p. 163), connotations of sexual deviance.

162 **love-prate** A possible pun on 'prat' (but-
tocks – see *OED* sv *sb²* 1a).

164 **bird . . . nest** Compare the proverb, 'It is
a foul bird that defiles his own nest' (Tilley B377);
the saying occurs in *Rosalind*, p. 125, Appendix 2,
p. 231.

166 **fathom** A unit for sounding of six feet; after
numerals the singular was often used.

167 **affection** sexual desire (*OED* sv 3).

167 **Bay of Portugal** 'The sea off the coast of
Portugal between Oporto and the Cape of Cintra.
The water is very deep, attaining 1400 fathoms
within 40 miles of the coast' (Sugden, p. 420).

168 **that** so that.

170 **bastard of Venus** Cupid was the son of
Venus, not by her husband Vulcan, but by Mercury or, according to another tradition, Zeus her
father (Cicero, *De Natura Deorum*, III, 23).

170 **begot of** procreated by.

thought, conceived of spleen, and born of madness, that blind
rascally boy that abuses everyone's eyes because his own are out, let
him be judge how deep I am in love. I'll tell thee, Aliena, I cannot
be out of the sight of Orlando. I'll go find a shadow and sigh till he
come.   175
CELIA And I'll sleep.

Exeunt

4.2 *Enter* JAQUES *and* LORDS, FORESTERS [*bearing the antlers and skin
of a deer*]

JAQUES Which is he that killed the deer?
I LORD Sir, it was I.
JAQUES Let's present him to the Duke like a Roman conqueror – and it

---

173 judge] *Eds.;* judge, F   **Act 4, Scene 2   4.2**] *Eds.; Scena Secunda.* F   **0** SD.1 LORDS] F *subst.;* lords, like
Collier   **0** SD.1–2 *bearing . . . deer*] *This edn; not in* F   **2** SH 1] *Malone; not in* F

171 thought anxiety, distress (*OED sb*^{1} 5a), or
possibly desire as at 112.

171 spleen The spleen was regarded variously
as the seat of melancholy and of mirth; the phrase
seems to have meant 'in jest' (*OED* Spleen 2a) or
'from a caprice' (4a).

171 madness For Ficino's opinion that 'bestial
love' was not a vice but a form of madness, see
Panofsky, p. 144.

172 rascally knavish.

172 abuses deceives (*OED* Abuse *v* 4a).

172 eyes . . . out For the topos of 'blind Cupid',
see Panofsky, pp. 95–128.

172 out out of use (not recorded in *OED*).

174 shadow (1) shady place (*OED* sv *sb* 11c), (2)
catamite (Rubinstein, pp. 234–5), (3) possibly, the
penthouse roof over a public playhouse stage.

175 come (1) arrives, (2) achieves orgasm (see
1.2.23 n.).

Act 4, Scene 2

4.2 The scene fills a two hours' interval (see
4.1.142) between scenes and sets off the wooing
scenes that frame it. With its cuckoldry jokes, it
may sound a sceptical note about marriage or, conversely, Peter Erickson may be right to argue that
'the expected negative meaning of horns as the sign
of a cuckold is transformed into a positive image of
phallic potency that unites men' (Peter B. Erickson,
Patriarchal Structures in Shakespeare's Drama, 1985,

p. 23). If the hunters are considered as poachers,
it may celebrate a ritual of inversion that matches
Rosalind's usurpation of the man's role in the wooing game. Compare the hunting scene in Chettle
and Munday's *Death of Robert Earl of Huntingdon*
(1598) in which Friar Tuck enters dancing 'carrying
a stag's head'.

0 SD.1 FORESTERS Either officers in charge of
the forest or natives of the forest (*OED* Forester
1 and 3); if the former, there may be a suggestion
that the officers have joined the cause of those who
appeared earlier as outlaws (2.7.0 SD.1). Alternatively, as Collier supposed (see collation) this may
indicate something about the dress of Duke Senior's
courtiers as at 2.1.0 SD.1–2.

1 A subtext for this line could be Jaques' memory
of the 'sobbing deer' about whose misfortunes it was
reported he had wept (2.1.26–66).

3 present bring into the presence of (*OED* sv *v*
1).

3 like a Roman conqueror Crowns of olives or
laurels were given in ancient triumphs to those who
had won victories. Sir Thomas Elyot, *The Governor*
(1531), notes that 'to them which, in [the hunting of
red deer], do show most prowess . . . a garland . . .
to be given, in sign of victory, and with a joyful
manner to be brought in the presence of him that
is chief in the company' (1, chap. 18). A 'Roman
conqueror' here has sexual connotations – compare
5.2.26 n. and *AWW* 4.2.57.

would do well to set the deer's horns upon his head for a branch of
victory. – Have you no song, forester, for this purpose?   5
I FORESTER Yes, sir.
JAQUES Sing it. 'Tis no matter how it be in tune, so it make noise enough.

Music
Song

LORDS   What shall he have that killed the deer?
               His leather skin and horns to wear.
               Then sing him home,   10
               The rest shall bear this burden:

               Take thou no scorn to wear the horn,
               It was a crest ere thou wast born;

---

6 SH] *This edn; Lord.* F; *Amiens / Wilson*   7 SD.2] F *subst.; Given a note, they sing / Latham*   8 SH] *Sisson; not in*
F; *1 Voice / Capell subst.; Amiens / Wilson subst.*   9 His] F; *2 Voice* His *Capell subst.*   10 Then] F; *1 Voice* Then
Capell   10–11] *This edn; Then . . . burthen; (one line)* F; *Then . . . home.* SD *The rest . . . burden. / Theobald;* Then . . .
home. (*a line of dialogue*) *The . . . burden. / Harbage subst.*   11 burden] *Eds.; burthen* F   12 Take] F; *Both* Take *Capell*
subst.   13 born] *Eds.; borne* F

4–5 set . . . victory For ritualised carrying of animal heads, see Ronald Hutton, *The Rise and Fall of
Merry England: The Ritual Year 1400–1700*, 1994,
p. 47; Hutton draws upon Robert Plot, *The Natural
History of Staffordshire* (1686), p. 434.

4 branch (1) of the antler, (2) of the garland of
victory.

5 forester This figure may well be Amiens (see
2.7.0 SD.1 n.), appearing as he does in another scene
(2.5) containing a song.

7 make noise create a clamour (*OED* Noise 1a).

7 SD.1 *Music* Possibly a book-holder's note to give
the pitch for the following song, or perhaps an indication that a consort of instruments (hunting horns?)
was available for the first performances.

8–17 The song seems to imitate a folk-mime in
which players, perhaps clad in foliage with animal
skins and antlers, performed burlesque and obscene
actions that recalled ancient fertility rites (see E. K.
Chambers, *The Mediaeval Stage*, 2 vols., 1903, 1,
166, for seasonal masquerades performed by mum-
mers dressed in animal skins and antlers). As the
two 'stanzas' are not symmetrical, and as many editors since Theobald have considered line 11 to be
a stage direction accidentally incorporated into the
song, there has been much dispute over how the
song was originally performed.

8–9, 14–15 Capell suggested that these lines
should be alternated between two voices.

9 The perquisites of the deer-killer, as in *Rosalind*
'What news, forester? Hast thou wounded some
deer, and lost him in the fall? Care not, man, for so
small a loss: thy fees was but the skin, the shoulder,
and the horns' (Bullough, p. 200). However, 'leather

skin' conceivably may mean that the protagonist of
the song is to be imagined naked as in *Edward III*
(1596) 'Since leathern Adam till this youngest hour'
(2.2.120).

10 Staunton took this to be the 'burden' or refrain
of the song.

11 This line does not appear in Hilton's version
of the song as a round for four voices (1652), and
may, therefore, have been a direction to the players.

11 *burden The word was in the period confused with 'bourdon' which generated a complex of
puns: (1) the bass, 'undersong', or accompaniment
(*OED* Bourdon² 1), or refrain (*OED* Burden *sb* 10),
(2) the cuckold's horns, (3) the stage property of the
slaughtered deer, (4) as is frequent in performance,
one of the lords carried on his fellows' shoulders
bearing horns.

12 Take thou no scorn Don't despise (*OED*
Scorn *sb* 4).

12 horn (1) ornamental (helmet) badge of honour
(*OED* SV *sb* 16), (2) sign of a cuckold (see the proverb,
'He wears the horns' (Tilley H625)); for examples of
ingenious sets of horns made for cuckolds, see D. E.
Underdown, 'The taming of the scold', in Anthony
Fletcher and John Stevenson (eds.), *Order and Dis-
order in Early Modern England*, 1985, pp. 116–36, at
128.

13 crest A heraldic figure or device originally
borne by a knight on his helmet; here, in the context
of horn-jokes, with phallic implications, as with the
'comb' of a cock (*OED* SV 1).

13 *thou wast born (1) began your life, (2) were
carried aloft (see 11 n.).

> Thy father's father wore it,
> And thy father bore it;   15
> The horn, the horn, the lusty horn,
> Is not a thing to laugh to scorn.

>   *Exeunt*

4.3 *Enter* ROSALIND [*as* GANYMEDE] *and* CELIA [*as* ALIENA]

ROSALIND How say you now, is it not past two o'clock? And here much
   Orlando!
CELIA I warrant you, with pure love and troubled brain he hath ta'en his
   bow and arrows and is gone forth – to sleep. Look who comes here.

>   *Enter* SILVIUS [*with a letter*]

SILVIUS My errand is to you, fair youth;   5
   My gentle Phoebe did bid me give you this:
   I know not the contents but, as I guess
   By the stern brow and waspish action
   Which she did use as she was writing of it,
   It bears an angry tenor. Pardon me,   10
   I am but as a guiltless messenger.
ROSALIND [*After reading the letter*] Patience herself would startle at this
   letter
   And play the swaggerer: bear this, bear all.

Act 4, Scene 3   4.3] *Eds.; Scæna Tertia.* F   1–4] *As prose, Pope; Ros. . . . clock? / And . . . Orlando. / Cel. . . .*
brain, / He . . . forth / To . . . heere. F   4 forth –] *Capell;* forth F   4 SD] *Enter* SILVIUS *Pope subst.; after* brain *in*
3 F   4 SD] *with . . . letter / Eds.; not in* F   6 Phoebe did] F; Phoebe F2   10 tenor] *Theobald;* tenure F   12 SD]
Hanmer; not in F

---

16 **lusty** (1) merry, pleasing, lustful (*OED* sv 1–4)
with the implication, from the context, that the word
celebrates woman's sexuality, (2) massive (*OED* sv 9,
although this meaning is recorded only from 1640).
   17 **laugh to scorn** ridicule.
   17 SD The scene ends so abruptly that we may
conjecture that lines (a comment by Jaques?) are
missing.

Act 4, Scene 3
   1 **much** not much (*OED* sv *adj* 2f).
   3 **warrant** assure.
   3 **with . . . brain** The phrase could designate the
condition of either Celia or Orlando.
   3–4 **he . . . sleep** Proverbial (Dent B564.1);
there may be a deprecating comparison with Cupid's
weapons.

7 **contents** Stressed on the second syllable (Cercignani, p. 38).
   8 **waspish** irascible, spiteful.
   8 **action** gesture (three syllables: Cercignani, p.
308).
   9 **writing of** For verbal nouns like this one, see
Abbott 178.
   10 *****tenor** F's 'tenure' was confused with 'tenor'
until the eighteenth century (*OED* Tenor *sb¹*).
   10–11 Compare the proverb, 'Messengers should
neither be headed nor hanged' (Tilley M905).
   11 **as** For this redundant usage, see Abbott 115.
   12–69 Rosalind, astounded by the letter's true
contents, seizes upon Silvius' intimation of its contents to cover her confusion.
   13 **swaggerer** quarreller.
   13 **bear this, bear all** Proverbial (Tilley A172).

She says I am not fair, that I lack manners;
She calls me proud, and that she could not love me   15
Were man as rare as phoenix. Od's my will,
Her love is not the hare that I do hunt –
Why writes she so to me? Well, shepherd, well?
This is a letter of your own device.

SILVIUS No, I protest, I know not the contents;   20
Phoebe did write it.

ROSALIND   Come, come, you are a fool
And turned into the extremity of love.
I saw her hand, she has a leathern hand,
A freestone-coloured hand. (I verily did think
That her old gloves were on, but 'twas her hands.)   25
She has a hussif's hand – but that's no matter.
I say she never did invent this letter:
This is a man's invention and his hand.

SILVIUS Sure, it is hers.

ROSALIND Why, 'tis a boisterous and a cruel style,   30
A style for challengers. Why, she defies me
Like Turk to Christian. Woman's gentle brain
Could not drop forth such giant-rude invention,
Such Ethiop words, blacker in their effect

---

18 well?] *Yale;* well, F   21 it.] F; it, with her own fair hand *Mason, conj. Rann*   21 you are] F; you're *Pope*   22 into] F; in *or* so in *conj. Capell*   32 Woman's] *Rowe;* vvomens F   33 giant-rude] *Eds.;* giant rude F

14 **fair** beautiful.

15 **that** states that (Abbott 382).

16 **Were . . . phoenix** Compare the proverb, 'As rare as the phoenix' (Tilley P256).

16 **phoenix** A mythical bird, reputed to be the only one of its kind, that lived five or six hundred years in the Arabian desert.

16 **Od's my will** See 3.6.43 n.

16 **will** The cant meanings of both penis and vagina are invoked here (Williams, pp. 337–9).

17 **hare** Hares were regarded as hermaphrodites, which suggests that Rosalind fears Phoebe's unwitting homo-erotic attentions (compare 4.1.124 n.).

18 **Well, shepherd, well** Compare the proverb, 'Well, well is a word of malice' (Tilley W269).

19 **device** invention (*OED* sv 1).

20 **protest** vow.

21 Rann's conjecture (see collation) is attractive since without it Rosalind's wilful confusion of 'hand' with 'handwriting' may be obscure.

22 **turned . . . love** transformed into the most foolish kind of lover.

23 **leathern** coarse, clumsy.

24 **freestone** 'any fine-grained sandstone or limestone that can be cut or sawn easily' (*OED*), i.e. cream or yellow-brown.

26 **hussif's** Dialect form of 'housewife's' or 'hussy's'.

27 **invent** compose.

28 **invention** style (*OED* sv 5).

31 **defies** challenges (*OED* Defy 2).

32 **Like Turk to Christian** In Christmas mumming plays the Turkish knight challenged the Christian in the name of 'Mahound'.

33 **drop forth** give birth to, although *OED* (Drop *v* 14) records this meaning only from 1662; compare 3.3.197–8 n.

33 **giant-rude** For the compound, see Abbott 430.

34 **Ethiop** Black, like a swarthy-skinned African.

34–5 **blacker . . . countenance** that are even more hurtful than they seem (being written in black ink).

Than in their countenance. Will you hear the letter?   35
SILVIUS So please you, for I never heard it yet,
    Yet heard too much of Phoebe's cruelty.
ROSALIND She Phoebes me. Mark how the tyrant writes:
    Reads 'Art thou god to shepherd turned,
        That a maiden's heart hath burned?'   40
    Can a woman rail thus?
SILVIUS   Call you this railing?
ROSALIND *Reads* 'Why, thy godhead laid apart,
        Warr'st thou with a woman's heart?' –
    Did you ever hear such railing? –
        'Whiles the eye of man did woo me,   45
        That could do no vengeance to me.' –
    Meaning me a beast!
        'If the scorn of your bright eyne
        Have power to raise such love in mine,
        Alack, in me what strange effect   50
        Would they work in mild aspect?
        Whiles you chid me, I did love;
        How then might your prayers move?
        He that brings this love to thee
        Little knows this love in me;   55
        And by him seal up thy mind,
        Whether that thy youth and kind
        Will the faithful offer take
        Of me and all that I can make,

---

39 SD, **42** SD] *Rowe;* Read. F   **39** god] *Eds.; god,* F

35 countenance Pronounced as two syllables (Cercignani, p. 274).

36 heard have heard (Abbott 347).

38 She Phoebes me She dares to write to me with her customary disdain.

38 tyrant usurper (*OED* sv 1) – in the sense that she is using a style she was not born to.

41 rail thus use such abusive language.

42 thy godhead laid apart having taken up human shape again.

45 Whiles While (*OED* sv 4).

45 man As contrasted with the 'god' of 39.

46 vengeance mischief (Johnson).

47 Since, she says, men could not harm her, she is implying that I am a sexual predator (see Williams, 'beast', pp. 39–40).

48–51 This is highly ironic, given Phoebe's scorn of this kind of conceit at 3.6.10–14.

48 eyne A poetically archaic plural.

49 Have Plural (as though 'eyne' were the subject; see Abbott 412).

51 in mild aspect if your look was more merciful or, possibly, were the planets to be in a favourable conjunction, as in Drayton's *Heroic Epistles*, Isabella to Mortimer, 17 'That blessed night, that mild-aspected hour, / Wherein thou mad'st escape out of the Tower' (1597; cited *OED* Mild *adj* 11).

51 aspect Accented on the second syllable (Cercignani, p. 37).

53 prayers Two syllables (Cercignani, p. 357).

56 seal up thy mind (1) make up your mind, (2) convey your thoughts in a letter.

57 kind natural affection.

59 make earn (*OED* sv *v* 29a).

Or else by him my love deny, 60
And then I'll study how to die.'
SILVIUS Call you this chiding?
CELIA   Alas, poor shepherd.
ROSALIND Do you pity him? No, he deserves no pity. – Wilt thou love
such a woman? What, to make thee an instrument and play false
strains upon thee? Not to be endured! Well, go your way to her – for 65
I see love hath made thee a tame snake – and say this to her: that if
she love me, I charge her to love thee; if she will not, I will never
have her, unless thou entreat for her. If you be a true lover, hence,
and not a word; for here comes more company.

Exit Silvius

Enter OLIVER

OLIVER Good morrow, fair ones. Pray you, if you know 70
Where in the purlieus of this forest stands
A sheepcote fenced about with olive-trees.
CELIA West of this place, down in the neighbour bottom;
The rank of osiers by the murmuring stream,
Left on your right hand, brings you to the place. 75
But at this hour the house doth keep itself:
There's none within.
OLIVER If that an eye may profit by a tongue,
Then should I know you by description:
Such garments, and such years. 'The boy is fair, 80
Of female favour, and bestows himself
Like a ripe sister; the woman low

---

65 strains] F *subst.;* strings F2   70 know] *Theobald³;* know) F   73 bottom;] *Capell;* bottom F   74 stream] F *subst.;* stream, *Theobald*   81 and] F; but *conj. Lettsom in Walker*   82 ripe sister] F; ripe sister, but F2 *subst.;* right forester *Hudson, conj. Lettsom*

64 **make thee an instrument** use you.
65 **strains** parts of a piece of music (*OED* Strain *sb²* 12).
66 **snake** drudge (*OED sv sb* 3b).
70 **fair** The adjective could be applied to either sex as at 14 above.
71 **purlieus** borders; purlieus or 'pourallees' were places where persons other than the monarch might hunt: see John Manwood, *A Treatise of the Laws of the Forest* (1592), chap. 20.
72 **sheepcote** See 2.4.77 n.
72 **olive-trees** Compare the palm-tree of 3.3.146, and see Curtius, p. 184.

73 **bottom** water-meadow or low-lying pasture.
74 **rank of osiers** row of willows.
75 **Left . . . hand** Having left (the rank of osiers) on your right hand.
76 **keep** guard (*OED sv v* 16d).
78 **eye . . . tongue** See 4.1.19 n. and 4.1.139 n.
79 **description** Probably four syllables.
81 **favour** feature (*OED sv sb* 9c).
81 **bestows** acquits, comports.
82 **ripe** marriageable (*OED sv adj* 2b); although if, as Hudson thought (see collation), 'sister' was a misreading of 'forester', it could mean 'mature'.
82 **low** short (see 1.2.224 n.).

And browner than her brother.' Are not you
The owners of the house I did enquire for?
CELIA It is no boast, being asked, to say we are.   85
OLIVER Orlando doth commend him to you both,
And to that youth he calls his Rosalind
He sends this bloody napkin. Are you he?
ROSALIND I am. What must we understand by this?
OLIVER Some of my shame, if you will know of me   90
What man I am, and how, and why, and where
This handkerchief was stained.
CELIA   I pray you tell it.
OLIVER When last the young Orlando parted from you,
He left a promise to return again
Within an hour and, pacing through the forest,   95
Chewing the food of sweet and bitter fancy,
Lo what befell. He threw his eye aside
And mark what object did present itself.
Under an old oak whose boughs were mossed with age,
And high top bald with dry antiquity,   100
A wretched ragged man, o'ergrown with hair,
Lay sleeping on his back; about his neck
A green and gilded snake had wreathed itself,
Who, with her head, nimble in threats, approached
The opening of his mouth. But suddenly   105
Seeing Orlando, it unlinked itself
And with indented glides did slip away

---

84 owners] *conj. Capell;* owner F   92 handkerchief] *Rowe;* handkercher F   98 itself.] *Theobald subst.;* it selfe F   99
an old] F; an *Pope*   100 antiquity,] *Rann;* antiquitie: F   104 threats,] *Rowe;* threats F

83 **And . . . brother** Celia had smirched her face
with umber (1.3.102); brown was a sign of amorous-
ness (Williams, p. 56).

84 ***owners** Capell's emendation (see collation)
is justified by the next line.

88 **napkin** handkerchief (*OED sv* 2a).

94 **again** back (*OED sv* 3).

95 **Within an hour** Before too long (at 4.1.144–5
Orlando had promised to return within two hours).

96 **Chewing the food of** Ruminating upon
(*OED sv* Food 1c and 3a).

96 **sweet and bitter** The oxymoron is typical of
post-Petrarchan love discourse.

96 **fancy** love.

97 **threw** turned, cast.

98 **object** sight (*OED sv sb* 3a).

99 **old** Pope's omission of this pleonasm (see collation) improves the metre.

100 **bald** leafless (*OED sv* 4a).

103 **gilded** yellow (*OED sv* 2).

103–4 **snake . . . head** The detail recalls Gen. 3
as well as the snake that was sent by Hera and stran-
gled by Hercules; figurative snakes are often feminine, and compare *Mac.* 3.2.13–14 for the alterna-
tion with the neutral pronoun.

103 **wreathed** coiled.

104 **Who** Which (Abbott 264).

105 **suddenly** immediately (*OED sv* 2).

107 **with indented glides** sliding in a zig-zag
pattern.

Into a bush; under which bush's shade
A lioness, with udders all drawn dry,
Lay couching head on ground, with cat-like watch   110
When that the sleeping man should stir – for 'tis
The royal disposition of that beast
To prey on nothing that doth seem as dead.
This seen, Orlando did approach the man
And found it was his brother, his elder brother.   115

CELIA O I have heard him speak of that same brother,
And he did render him the most unnatural
That lived amongst men.

OLIVER   And well he might so do,
For well I know he was unnatural.

ROSALIND But to Orlando – did he leave him there,   120
Food to the sucked and hungry lioness?

OLIVER Twice did he turn his back and purposed so.
But kindness, nobler ever than revenge,
And nature, stronger than his just occasion,
Made him give battle to the lioness,   125
Who quickly fell before him; in which hurtling
From miserable slumber I awaked.

CELIA Are you his brother?

ROSALIND   Was't you he rescued?

CELIA Was't you that did so oft contrive to kill him?

OLIVER 'Twas I, but 'tis not I. I do not shame   130

---

108 bush;] *This edn;* bush, F   115 elder] F; *eldest Theobald*² 118 amongst] F; *'mongst Rowe*³

109 with udders all drawn dry hungry because she had fed her cubs.
110 couching lying (used mainly with animals: see *OED* Couch *v* 1c).
110–11 Lay . . . should For the tenses, see Abbott 326.
111 that For this conjunctional affix, see Abbot 287.
112 royal Lions were monarchs of the animal world.
112–13 disposition . . . dead This lore is found in Pliny, *Natural History*, VIII, 16.
117 render depict (*OED* sv *v* 5).
122 so to do so.
123 kindness . . . revenge Compare the proverbs, 'To be able to do harm and not to do it is noble' and 'To pardon is a divine revenge' (Tilley H170 and R92).
123 kindness familial affection, natural inclination (*OED* sv 1, 3).

124 occasion grounds, reason (*OED* sv *sb*¹ 2).
125 give battle attack; we might imagine Orlando killing the lioness with his bare hands as Hercules wrestled with the Nemean lion.
126 hurtling conflict.
127 miserable slumber The phrase designates not simply Oliver asleep but his spiritual state before his conversion.
127 I This pronoun may be identified as a means by which Oliver tactfully identifies himself, or as a slip of the tongue.
129 contrive plot (*OED* sv *v*¹ 1c).
130 'Twas . . . not I Compare St Paul's description of his conversion: 'Thus I live yet, not I now, but Christ liveth in me' (Gal. 2.20).
130 do not shame am not ashamed (*OED* sv *v* 1c).

To tell you what I was, since my conversion
So sweetly tastes, being the thing I am.
ROSALIND But for the bloody napkin?
OLIVER   By and by.
When from the first to last betwixt us two,
Tears our recountments had most kindly bathed –   135
As how I came into that desert place –
In brief, he led me to the gentle Duke
Who gave me fresh array and entertainment,
Committing me unto my brother's love,
Who led me instantly unto his cave;   140
There stripped himself and here, upon his arm,
The lioness had torn some flesh away,
Which all this while had bled; and now he fainted,
And cried in fainting upon Rosalind.
Brief, I recovered him, bound up his wound,   145
And, after some small space, being strong at heart,
He sent me hither, stranger as I am,
To tell this story that you might excuse
His broken promise, and to give this napkin,
Dyed in this blood, unto the shepherd youth   150
That he in sport doth call his Rosalind.
                    [Rosalind faints]
CELIA Why, how now? Ganymede, sweet Ganymede!
OLIVER Many will swoon when they do look on blood.
CELIA There is more in it. – Cousin! Ganymede!
OLIVER *[Raising Rosalind]* Look, he recovers.   155
ROSALIND I would I were at home.
CELIA We'll lead you thither. – I pray you, will you take him by the arm.

---

136 place –] *Johnson Var.;* place. F   137 In] F2; I F   150 this] F; his F2   151 SD] *Pope; not in* F   152 now?] *Johnson;*
now F   154 Cousin!] *This edn;* Cosen F   155 SD] *Collier subst.; not in* F   157] *This edn; Cel. . . .* thither: / I . . .
arme. F

133 **for** what about.

135 **recountments** tales, the only example of the
word recorded in *OED*.

135 **kindly** naturally, sweetly.

136 **As** For example (*OED* sv *conj* 26).

136 **desert** unpeopled.

137 **gentle** noble.

138 **array** clothing.

138 **entertainment** provision, sustenance.

144 **cried . . . upon** reverentially invoked (*OED*
Cry *v* 2).

145 **Brief** In brief.

145 **recovered** revived.

146 **space** time.

149–50 **napkin . . . blood** For the genealogy
and uses of this stock property, see Marion Lomax,
Stage Images and Traditions: Shakespeare to Ford,
1987, pp. 34–6.

150 **this** F's reading (see collation) may be
dittography.

154 **Cousin** Although 'cousin' served as a common form of familial address, it could be that 'Celia,
in her first fright, forgets Rosalind's character and
disguise' (Johnson).

156 **were** The subjunctive after a verb of
wishing.

OLIVER Be of good cheer, youth. You a man? You lack a man's heart.

ROSALIND I do so, I confess it. Ah, sirrah, a body would think this was
    well counterfeited. I pray you tell your brother how well I counter–   160
    feited. Heigh-ho!

OLIVER This was not counterfeit: there is too great testimony in your
    complexion that it was a passion of earnest.

ROSALIND Counterfeit, I assure you.

OLIVER Well then, take a good heart, and counterfeit to be a man.   165

ROSALIND So I do. But, i'faith, I should have been a woman by right.

CELIA Come, you look paler and paler: pray you, draw homewards. –
    Good sir, go with us.

OLIVER That will I. For I must bear answer back how you excuse my
    brother, Rosalind.   170

ROSALIND I shall devise something. But I pray you commend my
    counterfeiting to him. Will you go?

Exeunt

5.1 *Enter* TOUCHSTONE *and* AUDREY

TOUCHSTONE We shall find a time, Audrey; patience, gentle Audrey.

AUDREY Faith, the priest was good enough, for all the old gentleman's
    saying.

TOUCHSTONE A most wicked Sir Oliver, Audrey, a most vile Martext.
    But, Audrey, there is a youth here in the forest lays claim to you.   5

AUDREY Aye, I know who 'tis. He hath no interest in me in the world.

158–9 OLIVER . . . it.] *As prose, Pope; Oli. . . . man? / You . . . heart. / Ros. . . . it;* F   169–70] *As prose, White; Oli. . . . backe / How . . . Rosalind.* F   **Act 5, Scene 1** 5.1] *Eds.; Actus Quintus. Scena Prima.* F   6 SD] *Sisson; after* 7 F

158 You lack a man's heart Compare the proverb, 'Take a man's heart to thee' (Dent H328.1).

158 lack (1) do not possess, (2) desire.

159 Ah, sirrah 'Sometimes forming part of a soliloquy and addressed . . . to the speaker himself' (Schmidt).

159 a body anyone.

160–1 I pray . . . counterfeited This could well be played as an aside.

163 complexion (1) appearance, (2) psychological constitution.

163 passion of earnest serious emotion.

167–8 These are Celia's last lines in the play, although she appears in 5.4.

167 draw let's turn.

169 excuse forgive.

170 Rosalind Oliver's use of Rosalind's proper name may be a good-humoured signal that he has seen through her disguise.

Act 5, Scene 1

1 gentle kind, although Touchstone may be gently mocking Audrey's new 'gentle' rank now she is 'married'.

2 old gentleman's Jaques'.

6 interest in legal right to (*OED* 1a).

Enter WILLIAM

Here comes the man you mean.

TOUCHSTONE It is meat and drink to me to see a clown. By my troth,
we that have good wits have much to answer for. We shall be
flouting; we cannot hold.   10

WILLIAM Good ev'n, Audrey.

AUDREY God ye good ev'n, William.

WILLIAM [*Taking off his hat*] And good ev'n to you, sir.

TOUCHSTONE Good ev'n, gentle friend. Cover thy head, cover thy
head. Nay prithee, be covered. How old are you, friend?   15

WILLIAM Five and twenty, sir.

TOUCHSTONE A ripe age. Is thy name William?

WILLIAM William, sir.

TOUCHSTONE A fair name. Wast born i'th'forest here?

WILLIAM Aye, sir, I thank God.   20

TOUCHSTONE 'Thank God': a good answer. Art rich?

WILLIAM Faith, sir, so-so.

TOUCHSTONE 'So-so' is good, very good, very excellent good – and yet
it is not: it is but so-so. Art thou wise?

WILLIAM Aye, sir, I have a pretty wit.   25

TOUCHSTONE Why, thou say'st well. I do now remember a saying:
'The fool doth think he is wise, but the wise man knows himself to
be a fool.'

---

8 clown.] F3 *subst.;* Clowne, F   13 SD] *This edn; not in* F   17 SH] F *subst.; Orl.* F^u   18 SH] F *subst.; Clo.* F^u   21–2] *As
prose, Pope; Clo. . . . answer: / Art . . . so* F   23 'So-so' is] F *subst.;* 'So-so'. 'Tis *Capell subst.*   23–4 and . . . wise?] *As
prose, Pope; and . . . so: / Art . . . wise?* F   27 wise man] *Rowe;* wiseman F

8 **meat and drink** Proverbial (Tilley M842).

8 **clown** yokel, but also ironic since the word designates Touchstone's role.

8 **troth** faith.

9 **good wits** keen intelligence.

9–10 **shall be flouting** are sure to be mocking,
jeering (Abbott 315).

10 **hold** desist.

11 **Good ev'n** See 2.4.62 n.

12 **ye** give you (the pronoun elided with an
archaic dialect form of 'give').

14 **gentle** noble (ironic).

14 **Cover thy head** Replace your hat.

17 **ripe** fine. William in fact is not older than most
would-be bridegrooms as the average age for marriage for men in the period was between 26 and 29
(Keith Wrightson, *English Society 1580–1680*, 1982,
p. 68).

21 **Thank . . . answer** Touchstone may be
mocking William's rustic accent with a quibble on
God/good.

21–2 **Art . . . so-so** For the increasing wealth
of the landed peasantry near Stratford, see V. H.
T. Skipp, *Crisis and Development: An Ecological
Case Study of the Forest of Arden, 1570–1674*, 1978,
pp. 68–79.

25 **wit** A probable *double entendre* (see 3.4.9 n.).

27–8 **The . . . fool** Compare the proverb, 'Who
weens himself wise, wisdom wots him a fool' (Tilley
W522); and compare 1 Cor. 3.18: 'Let no man
deceive himself. If any man among you seem to be
wise in this world, let him be a fool, that he may be
wise'; and Plato, *Apology*, 21d.

[*William gapes*]

The heathen philosopher, when he had a desire to eat a grape,
would open his lips when he put it into his mouth, meaning thereby   30
that grapes were made to eat and lips to open. You do love this
maid?

WILLIAM I do, sir.

TOUCHSTONE Give me your hand. Art thou learned?

WILLIAM No, sir.   35

TOUCHSTONE Then learn this of me: to have is to have. For it is a figure
in rhetoric that drink, being poured out of a cup into a glass, by
filling the one doth empty the other. For all your writers do consent
that '*ipse*' is he. Now you are not *ipse*, for I am he.

WILLIAM Which he, sir?   40

TOUCHSTONE He, sir, that must marry this woman. Therefore, you
clown, abandon, which is in the vulgar 'leave', the society, which in
the boorish is 'company', of this female, which in the common is
'woman': which together is 'abandon the society of this female'; or,
clown, thou perishest or, to thy better understanding, 'diest', or, to   45
wit, 'I kill thee', 'make thee away', 'translate thy life into death, thy
liberty into bondage'! I will deal in poison with thee, or in bastinado,
or in steel! I will bandy with thee in faction, I will o'errun thee with
policy – I will kill thee a hundred and fifty ways! Therefore, tremble
and depart.   50

---

28 SD] *Wilson, conj. Capell; not in* F   33 sir] F2; sit F   42 'leave',] *Eds.;* leaue F   45 'diest', or] F *subst.;* diest *Steevens,
conj. Farmer*   49 policy] F2; police F

29–31 The . . . open This may have connection
with the Italian proverb, reported by Giovanni Tor-
riano in 1666, 'A woman at a window as grapes on
the highway' (Tilley w647), i.e. both are reached
after. The lines might also suggest that Touchstone
is reacting to William's gaping mouth. The whole
passage, however, is basically a pastiche of euphuistic style.

31–9 You . . . he It may be that Touchstone cons
William into thinking that he is going to marry the
pair, but instead plays the tetchy schoolmaster, even
striking his pupil's hand with his bauble.

34 learned literate, educated.

36–9 This passage of chop-logic contains faint
echoes of Cicero's *Topics* and Quintilian's *Institutio
Oratoria*: see Baldwin, II, 116 ff.

36 to have is to have Proverbial (Tilley H215);
in the context of wooing, there is a bawdy suggestion
as 'have' can mean to possess sexually (Williams, p.
153); Baldwin, II, 120, derives this phrase from Aristotle.

36 figure figure of speech.

38 your See 3.3.37 n.

38 consent agree together.

39 you are not *ipse* Compare the proverb, 'You
are *ipse*' (Tilley 188); *ipse* is Latin for 'he'; there is a
possible quibble on 'tipsy', implying that William is
no longer drunk with the love of Audrey.

42 vulgar vernacular.

43 boorish A nonce-word in this context, meaning the speech of a boor.

46 translate convert, change (*OED* sv 4).

47 deal in make use of (*OED* Deal *v* 15).

47 bastinado beating with a cudgel, especially
on the soles of the feet.

48 in steel with a sword.

48 bandy give and take blows, fight (*OED* sv 8).

48 faction a factious quarrel (*OED* sv 4b).

48 o'errun overwhelm.

49 *policy craft.

AUDREY Do, good William.

WILLIAM God rest you merry, sir.   *Exit*

Enter CORIN

CORIN Our master and mistress seeks you. Come away, away.

TOUCHSTONE Trip, Audrey, trip, Audrey. – I attend, I attend.

Exeunt

5.2 *Enter* ORLANDO *and* OLIVER

ORLANDO Is't possible that on so little acquaintance you should like
      her, that, but seeing, you should love her, and, loving, woo, and,
      wooing, she should grant? And will you persevere to enjoy her?

OLIVER Neither call the giddiness of it in question, the poverty of her,
      the small acquaintance, my sudden wooing, nor her sudden con-   5
      senting. But say with me I love Aliena; say with her that she loves
      me; consent with both that we may enjoy each other. It shall be to
      your good, for my father's house and all the revenue that was old Sir
      Roland's will I estate upon you, and here live and die a shepherd.

Enter ROSALIND [*as* GANYMEDE]

ORLANDO You have my consent. Let your wedding be tomorrow;   10
      thither will I invite the Duke and all's contented followers. Go you,
      and prepare Aliena, for look you, here comes my 'Rosalind'.

ROSALIND God save you, brother.

54] *As prose, Pope; Clo.* . . . attend, / I attend. F   **Act 5, Scene 2 5.2]** *Eds.; Scæna Secunda* F   **5** nor her] *Rowe;* nor
F   **10–12]** *Pope subst.; Orl.* . . . consent. / Let . . . I / Inuite . . . followers: / Go . . . looke you, / Heere . . . *Rosalinde.*
F   **12** 'Rosalind'] *This edn; Rosalinde* F   **13** SH] F *subst.; Orl.* F3   **13** you,] F *subst.;* you and your *conj. Johnson*

53 seeks For the singular inflection, see Abbott
336.

54 Trip Move nimbly.

54 attend follow (*OED* sv 4).

Act 5, Scene 2

1–3 Is't . . . grant In *Rosalind* the older brother
wins Aliena's love by being instrumental in saving
her from a gang of ruffians.

3 persevere Accented on the second syllable
(Cercignani, p. 41).

3 enjoy have your will of (*OED* sv v 4b).

4 giddiness flightiness, suddenness.

4 the poverty of her her poverty (Abbott 225),
the fact that she lacks a dowry.

5 *her Rowe's emendation (see collation) restores
the balance of the sentence.

5 sudden hasty.

7 consent agree.

9 estate settle, bestow (*OED* sv v 3).

10 You have my consent Orlando immediately
assents to the patriarchal privilege of giving away
the bride.

13 brother brother-in-law (i.e. the future husband of her 'sister' Aliena).

OLIVER And you, fair 'sister'.   [*Exit*]

ROSALIND O, my dear Orlando, how it grieves me to see thee wear thy   15
heart in a scarf.

ORLANDO It is my arm.

ROSALIND I thought thy heart had been wounded with the claws of a
lion.

ORLANDO Wounded it is, but with the eyes of a lady.   20

ROSALIND Did your brother tell you how I counterfeited to swoon
when he showed me your handkerchief?

ORLANDO Aye, and greater wonders than that.

ROSALIND O, I know where you are. Nay, 'tis true, there was never
anything so sudden but the fight of two rams, and Caesar's   25
thrasonical brag of 'I came, saw, and overcame.' For your brother
and my sister no sooner met but they looked; no sooner looked, but
they loved; no sooner loved, but they sighed; no sooner sighed,
but they asked one another the reason; no sooner knew the reason,
but they sought the remedy; and in these degrees have they made a   30
pair of stairs to marriage, which they will climb incontinent – or else
be incontinent before marriage. They are in the very wrath of love,
and they will together – clubs cannot part them.

ORLANDO They shall be married tomorrow and I will bid the Duke to

---

14 'sister'] *This edn;* sister F 14 SD] *Capell; not in* F 21 SWOON] *Eds.;* sound F 22 handkerchief] *Eds.;* handkercher
F 25 fight] F (*probably*); sight F4 26 overcame] F2; ouercome F

14 *fair 'sister' Either the text is corrupt (see
collation), or this is a witty signal that Oliver has seen
through Rosalind's disguise – or perhaps Shakespeare made a mistake; see 4.3.170 n.

16 scarf sling (*OED* sv 4).

18 with by (Abbott 193).

21 *counterfeited to swoon See 3.6.17 n. and
4.3.160–1.

23 Referring to Oliver's falling in love with Celia.

24 I know where you are I know what you mean
(Dent W295.1).

25 fight F's ligature could be read as 'si' or 'fi'
(see collation).

26 thrasonical vainglorious, like the behaviour
of the braggart soldier Thraso in Terence's
Eunuchus.

26 I came, saw, and overcame Caesar's boast
was frequently quoted (Bullough, v, 75; Tilley
C540), often in the context of sexual predation (see
LLL 4.1.67–75).

26–32 For . . . marriage The passage is a gentle
parody of neo-platonic schemes of love that derived

from Plato's *Symposium*, 201d–212c, wherein the
virtuous soul, attracted by beauty, ascends towards
the good and ultimate union with godhead.

30 degrees Punning on the original meaning of
the word ('steps'), apt because it occurs in the climax to a bravura display of the rhetorical figure
called 'climax' or the 'marching' or 'climbing' figure (George Puttenham, *The Arte of English Poesie*
(1589), p. 173).

31 pair flight (*OED* sv *sb*[1] 6b).

31 climb incontinent ascend immediately.

32 be incontinent be unchaste.

32 wrath ardour (*OED* sv 3b).

33 will together For the suppression of a verb
of motion (in this context 'come'?) following will,
shall, etc., see Abbott 405.

33 clubs physical force (*OED* Club *sb* 1b), or
alluding to clubs borne by the watch (men who
patrolled the streets at night) and used in frays.
Alternatively this may be an allusion 'to the way
of parting dogs in wrath' (Johnson).

34 the Duke i.e. Duke Senior.

the nuptial. But O, how bitter a thing it is to look into happiness   35
through another man's eyes. By so much the more shall I tomorrow
be at the height of heart-heaviness, by how much I shall think my
brother happy in having what he wishes for.

ROSALIND Why then, tomorrow, I cannot serve your turn for Rosalind?

ORLANDO I can live no longer by thinking.   40

ROSALIND I will weary you then no longer with idle talking. Know of
me, then – for now I speak to some purpose – that I know you are
a gentleman of good conceit. I speak not this that you should bear a
good opinion of my knowledge, insomuch, I say, I know you are;
neither do I labour for a greater esteem than may in some little   45
measure draw a belief from you to do yourself good, and not to
grace me. Believe then, if you please, that I can do strange things. I
have, since I was three year old, conversed with a magician, most
profound in his art, and yet not damnable. If you do love Rosalind
so near the heart as your gesture cries it out, when your brother   50
marries Aliena shall you marry her. I know into what straits of
fortune she is driven, and it is not impossible to me, if it appear not
inconvenient to you, to set her before your eyes tomorrow, human
as she is, and without any danger.

ORLANDO Speak'st thou in sober meanings?   55

ROSALIND By my life, I do, which I tender dearly, though I say I am a
magician. Therefore put you in your best array, bid your friends.

---

44 know] F; know what *Rowe*   44 are] F2; arc F   55 meanings] F; meaning *Johnson*

35 nuptial The only time Shakespeare uses the more common plural form of the word is in *Per.* 5.3.80.

35 bitter injurious (*OED* sv 5a).

39 turn needs (with a sexual sense as well: see Williams, pp. 273–4, 280).

42 I speak to some purpose I am in earnest.

43 conceit understanding (*OED* sv 2), i.e. able to comprehend the 'mysteries' she goes on to describe.

43 that so that (Abbott 203).

44 insomuch in that (*OED* sv 4).

47 grace me do credit to myself.

47 strange wonderful.

48 year For the survival of the Old English inflexionless form, see *OED* sv 1b.

48 conversed communed, spent time with (*OED* sv 4b).

48 magician Orlando later (5.4.32–3) identifies the magician with Rosalind's uncle (3.3.288–9).

49 art magical knowledge.

49 not damnable i.e. because he was a practitioner of white and not black magic – unlike Marlowe's Faustus; see Frances A. Yates, *The Occult Philosophy*, 1979.

50 gesture bearing (*OED* sv 1a).

50 it On this indefinite object, see Abbott 226.

53 inconvenient unfitting.

53–4 human . . . danger 'That is, not a phantom [like the figure of Helen in Marlowe's *Doctor Faustus*], but the real Rosalind, without any of the danger generally conceived to attend the rites of incantation' (Johnson).

55 sober serious.

56–7 By . . . magician Conjuration and witchcraft generally were felonies (capital offences).

56 tender dearly hold precious.

57 you yourself (Abbott 223).

57 bid invite (*OED* sv *v* 8).

57 friends relatives (*OED* Friend 3).

For if you will be married tomorrow, you shall, and to Rosalind, if
you will.

Enter SILVIUS *and* PHOEBE

Look, here comes a lover of mine and a lover of hers.   60
PHOEBE Youth, you have done me much ungentleness
    To show the letter that I writ to you.
ROSALIND I care not if I have. It is my study
    To seem despiteful and ungentle to you.
    You are there followed by a faithful shepherd;   65
    Look upon him, love him: he worships you.
PHOEBE Good shepherd, tell this youth what 'tis to love.
SILVIUS It is to be all made of sighs and tears,
    And so am I for Phoebe.
PHOEBE And I for Ganymede.   70
ORLANDO And I for Rosalind.
ROSALIND And I for no woman.
SILVIUS It is to be all made of faith and service,
    And so am I for Phoebe.
PHOEBE And I for Ganymede.   75
ORLANDO And I for Rosalind.
ROSALIND And I for no woman.
SILVIUS It is to be all made of fantasy,
    All made of passion, and all made of wishes,
    All adoration, duty, and observance,   80
    All humbleness, all patience, and impatience,
    All purity, all trial, all obedience.
    And so am I for Phoebe.
PHOEBE And so am I for Ganymede.
ORLANDO And so am I for Rosalind.   85
ROSALIND And so am I for no woman.

---

82 obedience] *Cowden Clarke, conj. Malone;* obseruance F; obeisance *Singer, conj. Ritson*

60 comes For the singular inflection, see Abbott 335.
  61 ungentleness discourtesy (*OED* sv 1).
  62 show reveal (*OED* sv *v* 22a).
  63 study deliberate intention (*OED* sv *sb* 4a).
  64 despiteful spiteful, cruel.
  65 followed (1) pursued, (2) attended upon.
  66 him . . . him 'A strong accent upon both "him's" alone makes this line metrical' (Wilson).

  73 service the devotion of a 'servant' or lover (*OED* sv *sb*[1] 10).
  78 fantasy fancy, imagination.
  79 passion the feeling of love (*OED* sv 8a).
  80 observance observant care (*OED* sv 4).
  82 trial the suffering caused by devotion.
  82 *obedience Malone's conjecture is justified (see collation), as F's 'observance' was probably caught from 80.

PHOEBE [*To Rosalind*] If this be so, why blame you me to love you?
SILVIUS [*To Phoebe*] If this be so, why blame you me to love you?
ORLANDO If this be so, why blame you me to love you?
ROSALIND Who do you speak to 'Why blame you me to love you'?   90
ORLANDO To her that is not here nor doth not hear.
ROSALIND Pray you no more of this: 'tis like the howling of Irish wolves
    against the moon. [*To Silvius*] I will help you, if I can. [*To Phoebe*]
    I would love you, if I could. – Tomorrow meet me all together. –
    [*To Phoebe*] I will marry you, if ever I marry woman, and I'll be   95
    married tomorrow. [*To Orlando*] I will satisfy you, if ever I satisfy
    man, and you shall be married tomorrow. [*To Silvius*] I will con-
    tent you, if what pleases you contents you, and you shall be married
    tomorrow. [*To Orlando*] As you love Rosalind, meet; [*To Silvius*]
    as you love Phoebe, meet – and as I love no woman, I'll meet. So   100
    fare you well: I have left you commands.
SILVIUS I'll not fail, if I live.
PHOEBE Nor I.
ORLANDO Nor I.

                                                    Exeunt

5.3 *Enter* TOUCHSTONE *and* AUDREY

TOUCHSTONE Tomorrow is the joyful day, Audrey; tomorrow will we
    be married.
AUDREY I do desire it with all my heart, and I hope it is no dishonest
    desire to desire to be a woman of the world?

---

87 SD] *Oxford; not in* F   88 SD] *Pope subst.; not in* F   90 Who . . . to] *Rowe;* Why do you speake too, F   93 SD *To Silvius*]
Capell; Spoken to Orlando / Johnson; not in F   93 SD, 95 SD *To Phoebe*] *Johnson subst.; not in* F   96 SD] *Pope subst.; not
in* F   96 I satisfy] *Dyce²*, *conj. Douce;* I satisfi'd F   97 SD] *Pope subst.; not in* F   99 SDD] *Johnson subst.; not in* F   Act 5,
Scene 3 5.3] *Eds.; Scœna Tertia.* F

87 **to love** for loving.
90 ***Who do you speak to** Rowe's emendation
(see collation) is justified by Orlando's response.
92–3 **'tis . . . moon** Compare the proverbs, 'The
wolf barks in vain at the moon' and 'To bark against
the moon' (Tilley D449 and M1123), and *Rosalind*:
'I tell thee, Montanus, in courting Phoebe, thou
barkest with the wolves of Syria against the moon'
(p. 208).
92 **Irish** Possibly an allusion to a belief that the
Irish could change shape with wolves, or even a reference to the Irish rebellion against Elizabeth (figured in the 'moon' of 93) in 1598, but more likely a
rhetorical gesture.
93–9 **I will . . . tomorrow** Rosalind's riddles
are characteristic of the magician she has professed
herself to be (56–7).

96 ***I satisfy** F's 'satisfi'd' (see collation) is an
easy mistake for 'satisfie': there is no need to infer
that Rosalind was not a virgin. 'Satisfy' means 'pay
a sexual debt' (Williams, pp. 267–8).
102 **fail** be missing (*OED* sv 1a).

Act 5, Scene 3
3 **dishonest** unchaste.
4 **a woman of the world** Proverbial (Dent
w637.4) – the phrase means 'married' (*OED* World
4c), and probably derives ultimately from the
differences between virgins and wives, who care
'for the things of the world, how she may please her
husband' (1 Cor. 7.34).

Enter two PAGES

Here come two of the banished Duke's pages.   5
1 PAGE Well met, honest gentleman.
TOUCHSTONE By my troth, well met. Come, sit, sit, and a song.
2 PAGE We are for you; sit i'th'middle.
1 PAGE Shall we clap into't roundly, without hawking, or spitting, or
    saying we are hoarse, which are the only prologues to a bad voice?   10
2 PAGE Aye, faith, i'faith, and both in a tune like two gipsies on a horse.
1 AND 2 PAGE It was a lover and his lass,
    With a hey, and a ho, and a hey nonny-no,
    That o'er the green cornfield did pass,
      In spring-time,   15
      The only pretty ring-time,
        When birds do sing;
      Hey ding-a-ding, ding,
        Sweet lovers love the spring.

    Between the acres of the rye,   20
    With a hey, and a ho, and a hey nonny-no,
    These pretty country folks would lie,

---

4 SD] *Sisson; after 5* F **11** Aye, faith, i'faith] *This edn;* I faith, y'faith F; I'faith *conj. this edn* **12**] It *This edn;* Song. / It F **13** and a ho, and] F; with a hoe and *Morley* **14** cornfield] F *subst.;* corn fields *Morley* **15–16**] Capell *subst.; one line in* F **15** In] *Rowe (following* F *at 23), Morley;* In the F **16** pretty ring-time] *Eds.;* pretiring time *Morley* **16, 24, 32, 40** ring-] Rann, *conj. Steevens²; rang* F; range- *conj. Whiter* **17–18, 25–6, 33–4, 41–2** sing; / Hey] *Capell; sing, hey* F **17** do] F; did *Johnson* **22** folks] F *subst.;* fooles *Morley*

6 honest honourable.
8 i'th'middle 'This is clearly a reference to an old English proverb, "hey diddle diddle, fool in the middle"' (Franz von Dingelstedt (trans.), *Wie es euch gefällt*, 1868, p. 229).
9–10 Compare the proverb, 'All good singers have colds' (Tilley S482).
9 clap into't begin briskly.
9 hawking clearing our throats noisily.
10 only principal.
11 *Aye faith, i'faith F's version (see collation) suggests an uncorrected change of mind on the part of the compositor.
11 a tune unison (*OED* sv *sb* 3a).
11 like two gipsies on a horse Obscure: either in unison or as a canon.
11 gipsies Romanies had appeared in England at the beginning of the sixteenth century and were regarded as untrustworthy vagabonds.
11 a one.

12–43 The original music for this song is contained in Morley, sigs. B4ᵛ–C1.
13, 21, 29, 37 nonny-no A meaningless refrain, like 'nonny-nonny', often used in a sexually suggestive manner (Williams, p. 218).
14 cornfield wheatfield.
15 *In F's 'In the' occurs only in this stanza and not in Morley so we may presume it to be a compositorial error.
16, 24, 32, 40 only unique, special.
16, 24, 32, 40 *ring-time A nonce-word, referring to the exchanging of rings, or possibly to the vagina or anus (compare *MV* 5.1.307); F's 'rang' may be an obsolete form of 'rank', but retaining it destroys the rhyme.
*17, 25, 33, 41 This line would seem to be a general exaltation rather than an imitation of bird-song.
20 Between the acres On the grassy balks between the ploughed strips.

In spring-time,
The only pretty ring-time,
    When birds do sing;   25
Hey ding-a-ding, ding,
    Sweet lovers love the spring.

This carol they began that hour,
With a hey, and a ho, and a hey nonny-no,
How that a life was but a flower;   30
    In spring-time,
    The only pretty ring-time,
        When birds do sing;
Hey ding-a-ding, ding,
        Sweet lovers love the spring.   35

And therefore take the present time;
With a hey, and a ho, and a hey nonny-no,
For love is crownèd with the prime,
    In spring-time,
    The only pretty ring-time,   40
        When birds do sing;
Hey ding-a-ding, ding,
        Sweet lovers love the spring.

TOUCHSTONE Truly, young gentlemen, though there was no great
    matter in the ditty, yet the note was very untunable.   45
1 PAGE You are deceived, sir: we kept time; we lost not our time.
TOUCHSTONE By my troth, yes. I count it but time lost to hear such a
    foolish song. God buy you, and God mend your voices. – Come,
    Audrey.

Exeunt

23–7, 31–5, 39–43] *Eds.; In spring time, &c.* F   30 a life] F; *our life Hanmer*   36–43] *As Johnson; after 19* F   36] F
subst; Then prettie Lovers take the tyme *Morley*   45 untunable] F *subst.;* untimeable *Theobald*

28 carol song, originally designed to accompany
dancing in a ring.

30 life was but a flower Proverbial (Dent
L248.1), derived from 1 Pet. 1.24 and Ps. 103.15.

*36–43 This stanza appears after 19 in F; it is, as
Johnson observed, more likely to have formed the
conclusion of a *carpe diem* ditty of this kind – as it
does in Morley.

36 Compare the proverb, 'Take time when time
comes' (Tilley T312).

38 prime (1) spring (*OED* sv *sb*¹ 7), (2) sexual
excitement (Williams, p. 246).

45 matter good sense (*OED* sv *sb* 11b – the only
examples are Shakespearean).

45 ditty words, composition.

45 note tune (*OED* sv *sb*² 3a).

45 untunable unmelodious, harsh-sounding
(*OED* sv 1).

46 deceived mistaken.

46 lost not (1) did not get out of, (2) did not
waste (*OED* Lose *v* 6a).

47 yes indeed you did.

48 God buy you See 3.3.217 n.

48 mend improve.

5.4 *Enter* DUKE SENIOR, AMIENS, JAQUES, ORLANDO, OLIVER, CELIA [*as* ALIENA]

DUKE SENIOR Dost thou believe, Orlando, that the boy
        Can do all this that he hath promisèd?
ORLANDO I sometimes do believe and sometimes do not,
        As those that fear they hope and know they fear.

     Enter ROSALIND [*as* GANYMEDE], SILVIUS, *and* PHOEBE

ROSALIND Patience once more whiles our compact is urged. –   5
        You say, if I bring in your Rosalind,
        You will bestow her on Orlando here?
DUKE SENIOR That would I, had I kingdoms to give with her.
ROSALIND And you say you will have her, when I bring her?
ORLANDO That would I, were I of all kingdoms king.   10
ROSALIND You say you'll marry me, if I be willing.
PHOEBE That will I, should I die the hour after.
ROSALIND But if you do refuse to marry me,
        You'll give yourself to this most faithful shepherd.
PHOEBE So is the bargain.   15
ROSALIND You say that you'll have Phoebe if she will.
SILVIUS Though to have her and death were both one thing.
ROSALIND I have promised to make all this matter even. –
        Keep you your word, O Duke, to give your daughter. –
        You yours, Orlando, to receive his daughter. –   20
        Keep your word, Phoebe, that you'll marry me
        Or else, refusing me, to wed this shepherd. –
        Keep your word, Silvius, that you'll marry her

Act 5, Scene 4 5.4] *Eds.; Scena Quarta.* F 4 fear . . . fear] F *subst.;* think they hope, and know they fear *Hanmer;* fear, they hope, and know their fear *Johnson;* fear their hope, and know their fear *Heath* 4 hope] F; hap *Warburton* 11 say] F; say that *Yale* 18 I have] F; I've *Pope* 21 Keep your] *Rowe³;* Keep you your F

Act 5, Scene 4

1 **boy** 'Ganymede'.

4 The line has been much amended (see collation), but there is no reason why we should not take it to mean 'like those who know only too well that what they desire is vain expectation, and know that they fear their hopes will not come to pass'.

4 **hope** are hoping against hope.

4 **fear** i.e. that what they hope for will not come to pass.

5 **compact** covenant, contract; accented on the second syllable (Cercignani, p. 37).

5 **urged** pressed, enforced.

7 **bestow her** give her in marriage.

11 **be** The subjunctive in a conditional clause.

12 **hour** Two syllables.

18 **make all this matter even** straighten everything out.

19 **give** give away (in marriage).

21 ***your** F's 'you' (see collation) was probably caught from 19 above.

If she refuse me – and from hence I go
To make these doubts all even.   25

Exeunt Rosalind and Celia

DUKE SENIOR I do remember in this shepherd boy
Some lively touches of my daughter's favour.
ORLANDO My lord, the first time that I ever saw him,
Methought he was a brother to your daughter;
But, my good lord, this boy is forest-born   30
And hath been tutored in the rudiments
Of many desperate studies by his uncle
Whom he reports to be a great magician,
Obscurèd in the circle of this forest.

Enter TOUCHSTONE *and* AUDREY

JAQUES There is sure another flood toward, and these couples are com-   35
ing to the ark. Here comes a pair of very strange beasts which, in all
tongues, are called fools.
TOUCHSTONE Salutation and greeting to you all.
JAQUES Good my lord, bid him welcome. This is the motley-minded
gentleman that I have so often met in the forest: he hath been a   40
courtier, he swears.
TOUCHSTONE If any man doubt that, let him put me to my purgation.
I have trod a measure; I have flattered a lady; I have been politic
with my friend, smooth with mine enemy; I have undone three
tailors; I have had four quarrels, and like to have fought one.   45
JAQUES And how was that ta'en up?

---

25 SD *Exeunt*] *Eds.; Exit* F   28 ever] F; e'er *Yale*   34 SD] *Rowe³; after 33* F

27 **lively touches** lifelike traits.
27 **favour** features.
31 **rudiments** first principles.
32 **desperate** dangerous – because the practice of magic was a felony (*OED* sv 5b).
34 **Obscurèd** Hidden.
34 **circle** compass (*OED* sv 16a), with, possibly, an allusion to the magic circle of a conjurer.
35 **toward** about to take place.
36 **strange beasts** A witty variation on God's command to Noah: 'Of every clean beast thou shalt take to thee by sevens, the male and his female; but of unclean beasts by couples, the male and his female' (Gen. 7.2; see Shaheen, p. 170).

37 **fools** A piece of self-deprecation by Jaques, since a jester was also termed a fool.
42 **purgation** test (compare 1.3.43 n.).
43–5 Satirical glances at life at court.
43 **measure** grave or stately dance (*OED* sv *sb* 20a).
43 **politic** hypocritical (like a 'Machiavel' or politician).
43–4 **been . . . smooth** spoken speciously (*OED* Smooth *adj* 6b).
44 **undone** ruined (by not paying their bills).
45 **like** was likely.
45 **fought** fought over.
46 **ta'en** made.

TOUCHSTONE Faith, we met and found the quarrel was upon the seventh cause.

JAQUES How, 'seventh cause'? – Good my lord, like this fellow.

DUKE SENIOR I like him very well.   50

TOUCHSTONE God'ild you, sir; I desire you of the like. I press in here, sir, amongst the rest of the country copulatives, to swear and to forswear according as marriage binds and blood breaks. A poor virgin, sir, an ill-favoured thing, sir, but mine own. A poor humour of mine, sir, to take that that no man else will. Rich honesty dwells   55 like a miser, sir, in a poor house, as your pearl in your foul oyster.

DUKE SENIOR By my faith, he is very swift and sententious.

TOUCHSTONE According to 'the fool's bolt', sir, and such dulcet diseases.

JAQUES But, for 'the seventh cause': how did you find the quarrel on   60 'the seventh cause'?

TOUCHSTONE Upon a lie seven times removed. – Bear your body more seeming, Audrey. – As thus, sir: I did dislike the cut of a certain courtier's beard. He sent me word, if I said his beard was not cut well, he was in the mind it was: this is called 'the retort courteous'.   65 If I sent him word again it was not well cut, he would send me word

---

54 poor] F *subst.*; rare *conj. this edn*   59 diseases] F; discourses *conj. Johnson;* deceases *or* dieses *conj. this edn*   60 on] F; upon *Capell*

---

48 seventh cause 'By "the seventh cause" Touchstone . . . means the lie seven times removed; i.e. "the retort courteous", which is *removed* seven times (counted backwards) from the *lie direct*, the last and most aggravated species of lie' (Malone) – it is, however, verging on pedantry to explicate this amiable nonsense.

48 cause consideration (*OED* sv 3).

51 God'ild See 3.4.56 n.

51 desire you of the like return the compliment (*OED* Desire *v* 6b).

52 copulatives A nonce-word, derived from a technical term in grammar, for those about to be coupled in marriage.

52–3 to swear and to forswear Proverbial (Dent S1031.1).

53 blood breaks desire bursts forth (so destroying the marriage bond).

54 an . . . own Compare the proverb, 'Every man likes his own thing best' (Tilley M131).

54 poor This may have been caught from the preceding and succeeding sentences: a word like 'rare' may have been what Shakespeare wrote.

54 humour whim.

55 honesty (1) virtue, (2) chastity.

56 pearl . . . oyster Compare the proverb, 'Rich pearls are found in homely shells' (Dent P166.1).

56 foul dirty-coloured (*OED* sv *adj* 4b).

57 swift quick-witted.

57 sententious good at aphorisms.

58 fool's bolt A reference to the proverb, 'A fool's bolt is soon shot' (Tilley F515); 'bolt' probably means 'penis' here.

58 dulcet (1) sweet, (2) punning on 'doucets' = [deer's] testicles.

59 diseases Perhaps an indirect reference to a surfeit of fools, to a plethora of proverbs, to venereal diseases – but (see collation) it may be an obsolete form of 'deceases', 'departures' or 'deaths' – or an error for 'dieses' or quarter-tones (see *OED* Diesis).

62–72 'Giving the lie' was a prelude to a duel, and Shakespeare was satirising trivial offences of the type which provoked a plague of duels in the period (see *Shakespeare's England*, II, 402–3).

63 seeming in a more becoming manner.

63 As For instance.

63 dislike express an aversion to (*OED* sv *v* 3b).

65 in the mind of the opinion that (*OED* Mind *sb¹* 9b).

66 again in reply (*OED* sv *adv* 2).

he cut it to please himself: this is called 'the quip modest'. If again
it was not well cut, he disabled my judgement: this is called 'the
reply churlish'. If again it was not well cut, he would answer I spake
not true: this is called 'the reproof valiant'. If again it was not well   70
cut, he would say I lied: this is called 'the countercheck quarrelsome'. And so to 'the lie circumstantial' and 'the lie direct'.

JAQUES And how oft did you say his beard was not well cut?

TOUCHSTONE I durst go no further than the lie circumstantial, nor he
durst not give me the lie direct; and so we measured swords, and   75
parted.

JAQUES Can you nominate, in order now, the degrees of the lie?

TOUCHSTONE O, sir, we quarrel in print, by the book – as you have
books for good manners. I will name you the degrees: the first, the
retort courteous; the second, the quip modest; the third, the reply   80
churlish; the fourth, the reproof valiant; the fifth, the countercheck
quarrelsome; the sixth, the lie with circumstance; the seventh, the
lie direct. All these you may avoid but the lie direct, and you may
avoid that too with an 'if'. I knew when seven justices could not take
up a quarrel but, when the parties were met themselves, one of them   85
thought but of an 'if': as, 'If you said so, then I said so.' And they
shook hands and swore brothers. Your 'if' is the only peacemaker:
much virtue in 'if'.

JAQUES Is not this a rare fellow, my lord? He's as good at anything, and
yet a fool.   90

DUKE SENIOR He uses his folly like a stalking-horse, and under the
presentation of that he shoots his wit.

---

71 lied] *Hanmer;* lie F   72 to the] F2; ro F   89 He's as] F; He's *Rowe*

67 **modest** moderate.

68 **disabled** disparaged (*OED* Disable *v* 3).

71 *****lied** Hanmer's emendation (see collation)
aligns this verb with the other tenses in the passage.

71 **countercheck** rebuke.

72 **circumstantial** 'a contradiction given indi-
rectly by circumstances or details' (*OED* sv *adj* 1).

75 **measured swords** Before a duel swords were
measured; the phrase could mean literally this or to
fight (*OED* Measure *v* 2j). Given that Armin who
played Touchstone was dwarfish, it is probable that
the first sense is meant here.

77 **nominate** name.

78 **we . . . book** Something 'in print' was regular or defined (Tilley M239); there may be a specific
reference to Vicentio Saviolo's *Saviolo his Practice*
(1594–5), the second book of which is entitled 'Of
Honour and Honourable Quarrels'; this contains a
catalogue of types of lie which had been set out

in William Segar, *The Book of Honour and Arms*
(1590).

79 **books for good manners** Such works, 'courtesy books', were common in the period.

82 **circumstance** circumlocution, beating about
the bush (*OED* sv 6).

84 **knew** have known.

84–5 **take up** resolve.

86 **as** to wit, namely.

87 **brothers** a joint oath.

87 **only** unique.

89 **anything** all he says and does (with bawdy
innuendo).

91–2 Compare the proverb, 'Religion a stalking-
horse to shoot other fowl' (Tilley R63).

91 **stalking-horse** horse trained to conceal
hunters as they move towards game.

92 **presentation** display, show (*OED* sv 5a).

92 **wit** (1) witticisms, (2) penis (see 3.4.9 n.).

Still music. Enter HYMEN, [*with*] ROSALIND *and* CELIA
[*as themselves*]

HYMEN   Then is there mirth in heaven,
                   When earthly things made even
                        Atone together.   95
                   Good Duke, receive thy daughter;
                   Hymen from heaven brought her,
                        Yea, brought her hither
                   That thou might'st join her hand with his,
                   Whose heart within his bosom is.   100
ROSALIND   [*To the Duke*] To you I give myself, for I am yours.
           [*To Orlando*] To you I give myself, for I am yours.
DUKE SENIOR If there be truth in sight, you are my daughter.

---

92 SD.I *Still music*] *Dyce; after* CELIA F *subst.*   92 SD.2 *as themselves*] *Eds.; not in* F   98 hither] *Eds.; hether* F   99 join her] F3; *ioyne his* F   100 his] F; her *Malone*   101 SD, 102 SD] *Rowe; not in* F   102 To] F; *Or.* To F3

92 SD.I *Still* Soft, quiet (*OED* sv *adj* 3b), probably played on recorders. An appropriate pavane from the period is reprinted by Long, p. 157. It seems appropriate that the music should accompany the masque-like entrance, rather than coming after it, for although 92–7 appear in italics in F, so do, for example, Orlando's verses, and there is no indication that these lines were originally sung, although they have been set to music.

92 SD.I HYMEN It might be appropriate to have the god bearing a torch and attended by Cupid figures, as in Marston's *The Wonder of Women, or the Tragedy of Sophonisba* (1606?): '*Enter four boys, antiquely attired, with bows and quivers, dancing to the cornets a fantastic measure*' (1.2.35 SD; Prol. 16; *Three Jacobean Witchcraft Plays*, ed. Peter Corbin and Douglas Sedge, 1986). If *AYLI* was first performed at the Globe, the god may have descended in a throne from the 'cover' over the stage as does Jupiter in *Cym.* 5.5.186, or appeared on the upper level with music played in the adjacent music rooms (Hattaway, pp. 29–30).

92 SD.2 * *as themselves* There is no certain evidence from the text that Rosalind did put off her Ganymede costume at this point (see 104 n., 105 n. 'shape'), although it may be that Touchstone's 'lie' routine served in part to allow for a costume change (but see Maura Slattery Kuhn, 'Much virtue in *if*', *SQ* 28 (1977), 40–50). A bride's appearance, one that interestingly contains pastoral elements, is described thus in Jonson's *Hymenaei*: '*her hair flowing and loose, sprinkled with grey; on her head a garland of roses like a turret; her garments white, and on her back a wether's*

fleece hanging down; her zone, or girdle about her waist, of white wool, fastened with the Herculean knot' (49–52).

93–5 The lines were set to music by Thomas Arne (see Seng, p. 93).

93 mirth joy (*OED* sv 1); compare Luke 15.10: 'There is joy in the presence of the angels of god for one sinner that converteth.'

94 made even reconciled.

95 Atone Come into concord (*OED* sv *v* 2); the metaphor recalls the Ovidian conceit of *concordia discors* (*Metamorphoses*, 1, 517–18) that is enacted, for example, by the encounter with Owl and Cuckoo, Winter and Spring, at the end of *LLL*.

98 *hither F's 'hether' (see collation) indicates the original pronunciation (Cercignani, p. 51).

99 *join her F's 'his' (see collation) may have been a misreading of 'hir', although if Rosalind was still dressed as Ganymede the original reading could stand. It is also conceivable that Hymen is speaking of uniting 'Rosalind' with her 'Ganymede' persona.

100 Whose Given the uncertain status of the preceding line, the antecedent of 'Whose' could be 'her hand' or 'his [hand]'.

101–2 Anna Seward, reporting on Mrs Siddons' delivery of these lines in 1786, noted: 'The tender joy of filial love was in the first ['yours']; the whole soul of enamoured transport in the second' (Gamini Salgado (ed.), *Eyewitnesses of Shakespeare*, 1975, p. 163).

103, 104, 105 If The repetition of 'If' creates a sense of scepticism, even provisionality, concerning the play's resolution.

ORLANDO If there be truth in sight, you are my Rosalind.

PHOEBE If sight and shape be true, why then, my love, adieu.   105

ROSALIND [*To the Duke*] I'll have no father, if you be not he.

    [*To Orlando*] I'll have no husband, if you be not he.

    [*To Phoebe*] Nor ne'er wed woman, if you be not she.

HYMEN   Peace, ho: I bar confusion,

    'Tis I must make conclusion   110

    Of these most strange events.

    Here's eight that must take hands

    To join in Hymen's bands,

    If truth holds true contents.

    [*To Orlando and Rosalind*] You and you no cross

        shall part.   115

    [*To Oliver and Celia*] You and you are heart in heart.

    [*To Phoebe*] You to his love must accord,

    Or have a woman to your lord.

    [*To Touchstone and Audrey*] You and you are sure together

    As the winter to foul weather. –   120

    Whiles a wedlock hymn we sing,

    Feed yourselves with questioning,

    That reason, wonder may diminish

    How thus we met and these things finish.

---

104 sight] F; shape *Johnson*   105] F *subst.*; PHOEBE . . . true, / Why . . . adieu *Pope*   106–8 SDD] *Eds.*; *not in* F   114 truth] F; troth *conj. this edn*   114–18 SDD] *Johnson subst.*; *not in* F   124 met] F; meet *Theobald*[2]

104 It is notable that Orlando does not make explicit any recognition that 'Ganymede' was in fact Rosalind (compare *MV* 5.1.280–2, *Ado* 5.4.60–1, 65).

104 **sight** Johnson's emendation 'shape' is attractive, given the next line.

105 There is no way of telling from the line whether Phoebe is appalled that she has given her love to a woman and turns to Silvius with alacrity, or whether she abandons her love for Rosalind only with reluctance.

105 **shape** (1) appearance, (2) theatrical costume (*OED* sv *sb*[1] 8b, although the meaning is recorded only from 1603), (3) the female sexual organ (*OED* sv *sb*[1] 16).

109–10 If Hymen puts the stress on the two 'I's, the lines suggest that he feels Rosalind is usurping his role, or possibly violating a version of the wedding ceremony by denying her father the rite of 'giving her away'; if 'confusion' and 'conclusion' are stressed, the effect is of the enactment of due ceremony.

109 **Peace, ho** Be silent.

111 **events** outcomes (*OED* Event 3a).

112 **take hands** part of the marriage service.

113 **bands** bonds (*OED* Band *sb* 8).

114 'That is, if there be truth in truth, unless truth fails of veracity' (Johnson); compare: 'When my love swears that she is made of truth / I do believe her though I know she lies' (*Son.* 138.1–2); perhaps we should read 'troth' (fidelity) for 'truth'.

114 **contents** There could be a secondary meaning of 'happiness'.

115 **cross** quarrel, vexation.

117 **accord** attune yourself, agree (*OED* sv *v* 6).

118 **to** for.

119 **sure** indissolubly united.

121 **Whiles** Until.

122 **questioning** conversation (*OED* Question *v* 2).

123 **reason, wonder** Either word could be the grammatical subject of 'may diminish'.

Song

Wedding is great Juno's crown,   125
   O blessed bond of board and bed.
'Tis Hymen peoples every town,
   High wedlock then be honourèd.
Honour, high honour, and renown
To Hymen, god of every town.   130

DUKE SENIOR   O my dear niece: welcome thou art to me
   Even daughter; welcome in no less degree.
PHOEBE   I will not eat my word now thou art mine:
   Thy faith my fancy to thee doth combine.

Enter [JACQUES DE BOYS, *the*] *second brother*

JACQUES DE BOYS   Let me have audience for a word or two.   135
I am the second son of old Sir Roland,
That bring these tidings to this fair assembly.
Duke Frederick, hearing how that every day
Men of great worth resorted to this forest,
Addressed a mighty power which were on foot   140
In his own conduct, purposely to take
His brother here and put him to the sword;
And to the skirts of this wild wood he came,
Where, meeting with an old religious man,

---

131 me] *This edn;* me, F   132 Even daughter] F *subst.;* Even-daughter *Brissenden, conj. Knowles*   132 daughter; welcome] *Hanmer;* daughter welcome, F; daughter, welcome, F4   134 combine] F; combind *conj. this edn*   134 SD JACQUES DE BOYS] *Rowe subst.; not in* F   135 SH, 167 SH] *Rowe;* 2. *Bro.* F

125–30 There is no indication in the text as to who sang this song; hymns to Hymen ('hymen hymenaee o hymen') accompanied wedding processions in classical times (see Plautus, *Casina*, 4.3, and Ovid, *Heroides*, xv, 143–52).

125–6 Compare *Aeneid*, IV, 59: 'Iunoni ante omnis, cui vincla iugalia curae' (To Juno, above all, who has the care of marriage bonds).

126 **board and bed** The phrase 'bed and board' meant, in relation to a wife, 'full connubial relations, as wife and mistress of the household' (*OED* Bed *sb* 1c).

127 **Hymen** Marriage (*OED* sv 2).

127 **peoples** populates.

128 **High** Solemn – although it could be an adverb modifying 'honourèd'.

131–2 The lines are awkward, and we have to presume that they are addressed to Celia since Rosalind has already been 'welcomed' by her father at 103.

132 **Even** Exactly as a (see collation).

132 **in no less degree** i.e. in no lower degree than that of a daughter.

133 **eat my word** Proverbial (Tilley w825).

134 **my … combine** binds my love to you (*OED* Combine *v* 6); 'combine' may be an error for 'combind' (= combined), itself a form that arose from confusion between 'combine' and 'bind'; compare *MM* 4.3.149.

138 **how that** that (*OED* How *adv* 10).

140 **Addressed** Prepared (*OED* Address *v* 2a).

140 **power** force, army.

141 **In his own conduct** Under his own command.

143 **skirts** edges.

144 **religious man** This may be Rosalind's mysterious uncle, the magician (see 3.3.288–9, 5.2.48 n., 5.4.32–3); alternatively since Adam has now disappeared from the play, this may be a vestige of his role.

After some question with him, was converted   145
Both from his enterprise and from the world,
His crown bequeathing to his banished brother,
And all their lands restored to them again
That were with him exiled. This to be true,
I do engage my life.

DUKE SENIOR   Welcome, young man.   150
Thou offer'st fairly to thy brother's wedding:
To one his lands withheld, and to the other
A land itself at large, a potent dukedom. –
First, in this forest, let us do those ends
That here were well begun and well begot;   155
And, after, every of this happy number
That have endured shrewd days and nights with us
Shall share the good of our returnèd fortune
According to the measure of their states.
Meantime forget this new-fall'n dignity   160
And fall into our rustic revelry. –
Play, music – and, you brides and bridegrooms all,
With measure heaped in joy to th'measures fall.

JAQUES Sir, by your patience. [*To Jacques de Boys*] If I heard you rightly,
The Duke hath put on a religious life   165
And thrown into neglect the pompous court.

---

148 them] *Rowe;* him F   150 Welcome,] F4*;* Welcome F   151 brother's] F4*;* brothers F*;* brothers' *Johnson*² 155 were] F2*;* vvete F   162 Play,] *Theobald;* Play F   162 and, you] *Eds.;* and F   164 SD] *Wilson; not in* F

145 **question** See 122 n. above.
145 **was converted** For the omission of the subject, see Abbott 399–400.
146 **the world** all worldly things.
147 **crown** sovereignty (*OED* sv *sb* 3).
147 **bequeathing** assigning (*OED* sv *v* 3).
148 **restored** being restored.
148 ***them** Rowe's emendation (see collation), but F's reading ('him') could stand if we took 'states' in 159 to mean 'conditions' and not 'estates': it would then mean that Duke Senior would redistribute the land of the exiles according to their worth.
149 **exiled** Stressed on the second syllable (Cercignani, p. 38).
149 **This to be** That this is (Abbott 354).
150 **engage** pledge.
151 **offer'st fairly** bring fine gifts.
152 **To one his lands withheld** Orlando in fact already knows of Oliver's design to become a 'shepherd' (5.2.9).
152 **the other** i.e. myself.
153 **at large** entire (*OED* Large *sb* 5d).
153 **potent** mighty.

153 **dukedom** ducal office.
154 **do those ends** realise those intentions.
155 **begot** begotten (see Abbott 343).
156 **every** every one.
157 **shrewd** hard, piercingly cold (*OED* sv 9b).
159 **measure** nature, rank.
159 **states** See 148 n.
160 **new-fall'n dignity** newly acquired honour.
162–3 The play will end, in the manner of a court masque, with a dance. 'It would be inappropriate to end this play with a country dance like the hay . . . The celebration is . . . joyous, but it is also solemn' (Alan Brissenden, *Shakespeare and the Dance*, 1981, p. 54). A suitable melody from the period is reprinted in Long, p. 161.
162 **music** band of musicians (*OED* sv 5).
163 **measure heaped in** a full complement of.
163 **measures** steps of the stately dances (*OED* Measure *sb* 20a).
164 **by your patience** give me leave: a request that the dancing should be delayed.
166 **thrown . . . court** given up the ceremonious life of the court.

JACQUES DE BOYS He hath.

JAQUES To him will I: out of these convertites
        There is much matter to be heard and learned.
        [*To the Duke*] You to your former honour I bequeath: 170
        Your patience and your virtue well deserves it.
        [*To Orlando*] You to a love that your true faith doth merit.
        [*To Oliver*] You to your land and love and great allies.
        [*To Silvius*] You to a long and well-deservèd bed.
        [*To Touchstone*] And you to wrangling, for thy loving voyage   175
        Is but for two months victualled. – So to your pleasures;
        I am for other than for dancing measures.

DUKE SENIOR Stay, Jaques, stay.

JAQUES To see no pastime, I. What you would have
        I'll stay to know at your abandoned cave.   *Exit*   180

DUKE SENIOR Proceed, proceed. – We will begin these rites
        As we do trust they'll end, in true delights.

                   [*They dance.*] *Exeunt all but Rosalind*

[Epilogue]

ROSALIND It is not the fashion to see the lady the Epilogue, but it is no
    more unhandsome than to see the lord the Prologue. If it be true
    that good wine needs no bush, 'tis true that a good play needs no
    Epilogue. Yet to good wine they do use good bushes, and good plays

---

170 SD, 172 SD, 173 SD, 174 SD, 175 SD] *Rowe subst.; not in* F   181 We will] F2; *Wee'l* F; *We'll so Oxford, conj. Maxwell*   181 rites] *Rowe;* rights F   182 trust they'll end,] *Pope;* trust, they'l end F   182 SD *They dance*] *Capell subst.; not in* F   182 SD *Exeunt . . . Rosalind*] *Eds.; Exit* F; *not in* F2   **Epilogue** Epilogue] *Theobald²; not in* F

168–9 Jaques, who seems to have felt love for Rosalind / Ganymede, has been driven 'from his mad humour of love to a living humour of madness . . . to live in a nook, merely monastic' (3.3.344–6).

  168 will I For the omission of the verb of motion, see Abbott 405.

  168 convertites people converted to a religious life.

  169 matter good sense (*OED* 11b).

  170 bequeath entrust (*OED* sv 4).

  171 deserves For the singular termination, see Abbott 170.

  173 allies relatives, kinsmen (*OED* Ally *sb¹* 5).

  179 pastime frivolity.

  180 stay wait.

  182 SD *They dance* This is indicated by the Duke's command at 162–3; a suggestion for staging

could be taken from the end of *Hymenaei*: 'Here they danced their last dances, full of excellent delight and change, and in their latter strain fell into a fair orb or circle, Reason standing in the midst . . . and then dissolving, went down in couples led on by Hymen, the bride . . . following (358–60, 390–2).

Epilogue

  1 not . . . Epilogue Lyly's *Gallathea* (1585) also gives the Epilogue to the principal female character.

  2 unhandsome unbecoming (however, *OED* sv 4, offers no example before 1645).

  2 than . . . Prologue i.e. lords should not go before ladies.

  3 good wine needs no bush Proverbial (Tilley w462). An ivy-bush or garland was hung outside an inn to signify good wine within.

prove the better by the help of good Epilogues. What a case am I in,   5
then, that am neither a good Epilogue nor cannot insinuate with you
in the behalf of a good play? I am not furnished like a beggar,
therefore to beg will not become me. My way is to conjure you, and
I'll begin with the women. I charge you, O women, for the love you
bear to men, to like as much of this play as please you. – And I   10
charge you, O men, for the love you bear to women – as I perceive
by your simpering none of you hates them – that between you and
the women the play may please. If I were a woman, I would kiss as
many of you as had beards that pleased me, complexions that liked
me, and breaths that I defied not. And I am sure as many as have   15
good beards, or good faces, or sweet breaths will, for my kind offer,
when I make curtsey, bid me farewell.   *Exit*

FINIS

10 you] F; them *Hanmer*   17 SD] F; *Exeunt* F2

5 **case** state.

6 **then** 'Here seems to be a chasm, or some
other depravation, which destroys the sentiment
he intended. The reasoning probably stood thus:
"Good wine needs no bush, good plays need no
Epilogue"; but bad wine requires good bush, and a
bad play a good Epilogue. What a case . . .' (Johnson).

6 **nor cannot** For the double negative, see
Abbott 406.

6 **insinuate** ingratiate myself (*OED* sv *v* 2b).

7 **furnished** costumed.

8 **conjure** (1) solemnly enjoin, (2) charm by
magic – extending Rosalind's witty presentation of
herself as a kind of magician (see 5.2.47–9), whose
magic circle may have been the 'wooden O' of the
Globe playhouse (see 2.5.51 n.).

9 **women** For evidence about women in audiences see Andrew Gurr, *Playgoing in Shakespeare's
London*, 1987, *passim*. It is notable that Rosalind speaks not of 'ladies' who frequented court
performances: 'women' might well include citizens'
wives.

10 **this play** (1) today's dramatic offering, (2)
amorous dalliance.

10 **please** may please (Abbott 367); the sentence
contains a deft allusion to the title of the play.

12 **simpering** smirking (in an effeminate
manner?).

13 **play** A sexual quibble (Williams, p. 238).

13 **If I were a woman** Rosalind was played by
a boy player, but there can be no certainty as to
whether he was in male or female attire at this point
(see 5.4.92 SD.2 n. and 99 n.); 'One suspects that this
change [in gender] was signalled or accompanied
by a physical gesture such as the removal of a wig
or some article of female attire' (Michael Shapiro,
Gender in Play on the Shakespearean Stage, 1994,
p. 132); '"If I were among you" is often substituted
when the part is taken by a woman in modern productions' (Knowles).

14 **liked** pleased.

15 **defied** despised, found revolting (*OED* Defy
v^1 5).

16 **offer** i.e. to kiss spectators.

17 **bid me farewell** applaud.

TEXTUAL ANALYSIS

As You Like It was entered in the Stationers' Register on 4 August [1600]. The form of entry is unusual: it is listed 'to be staied' on a fly-leaf, along with *Henry V*, *Every Man in his Humour*, and *Much Ado About Nothing*. No stationer is named, and there is no record of any fee having been paid.[1] The other three plays appeared in print shortly afterwards, but *As You Like It* was not published before it appeared in the First Folio collection of works by Shakespeare (F), which was printed in William Jaggard's shop in 1623.[2]

Many explanations are possible for the non-appearance of the play in print: perhaps the players wanted to prevent unauthorised publication of a play so popular that they were unwilling to put the text into circulation; perhaps the entry is a clerk's memorandum signifying that the entry is to await further consideration;[3] perhaps the text was affected by the decree prohibiting the printing of satires and epigrams published by the Archbishop of Canterbury and the Bishop of London on 1 June 1599.[4] It may have fallen foul of the censors by virtue of containing, in the figure of Jaques, a satirical portrait of the queen's godson Sir John Harington who, in 1596, had published a witty and scatological treatise on his recently invented water-closet, *The Metamorphosis of Ajax*, and who, in consequence, was referred to as 'Sir Ajax Harington'.[5] Harington had served under the Earl of Essex in the Irish campaign of 1599, but he and his patron were out of favour with the Queen at the probable time of the play's composition.[6] Whether the mere evocation of Harington, even in an unfavourable guise, was enough to provoke censorship, or whether in these months any form of satire generated an official reaction is unknowable. Neither hypothesis is provable since there is no record of performance before one that may have taken place in 1603[7] – but equally no evidence to suggest that it was not performed – and there is nothing to clinch the identification with Harington.

In the Folio the play appears after *The Merchant of Venice* and before *The Taming of the Shrew*, occupying sigs. Q3^r–S2^r, pp. 185–207[8] of the section of the volume devoted to the comedies. The text is a good one and must have been set up from

---

[1] Arber, III, 37.

[2] It next appears on a list of sixteen plays entered in the Register on 8 November 1623 (Arber, IV, 107).

[3] This and other explanations are very fully discussed by Knowles, pp. 353–64.

[4] Richard A. McCabe, 'Elizabethan satire and the bishops' ban of 1599', *Yearbook of English Studies* 11 (1981), 188–94; Janet Clare, *'Art Made Tongue-tied by Authority': Elizabethan and Jacobean Dramatic Censorship*, 1990, pp. 60–97.

[5] Norman E. McClure (ed.), *Letters of John Chamberlain*, 1939, pp. 84, 397.

[6] Clare, *Art Made Tongue-tied*, notes that when *H5* was first published in quarto in 1600 passages favourable to Essex were omitted, pp. 72–3.

[7] See Stage History, p. 43.

[8] In all copies p. 189 is misnumbered 187.

a manuscript that presented few problems of legibility and which had undergone some process of editing: in particular, there are few problems of lineation, most deriving from compositorial decisions to print short passages of prose as verse.[1]

In order to determine what kind of manuscript the compositors worked from, we must consider what may have happened to copy as it was transmitted from manuscript(s) to printed book.

The text of a play from the early modern period was subject to alteration or corruption at up to seven stages:[2] by the author (or authors) while still in preliminary drafts; by authors or scribes preparing a 'fair copy' for delivery to a company;[3] by an adapter connected with the company by whom it was performed; by the book-holder (who doubled as a prompter)[4] annotating the 'foul papers' (or author's manuscript)[5] or preparing a prompt-book or 'play-book' for performance; by an editor preparing copy for the printer;[6] by the compositors; and by the proof-reader who scanned sheets as they came from the press. It is logical to look for evidence of changes of these kinds in reverse order and so produce a theory about the nature and authority of the copy used by the compositors who turned the manuscript into the printed texts that survive. The end of my endeavour as an editor is not to recover or reproduce an authoritative[7] or even permanently 'stable' text, but one that responds deliberatively to any textual signals that we may detect from the 'recorded forms'[8] of the past and one that establishes a degree of consistency by means of regularisation and normalisation. I give serious consideration to other readings by considering texts contemporary with *As You Like It* or readings suggested by informed and responsible modern readers and directors.

As a preliminary, we should note that proof-readers did not always or thoroughly check proofs against copy, that their main aim was to correct typographical inaccuracies or irregularities,[9] and that they might well thereby introduce corruption by correction. In the case of *As You Like It* there are textual and non-textual variants on pp. 193, 204, and 207; these involve the correction of inking problems, page

---

[1] These are listed in Wells and Taylor, *Textual Companion*, pp. 647–8.

[2] See Fredson Bowers, *On Editing Shakespeare*, 1966.

[3] T. J. King, *Casting Shakespeare's Plays: London Actors and their Roles, 1590–1642*, 1992, p. 9.

[4] W. W. Greg, *The Shakespeare First Folio*, 1955, p. 100; King, *Casting Shakespeare's Plays*, pp. 10–11; Patrick Tucker and Michael Holden (eds.), *As You Like It* (Shakespeare's Globe Acting Edition), 1991, reprints the F text in an 'acting' edition consisting of a platt (plot), prompt script (with exits and entrances noted), a part script for each role, and textual and explanatory notes.

[5] Greg, *First Folio*, p. 109.

[6] These have been studied by S. W. Reid, 'The editing of Folio *Romeo and Juliet*', *SB* 35 (1982), 43–66; Eleanor Prosser, *Shakespeare's Anonymous Editors*, 1981; T. H. Howard-Hill, 'Shakespeare's earliest editor, Ralph Crane', *S.Sur.* 44 (1992), 113–29.

[7] For the problematisation of this notion see Margreta de Grazia, *Shakespeare Verbatim: The Reproduction of Authority and the 1790 Apparatus*, 1991; G. Thomas Tanselle, 'Editing without a copy-text', *SB* 47 (1994), 1–22, and 'Textual stability and editorial idealism', *SB* 49 (1996), 1–60.

[8] I owe this formulation to Professor D. F. McKenzie.

[9] However, see Elizabeth Story Donno, 'Abraham Fleming: a learned corrector in 1586–7', *SB* 42 (1989), 200–11.

or signature errors, transposed speech headings, and, on p. 207, four insignificant literals.[1]

It was established by Charlton Hinman that *As You Like It* was set by three of Jaggard's compositors, B, C, and D. Spelling tests (B preferred the forms 'do', 'go', 'heere'; C the forms 'doe', 'goe', 'heere'; D the forms 'doe', 'goe', here')[2] and the tracing of individual pieces of type allowed Hinman to assign C (working from case x), B (working from case y), D (working from case z), the following stints:[3]

Cx set Q3^{r-v}	pp. 185–6	1–228	(1.1.1–1.2.48)[4]
By set Q4^r	p. 187	229–357	(1.2.49–153)
Dz set Q4^v–Q5^r	pp. 188–[9]	358–608	(1.2.154–2.1.2)
Cx set Q5^{v}a	p. 190a	609–74	(2.1.3–2.1.66 [deer])
Dz set Q5^{v}b–Q6^r	pp. 190b–191	675–852	(2.1.66 [DUKE . . .]–2.4.61)'
By set Q6^v–R3^v	pp. 192–8	853–1724	(2.4.62–3.5.12)
Cx set R4^r–R6^r	pp. 199–203	1725–2351	(3.5.13–5.1.8 [. . . By])
By set R6^v–S2^r	pp. 204–7	2352–2474	(5.1.8 [my . . .] – Epilogue 17)

Sometimes the casting-off of copy for compositors was inaccurate: B, for example, set 2.6 as verse – it occurs at the end of p. 192 – in order to eke out his copy.[5]

The results of compositorial analysis account for spelling inconsistencies that seemed to earlier scholars to point to manuscript copy that was either produced by more than one hand[6] or which indicated to them authorial revision or a text written by more than one author.

The next stage in our investigation must be to decide whether or not the copy from which the compositors worked derives from a manuscript that may have been used in the playhouse. Evidence of theatrical stage directions, added presumably by the book-holder, would suggest that the text passed through such a stage, although it is usually impossible to decide whether the copy is a holographic (or possibly scribal) text marked up by the book-holder in preparation for the copying-out of the play-book, or was copied by a scribe for the printer from a fully annotated play-book.

There is fairly firm evidence that behind copy used for *As You Like It* was a manuscript that was prepared for, served as, or copied from, a play-book. First, we find anticipated stage directions. Entrances are often marked for characters when they 'first come in view of those on stage, although it may be some while before

---

[1] Charlton Hinman, *The Printing and Proof-Reading of the First Folio of Shakespeare*, 2 vols., 1963, 1, 261–2.

[2] Hinman, *Printing and Proof-Reading*, 1, 182–200.

[3] *Ibid.*, 11, 434–49; these are confirmed by Trevor Howard-Hill, 'The compositors of Shakespeare's Folio comedies', *SB* 26 (1973), 61–106, and John O'Conner, 'Compositors D and F of the Shakespeare First Folio', *SB* 28 (1975), 81–117, except that O'Conner gives Q5^{v}a to D.

[4] In this table and the following text, act, scene, and line numbers as well as TLNS are given.

[5] See Paul Werstine, 'Compositor B of the Shakespeare First Folio', *AEB* 2 (1978), 241–63.

[6] 'Rosaline' appears only in the stints of Compositor D, 'who always uses this spelling, perhaps because he had set the name in *LLL* . . . a short time before his stint in *AYLI*' (Knowles, p. 326); for a general study, see Grace Ioppolo, *Revising Shakespeare*, 1991.

they join them':[1] 1.2.34 SD (212); 1.2.210 SD (426); 1.3.27 SD (494); 2.4.13 SD (801); 3.3.210 SD (1445); 4.3.0 SD (2151); 5.2.9 SD (2421); 5.4.34 SD (2610; see collation). Second, we find imperative stage directions, generally, but not always, a sign of prompt-book copy: 1.2.166 SD (373) ('*Wrastle*'); 1.2.168 SD (375) ('*Shout*'); 4.3.39 SD, 42 SD (2189, 2193) ('Read.').[2] The first two of these obviously appeared in the copy's margin, and belong in the same category as '*Song. Altogether heere*' 2.5.29 SD (926);[3] '*Song.*' 2.7.173 SD (1155), 5.3.12 (2546), 5.4.124 SD (2715); '*Musicke, Song.*' 4.2.7 SD (2136); and '*Still Musicke*' 5.4.92 SD (2682).[4] Third, speech headings and names in stage directions are generally consistent.[5] A version of 'Clown' is invariably used to designate Touchstone in stage directions and speech headings,[6] and the two Dukes are carefully distinguished in both stage directions and speech headings. (Paul Werstine, however, notes that this is not an entirely valid test for play-book copy – there are inconsistencies in play-book texts.)[7] The unusual stage direction '*Enter Rosaline for Ganimed, Celia for Aliena, and Clowne, alias Touchstone*' at 2.4.0 SD (781–2) is probably a clarifying note by either author or book-holder to distinguish Touchstone from William, another kind of 'clowne' (2351) – the word 'alias', however, appears in no other Shakespearean stage direction.[8] Fourth, we find a property note: '*Enter Celia with a writing*' at 3.3.98 (1321). This, however, could be authorial, especially since a line associated with Rosalind's earlier and parallel entrance at 3.3.64 (1285) is unglossed by a stage direction.

We must now look to F to see whether it presents possible signs of authorial copy.[9] It does. First, the text is carefully divided into acts and scenes.[10] (There are, however, good reasons for marking a new scene after Orlando's speech at 3.2.10 – see 3.3 n. Moreover, earlier editors found problems with 2.5–2.7 and directors rearranged the scenes because they were unwilling to concede that simultaneous staging

---

[1] Greg, *First Folio*, p. 294.

[2] See W. W. Greg, *The Editorial Problem in Shakespeare*, 1951, p. 37.

[3] See 2.5.29 SD n.

[4] Greg, *Editorial Problem*, p. 144; see also Patty S. Derrick, 'Stage directions in the Oxford Shakespeare: a view from the nineteenth century', *AEB* n.s. 4 (1990), 35–45.

[5] We might compare the case of *AWW*, a foul-papers text: see Fredson Bowers, 'Foul papers, Compositor B, and the speech-prefixes of *All's Well that Ends Well*', *SB* 32 (1979), 60–81.

[6] Compare the way Feste is designated in stage directions in *TN* as 'Clown' rather than as Feste or 'Fool': '*Enter Clowne. / And.* Heere comes the foole yfaith' (714–15).

[7] Paul Werstine, '"Foul papers" and "prompt-books": printer's copy for Shakespeare's *Comedy of Errors*', *SB* 41 (1988), 232–46.

[8] Greg notes that 'for' in a stage direction occurs in *MV* 4.1.169 and *LLL* 5.2.565, 592 – both texts that derive from foul papers (*Editorial Problem*, p. 144).

[9] Greg, *First Folio*, pp. 124–45; for a general defence of authorial SDs see Antony Hammond, 'Encounters of the third kind in stage-directions in Elizabethan and Jacobean drama', *Studies in Philology* 89 (1992), 71–99.

[10] On this factor as an indicator of authorial copy: see T. W. Baldwin, *On Act and Scene Division in the Shakespeare First Folio*, 1965, p. 12; Greg, *Editorial Problem*, pp. 35–6, implies that these divisions are likely to occur in play-books rather than foul papers. In Anthony Munday, *Fedele and Fortunio*, ed. Richard Hosley, 1981, the editor prints a table (pp. 68–73) that reveals that professional dramatists were scarcely consistent in this respect. Gary Taylor and John Jowett argue that the regular division into scenes suggests a 'literary transcript' which served as copy for the printer (Gary Taylor and John Jowett, *Shakespeare Reshaped 1606–1623*, 1993, pp. 241–2).

was probably used here.)[1] Second, the text contains permissive[2] or descriptive stage directions: 2.1.0 SD (604–5) *Enter . . . two or three Lords like Forresters*; 2.5.0 SD (889) *Enter, Amyens, Iaques, & others*; 2.7.0 SD (971) *Enter Duke Sen. & Lord, like Out-lawes*; 4.2.0 SD (2126) *Enter Iaques and Lords, Forresters*. Third, necessary entrances and exits are missing: 1.1.74 (94); 1.2.173 (382); 1.2.238 (454); 2.7.135 (1113); 3.3.249 (1486); or incorrect: 1.2.182 (393) does not name all who must leave the stage. Fourth, there are a few speech headings that are inconsistent or designate both names and roles. F's '1. *Lord*' in speech headings in 2.7 almost certainly refers to Amiens who would otherwise disappear after 2.5.[3] Jacques de Boys is named '*Iaques*' at 1.1.4, but is designated in a stage direction as '*second brother*' when he appears in 5.4.134 SD (2726).[4] It is, however, entirely possible that all of these survived transcription from foul papers into a play-book (the text used by the company's 'book-holder', who combined the roles of stage-manager and prompt): performances did not depend upon an absolutely rigorous or consistent master text,[5] and certainly some of the missing entrances and exits could be compositorial.

Finally, there is the possibility that F was printed from a manuscript version, parts of which were revised, other parts unrevised. John Dover Wilson and other editors suggested, on stylistic grounds, that Hymen's masque might have been added:[6] there is no textual evidence for this, and the alleged flatness of the verse in this sequence may have found compensation in the original music.[7] Likewise there is no textual evidence that the role of Jaques was an addition nor for the author's failure to include Adam in the dénouement. One of the key pieces of evidence for those looking for revision is Le Beau's description of Celia: 'indeede the taller is [Duke Frederick's] daughter'. Later it is Rosalind who describes herself as tall (1.3.105), and at 4.3.82 Celia is described as being 'low'.[8] The problem disappears, however, if we decide that the meaning of 'taller' here is 'more spirited'.[9] There is then need neither to conjecture authorial or compositorial error, nor that the text was revised to match the heights of a new set of boy players.

To conclude: the balance of probability is that F's text derives from a play-book. A sophisticated but entirely conjectural version of this would be that the manuscript

---

[1] See Alan C. Dessen, *Elizabethan Stage Conventions and Modern Interpreters*, 1984, p. 102.

[2] However, Werstine, '"Foul papers" and "prompt-books"' argues that permissive stage directions may on occasion have been added by one of the editors of the Folio text.

[3] In both 2.7 and 4.2 a 'Lord' is, like Amiens, required to sing; see 2.7.0 SD n.; Greg, *First Folio*, p. 294.

[4] R. B. McKerrow, 'A suggestion regarding Shakespeare's manuscripts', *RES* 11 (1935), 459–65, and Random Cloud, '"The very names of the persons": editing and the invention of dramatick character', in David Scott Kastan and Peter Stallybrass (eds.), *Staging the Renaissance*, 1991, 88–96, argue for the validity of this kind of evidence; Paul Werstine, 'McKerrow's "suggestion" and twentieth-century Shakespeare criticism', *Ren. Drama* n.s. 19 (1988), 149–73, argues against it.

[5] See S. P. Cerasano, 'Editing the theatre, translating the stage', *AEB* n.s. 4 (1990), 21–34.

[6] Wilson, p. 108; see Greg, *First Folio*, p. 295, for a rebuttal of Wilson's quaint theory that the play was originally written completely in verse in 1593.

[7] It might also be compared with the flat style of the apparitions in *Cym.* 5.4.30–92.

[8] Compare Wilson, pp. 101–3; Chambers, *Shakespeare*, 1, 403.

[9] See 1.2.224 n.

'As you like yt / a booke', possibly the original play-book, that was given to the Stationers' Company 'to be staied' or to the Master of the Revels to be seen and allowed may well not have been recovered by the Lord Chamberlain's Men. It is tempting to surmise that another play-book was produced from Shakespeare's manuscript (or a 'literary transcript' of it)[1] perhaps simply by marking up without re-copying, which would explain the combination of authorial and play-book characteristics. It would be from this play-book that the printers' copy derives.

[1] See p. 202 n. 9.

APPENDIX 1: AN EARLY COURT PERFORMANCE?

In her Arden 3 edition of the play (2006), Juliet Dusinberre drew attention to a record of a payment to Shakespeare's company for what may well have been a significant performance of *As You Like It* (although not necessarily its first), before the Queen and the court at Richmond on Shrove Tuesday, 20 February 1599.[1] Elizabeth herself liked to play a role in the deer-hunting – one of the play's prominent themes – which had taken place in Sheen Chase, the former name of Richmond Park, since medieval times. In addition, Dusinberre associated the poem's mention of a dial with the great dial in the outer court at Richmond and also noted the mention of a dial in the text (2.7.20). (Although the palace dial had been repainted and repaired in 1599, it was not a new construction.)[2] The payment is contained within a warrant of 2 October 1599 for three performances on the feasts of St Stephen (26 December [1598]), New Year's Day [1599], and Shrove Tuesday [1599]. It was augmented because the Queen had offered the traditional extra remuneration for a performance at which she was present:

To Iohn Heminges and Thomas Pope servant[es] vnto the Lorde Chamberleyne vppon the Councells warraunt dated at the Courte at Nonesuche s[ecun]do die Octobris 1599 for three Enterludes or playes played before her Matie vppon St Stephens daye at nighte Newyeares daye at nighte and shrove-tuesdaye at nighte laste paste xx^li [£20] and to them more by waye of her Ma^ts rewarde x^li In all amounting to xxx^li3

Dusinberre selects the last of these, Shrove Tuesday, because of Touchstone's pancake joke – pancakes filled with minced meat were, she claims, eaten on that day: 'a certain knight . . . swore, by his honour, they were good pancakes, and swore, by his honour, the mustard was naught' (1.2.50–1). However, although Shrove Tuesday was indeed 'Pancake Day',[4] pancakes were eaten throughout the year, and there is no known reference in the period to this sort of savoury fritter.[5] The laborious jest does have the feel of a topical reference, but it might recall a well-known incident, of which we have no record, that had occurred several months before an early performance. Apart from that jest, however, which does not

---

[1] Dusinberre, pp. 36–46; Juliet Dusinberre, 'Pancakes and a date for *As You Like It*', *SQ* 54 (2003), 371–405. In the period, although New Year gifts were exchanged on 1 January, the calendar year began on Lady Day, 25 March, so that day (20 February) would have been dated 1598. The Queen and court had moved to Richmond on 10 February (John Chamberlain, *The Letters of John Chamberlain*, ed. N. E. McClure, 2 vols., 1939, I, 68). She was at Nonesuch for the summer of that year.

[2] Dusinberre, pp. 37–42.

[3] David Cook and F. P. Wilson (eds.), *Dramatic Records in the Declared Accounts of the Treasurer of the Chamber, 1558–1642*, Malone Society Collections 6, 1962, 55a, p. 30; the Lord Admiral's Men were, as was customary, playing at court at the same time (John Astington, *English Court Theatre, 1558–1642*, 1999, pp. 235–6).

[4] See Thomas Dekker, *The Shoemaker's Holiday*, ed. R. L. Smallwood and Stanley Wells, 1979, xvii 53 and p. 218.

[5] Knowles, p. 33 n. However, in Deloney's *The Gentle Craft* (1597–8), there is a mention of a Shrovetide feast of 'pudding-pies and pancakes' (quoted in Smallwood and Wells (eds.), *Shoemaker's Holiday*, p. 218), and see *OED*, 'pudding-pie' (generally contained meat). In John Taylor, *The Great Eater of Kent* (1630) 'pancakes' are included in a list of sweetmeats, not savouries (p. 13).

clinch the case (see 1.2.50–1 n.), there is nothing to associate this play with that payment, or indeed with the payments for other Christmas and Shrovetide court performances by the Chamberlain's Men in 1598–9.[1] Another entry the next year when the court was again at Richmond records a similar payment for performances by Shakespeare's company at Christmas 1599 and Shrove Sunday (3 February 1600):

To Iohn Hemynge servaunt to the Lorde Chamberlaine vppon the Councells Warraunt dated at the Courte at Richmond xvij^mo die Februarij 1599 [i.e. 1600] for three Enterludes or playes played before her Matie on St Stephens daye at nighte, Twelfth daye at night and Shroue sondaye [i.e. 3 February 1600] at night laste paste xxx^li2

This suggests that if indeed the first performance of *As You Like It* was at court, it could have been in late 1598, 1599, or 1600.

In 1972 news had been published of an unattributed poem, dated 1598 [–1599], but detached from any play. The poem was found in the commonplace book of Henry Stanford. Stanford was chaplain and tutor in the household of the Lord Chamberlain, George Carey, Lord Hunsdon, who, in 1603, was to leave him £40 in his will:[3]

'To the Queen, by the players, 1598'

As the *dial* hand tells o'er
    The same hours it had before,
    Still beginning in the ending,
    Circular account still lending.
So, most almighty *Queen*, we pray,
    Like the dial day by day,
    You may lead the seasons on,
    Making new when old are gone.
That the babe which now is young
    And hath yet no use of tongue,
    Many a *Shrovetide* here may bow
    To that Empress I do now:
    That the children of these lords,
    Sitting at your *council* boards,
    May be, grave and agèd, seen
    Of her that was their father [*sic*] Queen.
Once I wish this wish again:
    Heaven subscribe it with '*Amen*' [emphases added].

The anthology's editors tentatively ascribed the poem to Shakespeare.[4]

---

[1] Cook and Wilson (eds.), *Dramatic Records*, 39b and 57a, pp. 30–1.

[2] *Ibid.*, 57a, p. 31; Chambers, IV, 112. This is puzzling, because a subsequent payment is given to Derby's Men for another evening performance on Shrove Sunday (3 February): 'To Robert Browne servaunt to Therle of Darby vppon the Councells Warraunt dated at the Courte at Richmond xviij^uo die Februarij 1599 [i.e. 1600] for one Enterlude or playe playde before her highnes on Shrove sondaye at nighte laste paste x^li' (Cook and Wilson (eds.), *Dramatic Records*, 57a, p. 31). However, the *Acts of the Privy Council* show that it was the Chamberlain's Men who performed on Shrove Sunday and that Derby's Men played on Shrove Tuesday (John Roche Dasent *et al.*, *Acts of the Privy Council of England 1542–1631*, 40 vols., 1890–, 30.89 – Prof. Steven W. May gave me this reference).

[3] See Steven W. May's Stanford entry in the *Oxford Dictionary of National Biography*.

[4] Cambridge University Library, ms. DD.5.75, f. 46; see William A. Ringler and Steven W. May, 'An epilogue possibly by Shakespeare', *MP* 70 (1972), 138–9; Steven W. May and William A. Ringler

The poem invokes 'Shrovetide', a season when, as records show, Shakespeare's company did perform before the court. As we have seen, Dusinberre related this hypothetical link between the poem and the 1599 Shrove Tuesday performance (proposed by Steven May) specifically to *As You Like It*.[1] However, there is also a warrant (of the same date) for a Shrovetide performance at Richmond by the Lord Admiral's Men two days earlier, on Shrove Sunday – as usual the two companies played before the Queen that Shrovetide.[2] The epilogue could be linked to either one of these 1599 Shrovetide performances, which performances cannot therefore be used for resolving the poem's provenance.

Conversely, the argument for Shakespearean authorship cannot be reinforced by this kind of contextualizing. The poem's trochaic metre and grammar could indeed be Shakespearean – although Shakespeare might conceivably have penned it for a play he did not write himself. Despite the fact that Shakespeare and Stanford were both associated with Lord Hunsdon – as was Morley[3] – it may be significant that Stanford's anthology contains nothing that is indubitably by Shakespeare, although there are many poems by the courtier poets of the age.

Jonson seems to me to be a stronger candidate for authorship. The trochaic tetrameters used by Jonson in, for example, the songs from Lord Haddington's wedding masque that were to be performed at court on Shrove Tuesday at night in 1608 and the satyr songs in his *Oberon* of 1611 are very close in style to the dial poem and have roughly the same proportion of feminine endings. The forms 'dial' and 'father' are probably uninflected genitives, as in F1's version of *AC*, 2.7.129 ('father house').[4] However, this is not a Shakespearean idiosyncrasy: 'father' was both inflected and uninflected in Old English, although the *OED* claims, erroneously it would seem, that the uninflected form had disappeared in the fifteenth century. Jonson also occasionally uses the form.[5] Moreover, the neo-platonic conceit of the 'circular' is more likely to be Jonsonian than Shakespearean.[6] Jonson was a member of the Admiral's Men in 1598, although his career had been lately jeopardised by his killing of Gabriel Spenser. So this poem could have been affixed to a court performance of one of his plays, perhaps *The Case is Altered*, sold earlier to Henslowe, or the tragedy, the plot of which he had supplied to Henslowe, which was revised by Chapman.[7]

(eds.), *Elizabethan Poetry: A Bibliography and First-Line Index of English Verse, 1559–1603*, 3 vols., 2004, EV2916, III, 363; Steven W. May, *Henry Stanford's Anthology: An Edition of Cambridge University Library Manuscript Dd.5.75*, 1988, pp. xx, lxiii, 162 (item 228), and 373. In this later book May considers that the poem 'could hardly be Shakespeare's' (p. xx). Brian Vickers, *Counterfeiting Shakespeare: Evidence, Authorship and John Ford's Funerall Elegye*, 2002, pp. 428–9 reviews the evidence but does not endorse the attribution. However, in William Shakespeare, *Complete Works*, ed. Jonathan Bate and Eric Rasmussen, 2007, p. 2433, it is accorded canonical status.

[1] Ringler and May, 'Epilogue', p. 138; James Shapiro guesses that the poem was written not for the first performance of *As You Like It* but for a revival of *A Midsummer Night's Dream* at Shrovetide 1599. It was, he argues, a substitution for Puck's epilogue, which matches it almost exactly in metre – the reason for Shapiro's attribution (Shapiro, *1599*, pp. 84–6).

[2] Cook and Wilson (eds.), *Dramatic Records*, 55b, p. 31.

[3] May, *Anthology*, pp. xix and 313–14.

[4] Some editors ascribe this to compositorial error; it could derive equally from the author or copyists.

[5] See A. C. Partridge, *The Accidence of Ben Jonson's Plays, Masques and Entertainments*, 1953, pp. 61 and 278–81, and N. F. Blake, *A Grammar of Shakespeare's Language*, 2002, pp. 38–9.

[6] See Ben Jonson, 'To . . . Sir Lucius Cary and Sir H. Morison' and 'The vision of Ben Jonson', *Poems*, ed. Ian Donaldson, 1975, pp. 233 line 9 n. and 313 line 19; *Hymenaei*, 363–4; and *The New Inn*, ed. Michael Hattaway, 1984, 3.2.106 n., p. 146.

[7] Carol Chillington Rutter (ed.), *Documents of the Rose Playhouse*, 1984, p. 153; Gurr, *Playing Companies*, p. 241; for a link between Jonson and Stanford, see Katherine Duncan-Jones, '"They say a made a good end": Ben Jonson's Epitaph on Thomas Nashe', *Ben Jonson Journal* 3 (1996), 1–20.

However, the poem raises as many problems as it offers suggestions. First, the date: Henry Stanford dates only some of the entries in his anthology. There are many items of later dates that are entered *before* 'As the dial hand tells o'er'. An example is item 93 of 1612, which was inserted after the publication in English of the works of Du Bartas in 1611.[1] We cannot therefore be sure that the dial poem was copied as soon as Stanford received it, and its dating must be treated with caution. Given that it wishes the Queen another fifty or so years of life, excessive even by the hyperbolic standards of the day, it might have been *written* well before, perhaps soon after one or other of the attempts on the life of Elizabeth. Second, it may contain dangerous matter: '*En ma fin est mon commencement*' ('In my end is my beginning') was the motto of Mary Queen of Scots, whom Elizabeth had had executed in 1587. Would it have been tactful to broadcast these words from the stage at any time after this? Third, there is no connection with any playing company. Fourth, and most significantly, it is obviously not primarily an *epilogue*. Yet its commentators have assumed that it is.

What is distinctive about this poem is that it compliments the Queen but does not invite her or the audience to think favourably of the play in the manner of most epilogues.[2] Most probably it was a *prayer* of the sort that was sometimes offered up at court or private performances by the players (it does, after all, end with 'Amen'), perhaps to redeem themselves in the eyes of a society apt to regard them as vagabonds. In 1596 the Queen's godson Sir John Harington wrote at the end of his *The Metamorphosis of Ajax*:

. . . I will neither end with sermon nor prayer, lest some wags like me to my Lord ( )'s Players who, when they have ended a bawdy comedy, as though that were a preparative to devotion, kneel down solemnly and pray all the company to pray with them for their good lord and master.[3]

A quotation cited by Harington's editor, Elizabeth Story Donno, reveals that the prayer for Queen and Council in the new poem was formulaic (see below) and should not be read as having a connection with the action of any particular play. Conceivably, it may not even imply composition for a performance before the Queen. Writing of Sir William Holles of Houghton, Nottinghamshire (1509–91), Gervase Holles (1547–1627) observed:

he always kept a company of stage players of his own which presented him masques and plays at festival times and upon days of solemnity . . . always at the end of the play praying (as the custom then was) for the Queen's majesty, the Council, and their right worshipful good master, Sir William Holles.[4]

In Middleton's *A Mad World, My Masters*, a Paul's play of 1606(?), Folly begs his grandfather for a blessing: 'This shows much like kneeling after the play: I praying for my Lord Owemuch

---

[1] May, *Anthology*, p. 261.

[2] Tiffany Stern, *Making Shakespeare: From Stage to Page*, 2004, p. 120; Tiffany Stern, '"A small-beer health to his second day": playwrights, prologues, and first performances in the early modern theater', *SP* 101 (2004), 172–99.

[3] Sir John Harington, *The Metamorphosis of Ajax*, ed. Elizabeth Story Donno, 1962, p. 185. Peter Roberts suggests privately that this could be a reference to Leicester's Men. The Queen disapproved not only of the indelicate subject matter of Harington's book but also of alleged slighting references to Leicester in the text. The Earl had died in 1588: Harrington's jest, in the present tense, suggests 'deliberate obfuscation to cloak a dig at the hypocrisy of the patron of puritans and players'.

[4] Gervase Holles, *Memorials of the Holles Family, 1493–1656*, ed. A. C. Wood, vol. 5 of *Camden third series*, 1937, p. 42; see also Bernard Capp, 'A lost Elizabethan actors' company', *NQ* 242 (1997), 95–6; Peter Roberts, 'Elizabethan players and minstrels and the legislation of 1572 against retainers and vagabonds', in Anthony Fletcher and Peter Roberts (eds.), *Religion, Culture and Society in Early Modern Britain*, 1994, 29–55.

and his good countess, our honourable lady and mistress.'[1] Such a prayer could have been attached to any one of a handful of performances by the Admiral's or the Lord Chamberlain's Men at Shrovetide.

Although Henry Stanford was associated with the Carey family – George Carey, Lord Hunsdon was patron to the company generally known as the Chamberlain's Men, and the Queen sometimes stayed in the Chamberlain's residence in Blackfriars[2] – his anthology contains a poem by Ferdinando Stanley, Lord Strange, later Earl of Derby.[3] Its editor dates that entry around the end of 1588. Could Stanley, who, like Stanford, had Catholic connections and who had died suddenly in 1594, have written the prayer for his troupe who used it in 1599–1600 when they too were performing on Shrove Sunday at Richmond?[4] Or could it perhaps be by Ferdinando's brother William, sixth Earl of Derby, who wrote poems and plays himself, or by one of his large circle of literary associates?[5]

The dialogue 'Epilogue at Court' to Dekker's *Old Fortunatus* (probably performed at court by the Admiral's Men on 27 December 1599), which doubles as a prayer, contains conceits so closely resembling those in 'As the dial hand tells o'er' (the wish for a life so long for the Queen that she might see the locks of boys [boy players?] turn white and mathematical imagery) that Dekker may also be the author of the poem. Within his corpus, at least eight songs are written in trochaics.[6] Ringler and May note that the only *dramatists* known to have used trochaics in the period were Shakespeare, Dekker, and Jonson,[7] although they identified no fewer than 112 poems from the period with the same rhyme and metrical schemes as the dial poem.[8] As we have seen, the Admiral's Men, the company to which Jonson and Dekker

---

[1] Thomas Middleton, *A Mad World, My Masters* (1608), sig. H4ᵛ. Epilogues followed by prayers, or epilogues that incorporate prayers (often for King or Queen and Council), appear in Skelton's *Magnificence* (1515), Rastell's *Calisto and Melebea* (1527), Heywood's *Witty and Witless* (1533) and *A Play of Love* (1534), Udall's *Thersites* (1537), Bale's *Three Laws of Nature* (1538), Redford's *Wit and Science* (1539), Udall's *Rafe Roister Doister* (1552), *Nice Wanton* (1560), *King Darius* (1565), Wager's *The Trial of Treasure* (1567), *The History of Jacob and Esau* (1568), Preston's *Cambises* (ca 1569), Garter's *Susanna* (1569), Golding's *Abraham's Sacrifice* (1577), Fulwell's *Like Will to Like* (1587), *The Pedlar's Prophecy* (1595), and Greene and Lodge's *A Looking-Glass for London and England* (1588). James Shapiro argues that the first part of the Epilogue to *2H4* was spoken by Shakespeare himself at a court performance at Whitehall in the same season during which the Admiral's Men were performing a Robin Hood play (*1599*, p. 39). In the quarto version of the play, this section ends, 'And so I kneel down before you, but, indeed, to pray for the queen' (Giorgio Melchiori (ed.), *2H4*, 1989, Epilogue, 12–13). The rest of the epilogue may combine two further epilogues (14–19 and 20–26), each composed for delivery before terminal jigs in amphitheatre performances. The actual words of that prayer, of course, are lost. Rastell's *Of Gentleness and Nobility* (1527) has prayers at the end of each of its three parts. Terminal prayers may have been more common in the early Tudor period, but obviously still occurred.

[2] May, *Anthology*, pp. xiii–xiv; for Dudley Carleton's cryptic reference to the Queen dining with Lord Hunsdon on 29 December 1601 when she saw a play, probably performed by the Chamberlain's Men, in Blackfriars, either in Hunsdon's own great chamber or in the adjacent playhouse, see Chambers, *Shakespeare*, II, 48. There is, however, no evidence that other performances of this nature in Blackfriars, for which *AYLI* may have been deemed suitable, had taken place earlier. (Peter Roberts supplied me with this reference.)

[3] May, *Anthology*, item 165 (see pp. 304–5).

[4] Cook and Wilson, *Dramatic Records*, 57a, p. 31; Astington, *Court Theatre*, p. 236.

[5] *DNB*, 52, p. 249; the dial poem resembles many of the simile poems printed in John Bodenham *et al.*, *Bel-vedére or The garden of the Muses*, 1600.

[6] *Old Fortunatus*, 1600, sigs. A4ʳ, L3ʳ; *The Shoemaker's Holiday*, 1600, sig. A4ʳ; *Patient Grissil*, 1603, sigs. A4ᵛ, H1ᵛ; *Troia Nova*, 1612, sig. C3ᵛ; *The Noble Spanish Soldier*, 1634, sig. B2ʳ; *The Sun's Darling*, 1656, sig. G1ʳ. Shakespeare used trochaics more than twenty times (Ringler and May, 'Epilogue', p. 139).

[7] Ringler and May, 'Epilogue', p. 139.

[8] May and Ringler, *Bibliography*, aa4troch, III, 2121; Campion devotes Chapter 6 of his *Observations in the Art of English Poesy* (1602) to the metre.

belonged at the time, had performed at court earlier that year on Shrove Sunday 1599, two days before the performance by the Chamberlain's Men, and, although we know no more about what they performed than we do about the offering of the Chamberlain's Men, we must entertain the conjecture that the epilogue could have been for that performance.[1] If the poem was indeed by Jonson or Shakespeare, Dekker could have borrowed from it for his *Old Fortunatus* epilogue. It is, of course, also the case that 'Rosalind's' epilogue, which is customarily printed and performed at the end of *As You Like It*, could have been used at only one performance, and equally possible that a prayer was spoken after that.[2]

[1] Gurr, *Playing Companies*, p. 254; Astington, *Court Theatre*, p. 236.
[2] Tiffany Stern, 'Re-patching the Play', in Peter Holland and Stephen Orgel (eds.), *From Script to Stage in Early Modern England*, 2004, 151–77 at 161.

APPENDIX 2: EXTRACTS FROM SHAKESPEARE'S PRINCIPAL SOURCE, LODGE'S *ROSALIND*

The misogyny of Lodge's Sir John of Bordeaux

'But above all,' and with that he fetched a deep sigh, 'beware of love, for it is far more perilous than pleasant, and yet I tell you it allureth as ill as the sirens. Oh my sons, fancy is a fickle thing, and beauty's paintings are tricked up with time's colours, which being set to dry in the sun, perish with the same. Venus is a wanton, and though her laws pretend liberty, yet there is nothing but loss and glistering misery. Cupid's wings are plumed with the feathers of vanity and his arrows, where they pierce, enforce nothing but deadly desires. A woman's eye, as it is precious to behold, so it is prejudicial to gaze upon, for as it affordeth delight so it snareth unto death. Trust not their fawning favours, for their loves are like the breath of a man upon steel, which no sooner lighteth on but it leapeth off; and their passions are as momentary as the colours of a polyp [octopus or cuttlefish] which changeth at the sight of every object. My breath waxeth short and mine eyes dim; the hour is come and I must away. Therefore let this suffice: women are wantons, and yet men cannot want [be without] one, and therefore if you love, choose her that hath her eyes of adamant that will turn only to one point; her heart of a diamond that will receive but one form; her tongue of a shittim [acacia] leaf that never wags but with a south-east wind. And yet, my sons, if she have all these qualities – to be chaste, obedient, and silent – yet, for that she is a woman, shalt thou find in her sufficient vanities to countervail her virtues.

'Oh now, my sons, even now take these my last words as my latest legacy, for my thread is spun and my foot is in the grave. Keep my precepts as memorials of your father's counsels, and let them be lodged in the secret of your hearts, for wisdom is better than wealth, and a golden sentence worth a world of treasure. In my fall see and mark, my sons, the folly of man, that being dust climbeth with [Briareus] to reach at the heavens, and ready every minute to die, yet hopeth for an age of pleasures. Oh, man's life is like lightning that is but a flash, and the longest date of his years but as a bavin's [bundle of brushwood's] blaze. Seeing, then, man is so mortal, be careful that thy life be virtuous, that thy death may be full of admirable honours; so shalt thou challenge fame to be thy fautor [protector], and put oblivion to exile with thine honourable actions. But, my sons, lest you should forget your father's axioms, take this scroll wherein read what your father, dying, wills you to execute, living.'

At this he shrunk down in his bed and gave up the ghost.[1]

The miseries of Rosader

In this humour was Saladyne making his brother Rosader his footboy [page] for the space of two or three years, keeping him in such servile subjection as if he had been the son of any country vassal. The young gentleman bare all with patience, till on a day, walking

---

[1] *Rosalind*, pp. 100–1.

in the garden by himself, he began to consider how he was the son of John of Bordeaux, a knight renowned for many victories, and a gentleman famoused for his virtues, how, contrary to the testament of his father, he was not only kept from his land and entreated as a servant, but smothered in such secret slavery as he might not attain to any honourable actions.

'Ah,' quoth he to himself (Nature working these effectual passions), 'why should I, that am a gentleman born, pass my time in such unnatural drudgery? Were it not better either in Paris to become a scholar, or in the court a courtier, or in the field a soldier, than to live a footboy to my own brother? Nature hath lent me wit to conceive, but my brother denied me art to contemplate. I have strength to perform any honourable exploit, but no liberty to accomplish my virtuous endeavours. Those good parts that God hath bestowed upon me, the envy of my brother doth smother in obscurity. The harder is my fortune, and the more his frowardness.'

With that, casting up his hand he felt hair on his face, and perceiving his beard to bud, for choler he began to blush and swore to himself he would be no more subject to such slavery. As thus he was ruminating of his melancholy passions, in came Saladyne with his men and, seeing his brother in a brown study, and to forget his wonted reverence, thought to shake him out of his dumps thus:

'Sirrah,' quoth he, 'what, is your heart on your halfpenny, or are you saying a dirge for your father's soul? What, is my dinner ready?'

At this question Rosader, turning his head askance and bending his brows as if anger there had ploughed the furrows of her wrath, with his eyes full of fire, he made this reply:

'Dost thou ask me, Saladyne, for thy cates [delicacies]? Ask some of thy churls who are fit for such an office. I am thine equal by nature, though not by birth, and though thou hast more cards in the bunch [pack of cards], I have as many trumps in my hands as thyself. Let me question with thee why thou hast felled my woods, spoiled my manor-houses, and made havoc of such utensils as my father bequeathed unto me? I tell thee, Saladyne, either answer me as a brother, or I will trouble thee as an enemy.'

At this reply of Rosader's, Saladyne smiled as laughing at his presumption and frowned as checking his folly. He therefore took him up thus shortly:

'What, sirrah! Well, I see early pricks the tree that will prove a thorn. Hath my familiar conversing with you made you coy [disdainful], or my good looks [generosity] drawn you to be thus contemptuous? I can quickly remedy such a fault, and I will bend the tree while it is a wand. In faith, sir boy, I have a snaffle [bridle-bit] for such a headstrong colt . . . You, sirs, lay hold on him and bind him, and then I will give him a cooling card for his choler.'

This made Rosader half mad that, stepping to a great rake that stood in the garden, he laid such load [heavy blows] upon his brother's men that he hurt some of them and made the rest of them run away. Saladyne, seeing Rosader so resolute and with his resolution so valiant, thought his heels his best safety and took him to a loft adjoining to the garden, whither Rosader pursued him hotly. Saladyne, afraid of his brother's fury, cried out to him thus:

'Rosader, be not so rash. I am thy brother and thine elder, and if I have done thee wrong I'll make thee amends. Revenge not anger in blood, for so shalt thou stain the virtue of old Sir John of Bordeaux. Say wherein thou art discontent and thou shalt be satisfied. Brothers' frowns ought not to be periods of wrath. What, man, look not so sourly, I know we shall be friends, and better friends than we have been. For, *amantium ira amoris redintegratio est* [anger between lovers brings the renewal of love].[1]

---

[1] *Ibid.*, pp. 104–6.

The wrestling

The franklin, seeing so goodly a gentleman to give him such courteous comfort, gave him hearty thanks with promise to pray for his happy success. With that Rosader vailed bonnet [took off his cap] to the king, and lightly leaped within the lists where, noting more the company than the combatant, he cast his eye upon the troop of ladies that glistered there like the stars of heaven; but at last Love, willing to make him as amorous as he was valiant, presented him with the sight of Rosalind, whose admirable beauty so inveigled the eye of Rosader, that, forgetting himself, he stood and fed his looks on the favour of Rosalind's face, which, she perceiving, blushed: which was such a doubling of her beauteous excellence that the bashful red of Aurora [at] her sight of unacquainted Phaeton was not half so glorious.

The Norman, seeing this young gentleman fettered in the looks of the ladies, drove him out of his memento [reverie] with a shake by the shoulder; Rosader, looking back with an angry frown, as if he had been awakened from some pleasant dream, discovered to all by the fury of his countenance that he was a man of some high thoughts: but when they all noted his youth and the sweetness of his visage, with a general applause of favours they grieved that so goodly a young man should venture in so base an action. But seeing it were to his dishonour to hinder him from his enterprise, they wished him to be graced with the palm of victory. After Rosader was thus called out of his memento by the Norman, he roughly clapped to him with so fierce an encounter that they both fell to the ground, and with the violence of the fall were forced to breathe, in which space the Norman called to mind by all tokens [signs] that this was he whom Saladyne had appointed him to kill; which conjecture made him stretch every limb and try every sinew that, working his death, he might recover the gold which so bountifully was promised him.

On the contrary part, Rosader while he breathed was not idle, but still cast his eye upon Rosalind, who, to encourage him with a favour, lent him such an amorous look as might have made the most coward desperate; which glance of Rosalind so fired the passionate desires of Rosader that, turning to the Norman, he ran upon him and braved him with a strong encounter; the Norman received him as valiantly that there was a sore combat, hard to judge on whose side Fortune would be prodigal [lavish]. At last Rosader, calling to mind the beauty of his new mistress, the fame of his father's honours, and the disgrace that should fall to his house by his misfortune, roused himself and threw the Norman against the ground, falling upon his chest with so willing a weight that the Norman yielded Nature her due and Rosader the victory.

The death of this champion, as it highly contented the franklin as a man satisfied with revenge, so it drew the king and all the peers into a great admiration that so young years and so beautiful a personage should contain such martial excellence: but when they knew him to be the youngest son of Sir John of Bordeaux, the king rose from his seat and embraced him, and the peers entreated him with all favourable courtesy, commending both his valour and his virtues, wishing him to go forward in such haughty [high-minded] deeds that he might attain to the glory of his father's honourable fortunes.

As the king and lords graced him with embracing, so the ladies favoured him with their looks, especially Rosalind, whom the beauty and valour of Rosader had already touched. But she accounted love a toy and fancy a momentary passion, that as it was taken in with a gaze might be shaken off with a wink; and therefore feared not to dally in the flame, and to make Rosader know she affected him took from her neck a jewel and sent it by a page to the young gentleman. The prize that Venus gave to Paris was not half so pleasing to the Trojan as this gem was to Rosader, for if Fortune had sworn to make him sole monarch of the world, he would rather have refused such dignity than have lost the jewel sent him by Rosalind.[1]

---

[1] *Ibid.*, pp. 111–13.

Alinda's comfort to perplexed Rosalind

'Why, how now, Rosalind, dismayed with a frown of contrary fortune? Have I not oft heard thee say that high minds were rediscovered in Fortune's contempt, and heroical seen in the depth of extremities? Thou wert wont to tell others that complained of distress that the sweetest salve for misery was patience, and the only medicine for want, that precious emplaster [plaster] of content. Being such a good physician to others, wilt thou not minister receipts [prescriptions] to thyself? But perchance thou wilt say: *consulenti nunquam caput doluit* [the advice-giver does not have a headache of her own].

'Why, then, if the patients that are sick of this disease can find in themselves neither reason to persuade nor art to cure, yet, Rosalind, admit of the counsel of a friend and apply the salves that may appease thy passions. If thou grievest that being the daughter of a prince and envy thwarteth thee with such hard exigents [extremities], think that royalty is a fair mark, that crowns have crosses when mirth is in cottages, that the fairer the rose is the sooner it is bitten with caterpillars, the more orient the pearl is the more apt to take a blemish, and the greatest birth, as it hath most honour, so it hath much envy. If, then, Fortune aimeth at the fairest, be patient, Rosalind, for first by thine exile thou goest to thy father. Nature is higher prized than wealth, and the love of one's parents ought to be more precious than all dignities. Why then doth my Rosalind grieve at the frown of Torismond, who, by offering her a prejudice [injury], proffers her a greater pleasure? And more, mad lass, to be melancholy, when thou hast with thee Alinda, a friend who will be a faithful copartner of all thy misfortunes, who hath left her father to follow thee, and chooseth rather to brook all extremities than to forsake thy presence.'[1]

Rosalind's response to Montanus' poem

MONTANUS' PASSION

Hadst thou been born whereas perpetual cold
Makes Tanais[2] hard and mountains silver old:
Had I complained unto a marble stone
Or to the floods bewrayed my bitter moan,
   I then could bear the burden of my grief.
But even the pride of countries at thy birth,
Whilst heavens did smile, did new array the earth
    With flowers chief.
Yet thou, the flower of beauty blessèd born,
Hast pretty looks, but all attired in scorn.
Had I the power to weep sweet Myrrha's[3] tears,
Or by my plaints to pierce repining ears;
Hadst thou the heart to smile at my complaint,
To scorn the woes that doth my heart attaint,
   I then could bear the burden of my grief:
But not my tears, but truth with thee prevails,
And, seeming sour, my sorrows thee assails:
    Yet small relief.
For if thou wilt, thou art of marble hard;
And if thou please my suit shall soon be heard.

---

[1] *Ibid.*, pp. 121–2.
[2] The river Don.
[3] Myrrha was the mother of Adonis.

'No doubt,' quoth Aliena, 'this poesy is the passion of some perplexed shepherd that, being enamoured of some fair and beautiful shepherdess, suffered some sharp repulse, and therefore complained of the cruelty of his mistress.'

'You may see,' quoth Ganymede, 'what mad cattle you women be, whose hearts sometimes are made of adamant that will touch with no impression, and sometime of wax that is fit for every form. They delight to be courted, and then they glory to seem coy; and when they are most desired then they freeze with disdain. And this fault is so common to the sex that you see it painted out in the shepherd's passions, who found his mistress as froward as he was enamoured.'

'And I pray you,' quoth Aliena, 'if your robes were off, what metal are you made of that you are so satirical against women? Is it not a foul bird defiles [its] own nest? Beware, Ganymede, that Rosader hear you not; if he do, perchance you will make him leap so far from love that he will anger every vein in your heart.'

'Thus,' quoth Ganymede, 'I keep decorum: I speak now as I am Aliena's page, not as I am Gerismond's daughter; for put me but into a petticoat, and I will stand in defiance to the uttermost that women are courteous, constant, virtuous, and whatnot.'

'Stay there,' quoth Aliena, 'and no more words, for yonder be characters graven upon the bark of the tall beech tree.'

'Let us see,' quoth Ganymede, and with that they read a fancy written to this effect:

> First shall the heavens want starry light,
> The seas be robbèd of their waves,
> The day want sun, and sun want bright,
> The night want shade, the dead men graves,
>   The April, flowers and leaf and tree,
>   Before I false my faith to thee.
>
> First shall the tops of highest hills
> By humble plains be overpried,
> And poets scorn the Muses' quills,
> And fish forsake the water glide;
>   And Iris lose her coloured weed,
>   Before I fail thee at thy need.
>
> First direful hate shall turn to peace,
> And love relent in deep disdain,
> And death his fatal stroke shall cease,
> And envy pity every pain,
>   And pleasure mourn, and sorrow smile,
>   Before I talk of any guile.
>
> First time shall stay his stayless race,
> And winter bless his brows with corn,
> And snow bemoisten July's face,
> And winter, spring, and summer mourn,
>   Before my pen, by help of fame,
>   Cease to recite thy sacred name.
>   Montanus

'No doubt', quoth Ganymede, 'this protestation grew from one full of passions.'

'I am of that mind too,' quoth Aliena, 'but see, I pray, when poor women seek to keep themselves chaste, how men woo them with many feigned promises, alluring with sweet

words as the Sirens, and after proving as trothless as Aeneas. Thus promised Demophoön
to his Phyllis, but who at last grew more false?'

'The reason was,' quoth Ganymede, 'that they were women's sons, and took that fault of
their mother; for if man had grown from man, as Adam did from the earth, men had never
been troubled with inconstancy.'

'Leave off,' quoth Aliena, 'to taunt thus bitterly, or else I'll pull off your page's apparel
and whip you, as Venus doth her wantons, with nettles.'

'So you will,' quoth Ganymede, 'persuade me to flattery, and that needs not. But come,
seeing we have found here by this fount the tract of shepherds by their madrigals and
roundelays, let us forward, for either we shall find some folds, sheepcots, or else some
cottages wherein for a day or two to rest.'[1]

The shepherd's lot

'If I should not, fair damsel, occasionate offence, or renew your griefs by rubbing the scar,
I would fain crave so much favour as to know the cause of your misfortune, and why, and
whither you wander with your page in so dangerous a forest.'

Aliena, that was as courteous as she was fair, made this reply: 'Shepherd, a friendly
demand ought never to be offensive, and questions of courtesy carry privileged pardons in
their foreheads. Know, therefore, to discover my fortunes were to renew my sorrows, and I
should by discoursing my mishaps but rake fire out of the cinders. Therefore let this suffice,
gentle shepherd: my distress is as great as my travel is dangerous, and I wander in this forest
to light on some cottage where I and my page may dwell. For I mean to buy some farm and
a flock of sheep and so become a shepherdess, meaning to live low and content me with a
country life; for I have heard the swains say that they drunk without suspicion and slept
without care.'

'Marry, mistress,' quoth Corydon, 'if you mean so you came in a good time, for my
landlord intends to sell both the farm I till and the flock I keep, and cheap you may have
them for ready money. And for a shepherd's life, oh mistress, did you but live a while in their
content you would say the court were rather a place of sorrow, than of solace. Here, mistress,
shall not Fortune thwart you, but in mean misfortunes, as the loss of a few sheep which, as
it breeds no beggary, so it can be no extreme prejudice. The next year may mend all with
a fresh increase. Envy stirs not us, we covet not to climb, our desires mount not above our
degrees, nor our thoughts above our fortunes. Care cannot harbour in our cottages, nor do
our homely couches know broken slumbers. As we exceed not in diet, so we have enough to
satisfy. And, mistress, I have so much Latin: *satis est quod sufficit* [sufficient is enough].'

'By my troth, shepherd,' quoth Aliena, 'thou makest me in love with your country life;
and therefore send for thy landlord and I will buy thy farm and thy flocks, and thou shalt still,
under me, be overseer of them both. Only for pleasure sake, I and my page will serve you,
lead the flocks to the field, and fold them. Thus will I live quiet, unknown, and contented.'[2]

Adam Spencer's speech

'Oh, how the life of man may well be compared to the state of the ocean seas, that for every
calm hath a thousand storms, resembling the rose tree that, for a few fair flowers, hath
a multitude of sharp prickles. All our pleasures end in pain, and our highest delights are
crossed with deepest discontents. The joys of man, as they are few, so are they momentary,

---

[1] *Rosalind*, pp. 124–7.
[2] *Ibid.*, pp. 133–4.

scarce ripe before they are rotten and, withering in the blossom, either parched with the heat of envy or Fortune. Fortune – oh inconstant friend – that in all thy deeds are froward and fickle, delighting in the poverty of the lowest and the overthrow of the highest to decipher [reveal] thy inconstancy. Thou standst upon a globe, and thy wings are plumed with Time's feathers that thou mayst ever be restless. Thou art double-faced like Janus, carrying frowns in the one to threaten and smiles in the other to betray. Thou profferest an eel and performest a scorpion, and where thy greatest favours be, there is the fear of the extremest misfortunes, so variable are all thy actions.

'But why, Adam, dost thou exclaim against Fortune? She laughs at the plaints of the distressed, and there is nothing more pleasing unto her than to hear fools boast in her fading allurements or sorrowful men to discover the sower of their passions. Glut her not, Adam, then, with content, but thwart her with brooking all mishaps with patience. For there is no greater check to the pride of Fortune than with a resolute courage to pass over her crosses without care. Thou art old, Adam, and thy hairs wax white, the palm-tree is already full of blooms, and in the furrows of thy face appears the calendars [signs] of death. Wert thou blessed by Fortune, thy years could not be many nor the date of thy life long. Then, sith Nature must have her due, what is it for thee to resign her debt a little before the day?

'Ah, it is not this which grieveth me, nor do I care what mishaps Fortune can wage against me, but the sight of Rosader, that galleth unto the quick. When I remember the worships of his house, the honour of his fathers, and the virtues of himself, then do I say that Fortune and the Fates are most injurious to censure so hard extremes against a youth of so great hope. Oh Rosader, thou art in the flower of thine age and in the pride of thy years, buxom [gracious] and full of May. Nature hath prodigally enriched thee with her favours and Virtue made thee the mirror of her excellence, and now, through the decree of the unjust stars, to have all these good parts nipped in the blade and blemished by the inconstancy of Fortune! Ah Rosader, could I help thee, my grief were the less, and happy should my death be, if it might be the beginning of thy relief. But seeing we perish both in one extreme [extremity], it is a double sorrow. What shall I do? Prevent the sight of his further misfortune with a present dispatch of mine own life? Ah, despair is a merciless sin.'[1]

Rosalind's description

> Like to the clear in highest sphere,
> Where all imperial glory shines,
> Of selfsame colour is her hair,
> Whether unfolded or in twines.
>   Heigh ho, fair Rosalind.
> Her eyes are sapphires set in snow,
> Refining heaven by every wink;
> The gods do fear whenas they glow,
> And I do tremble when I think.
>   Heigh ho, would she were mine.
>
> Her cheeks are like the blushing cloud
> That beautifies Aurora's face,
> Or like the silver crimson shroud
> That Phoebus' smiling looks doth grace.
>   Heigh ho, fair Rosalind.

---

[1] *Ibid.*, pp. 141–3.

Her lips are like two budded roses
Whom ranks of lilies neighbour nigh,
Within which bounds she balm encloses,
Apt to entice a deity:
   Heigh ho, would she were mine.

Her neck like to a stately tower
Where Love himself imprisoned lies,
To watch for glances every hour
From her divine and sacred eyes.
   Heigh ho, fair Rosalind.
Her paps are centres of delight,
Her paps are orbs of heavenly frame
Where Nature moulds the dew of light
To feed perfection with the same.
   Heigh ho, would she were mine.

With orient pearl, with ruby red,
With marble white, with sapphire blue,
Her body every way is fed,
Yet soft in touch and sweet in view:
   Heigh ho, fair Rosalind.
Nature herself her shape admires,
The gods are wounded in her sight,
And Love forsakes his heavenly fires
And at her eyes his brand doth light.
   Heigh ho, would she were mine.

Then muse not, nymphs, though I bemoan
The absence of fair Rosalind,
Since for her fair there is fairer none,
Nor for her virtues so divine.
   Heigh ho fair Rosalind;
   Heigh ho, my heart, would God that she were mine.
               Periit, quia deperibat [He died because he was despairing in love].[1]

Mock marriage by Aliena

When thus they had finished their courting eclogue in such a familiar clause, Ganymede, as augur of some good fortunes to light upon their affections, began to be thus pleasant:

'How now, forester, have I not fitted your turn? Have I not played the woman handsomely and showed myself as coy in grants, as courteous in desires, and been as full of suspicion as men of flattery? And yet to salve all, jumped I not all up with the sweet union of love? Did not Rosalind content her Rosader?'

The forester, at this smiling, shook his head and, folding his arms, made this merry reply:

'Truth, gentle swain, Rosader hath his Rosalind but as Ixion had Juno, who thinking to possess a goddess, only embraced a cloud. In these imaginary fruitions of fancy I resemble the birds that fed themselves with Zeuxis' painted grapes, but they grew so lean with pecking at shadows that they were glad with Aesop's cock to scrape for a barley cornel [granule]. So

---

[1] *Ibid.*, pp. 152–3; compare this with Orlando's poem 3.3.65–72.

fareth it with me, who, to feed myself with the hope of my mistress' favours, soothe myself in thy suits, and only in conceit reap a wished-for content. But if my food be no better than such amorous dreams, Venus at the year's end shall find me but a lean lover. Yet do I take these follies for high fortunes and hope these feigned affections do divine some unfeigned end of ensuing fancies.'

'And thereupon,' quoth Aliena, 'I'll play the priest. From this day forth Ganymede shall call thee husband and thou shalt call Ganymede wife, and so we'll have a marriage.'

'Content,' quoth Rosader, and laughed.

'Content,' quoth Ganymede, and changed as red as a rose.

And so with a smile and a blush, they made up this jesting match that after proved to a marriage in earnest, Rosader full little thinking he had wooed and won his Rosalind.[1]

The episode of the lion

All this while did poor Saladyne, banished from Bordeaux and the court of France by Torismond, wander up and down in the forest of Arden, thinking to get to Lyons, and so travel through Germany into Italy. But the forest being full of by-paths, and he unskilful of the country coast [region], slipped out of the way, and chanced up into the desert, not far from the place where Gerismond was, and his brother Rosader.

Saladyne, weary with wandering up and down and hungry with long fasting, finding a little cave by the side of a thicket, eating such fruit as the forest did afford and contenting himself with such drink as Nature had provided and thirst made delicate, after his repast he fell in a dead sleep. As thus he lay, a hungry lion came hunting down the edge of the grove for prey and, espying Saladyne, began to seize upon him; but seeing he lay still without any motion, he left to touch him – for that lions hate to prey on dead carcasses – and yet desirous to have some food, the lion lay down and watched to see if he would stir.

While thus Saladyne slept secure, Fortune, that was careful over her champion, began to smile and brought it so to pass, that Rosader – having stricken a deer that, but lightly hurt, fled through the thicket – came pacing down by the grove with a boarspear in his hand in great haste. He spied where a man lay asleep and a lion fast by him. Amazed at this sight, as he stood gazing his nose on the sudden bled, which made him conjecture it was some friend of his. Whereupon, drawing more nigh, he might easily discern his visage, and perceived by his physiognomy that it was his brother Saladyne, which drove Rosader into a deep passion, as a man perplexed at the sight of so unexpected a chance, marvelling what should drive his brother to traverse those secret deserts without any company in such distress and forlorn sort. But the present time craved no such doubting ambages [roundabout thoughts], for either he must resolve to hazard his life for his relief or else steal away and leave him to the cruelty of the lion – in which doubt, he thus briefly debated with himself:

ROSADER'S MEDITATION

'Now, Rosader, Fortune that long hath whipped thee with nettles means to salve thee with roses and, having crossed thee with many frowns, now she presents thee with the brightness of her favours. Thou, that didst count thyself the most distressed of all men, mayst account thyself now the most fortunate amongst men, if Fortune can make men happy or sweet revenge be wrapped in a pleasing content. Thou seest Saladyne, thine enemy, the worker of thy misfortunes, and the efficient cause of thine exile, subject to the cruelty of a merciless lion, brought into this misery by the gods that they might seem just in revenging his rigour and thy injuries. Seest thou not how the stars are in a favourable aspect, the planets in some

---

[1] *Ibid.*, pp. 168–9.

pleasing conjunction, the Fates agreeable to thy thoughts, and the destinies performers of thy desires in that Saladyne shall die and thou [be] free of his blood, he receive meed for his amiss and thou erect his tomb with innocent hands? Now, Rosader, shalt thou return to Bordeaux and enjoy thy possessions by birth and his revenues by inheritance. Now mayst thou triumph in love and hang Fortune's altars with garlands. For when Rosalind hears of thy wealth, it will make her love thee more willingly, for women's eyes are made of chrysocolla [borax or malachite] that is ever unperfect unless tempered with gold, and Jupiter soonest enjoyed Danaë because he came to her in so rich a shower. Thus shall this lion, Rosader, end the life of a miserable man, and from distress raise thee to be most fortunate.'

And with that, casting his boar-spear on his neck, away he began to trudge. But he had not stepped back two or three paces but a new motion stroke him to the very heart that, resting his boar-spear against his breast, he fell into this passionate humour:

'Ah, Rosader, wert thou the son of Sir John of Bordeaux, whose virtues exceeded his valour and yet the most hardiest knight in all Europe? Should the honour of the father shine in the actions of the son? And wilt thou dishonour thy parentage in forgetting the nature of a gentleman? Did not thy father at his last gasp breathe out this golden principle: brothers' amity is like the drops of balsam, that salveth the most dangerous sores? Did he make a large exhort unto concord, and wilt thou show thyself careless? Oh, Rosader, what though Saladyne hath wronged thee and made thee live an exile in the forest? Shall thy nature be so cruel, or thy nurture so crooked, or thy thoughts so savage, as to suffer so dismal a revenge? What, to let him be devoured by wild beasts? *Non sapit, qui non sibi sapit* [He is not wise who is not wise for himself] is fondly spoken in such bitter extremes. Lose not his life, Rosader, to win a world of treasure, for in having him thou hast a brother, and by hazarding for his life, thou gettest a friend, and reconcilest an enemy, and more honour shalt thou purchase by pleasuring a foe than revenging a thousand injuries.'

With that his brother began to stir and the lion to rouse himself, whereupon Rosader suddenly charged him with the boar-spear and wounded the lion very sore at the first stroke. The beast, feeling himself to have a mortal hurt, leapt at Rosader and with his paws gave him a sore pinch on the breast that he had almost fallen; yet, as a man most valiant, in whom the sparks of Sir John of Bordeaux remained, he recovered himself and in short combat slew the lion, who at his death roared so loud that Saladyne awaked and, starting up, was amazed at the sudden sight of so monstrous a beast lying slain by him and so sweet a gentleman wounded. He presently, as he was of a ripe conceit, began to conjecture that the gentleman had slain him in his defence. Whereupon, as a man in a trance, he stood staring on them both a good while, not knowing his brother being in that disguise. At last he burst into these terms:

'Sir, whatsoever thou be (as full of honour thou must needs be by the view of thy present valure [worthiness, might]), I perceive thou hast redressed my fortunes by thy courage and saved my life with thine own loss, which ties me to be thine in all humble service. Thanks thou shalt have as thy due, and more thou canst not have for my ability denies to perform a deeper debt. But if any ways it please thee to command me, use me as far as the power of a poor gentleman may stretch.'

Rosader, seeing he was unknown to his brother, wondered to hear such courteous words come from his crabbed nature; but, glad of such reformed nurture, he made this answer:

'I am, sir, whatsoever thou art, a forester and ranger of these walks who, following my deer to the fall, was conducted hither by some assenting Fate that I might save thee and disparage [discredit] myself. For, coming into this place, I saw thee asleep and the lion watching thy awake that at thy rising he might prey upon thy carcass. At the first sight I conjectured thee a gentleman – for all men's thoughts ought to be favourable in imagination – and I counted it the part of a resolute man to purchase a stranger's relief, though with the loss of his own blood, which I have performed, thou seest, to mine own prejudice. If, therefore, thou be a man of such worth as I value thee by thy exterior lineaments, make discourse unto me what is the cause of thy present fortunes. For by the furrows in thy face thou seemest to be crossed with her frowns. But whatsoever or howsoever, let me crave that favour, to hear the tragic cause of thy estate.' Saladyne sitting down and fetching a deep sigh, began thus.[1]

Resolution

Corydon having thus made them merry, as they were in the midst of all their jollity, word was brought in to Saladyne and Rosader that a brother of theirs, one Fernandyne, was arrived and desired to speak with them. Gerismond, overhearing this news, demanded who it was.

'It is, sir,' quoth Rosader, 'our middle brother that lives a scholar in Paris; but what fortune hath driven him to seek us out I know not.'

With that Saladyne went and met his brother, whom he welcomed with all courtesy, and Rosader gave him no less friendly entertainment; brought he was by his two brothers into the parlour where they all sat at dinner. Fernandyne, as one that knew as many manners as he could [knew] points of sophistry, and was as well brought up as well lettered, saluted them all. But when he espied Gerismond, kneeling on his knee, he did him what reverence belonged to his estate, and with that burst forth into these speeches:

'Although, right mighty prince, this day of my brothers' marriage be a day of mirth, yet time craves another course, and therefore from dainty cates rise to sharp weapons. And you, the sons of Sir John of Bordeaux, leave off your amours and fall to arms; change your loves into lances and now this day show yourselves as valiant as hitherto you have been passionate. For know, Gerismond, that hard by at the edge of this forest the twelve peers of France are up in arms to recover thy right, and Torismond, trooped with a crew of desperate runagates [renegades], is ready to bid them battle. The armies are ready to join; therefore show thyself in the field to encourage thy subjects. And you, Saladyne and Rosader, mount you and show yourselves as hardy soldiers as you have been hearty lovers. So shall you for the benefit of your country discover the idea of your father's virtues to be stamped in your thoughts, and prove children worthy of so honourable a parent.'

At this alarum given by Fernandyne, Gerismond leaped from the board, and Saladyne and Rosader betook themselves to their weapons.

'Nay,' quoth Gerismond, 'go with me. I have horse and armour for us all, and then, being well mounted, let us show that we carry revenge and honour at our falchions' [broad-swords'] points.'

Thus they leave the brides full of sorrow, especially Alinda, who desired Gerismond to be good to her father. He, not returning a word because his haste was great, hied him home to his lodge where he delivered Saladyne and Rosader horse and armour and, himself armed, royally led the way – not having ridden two leagues before they discovered where, in a valley, both the battles were joined. Gerismond, seeing the wing wherein the peers fought, thrust in there, and cried 'Saint Denis' – Gerismond laying on such load [heavy blows] upon his enemies that he showed how highly he did estimate of a crown. When the peers perceived that their lawful king was there they grew more eager, and Saladyne and Rosader so behaved themselves that none durst stand in their way nor abide the fury of their weapons. To be short, the peers were conquerors, Torismond's army put to flight, and himself slain in battle. The peers then gathered themselves together and, saluting their king, conducted him royally into Paris where he was received with great joy of all the citizens. As soon as all was quiet and he had received again the crown, he sent for Alinda and Rosalind to the court, Alinda

---

[1]   *Ibid.*, pp. 171–4.

being very passionate for the death of her father, yet brooking it with the more patience in that she was contented with the welfare of her Saladyne.

Well, as soon as they were come to Paris, Gerismond made a royal feast for the peers and lords of his land which continued thirty days, in which time, summoning a parliament, by the consent of his nobles he created Rosader heir apparent to the kingdom; he restored Saladyne to all his father's land, and gave him the dukedom of Nemours; he made Fernandyne principal secretary to himself; and that Fortune might every way seem frolic, he made Montanus lord over all the forest of Arden, Adam Spencer captain of the king's guard, and Corydon master of Alinda's flocks.[1]

---

[1] *Ibid.*, pp. 225–7.

APPENDIX 3: THE SONGS

Many pastoral works, Sidney's *Arcadia* and Lodge's *Rosalind* included, contain songs, and productions of *As You Like It*, which contains five songs, are often remarkable for their music. In fact there was a vogue for 'operatised' versions of the play in the first half of the eighteenth century.[1] No settings of 'Under the greenwood tree' (2.5.1–8, 30–7, 42–9) or 'Blow, blow, thou winter wind' (2.7.174–97) have survived from Shakespeare's period; the earliest are those of Thomas Arne for the production of 1740 at Drury Lane.[2] 'O sweet Oliver' from which Touchstone sings (3.4.75–81) is the name given in a lute-book compiled by Adrian Smout in Leyden to the tune 'The hunt is up'.[3] There is an arrangement of 'What shall he have that killed the deer?' (4.2.8–17) as a catch for four voices that was made by John Hilton, organist of St Margaret's Westminster (1599–1657), although it was not published until 1652. (It also appeared in J. Playford's *The Musical Companion* in 1667.) The fact that it does not contain the song's slightly puzzling 'Then sing him home, / The rest shall bear this burden' (see 4.2.10 n., 11 n.) implies that it may not have been used in theatrical performances.[4]

'It was a lover and his lass' (5.3.12–43), which is very close to Corydon's song 'A blithe and bonny country lass',[5] was set by Thomas Morley for voice, lute, and bass-viol, and appeared in his *First Book of Airs, or Little Short Songs*, 1600, sigs. B4ᵛ–C1ʳ.[6] We cannot tell whether it was written specially for the play, or taken over by Shakespeare. The order in which the stanzas are printed in the song-book would seem to be more appropriate than that in which they appear in the Folio text (see 5.3.36–43 n.). There is no extant contemporary music for 'Wedding is great Juno's crown' (5.4.125–30).[7]

[1] See Stage History, p. 57; musical settings of the songs and related music are listed in Bryan N. S. Gooch, David Thatcher, and Odean Long (eds.), *A Shakespeare Music Catalogue*, 5 vols., 1991, entries 387–2017; see also Randy L. Neighbarger, *An Outward Show: Music for Shakespeare on the London Stage, 1660–1830*, 1992; David Lindley, 'Shakespeare's provoking music', in John Caldwell, Edward Olleson, and Susan Wollenberg (eds.), *The Well Enchanting Skill: Music, Poetry, and Drama in the Culture of the Renaissance: Essays in Honour of F. W. Sternfeld*, 1990, pp. 79–90.

[2] Thomas Arne, *The Songs in the Comedies called As You Like It, and Twelfth Night* (1741), reprinted in John Caulfield, *A Collection of the Vocal Music in Shakespeare's Plays*, 2 vols., [1864], II, 133, 138; Long describes the nature of the songs, and endorses the theory that tunes printed in J. Playford, *The English Dancing Master* (1650), may be contemporaneous with the play (pp. 141–5, 149); see also Seng, p. 75.

[3] J. P. N. Land (ed.), *Het Luitboek van Thysius*, 1882–92; 'The hunt is up' is printed by Claude M. Simpson, *The British Broadside Ballad and its Music*, 1966, pp. 323–5.

[4] John Hilton, *Catch that Catch Can* (1652); it is printed by Long, p. 151; see Seng, pp. 85–6.

[5] *Rosalind*, pp. 224–5.

[6] Morley's song is reproduced in facsimile by Long, p. 154; see E. Brennecke, 'Shakespeare's collaboration with Morley', *PMLA* 54 (1939), 139–52; there is a scholarly edition of Morley's *Book of Airs* by R. Thurston Dart, 1958; see Seng, pp. 89–90. The melody can be heard on http://www.obriencastle.com/EnglishMidi/lovrlass.htm.

[7] The earliest setting is by Thomas Chilcot, included in his *Twelve English Songs* [1750?], p. 31; see Seng, p. 92.

READING LIST

Anne Barton. '*As You Like It* and *Twelfth Night*: Shakespeare's "sense of an ending"' [1972], *Essays, Mainly Shakespearean*, 1994, pp. 91–112

William G. Carroll. *As You Like It; Twelfth Night; Much Ado about Nothing*, Pegasus Shakespeare Bibliographies, 1996

A. Stuart Daley. 'The dispraise of the country in *As You Like It*', *SQ* 36 (1985), 300–14

Juliet Dusinberre. 'As *who* liked it?', *S.Sur.* 46 (1994), 9–22

Peter Erickson. 'Sexual politics and social structure in *As You Like It*', in *Patriarchal Structures in Shakespeare's Drama*, 1985, pp. 15–38

Z. S. Fink. 'Jaques and the malcontent traveler', *PQ* 14 (1935), 237–52

Brian Gibbons. *Shakespeare and Multiplicity*, 1993, chap. 6

René Girard. *A Theater of Envy: William Shakespeare*, 1991, chaps. 10 and 11

Jay L. Halio and Barbara C. Millard. '*As You Like It*': *An Annotated Bibliography, 1940–1980*, 1985

Nancy K. Hayles. 'Sexual disguise in *As You Like It* and *Twelfth Night*', *S.Sur.* 32 (1979), 63–72

Barbara Hodgdon. 'Sexual disguise and the theatre of gender', in Alexander Leggatt (ed.), *The Cambridge Companion to Shakespearean Comedy*, 2002, pp. 179–97

Maurice A. Hunt. *Shakespeare's 'As You Like It': Late Elizabethan Culture and Literary Representation*, 2008

L. A. Montrose. 'Of gentlemen and shepherds: the politics of Elizabethan pastoral form', *ELH* 50 (1983), 415–59

Camille Paglia. 'Shakespeare and Dionysus: *As You Like It* and *Antony and Cleopatra*', in *Sexual Personae: Art and Decadence from Nefertiti to Emily Dickinson*, 1991, pp. 194–239

D. J. Palmer. 'Art and Nature in *As You Like It*', *PQ* 49 (1970), 30–40

Phyllis Rackin. 'Androgyny, mimesis, and the marriage of the boy heroine', *PMLA* 102 (1987), 29–41

Carol Rutter *et al. Clamorous Voices: Shakespeare's Women Today*, 1988

William Shakespeare. *As You Like It*, Shakespeare in Production, ed. Cynthia Marshall, 2004

Michael Shapiro. *Gender in Play on the Shakespearean Stage: Boy Heroines and Female Pages*, 1994

J. Shaw. 'Fortune and Nature in *As You Like It*', *SQ* 6 (1955), 45–50

Robert Smallwood. *As You Like It*, Shakespeare at Stratford, 2003

Peter Stallybrass. '"Drunk with the cup of liberty": Robin Hood, the carnivalesque, and the rhetoric of violence in early modern England', *Semiotica* 54 (1985), 113–45

Edward Tomarken (ed.). '*As You Like It' from 1600 to the Present: Critical Essays*, 1997

David Wiles. *Shakespeare's Clown: Actor and Text in the Elizabethan Playhouse*, 1987

CPSIA information can be obtained
at www.ICGtesting.com
Printed in the USA
LVHW011941150720
660782LV00015B/849

9 780521 732505